Listening

Processes, Functions, and Competency

DEBRA L. **WORTHINGTON**

Auburn University

MARGARET E. **FITCH-HAUSER**

Auburn University

Allyn & Bacon

Boston   Columbus   Indianapolis   New York   San Francisco   Upper Saddle River   Amsterdam
Cape Town   Dubai   London   Madrid   Milan   Munich   Paris   Montreal   Toronto   Delhi
Mexico City   São Paulo   Sydney   Hong Kong   Seoul   Singapore   Taipei   Tokyo

Editor-in-Chief, Communication: Karon Bowers
Project Editor: Toni Magyar
Editorial Assistant: Stephanie Chaisson
Marketing Manager: Blair Tuckman
Associate Managing Editor: Bayani Mendoza de Leon
Project Manager: Debbie Ryan
Art Director: Jayne Conte
Project Coordination, Text Design, and Electronic Page Makeup: Vishal Gaudhar/Aptara®, Inc.
Cover Designer: Suzanne Duda

Library of Congress Cataloging-in-Publication Data

Worthington, Debra L.
 Listening : processes, functions, and competency / Debra L. Worthington, Margaret E. Fitch-Hauser.
 p. cm.
 ISBN-13: 978-0-13-228854-5
 ISBN-10: 0-13-228854-0
 1. Listening. 2. Listening comprehension. 3. Listening—Social aspects. I. Fitch-Hauser, Margaret E. II. Title.
 BF323.L5W67 2012
 153.6'8—dc22   2011002924

1 2 3 4 5 6 7 8 9 10——13 12 11 10

Allyn & Bacon
is an imprint of

www.pearsonhighered.com

ISBN-10:   0-13-228854-0
ISBN-13: 978-0-13-228854-5

BRIEF CONTENTS

CONTENTS

PART IV Listening: New Frontiers

CHAPTER 12
Transforming Listening: Future Directions 263

PREFACE

We went into the project of writing this book with the firm belief that listening is a critical life competency. Support for our belief can be found in the numerous business articles that are written about the importance of listening in various occupations. Even the American Medical Association has recognized the importance of listening by mandating listening training for future physicians. Unfortunately, however, listening is so embedded in our daily communication processes that few of us take the time to contemplate how it contributes (or detracts) from our ability to communicate effectively with others. Our primary motivation, as active researchers in listening processes, is to provide a vehicle to spur student awareness of and interest in listening as a critical communication competency and as a field of study.

As educators we know that today's college students are very pragmatic. Therefore, we address how listening can contribute to their future success in life as well as careers. Specifically our text addresses the role and effect of listening in four selected academic and professional contexts. However, our text also has a significant theoretical focus. We provide a review of the progression of more than 50 years of listening research to provide an overview of theory and application. We believe it is important to understand what works but, more important, why it works. An understanding of theory will allow students to adapt their skills, not only in the areas covered in the text, but also in other situations, thus greatly extending their ability to apply skilled listening to a variety of personal and professional challenges.

ORGANIZATION OF THE BOOK

Our approach to this textbook provides a theory and research-based discussion of listening as a cognitive process, as a social function, and as a critical professional competency. To achieve the above goals, we have organized the text into three sections. The first section introduces foundational concepts, such as types of listening, as well as cognitive and individual-related factors that might affect listening processes. The second section addresses social aspects of listening such as how it affects and is affected by the important relationships in our lives. The third section addresses listening in selected professional contexts, while the final chapter focuses on the future of listening: emerging contexts and research.

Pedagogical Features

Each chapter begins with a brief Case Study vignette based on a set of hypothetical students enrolled in a college listening course. Their interactions with each other and family members form the basis for examples and topic-specific discussions.

Key concepts are identified in bold or italicized. At the end of each chapter are a list of key concepts, discussion questions, and additional readings and resources. Instructors can use the discussion questions as the basis for reading responses to assess comprehension and recall of material, to spark additional in-class discussion, or to assess students' ability to apply and critique concepts. *Think on It* boxes are located throughout the text, providing students with the opportunity to consider how a concept directly applies to them. Some boxes identify Internet sites where students can take self-tests associated with the personality or communication construct under discussion. Finally each chapter is well supported by research as evidenced by extensive endnotes and bibliographies.

ACKNOWLEDGMENTS

We would like to thank the many people who helped make this book possible. First, we would like to thank our family members, Don, Jerry, and Kathryn, for their patience and understanding as we spent time and energy on researching, writing, and editing this book. We would also like to thank the many graduate students who aided us in our research as well as undergraduates who reviewed and gave us feedback on individual chapters. Finally we'd like to thank everyone at Pearson who contributed to bringing this project to fruition, and especially the reviewers of early drafts of the text: Richard Bommelje, Rollins College; Jerry Catt-Oliason, Boise State University; Mary Etta Cook, Belmont University; Marshall G. Most, Boise State University; Brent Northup, Carroll College Helena; Lisa M. Orick-Martinez, Central New Mexico Community College; James W. Pratt, University of Wisconsin-River Falls; Carolyn H. Rester, East Texas Baptist University; Jennifer Holly Sisk, Eastern Michigan University; Elizabeth Spradley, Stephen F. Austin State University; Willis M. Watt, Methodist University; Judith D. Willner, Copin State University; and Kent L. Zimmerman, Sinclair Community College.

ABOUT THE AUTHORS

Debra L. Worthington is an Associate Professor of Communication at Auburn University. Dr. Worthington's teaching and research reflect her interest in persuasion and social influence. She teaches a variety of undergraduate and graduate courses, including Small Group, Legal Communication, Health Communication, Persuasive Discourse, and Empirical Research Methods. Much of her research explores psychosocial factors affecting communication processes during juror decision making. Her listening research has primarily focused on extending and refining our understanding of individual listening style. Her research has appeared in a variety of journals, including the *International Journal of Listening, Law & Human Behavior, Behavioral Sciences & the Law, Communication Law Review,* and *Argument & Advocacy.* Her research has been recognized by the Burton Foundation for Legal Achievement, the Communication and Law Division of the National Communication Association, and the International Listening Association.

Margaret Fitch-Hauser, an Associate Professor of Communication at Auburn University, has been involved in listening research for more than 25 years. She has been an active member of the International Listening Association, including serving three years as the editor of the *International Journal of Listening.* Her listening research has focused on listening fidelity, information distortion in recall, the effect of schemata on the listening process, and other application-focused topics. She currently chairs the Department of Communication and Journalism and teaches at the undergraduate and graduate level. Her current research is focused on listening fidelity and developing two new measures of listening. Dr. Fitch-Hauser has authored one textbook on business writing and a number of book chapters and cases studies, as well as numerous scholastic papers.

Introduction and Overview

Walk into any student union on a college campus and you'll find a group of students working on a project or discussing a class. Today, at a large table, we see a group involved in an intense discussion. They are all students in Professor Jackie Merritt's Listening class who learned today that they had to, as a group, write and perform a skit about listening in the workplace. Since this is the first week of school, they decided to meet so they could get to know each other better. Around the table we have Ben Goleman, Tamarah Jackson, Nolvia Gutierrez, NaMii Kim, Carter Bishop, and Radley Monroe. Let's listen to part of their conversation.

CASE STUDY 1.1

Getting to Know Our Students

Well, since I appear to be the oldest in this group, why don't I get things started? As you know, I'm **Tamarah Jackson** and I really appreciate you agreeing to meet at this time. Since I work full time in the city's public safety department, I can only meet after five. I'm an only child and grew up surrounded by members of the Choctaw Nation since my dad is a tribal elder. My mom is a social worker, and my dad is a plumber.

Cool! That's interesting. I bet your background will add a lot to our class discussions about listening. I'm **Ben Goleman** and, like Tamarah, I have some time constraints. I can't meet between sundown on Friday and sundown on Saturday. Friday evening my family observes

Shabbat and then attends synagogue on Saturday. I'm a middle child, and my mother is a physician and Dad is the VP of human resources at the auto plant here in town. He thought I picked a good class when I told him I was taking a listening class. He thinks it's a skill that can really help me in all aspects of life. I sure hope he's right; I hate the idea of just taking a class to get a grade.

I know what you mean. Some classes can be a real waste of time. But I think this one will be different. My name is **Carter Bishop,** and I'm a "second batch" kid. My parents had three girls, and then fifteen years later I came along. They split up when I was four. My mom and sisters and I stayed here. Dad moved to Chicago and

(continued)

1

works for a PR firm there. Mom's a secretary in the dean's office. I know both of my parents think listening is important. Just last week, when I visited my dad, he talked about how important listening to his clients is to his success. He was giving me one of those get-your-act-together talks.

Oh, brother! You too, huh? I always thought the youngest kid was spared all of that. I'm the oldest of four, and my folks really seem to be zeroed in on me setting the bar for my sisters and little brother. I'm **Radley Monroe.** If you're from around here, you may have heard of my folks. Dad's the football coach at Mockingbird High. He was the first African-American to get a graduate degree from State U. He also teaches math, so he's pretty smart. Mom's Scout Monroe, one of the anchors of the six o'clock news on Channel 10.

Wow! My family never misses your mom's newscast. They will be so excited when I tell them that we are working on a project together. My name is **NaMii Kim,** and as you have probably figured out, I'm Korean. My grandparents immigrated here in the '50s. My dad is the eldest of their children and the only boy. My grandparents love to talk about Korean traditions. It's pretty interesting most of the time, but sometimes they don't exactly approve of the "modern" ideas my brothers and I have, and since they live with us, we get an earful. Maybe this class will help me listen to all the different viewpoints. My dad works at the auto plant as an accountant and business manager. And, Ben, I think my dad knows your dad. My mother works in the cosmetics department of Merc's department store. Let me know if you need anything; I can get a discount.

Well, it looks like I'm the only one left. I'm **Nolvia Gutierrez.** Yeah, I know what you mean, NaMii, about grandparents and their old-school ideas. Mine came from Honduras and live next door to my family. But it actually has been a good thing. My dad had an accident a few years ago, and now he's a paraplegic. Thank goodness my grandparents were there. They really helped while dad went through operations, therapy, and all that stuff. My mom works as a pharmacist with Rex Drugs, and she really relied on them a lot to help my dad and to look after my brother and me.

It looks like we will have plenty of viewpoints to draw on as we develop our skit. Any ideas about what we should do? Maybe we could do one of those infomercials. You know, "Do you want to be a better friend or family member? A better student? A more successful employee? Even a better communicator? There is a skill that will help you become all of these things and more. What is that skill? Listening."

Say, Nolvia, that's great idea. I think we can find someone to be the loudmouth spokesperson. My friend Sam can probably help out with props . . . ∎

INTRODUCTION

As children, we are often praised and reinforced for speaking well. But how many of you were praised for "listening well"? For not interrupting? For being attentive? In school you are assigned speeches to give, and you can even take speaking classes. However, it is unlikely that you have received formal listening training before now. At best, you were exposed to a unit of listening as part of another class you have taken—public speaking, interpersonal communication, or music education.

Chances are classes aren't the only way you've learned about communication. You have made a lifetime study of the communication behaviors of those around you, particularly the communication habits and behaviors of significant people, such as your parents and friends. All of us tend to model our communication behaviors after those we observe. This holds true for listening as well. But just because you model your communication and listening on others in your lives doesn't mean you can't learn a great deal more about useful and effective listening behaviors.

As scholars and consultants in the field of communication and listening, we feel that listening is not just a critical communication competency; it is an important life competency. As a listener, you receive information that helps you to reach personal goals and develop and support relationships. Business owners often report that one of the skills they value most is listening.[1] As consultants, we often hear them complain that they have a hard time finding employees who listen effectively.

LISTENING IS FUNDAMENTAL

The Importance of Listening Competency

One reason we believe listening is a critical life competency is it is fundamental to all other communication competencies—speaking, writing, and reading. Of these competencies, listening is the first communication skill we acquire and use. In fact, you began to listen before you were born. Researchers have found that during the last trimester of a pregnancy, the fetus actively processes incoming auditory input. Fetuses at this stage can clearly distinguish among music, language, and other sounds.[2] So even at the very beginnings of human consciousness, listening plays an important role.

Listening is also key to learning language.[3] In fact, "learning to speak a language is very largely a task of learning to hear it."[4] Infants are born with the ability to distinguish among all sounds—consonants and vowels—necessary to produce any human language.[5] However, if infants do not hear certain sounds, they eventually lose the ability to easily reproduce them. By 12 months, children have learned the sounds and rules of their native language. So an English-speaking child distinguishes between and can articulate both *R* and *L,* while a Japanese child does not. It is by listening that infants fine-tune their brains to Swahili instead of Spanish, or to English instead of Egyptian. Infants, then, learn to understand and master language by simply listening to us talk. This understanding of oral language becomes the basis for learning the details and language rules needed to accurately read and write. In fact, reading comprehension is highly correlated with listening comprehension.[6] This finding can be illustrated by how a number of children learn to read by first listening to others read aloud then listening to the words as they themselves read aloud. By reading aloud, children can recognize (by listening to their own voices) and self-correct their pronunciation.[7]

Ultimately your abilities to "speak, read, write, and reason" are influenced by your listening ability.[8] As students, listening is fundamental to your personal and academic success.[9] Educator Joseph Beatty went even further, arguing that good listening is both an intellectual as well as a moral virtue because it is fundamental to understanding both yourself and others. He went on to say that it is only with good listening that you have the ability to "transform" yourself (and others). In other words, through listening you have the opportunity to "be all that you can be" and can help others do the same.

THINK ON IT

Can you think of a time when listening led you to discover something new about yourself? How did you react? Do you think you would have learned this about yourself if you hadn't learned it by listening to others?

Listening Takes Time (Literally)

As the discussion and proposed skit at the beginning of this chapter suggest, listening is an important communication competency. But just how important is it? Of the many forms of communication—reading, writing, speaking, and listening—which is used the most?

Researcher Paul Rankin was the first to ask this question, in 1926. Results of Rankin's communication time study suggested that people in the early 20th century engaged in listening approximately 42 percent of their waking hours. Studies conducted since then have consistently supported Rankin's findings across a variety of populations and contexts. For example, research in the early 1970s showed that homemakers spent about 48 percent of their time listening, while businesspeople spent 33 percent of their time listening.[10] Another study assessing how students, employees, and homemakers spent their communication time found that 55 percent of that time was spent listening.[11] More recent studies found similar listening results.[12] Table 1.1 summarizes much of the time research that has been conducted over the past 70 years.

An interesting piece of information to keep in mind when looking at the results presented in this table is the effect of media usage on the time spent listening. As indicated in Table 1.1, some earlier studies included time spent listening to media in their calculation of the total percentage of time we spend listening. These studies were conducted before the explosion of computer and related communication technology over the past ten years. To get an accurate picture of how much time you and your colleagues actually spend listening, we must look at the effect of your use of the Internet, e-mail, Facebook, iPods, mobile phones, and so forth. The most recent time study available, reported in 2006 by listening scholars Laura Janusik and Andy Wolvin, measured media usage (including Internet and e-mail) and looked at communication in specific settings such as work and family/friend time.[13] They concluded that, on average, we spend at least 50 percent of our day listening to either another person or to media. However, given the ubiquitous nature of media technology, they speculate that the figure might actually be higher. Another interesting finding emerging from the Janusik and Wolvin study is that use of technology has affected how much time we interact face-to-face. Their research suggests that while overall communication time has increased, it appears that for the first time, we spend less than 50 percent of our communication time speaking (20 percent) and listening (24 percent). Listening associated with new media has apparently taken time from previous listening and speaking interactions. It is important to note that Janusik and Wolvin's study indicates that we still spend more time listening in a face-to-face context than we do in any other communication activity.

Taken as a whole, these studies indicate that you spend approximately half of your time communicating with others. And you spend at least half of your communication time listening.

Clearly, listening plays a significant role in our intellectual and social development as well as being critical to effective communication. To get us started in our exploration of this critical competency, we first discuss definitions of listening and review models of listening. We then introduce a new model of listening that we use throughout this book, and finally we provide an overview of the topics covered in this text.

TABLE 1.1

Time Studies Showing the Percentage of Time in Various Communication Activities[14]

Year	Study	Population	Time Listening	Time Speaking	Time Reading	Time Writing	Time with Media
1926	Rankin	Varied	.42	.32	.15	.11	
1971	Breiter	Homemakers	.48	.35	.10	.07	
1975	Weinrauch & Swanda	College students	.33	.26	.19	.23	
1975	Werner	Varied	.55	.23	.13	.08	
1980	Barker et al.	College students	.53*	.16	.17	.14	.20*
1990	Vickers	College students	.64*	.22	.08	.07	.31*
1999	Bohlken	College students	.53	.22	.13	.12	
2001	Davis	College students	.34	.31	.12	.10	
2006	Janusik & Wolvin	College students	.24**	.20	.08	.09	.39

*Time spent listening to media is also included in total time spent listening.
**Time spent listening doesn't include time spent listening to/using the media.

Defining Listening

Even though listening is one of the most important skills you can develop, scholars haven't always agreed on just what constitutes listening competency. Perhaps the best overview of definitions of listening was written by Ethel Glenn in 1989. In that article she analyzed the content of fifty definitions of listening.[15] These definitions came from a variety of sources, including listening scholars, speech communication texts, and other communication research. A handful of the definitions Glenn covered is presented in Table 1.2.

Glenn concluded her article by stating, "[a] universal definition of listening from which operational guidelines may be established will not be easy to formulate."[16] Her observations presented a challenge to scholars around the world involved in listening research. After much discussion and debate, in 1996 the members of the International Listening Association adopted the following definition: Listening is *"the process of receiving, constructing meaning from, and responding to spoken and/or nonverbal messages."*[17] Today it is one of the most used definitions in both professional and academic listening publications.

THINK ON IT

Looking at the definitions presented in Table 1.2, what do they have in common? How do they differ? How do they compare to the definition adopted by the members of the International Listening Association? Do you think the ILA definition should incorporate any other elements? Given the changes in technology since 1996, would you suggest any changes to the ILA's definition?

> ### TABLE 1.2
>
> **Definitions of Listening**
>
> - The ability to understand spoken language (Rankin, 1926).
> - The process of reacting to, interpreting, and relating the spoken language in terms of past experiences and further courses of action (Barbe & Meyers, 1954).
> - The aural assimilation of spoken symbols in a face-to-face speaker audience situation, with both oral and visual cues present (Brown & Carlsen, 1955).
> - The selective process of attending to, hearing, understanding, and remembering aural symbols (Barker, 1971).
> - The process by which spoken language is converted to meaning in the mind (Lundsteen, 1971).
> - A rather definite and deliberative ability to hear information, to analyze it, to recall it at a later time, and to draw conclusions from it (Kelly, 1975).
> - Three interwoven processes: (1) the physical reception of auditory stimuli, (2) the perception (symbolic classification) of the stimuli, and (3) the interpretation of the stimuli (Millar & Millar, 1976).
> - The process of receiving, attending to, and assigning meaning to aural stimuli (Wolvin & Coakley, 1985).
> - . . . an intellectual or active function that involves the mind, eyes, ears, and memory (Vasile & Mintz, 1986).

Models of Listening

Most of you are probably familiar with basic communication models that address the sender, receiver, message, feedback, and noise. These elements are combined with various others in a multitude of models. Based on these communication models, we have learned a great deal about constructing and sending messages. However, while you have spent much of your lives learning how to put together a message, this time is wasted if you don't also think about what happens when the other party receives it. So just as you are mindful about what goes into a message that you send, you need to be mindful of how incoming information is received and processed. To help us start down that road, we will next look at models of listening. The purpose of a **model** is to illustrate complex, abstract processes in such a way you have a clear understanding of how the process works.

Before introducing our model of listening (the WFH model), we need to look briefly at existing models. Belle Ruth Witkin reviewed a number of listening models in a 1990 article.[18] She divided the models into three broad areas: speech communication models, cognitive models, and speech science models.

Speech Communication Models

Speech communication models look at listening within the context of a communication setting or as a communication-specific skill. Well-known examples of this category include models by Larry Barker and Andy Wolvin and Carolyn Coakley.[19] Essentially these models go beyond traditional communication models to emphasize the skills and processes used to listen. For example, both models highlight the role and importance of receiving information and assigning meaning to messages. Most general communication models at the time tended to ignore these aspects of communication.

The root of speech communication models can be traced to the early work of Ralph Nichols. Nichols is known as the "father of listening" because his early research had a profound effect on how scholars viewed listening. Although other scholars had studied listening, Nichols's work motivated scholars to think of listening as a separate and identifiable aspect of communication. In a 1948 article, Nichols argued that an awakening was taking place in education about the importance of listening comprehension. He declared that (at that time) most educators felt "the process of communication is predominantly composed of four skills: reading, writing, speaking, and listening."[20] During this period, Nichols was mostly interested in listening as it related to the comprehension of lecture information. He constructed a test designed to tap listening comprehension of a lecture and compared the results with several standardized tests covering intelligence, social ease, and other mental and social variables. His results suggested that there are a number of **elements affecting listening comprehension,** including *cognitive factors* (e.g., intelligence, curiosity, inference-making ability, ability to concentrate), *language-related factors* (e.g., reading comprehension, recognition of correct English usage, size of the listener's vocabulary, ability to identify main ideas), *speaker-related factors* (e.g., speaker effectiveness, audibility of the speaker, admiration for the speaker), *contextual factors* (e.g., interest in the subject, importance of the subject, room ventilation and temperature, listener's physical fatigue), and *demographic factors* (e.g., listener sex, parental occupation, high school academic achievement).

Looking at Nichols's research, you can see that he was still focused on the overall communication process. While he begins to isolate or separate listening from other communication elements, he still includes the effect of the speaker. Thus, Nichols's approach still ultimately embeds listening in the sender-receiver mode.

One of the most important conclusions Nichols drew from his work was that "listening comprehension apparently involves a number of factors not operative in reading comprehension."[21] This statement suggested that listening was a separate receiving and information-processing skill that qualitatively differed from other communication skills studied at that time (e.g., reading, writing). So even though he focused on the communication aspect of listening, he laid important groundwork for the next generation of listening scholars to use in their development of cognitive models.

Cognitive Models

The cognitive models were developed in the field of cognitive psychology. While these models are not listening specific, they do include in-depth analyses of two essential elements of listening: attention and memory. In general, these models tend to focus on getting a receiver's attention and getting information into memory. With the exception of a memory-based listening model introduced by Bob Bostrom and Enid Waldhart, the concept of listening isn't considered as part of any of the specific cognitive models covered by Witkin.[22] Listening scholars

Bostrom and Waldhart felt that components of memory were essential to understanding the listening process. Perhaps the most important contribution of this model is its emphasis on short- and long-term memory and the functions they play in listening. Bostrom and Waldhart did find relationships between memory and listening and concluded that listening includes short- and long-term components.[23] Other cognitive and listening research has found listening to be related to inductive reasoning, verbal comprehension, memory, reading, cognitive complexity, and receiver apprehension.[24]

More recently Laura Janusik continued this line of research by going beyond just looking at related cognitive functions. She proposed a model of listening grounded in working memory (i.e., short-term memory). Her model addresses how we process information as well as how we store it.[25] Her research findings support claims that listening is a cognitive process. We discuss cognitive aspects of listening further in Chapter 3.

Speech Science Models

The third category of models that Witkin explored was speech science models, or auditory-processing models. These models seem to focus more on the physiological aspects of listening or hearing and the act of discriminating types of incoming stimulus. Through her research, Witkin identified a number of important auditory elements affecting listening, such as pitch/intonation and oral language processing.[26] While critics of these models suggest that they confuse the hearing process with listening (and we certainly don't want to do that), these models are important because they emphasize two critical aspects of listening: physical reception of the stimulus and the ability to discriminate among pieces of the stimulus. While knowing the physiology of listening is important, we must keep in mind that people who are profoundly deaf and those who have hearing disabilities are able to take in information and process it. This observation suggests that listening is much more than the physiological process of receiving and processing sound.

Current Listening Models

Recent models attempt to blend the three areas identified by Witkin. One of these models, Judy Brownell's **HURIER model,** includes elements of the cognitive and speech science perspectives.[27] The model looks at six interrelated processes:

1. Hearing—the accurate reception of sound. This element of the process includes focusing on the speaker, discriminating among sounds, and concentrating on the message.
2. Understanding—listening comprehension or understanding the message. This element involves information processing and inner speech.
3. Remembering—retaining and recalling information.
4. Interpreting—using the interaction context and knowledge of the other person to assign meaning to the message.
5. Evaluating—applying your own perspectives and biases to your interpretation.
6. Responding—appropriately responding to the message.

In the HURIER model, the above elements are situated in the context of the listening goal and the situation, making it an interpersonally based model.

Other models are more contextually based. For example, the **Integrative Listening model** (ILM), developed by Kathy Thompson and colleagues, is based on a specific definition of listening: "the dynamic, interactive process of integrating appropriate listening attitudes, knowledge, and behaviors to achieve the selected goal(s) of a listening event."[28] This model centers on four stages:

1. Preparing to listen—establishing listening goals ahead of time, analyzing the interaction context, and addressing potential listening filters
2. Applying the listening process model—using five distinct components of listening—receiving, comprehending, evaluating, interpreting, and responding—in ways that are appropriate for the specific listening setting
3. Assessing listening effectiveness—reflecting on one's listening performance by oneself and others
4. Establishing goals for future listening—ongoing development of listening goals based on self-assessment and feedback

The authors suggest that the stages are interrelated, discrete elements that are each uniquely important to the listening process. In addition to context, the ILM also emphasizes the role of assessment by each party.

The next model was developed to study cultural differences in listening. Professors Margarete Imhof of Germany and Laura Janusik of the United States developed a **systems model** of the listening process.[29] Their model explores the associations among three aspects of listening: presage, process, and product. *Presage* includes the interaction of context factors and the mental and motivational aspect of the listener, while *process* includes different courses of listening action. For example, they feel that listening for information and listening for relationship building are two very different things. Finally, *product* reflects the listening outcome the listener seeks and achieves. It is important to remember that presage, process, and product interact and affect each other.

> **THINK ON IT**
>
> Think back on a recent listening encounter. It can be a class lecture you found particularly interesting (or boring), a friend in distress, or a movie you were watching. Pick two of the previously described models. How would they help explain what occurred during your listening encounter? Did you find one model did a better job of explaining than the other?

The above discussion of existing models of listening gives you a good idea of the breadth of perspectives of the listening process. The next model we cover is our own model—the Worthington Fitch-Hauser (WFH) model—and the one that we will use to present listening as a critical communication and life competency. The **Listening MATERRS model** presents our perspective of the listening process. While we recognize that listening occurs in some type of communication context, we feel it is important to focus on what happens from the point the listener becomes aware of a stimulus. This starting point is the beginning of the conscious process of listening and acknowledges that there are many sounds "out there" that we choose to ignore. Before reading about our model, take a moment to *Think on It.*

> **THINK ON IT**
>
> Have you ever thought about how noisy our world is? To test this premise, get everyone in the room to stop talking for sixty seconds. During this time of silence, count the number of sounds you can identify.

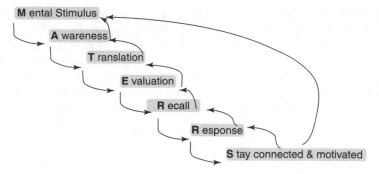

FIGURE 1.1
Elements of the Worthington Fitch-Hauser Model of Listening.

WORTHINGTON FITCH-HAUSER MODEL OF LISTENING: LISTENING MATERRS

WFH Model Elements

<u>M</u>ental Stimulus   In many ways, listening is a sorting process. We hear a tremendous amount of material every day, but as you know, we can't listen to all of it. **Mental stimulus** occurs when you begin to actively *attend* to a physical noise or stimulus. You make a conscious decision to focus and "listen" to a particular input. Thus, you hear your name from across the room, someone raises his voice and speaks angrily, or you see a quick movement and direct your focus to that particular listening event. Thus, hearing is the physiological process, while listening

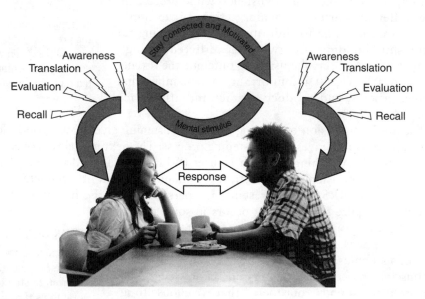

FIGURE 1.2
The Worthington Fitch-Hauser Model.

involves *intentionality* on the part of the receiver. We hear a great deal (i.e., physically receive stimulus) but attend to relatively little of it.

Awareness   Once you become fully aware or intentionally listen to a sound or message, you can then say you have moved to **awareness.** Here you engage in what can best be described as a mental sorting process, which means you have begun to listen more closely to the message or sound. Your decision to actively attend to a message is affected by any number of factors. One of these factors is **motivation.** If you are motivated by the subject matter, the situation, or the individual, you will find a way to focus and pay attention. Another factor is cognitive load. **Cognitive load** is the amount of information you are mentally processing at a given point in time.[30] For example, if you are experiencing a particularly high cognitive load, you might not be able to listen any further. The student who is worried about an exam; the woman driving and talking on her mobile phone; and the dad with a child jumping up and down, trying to get his attention will all have a higher cognitive load than the person who is sitting quietly, focused on a presentation. The higher the cognitive load, the fewer mental resources you have available to listen. Although most of us like to think we can multitask, multitasking simply does not work well when it comes to really listening to others. Multitasking is directly related to cognitive load, the more activities you engage in, the greater your cognitive load.

Cognitive filtering can also affect your ability to listen. Cognitive filtering addresses your ability to filter out common noises such as the ones you identified when you tried the 60-second exercise in the *Think on It* box. During that brief time, you heard any number of mental stimulus inputs. However, until that moment, you were probably unaware of them largely because you had no reason, or lacked motivation, to tune in to them.

Environmental factors can also affect your ability to listen. These factors can be internal or external. For example, a loud radio, uncomfortable temperatures, hunger pangs, and the like can distract you from listening. Finally cognitive filtering includes your **personal biases.** You might stop listening to a speaker because you think you have "heard it all before," you personally dislike him, or you think he is too young to offer insight into your conversation. Your biases can have a tremendous effect on your choice to engage in the next aspect of our model: translation.

Translation   Given sufficient motivation, you move from awareness to **translation.** At this level the listener begins to recognize the basic components of the message. Here language begins to be processed, nonverbals are interpreted,

---

THINK ON IT

Grammy Award–winning violinist Joshua Bell, one of the world's premier violinists, participated in a study conducted by the *Washington Post*. Would the people of Washington, D.C., stop and listen as they passed through L'Enfant Plaza, one of many subway stops in the city? Would they listen to a man who sells out concert halls and who owns and plays a $3.5 million Stradivarius violin? Would you stop and listen? As you watch the video clips embedded in the *Washington Post*'s story, you can tell that for some people, his music did not register enough with them for their listening to move to an awareness level. These people did not appear to hear him at all. Other individuals were obviously aware of Bell's playing. They looked over to him but continued walking. A few people stopped and put money in his violin case. Even fewer actually stopped and truly listened.

Reviewing the factors that may affect the first two levels of listening described above, what may be affecting their listening processes? Why would all the children who heard Bell play try to stop and listen, while their parents try to hurry them along?

A few individuals did stop and listen. What has to happen in terms of their listening for this to occur? Why would they stop? If you're interested in the explanations from individuals who heard Bell play that day, you can access the full article and video clips at the *Washington Post* Web site (www.washingtonpost.com). Gene Weingarten's article is titled "Pearls Before Breakfast."

schemata are triggered. Three types of processing of information might occur: affective processing, rational processing, and dual processing.

Affective processing occurs when you primarily focus on the emotional elements of what you are hearing. Is the person upset? Does the message make you happy? Sad? Angry? Is it uplifting or depressing? Some contexts require that you primarily focus on affective processing. At those times you are less concerned about whether a person's message makes sense and are more interested in determining how he or she is feeling. At other times you might need to suppress your own emotions and focus on fully understanding a message—grammar, logic, clarity, coherence, and so forth. At these times you engage in **rational processing**. Rational processing occurs when you focus on the information itself and the logic of that information. In this type of processing, you analyze, fairly objectively, the validity of the message and begin to connect it with what you have stored in your own information banks. You might also evaluate the credentials of the speaker and the appropriateness of the information for the situation. When you use your rational processing as a listener, you are assessing the information according to your individual understanding of the rules of logic. In other words, what seems logical to Ben might not seem logical to Tamarah. Thus, it's important for you to remember that like all information processing, this type of reasoning is governed by individual experiences and education. Finally you can also engage in **dual processing**. At times effective listening requires you to use both affective and rational processing to translate a message.

Evaluation   When you truly begin linking what you hear to what you know, you have moved to **evaluating** a message. This level involves the actual cognitive processing of the information. You use your schemata to aid in the interpretation of what you hear, to develop new mental models, and to categorize information. This level also includes value assessments. In judging the violin playing of Joshua Bell (see previous *Think on It* box), you might decide the music has a beautiful melody, too slow a beat, or just isn't your style. If you determine the information is important enough or novel enough, you are motivated to move to the next element in our model of listening: recalling.

Recall   Two important things happen at this point. First, you determine what gets stored in your memory. Second, you assess whether a message requires a response. In the context of this model, memory can be divided into two primary areas: working memory and long-term memory. **Working memory** is the information that is accessible to you during a listening event. Memory researchers would call this short-term memory (a concept discussed further in Chapter 3). In essence, working memory is short-term storage where you place information while you make decisions about what you are going to do with it.[31] For example, if you hear a professor say information is going to be covered on an exam, you will not only pay close attention, you will likely send the information to long-term memory. On the other hand, if you are engaging in a social conversation with the same professor, you will retain information just long enough to make an appropriate response; you might or might not send the information to long-term storage. **Long-term memory** is your storehouse of information. It contains all of the information you have learned in life. However, it is important to note that if you are not listening, information probably will never make it to long-term storage.

<u>Responding</u>   At this level you make decisions about how you will respond to the other party. Your internal response occurs at both the translation and the evaluation levels. When responding, you might decide against overtly responding to a message (i.e., ignore it), you might decide that a touch of the hand is enough, or you might verbally respond to the incoming message. Your decisions about responding can also be influenced by any number of factors: your knowledge of the topic, your history with that individual, the schemata stored in memory of what is appropriate in this particular type of situation, your mood. For example, if the other person is upset, you use your "how to respond to sadness schema" to help you determine what the right response is. If you are going to reply verbally, at this point you determine the best form and content for the message. Your memory of previous encounters will aid you in determining the best way to respond to a situation. A good listener will be aware of the entire message—words, emotions, and context—and will be able to react in a caring and appropriate manner.

<u>Staying Connected (and Motivated)</u>   Overarching the entire process is staying connected and being motivated. Staying connected implies that the listening process is more than "in one ear and out the other." Listening is built around relationships you have with others. As you listen, you identify what you know about the other person, what you have learned from past interactions, what the person's nonverbal messages are, and what the context is. In addition, you continue to pull in additional information during each listening episode with the person, context, event, and so forth, and use it in your future interactions. You use this information to help build schemata and scripts to help guide your behavior in future interactions and in similar contexts (using long-term memory). Here we focus on remaining engaged, truly listening to the other. To do so, you must be motivated to stay focused.

Motivation is of critical importance because it links each of the factors we have discussed. When receiving a mental stimulus, you must be motivated in some way to become fully aware of what you hear, and even greater motivation is needed to translate and evaluate the stimulus. Essentially motivation is the tie that binds all parts of the greater listening process.

Finally another overarching element of the listening process is your **personal biases.** As we mentioned above, biases can affect not only your choice to actually listen but your decision to continue listening, how you translate and evaluate what you hear, and what and how you remember what you attend to.

OVERVIEW OF THE TEXT

As we noted earlier, this textbook focuses on listening as more than just a critical communication competency, but also as a life skill. Consequently you will find that many of the chapters cover the role and function of listening in either important settings we find ourselves in or within certain occupational areas.

The book is divided into three major sections. The first addresses the cognitive processes associated with listening. Chapter 2 introduces you to the different types of listening, the role of empathy, and the importance of listening across the life span. It also examines the importance of listening competence, shows you how to measure your own listening competency, and concludes with a discussion of the importance of setting personal and professional listening goals. Chapter 3 addresses information processing issues. For example, we look at the role schemata play in listening as well as the effect that memory and recall have on listening. The next chapter focuses on individual differences that can affect our listening processes. In it we explore listening style preferences, personality types, communication apprehension, and emotional IQ.

The second section of the text explores the social functions of listening. Chapter 5 examines the fundamental role of listening to understanding ourselves, especially as related to daily conversations, conflict, and relationship building. Chapters 6 and 7 explore the effect listening has on specific relationships, including friendships, romance, and families.

The third section of the book looks at listening in specific contexts, such as organizations, health, education, and law. As students, you might find Chapter 8 particularly interesting as it addresses listening in the educational context. Here we explore connections between listening and topics such as learning and academic performance, teaching effectiveness, and note-taking. Chapter 9, the organizational chapter, explores the connection between listening and job satisfaction and the importance of listening to customer satisfaction. Chapter 10 addresses listening and the health industry. We explore listening links to patient health, medical error, and patient satisfaction and compliance. Finally Chapter 11 examines listening in the legal context. For example, we address listening theory and practice in the trial process, in attorney-client interviews, jury decision-making, and in alternative dispute resolution.

In Chapter 12 we conclude the book with a brief look at the future of listening, especially how new areas of listening research might expand our understanding of how we develop our listening skills, how we measure listening competency, and new ways of developing our listening competency.

CONCEPTS TO KNOW

Listening Models
    Speech Communication Models
    Cognitive Models
    Speech Science Models
    HURRIER Model
    Integrative Listening Model (ILM)
    Systems Model
Listening MATERRS (WFH) Model
    Mental Stimulus
    Awareness
        Cognitive Load
        Cognitive Filtering
        Environmental Factors
        Personal Biases

Translation
    Affective Processing
    Rational Processing
    Dual Processing
Evaluation
Recall
    Working Memory
    Long-term Memory
Response
Stay Connected
    Motivation

DISCUSSION QUESTIONS

1. Who are some of the significant people you believe affected your communication and listening? What communication and listening skills and habits (good and bad) do you engage in that you can trace back to them?
2. Do you think your culture or ethnic background has affected how you listen? If so, how? If not, why not?
3. We cover three primary types of models: speech communication models, cognitive models, and speech science models. What commonalities do they share? What do these commonalities suggest about the process of listening? What differences do you see? What do these differences suggest about how researchers perceive listening?

4. The WFH model of listening introduces the idea of different types of processing as part of the translation process. When are you most likely to engage in affective processing? Rational processing? Dual processing?

LISTENING ACTIVITIES

1. How do your communication and listening activities stack up against the studies described in Table 1.1? Chart your activities for a day or two or even a week. Do you spend more time on the computer? Talking face-to-face with friends? Using your mobile phone? How do your findings compare with your friends'? In a small group or with the entire class, average your findings together and compare them to those presented in Table 1.1.

2. Tinnitus (ringing in the ears) is one of the many factors that can affect listening. What are other hearing disabilities? Locate and interview someone with a hearing disability. How severe does she find the disability? How does it affect her life? Does it interfere with how she communicates with others? If yes, how does she compensate for it? If possible, also interview a friend or family member of the person with the hearing disability. Does he agree that his friend/loved one listens effectively?

ADDITIONAL READINGS

Bostrom, R. N., & Waldhart, E. S. (1980). Components in listening behavior: The role of short-term memory. *Human Communication Research, 6*, 222–227.

Holtgraves, T. M. (2002). *Language as social action: Social psychology and language use.* Mahwah, NJ: Erlbaum.

Johnson, A., & Proctor, R. W. (2004). *Attention: Theory and practice.* Thousand Oaks, CA: Sage.

Proctor, R. W., & Vu, K. P. L. (2006). The cognitive revolution at age 50: Has the promise of the human information-processing approach been fulfilled? *International Journal of Human-Computer Interaction, 21*, 253–284.

Spitzberg, B. H., & Cupach, W. R. (1984). *Interpersonal communication competence.* Beverly Hills: Sage.

ENDNOTES

1. Hansen & Hansen, 2007; Lloyd & Kennedy, 1997; "What are employers," 2006
2. Karmiloff-Smith, 1995; Wilkin, 1993
3. Vandergrift & Goh, 2009
4. Nida, 1957, p. 53, as cited in Peterson, 2001
5. "How babies acquire," 2001
6. Badian, 1999
7. De Jong & der Leij, 2002; Gough & Tunmer, 1986
8. Rubin & Morreale, 1996; Sandall, Schramm, & Seiber, 2002
9. Barr, Dittmar, Roberts, & Sheraden, 2002; Swanson, 1997
10. Brieter, 1971; Weinrauch & Swanda, 1975
11. Werner, 1975
12. Coakley, 1988 (as cited in Coakley & Wolvin, 1990); Perras & Weitzel, 1981; Rankin, 1926; Vickers, 1990
13. Janusik & Wolvin, 2006
14. Janusik & Wolvin, 2007. The full citation for each of the listed studies is presented in the chapter reference list.
15. Glenn, 1989
16. Glenn, 1989, p. 29
17. Listen, 2007
18. Witkin, 1990
19. Barker, 1971; Wolvin & Coakley, 1996
20. Nichols, 1948, p. 154
21. Nichols, 1948, p. 162
22. Bostrom & Waldhart, 1988
23. Bostrom & Waldhart, 1980
24. Beatty & Payne, 1984; Caffrey, 1953; Fitch-Hauser, Barker, & Hughes, 1990; Roberts, 1988; Spearrit, 1962
25. Janusik, 2005
26. Witkin, Butler, & Whalen, 1977
27. Brownell, 2009
28. Thompson, Leintz, Nevers, & Witkowski, 2004
29. Imhof & Janusik, 2006
30. Kalyuga, 2009
31. For an excellent discussion of working memory and problems with poor working memory, see Klingberg (2009).

REFERENCES

Badian, N. (1999). Reading disability defined as a discrepancy between listening and reading comprehension. *Journal of Learning Disabilities, 32,* 138–148.

Barker, L. (1971). *Listening Behavior.* Englewood Cliffs, NJ: Prentice-Hall.

Barker, L., Edwards, R., Gaines, C., Gladney, K., & Holley, F. (1980). An investigation of proportional time spent in various communication activities by college students. *Journal of Applied Communication Research 8,* 101–110.

Barr, L., Dittmar, M., Roberts, E., & Sheraden, M. (2002). *Enhancing student achievement through the improvement of listening skills.* (ERIC Document Reproduction Service No. ED465999)

Beatty, M., & Payne, S. (1984). Listening comprehension as a function of cognitive complexity: A research note. *Communication Monographs, 51,* 85–89.

Bohlken, B. (1999, Fall). Substantiating the fact that listening is proportionately most used language skill. *The Listening Post, 70,* 5.

Bostrom, R. N., & Waldhart, E. S. (1980). Components in listening behavior: The role of short-term memory. *Human Communication Research, 6,* 221–227.

Bostrom, R. N., & Waldhart, E. (1988). Memory models and the measurement of listening. *Communication Education, 37,* 1–13.

Brieter, L. R. (1971). Research in listening and its importance to literature. In L. Barker (ed.), *Listening Behavior.* Englewood Cliffs, NJ: Prentice-Hall.

Brownell, J. (2009). *Listening: Attitudes, principles and skills.* (4th ed.). Boston: Allyn & Bacon.

Caffrey, J. G. (1953). *Auding ability as a function of certain psychometric variables.* Unpublished doctoral dissertation, University of California, Berkeley.

Coakley, C. G., & Wolvin, A. D. (1990). Listening pedagogy and andragogy: The state of the art. *Journal of the International Listening Association, 4,* 33–61.

Davis, D. F. (2001, Summer). Two ears and one mouth: Two eyes and one hand. *The Listening Post, 77,* 10–13.

De Jong, P., & der Leij, A. (2002). Effects of phonological abilities and linguistics comprehension on the development of reading. *Scientific Studies of Reading, 6,* 51–77.

Fitch-Hauser, M., Barker, D. R., & Hughes, A. (1990). Receiver apprehension and listening comprehension: A linear or curvilinear relationship? *Southern Communication Journal, 56,* 62–71.

Glenn, E. (1989). A content analysis of fifty definitions of listening. *Journal of the International Listening Association, 3,* 21–31.

Gough, P., & Tunmer, W. (1986). Decoding, reading, and reading disability. *Remedial and Special Education, 7,* 6–16.

Greitemeyer, T. (2009). Effects of songs with prosocial lyrics on prosocial behavior: Further evidence and a mediating mechanism. *Personality and Social Psychology Bulletin, 35,* 1500–1511.

Hansen, R. S., & Hansen, K. (n.d.). What do employers really want? Top skills and values employers seek from job-seekers. *Quintessential Careers.* Retrieved from www.quintcareers.com/job_skills_values.html.

How babies acquire building blocks of speech affects later reading, language ability. (2001, July 30). *Science Daily.* Retrieved from www.sciencedaily.com.

Imhof, M., & Janusik, L. (2006, July). Development and validation of the Imhof-Janusik listening concepts inventory to measure listening conceptualization differences between cultures. *Journal of Intercultural Communication Research, 35,* 79–98.

Janusik, L. (2005). Conversational listening span: A proposed measure of conversational listening. *International Journal of Listening, 19,* 12–30.

Janusik, L., & Wolvin, A. (2006). *Time spent listening.* Paper presented to the annual meeting of the International Listening Association, Salem, OR.

Janusik, L., & Wolvin, A. (2009). 24 hours in a day: A listening update to the time study. *International Journal of Listening, 23,* 104–120.

Kalyuga, S. (2009). *Managing cognitive load in adaptive multimedia learning.* Hershey, PA: IGI Global.

Karmiloff-Smith, A. (1995). *Beyond modularity: A developmental perspective on cognitive science.* Cambridge, MA: MIT Press.

Klingberg, T. (2009). *The overflowing brain.* New York: Oxford University Press.

International Listening Association. (2007). *Listen and make the connection.* Retrieved from www.listen.org.

Lloyd, M. A., & Kennedy, J. H. (1997, August 28). Skills employers seek. Retrieved from PsychWeb www.psywww.com/careers/skills.htm.

Nichols, R. (1948). Factors in listening comprehension. *Speech Monographs, 15,* 154–163.

Perras, M. T., & Weitzel, A. R. (1981). Measuring daily communication activities. *Florida Speech Communication Journal, 9,* 19–23.

Peterson, P. W. (2001). Skills and strategies for proficient listening. *Teaching English as a second or foreign language.* (3rd ed.). Boston: Heinle & Heinle.

Rankin, P. T. (1926). *The measurement of the ability to understand spoken language.* Doctoral dissertation. Available from ProQuest Dissertations and Theses database. (AAT 0004362)

Roberts, C. V. (1988). The validation of listening tests: Cutting the Gordian knot. *Journal of the International Listening Association, 2,* 1–19.

Rubin, R. B., & Morreale, S. P. (1996). Setting expectations for speech communication and listening. *New Directions for Higher Education, 96,* 19–29.

Sandall, N., Schramm, K., & Seiber, A. (2003). *Improving listening skills through the use of children's literature.* Saint Xavier University & SkyLight Professional Development Field-based Masters Program, Chicago, IL. (ERIC Document Reproduction Service No. ED482002)

Spearrit, D. (1962). Listening comprehension: A factorial analysis. *ACER Research Series No. 76.* Melbourne, Australia: Australian Council for Educational Research.

Swanson, C. H. (1997). *Who's listening in the classroom? A research paradigm.* Paper presented at the annual meeting of the International Listening Association, Sacramento, CA. (ERIC Document Reproduction Service No. ED407659)

Thompson, K., Leintz, P., Nevers, B., & Witkowski, S. (2004). The integrative listening model: An approach to teaching and learning listening. *Journal of General Education, 53,* 225–246.

Vandergrift, L., & Goh, C. (2009). Teaching and testing listening comprehension. In M. H. Long & C. J. Doughty (eds.), *The handbook of language teaching* (395–411). Malden, MA: Wiley-Blackwell.

Vickers, L. M. (1990). *The relationship between listening ability and time spent engaging in communication activities.* Unpublished master's thesis, Auburn University, Auburn, AL.

Weingarten, G. (2007, April 8) Pearls before breakfast: Can one of the nation's great musicians cut through the fog of a D.C. rush hour? Let's find out. *Washington Post,* W10. Retrieved from www.washingtonpost.com.

Weinrauch, J. D., & Swanda Jr., R. (1975). Examining the significance of listening: An exploratory study of contemporary management. *Journal of Business Communication, 13,* 25–32.

Werner, E. (1975). *A study of communication time.* Unpublished master's thesis, University of Maryland, College Park.

"What are employers looking for?" (2006). Student Services. Retrieved from University of Wisconsin—Madison, College of Engineering Web site http://studentservices.engr.wisc.edu/international/employers.html.

Wilkin, P. E. (1993). Prenatal and postnatal responses to music and sound stimuli. In T. Blum (ed.), *Prenatal perception learning and bonding* (307–329). Berlin: Leonardo.

Witkin, B. R. (1990). Listening theory and research: The state of the art. *Journal of the International Listening Association, 4,* 7–32.

Witkin, B. R., Butler, K. G., & Whalen, T. E. (1977). Auditory processing in children: Two studies of component factors. *Language, Speech & Hearing Services in Schools, 8,* 140–154.

Wolvin, A., & Coakley, C. (1996). *Listening.* (5th ed.). Boston: McGraw-Hill.

Listening

Types and Competencies

Listening Is Hard to Do

Man, I just heard the best lecture ever this morning. My mechanical engineering prof was on target. She lectured on properties of ceramic materials—you know, like the tiles on the space shuttle—and made half of the class want to apply to the space program.

Oh, Carter, you are such a nerd! I don't see how you stay interested in technical topics like that.

I was thinking about that question on my way here, Radley. This listening class has me thinking about a lot of things. Don't you think it's odd that I find it so easy to listen to lectures on ceramics or other materials of engineering but have such a problem listening to my mom? I would think that if I'm a good listener in class, I would be a good listener in any situation. Just yesterday my mom caught me not listening when she was telling me about my sister, Clara—you know, the one who lives in Jackson Gap.

I know what you mean. Some information is just easier for me to listen to. Why is it that I have problems listening in music appreciation and none when I talk with your dad about his football team? ■

TYPES OF LISTENING

As a critical communication competency, listening is multifaceted. If we think about Listening MATERRS, it is easy to see that it will take a number of different skills to be a good listener. This chapter will focus on two topics that will clarify what skills we need to be competent listeners. First, we will discuss listening as a critical communication competency. Second, we will look at different types of listening and the situations in which you will want to use them. We will finish with a discussion of the importance of levels of listening as an additional layer of listening types.

LISTENING AS A CRITICAL COMMUNICATION COMPETENCY

As you know, we feel strongly that listening is both a critical communication competency and a critical life competency. In fact, listening may well be the "key for the development and enhancement of language and learning skills."[1] Think about what would happen if a piece of information were important to your success and you didn't have the skills or abilities to understand the message as the sender intended. As communication professor Charles Swanson said, "Those who listen, learn. Those who do not or cannot listen, find the classroom frustrating."[2] Of course, this frustration isn't limited to the classroom. It also extends to other aspects of our lives. When you find yourself in a situation where you have failed to get information you need to respond appropriately to a friend or to complete a task properly, don't you feel frustrated? Chances are you also feel frustrated when other people don't listen to you. For example, how do you feel when you tell someone something that is important to you but that person ignores you? Clearly we can't communicate at all if no one is listening. As the receiving component of the communication process, listening is essential to the completion of the act of communication. According to education professor Joseph Beatty, a "good listener focuses her attention on the other's communication in order to understand the other's meaning or experience."[3] He went on to say that we need to understand the other party to achieve "a kind of fidelity to the meaning or intention of the other."

To further underscore the importance of listening, the National Communication Association (NCA), the largest U.S. organization for scholars in the field of communication, has identified a number of competencies that are directly listening focused. The following section gives an overview of the competencies listed on the NCA Web site.[4] These competencies have been identified as essential to the success of all college graduates.

The NCA suggested that a competent listener should be proficient in two areas. The first of these is listening with **literal comprehension.** Literal comprehension includes the ability to identify main ideas, supporting details, and the relationships among ideas. A competent listener should also be able to recall the basic ideas and details. So as a competent listener, one level of listening in which you want to develop skills is focusing on the *denotative,* or literal, meaning of the message. In the example in the case at the beginning of the chapter, Carter must use literal comprehension to understand his professor's lecture on ceramic materials. However, if he uses this same type of listening in his exchange with Radley, he will completely miss the intended message. So a good listener must also be able to listen beyond the literal message itself.

The second area of competence the NCA labeled **critical comprehension.** Under critical comprehension, the NCA suggested that a competent listener listens with an open mind. Listening with an open mind means that you are aware of your biases and recognize that everyone has a unique perspective. (The affect of biases will be discussed more fully in Chapter 5.) Listening with an open mind also means that you will send feedback that indicates your willingness to listen.

Critical comprehension also includes identifying the speaker's purpose and pattern of organization of the ideas. You should also be able to identify the

THINK ON IT

Can you think of a situation where you listened critically when you should have listened literally or vice versa?

speaker's bias and prejudice, the effect of that bias and prejudice, and the speaker's attitude. By focusing on these elements, you will be able to pick up the connotative meanings, or meanings that are intended rather than literally stated. So when Radley refers to his friend as a nerd, he isn't being literal; he is engaging in light banter. Since Carter can listen beyond the words and pick up the entire message in the context, he understands Radley's intended meaning.

While their exchange is rather simplistic, it doesn't take much imagination to apply the principles to truly important aspects of your lives. Clearly competent listening involves much more than taking in only the words themselves; it is a complex process we use to take in the entire message and accurately assign meaning to an incoming piece of information. A truly effective listener must use a wide variety of knowledge sources, rapidly interpret incoming data, and make sense of the message.[5] One way to understand the complexity of listening is to look at the dimensions covered by those who measure listening.

MEASURING LISTENING

One of the challenges faced by listening scholars is how to measure something without physical properties. Listening is a *hypothetical construct,* something you know exists but you can't physically see. You can see only the behavioral indicators supporting its existence. For example, communication is also a hypothetical construct. You can see most of the behaviors we associate with the act but can't put your finger on anything that actually, literally is communication. Listening is the same. You can see behaviors and experience feeling associated with listening but can't actually point to something and say, "That's listening." So how do you measure something that is abstract, and how do you know it actually exists? Researchers do so by identifying definable aspects of the skill and developing ways to measure those aspects.

A number of years ago, a researcher examined 25 different listening tests in an attempt to identify exactly what aspects of listening were being measured. The research identified 22 listening components, among them following directions, judging others' moods, and overall comprehension.[6] We can draw two conclusions from this study. First, there is some disagreement over the exact components of listening. And second, listening has many dimensions.

In this next section, we will examine a few of the attempts that have been made to add a sense of concreteness to the construct of listening.

Listening Fidelity

The first way we will look at listening is to focus on the literal comprehension dimension of the skill. One way to do this is exploring the goodness of fit between what the receiver mentally processes and what the sender actually delivers. This goodness of fit is referred to as **listening fidelity.** When the concept of fidelity was first introduced, researchers David Brant and William Powers focused on how well a sender could communicate with a receiver.[7] They felt that a sender should be able to communicate clearly enough that the receiver could create a representation of the message that was very similar to the original. Early research on fidelity looked at both concrete and abstract messages but did so from the sender's perspective, focusing on how the message was structured.[8] More recently the research on fidelity has shifted to looking at the issue from the receiver's point of view.

The work of Alice Mulanax and William Powers shifted the focus of fidelity research when they introduced the concept of listening fidelity.[9] Subsequent work has expanded what we know about fidelity from the listening point of view.[10] Listening fidelity is defined as "the degree of congruence between the cognitions of a listener and the cognitions of a source following a communication event."[11] In the listening-focused fidelity studies, cognitions have been measured by the listeners' abilities to reproduce an orally presented geometric form. In other words, this particular measurement of listening focuses on the goodness of fit between the sent message and the received message.[12] While this research has helped us understand the nature of listening fidelity, it falls short of looking at the role listening fidelity plays in our daily listening.

To clearly understand the importance of high-fidelity listening, we need only look at a common occurrence: getting directions. Whether you are getting directions on how to get somewhere or how to perform a particular task, you know the importance of being able to faithfully re-create the information in your mind so you can follow through with your objective. Have you ever found yourself in a situation where you ended up in the wrong place because you forgot a step in the directions? This happened the first time Professor Margaret Fitch-Hauser went to Portland, Oregon. She stopped at a convenience store and asked for directions to a particular hotel. Unfortunately she missed one critical piece of information and ended up several miles in the opposite direction from her hotel and had to make another stop to ask for directions. She listened more closely the second time and was able to get to her intended destination. Chances are you have probably experienced a variation of this challenge.

Now let's look a little deeper into how listening fidelity can be important on a personal level. When you are talking with someone who is very important to you, aren't you motivated to listen? Or if you really need to be listened to, don't you want the other person to truly focus on what you mean and feel? Achieving listening fidelity on the interpersonal level is challenging. It calls for you to engage in the type of listening appropriate for the situation and the relationship. As you read the rest of this chapter, think about how each of the dimensions and types of listening discussed can help you be a higher-fidelity listener.

Multidimensional Listening

While it is important for a listener to focus on what the speaker says as you attempt to accurately reproduce the intended meaning, most messages require you to focus on more than just the spoken message itself to achieve fidelity. Usually other aspects of the message must be processed before you can understand what the sender

THINK ON IT

Identify two listening situations, one that is impersonal and one that is personal. What are the differences in the listening skills you need to use to be a high-fidelity listener?

really intended. As you recall from the definitions and models of listening discussed in Chapter 1, the skill of listening involves many dimensions, including the ones incorporated in the Worthington Fitch-Hauser model, Listening MATERRS. Some of these dimensions include translating, evaluating, and recalling information.

Because listening has been defined as a multidimensional skill, most listening tests stress more than reproducing the actual message; they stress cognitive elements as well.[13] By taking a quick look at the elements covered by some of the better-known traditional listening tests, you can get a better idea of many of the elements involved in listening. Table 2.1 lists four well-known listening tests and identifies the elements they are designed to test.

As you can see in the table, even listening scholars don't always agree on exactly what elements or dimensions should be included when measuring listening. It is fair to conclude that listening is multidimensional in nature, so any attempt to measure it should take into account as many of these dimensions as possible. Consequently, the listening fidelity test discussed above and the STEP III listed in Table 2.1 are probably insufficient to shed much light on the entire process of listening because they are one dimensional, looking at only a single aspect of listening. They are useful, however, in better understanding the particular aspect of listening they are designed to measure.

The reason that single-dimension measurements are inadequate can be more fully explained by the next section, which looks at different types of listening. Because you listen in many different contexts, ranging from classroom lectures to intimate personal conversations, you listen to a wide variety of information that calls for different skills and levels of involvement. Therefore, you need a variety of listening skills that will help you adapt to the shifts in listening demands you encounter. The following discussion of types of listening will introduce some of the critical listening skills you use.

TABLE 2.1

Dimensions of Listening Tests

Brown-Carlsen[14]	STEP III[15]	KCLT[16]	Watson Barker[17]
Immediate recall	Listening comprehension	Short-term listening	Evaluating message content
Following directions		Short-term listening with rehearsal	Understanding meanings in conversation
Recognizing transitions		Interpretation or understanding	Understanding and remembering information in lectures
Recognizing word meanings		Lecture listening	Evaluating emotional meanings in messages
Lecture comprehension		Distractions	Following instructions and directions

TYPES OF LISTENING

If you are committed to high-fidelity listening, you need to think about listening to all types of information. One way to cope with the variety of information and situations that you face is to realize that listening is a multifaceted skill that you use to gather many types of information. That is, one size doesn't fit all when it comes to listening. Just as you would use different clubs to hit golf balls, depending on the conditions of the course, the length of the needed shot, and your goal, you also use a variety of types of listening, depending on the situation.

Wolvin and Coakley identified five categories of listening in their textbook.[18] They felt that each category represented different purposes of listening. Using a tree as a metaphor for listening, they made discriminative listening the root that feeds the tree; comprehensive listening the trunk that supports the branches; and critical, appreciative, and therapeutic listening the branches. We will talk about these as well as other types of listening.

Discriminative Listening

Wolvin and Coakley defined **discriminative listening** as "listening to distinguish aural and sometimes visual stimuli." In essence, it is the reception of the stimulus. If you don't physically receive the stimulus, you can't listen. When you engage in discriminative listening, you focus on whether a stimulus is worthy of paying attention to or not; how you should classify the sound (language, large truck); and detecting changes and nuances in a speaker's pitch, volume, rate, and language-related sounds. Discriminative listening also helps you determine from where the sound is coming.

This type of listening involves distinguishing between aural and other types of stimuli. In essence, discriminative listening is about being tuned in to the variations and differences in the sounds and visual stimuli around you. Our world is filled with noises. As you are reading this chapter, cars might be driving by, people might be talking in the hallway, the ventilation system might be switching on and off, and you might have your MP3 player or television turned on. With all of this noise going on, how do you make the decision about what to pay attention to and which sounds to ignore? You make the decision by using discriminative listening.

Discriminative listening is also critical to our survival. When we pick up a sound, one of the first things we do is decide whether the sound is friend or foe. If we hear something that is threatening, our fight-or-flight instinct kicks in. Think about what you do when you are walking down a street and suddenly hear a loud horn honking. Chances are you jump a little or in some other way physically react to the unexpected sound. You will probably also look for the source of the horn. The purpose of your physical reaction is to help you get out of harm's way if you determine you are in danger.

Discriminative listening is so crucial to your survival that you develop this capability *in utero* and continue to develop it during the first few months of your life. Research indicates that a fetus can distinguish among music, language, and other sounds.[19] Measurement of heart rate and motor responses clearly show a fetus can tell the difference in sounds. For example, a sudden sharp noise elicits a different response than a Mozart sonata. It is interesting that this discriminative capability is also illustrated by a newborn's ability to distinguish its mother's voice from other female voices.[20] Further research indicates that by four days old, babies are able to differentiate their mother language from other languages.[21] In truth, your discriminative abilities might be at their peak early in your life. For example, a child up to four months old can distinguish all 150 sounds that make up human languages.[22] However, as we noted in Chapter 1, you soon lose this ability as you gain more experience in the language or languages used in your environment; you lose the ability to distinguish among all of the sounds. Consequently as an adult, you probably have difficulty picking up fine distinctions between sounds that are very close if your ears are unaccustomed to hearing them.

Another way you use discriminative listening is to make sense out of human sounds. If you are flying on a crowded plane and hear the person sitting next to you make a sound, you will try to determine whether the person is talking or simply making a noise. If you notice the person's eyes are closed and his head is lolling forward, you will conclude that he isn't trying to talk to you. If, however, you notice that the person is looking at you, you will probably try to come up with an appropriate answer. As you learn a language, whether it is your native language or another one, you begin to learn the patterns of sounds associated with the language and begin to listen for those sounds.

One concept that helps clarify discriminative listening is **speech intelligibility**.[23] Speech intelligibility involves a sender and a listener who processes the signal to arrive at some level of understanding or intelligibility.[24] When you use discriminative listening, you pick up speaker affect and voice quality as well as the words themselves. **Speaker affect** is perceived by listening to the pitch, precision, and patterns of emphasis. Research by audiologists indicates that processing paralinguistic cues of this type is a parallel process to hearing the words. These findings led researchers to conclude that listeners have to work extra hard to decode speech that is different from what they are accustomed to hearing.

Unfortunately this increased degree of difficulty can create a listening barrier. For example, both authors of this book have spent the majority of their lives in the southern part of the United States. Consequently our ears are very accustomed to Southern English. When we travel to other areas of the country, we sometimes have difficulty recognizing words because the sound structures are different. The same thing occurs when we travel internationally.

Every language has its own sounds. While we are able to hear the nuances of southern U.S. English, we have difficulty physically picking up (and producing) the nuances of a language such as Korean. Discriminative listening is one key to learning another language as adults. Research by Akiyo Hirai, an associate professor at the University of Tsukuba in Japan, found a relationship between listening and proficiency in a second language. He concluded that proficiency in a second language is dependent on the ability to process the spoken language, which we can get only through listening.[25]

Even though discriminative listening is physically receiving the stimulus, it is important that a listener doesn't use this first step in listening as an excuse not to listen. Many years ago, Professor Fitch-Hauser attended a speech

THINK ON IT

If you aren't personally familiar with one, get with a friend who is fluent in another language. What are some of the sounds that don't translate well into English? Or as in Chinese, a word whose meaning may change with a change in pitch? How can such differences affect how we listen and understand others?

in a large hall. The speaker chose not to use a microphone, and the acoustics of the hall didn't allow the speaker's voice to carry throughout. Since she couldn't hear what the speaker was saying, she couldn't listen completely. At that time she had to make some choices as a listener. First, she could watch the nonverbals: the facial expressions, the body postures, the gestures. Based on these visual elements as well as responses from the audience members who could hear, she could draw certain conclusions. Other options she had were to move to a location where she could hear or to inform the speaker that she couldn't hear. The main lesson of this example is that even at the discriminative level, an individual has the responsibility of making the choice of whether or not to attend to the stimulus or make an effort to attend to the stimulus.

Just as in the example of a nonnative language, discriminative listening also helps us distinguish among sounds in our own language. Many sounds are somewhat similar. For example, plosive sounds such as "p" and "b" take focus and concentration to distinguish in less-than-ideal conditions. The same can be said of distinguishing between "b" and "d." This problem can be extended even further as we think about how we pronounce certain words. For example, homonyms are words that sound alike *(to, two, too)*. Only by listening to the context are we able to determine which word is being used. We have similar problems with words that aren't really homonyms but are regionally pronounced alike. For example, *pen* and *pin* and *aunt* and *ant* are pronounced very similarly in many parts of the United States. A good discriminative listener will be able to distinguish among these similar sounds.

As seen here, discriminative listening is crucial to our survival and forms a basis for our ability to understand others' messages. While distinguishing stimuli is very important to listening, we must also be able to establish what the stimuli mean. We do this as we begin to listen comprehensively.

Comprehensive Listening

In comprehensive listening we strive for a level of listening fidelity that will allow us to assign meanings to a message that are as close as possible to what the sender intended. So we must learn to focus on the words plus all of the appropriate nonverbal elements that accompany the words. It is at this level that we try to truly achieve communication fidelity. According to Wolvin and Coakley, **comprehensive listening** is "listening for understanding of the message."[26] In comprehensive listening, then, we must pay attention to all of the information coming in: the words; the tone of voice and other paralinguistic cues; all nonverbal cues, including facial expressions; and the interactive situation itself.

Consider what happens in the following scenarios:

a. Ben overhears his parents talking after work. His father is talking about a confrontation he had with a disgruntled employee. As he gets into the details of the incident, his voice begins to sound angry.
b. Tamarah is taking a 911 call. Her voice is flat as she asks the caller to calm down and tell her where the accident has occurred.

As a listener to the first situation, one could conclude that Mr. Goleman, Ben's father, is angry. One might even assume that he is angry with Mrs. Goleman because she is the person he is talking with. However, Ben is a good comprehensive listener who sees both parties in the interaction. He also takes into account the situation. Consequently he is able to understand that his father is expressing emotions that were appropriate to the situation at work, not showing anger toward Mrs. Goleman. He can understand that his father is frustrated about certain things at work.

In the second case, the person on the other end of the phone call could assume that Tamarah is uncaring. But instead the individual probably picks up the message to remain as calm as possible so the important information about the accident can be relayed.

Both of these cases illustrate the importance of assigning meaning to a message based on more than just the words themselves. In the previous section, we talked about the importance of a discriminative listener paying attention to speaker affect. A good comprehensive listener is able to interpret this affect and determine how it influences what the message really means.

Of course, it is also important for us to understand the words used to express the message. If we don't understand the words a speaker is using, we will have great difficulty assigning meaning to the message. Wolvin and Coakley suggest that one thing we can do to be better comprehensive listeners is to build our vocabularies.

In addition to assigning meaning to the message, comprehensive listening also involves storing the information in our memory banks. When we focus on what is being said, we process that information in such a way that we can store it in the appropriate place. One way we do this is by using schemata to make sense of information. Schemata are patterns we use to organize and interpret information. The role of schema and memory is discussed more fully in Chapter 3. So when you hear one of your friends start talking about his or her date last night, you listen with the expectation of hearing information that fits your "date story" schema. You will also store the information using that set of expectations.

Comprehensive listening allows us to understand and remember information. However, we seldom simply just take information in; we also evaluate the stimuli in some way.

Critical Listening

The third type of listening described by Wolvin and Coakley is critical listening. Some listening scholars feel that this level of listening is the most important.[27] It is in **critical listening** that we think about the message, make inferences, and evaluate both the speaker and the message.[28] This type of listening is important any time we need to assess the value of information. It is perhaps most important when we are listening to information meant to persuade us.

One decision a listener should make when taking in a message concerns the type of information being heard. Is it factual or not? Whether listening to a newscast or to another individual, a competent critical listener will be able to distinguish between fact and information that isn't fact. Let's take a quick look at the difference in the types of information. Case Study 2.2 presents an actual news story about a college student. Read over the article and see if you can distinguish information that is fact from information that is opinion.

CASE STUDY 2.2

Distinguishing Facts from Opinion

Auburn Student Honored for Bravery
March 8, 2008
By AMY WEAVER

Daniel Brinson will probably never feel comfortable being regarded as a hero.

It's a title the Auburn University sophomore earned after he and a friend encountered a multiple-vehicle car accident on their way to the beach last fall. With some of the cars on fire, the pair jumped out of their vehicle and dashed to the scene. Brinson said it was clear they were too late for some, but then they heard voices.

One belonged to a young girl, trapped in a car.

"There was no telling when the car was going to explode, but we had to get her out," said Brinson, an agriculture business and economics major.

As the weeks and months have passed since then, it's gotten easier for Brinson to talk about that day's events and that young girl. He still remembers how they had to break her legs to free her from the wreck and how her passenger friend wasn't as lucky. She died at the scene, he said.

"I saw that she was young and pretty," Brinson said, "and I knew it was more important for her to live and go on than myself."

Congressman Mike Rogers heard the heroic tale of Brinson and Terrell Webb and shared it with his fellow legislators on the floor of the U.S. House of Representatives back in January. On Monday, he presented Brinson with a certificate of commendation at AU's Samford Hall.

"Any time we see extraordinary bravery, we should acknowledge it," Rogers said.

Perhaps Brinson's instincts as a former volunteer firefighter kicked in or it was just his inherent instinct to help others, but no matter what it was that drove him into that dangerous situation, he's glad he happened to be there and could do what he did.

"You can't pass burning cars and not stop," he said. "You just can't."

Since then, Brinson has learned more about the young girl whose life he saved, including how she had a young baby girl at home. She told the Brinson family how someone was looking out for her that September day and how she was meant to live her life for that little one.

News like that melts Brinson's big heart and puts a big grin on his face.

The last time he talked to her, he said he learned that she had started rehabilitation and is even enrolled at Southern Union State Community College. ∎

Reproduced with permission from the Opelika Auburn News.

Even in a news story, not all information is factual. A good listener will be able to distinguish what type of information is forthcoming.

Another aspect of competent critical listening is the ability to recognize discrepancies between verbal and nonverbal messages. In fact, this aspect of critical listening can help us be more sensitive to cultural differences in our multicultural society and can help us detect whether the speaker is being truthful. A good critical listener knows that the vast majority of a message is contained in the nonverbal behavior of the speaker.[29] Research by scholars Susan Timm and Betty Schroeder found a relationship between training in listening and nonverbal communication and cultural sensitivity.[30] It seems that people who learned to listen and focus on the nonverbal aspects of the message are more aware of and accepting of cultural differences. This finding suggests that if you are sensitive to the subtleties of the relationship between verbal and nonverbal messages, you will probably also be more aware of and open to cultural differences.

At the same time, research has shown that when there is a discrepancy between the verbal and the nonverbal, we should believe the nonverbal.[31] Consequently a good critical listener needs to understand the effect of nonverbal messages on the overall perception of the meaning of the message. Dale Leathers's research tells us that we respond to inconsistent messages in one of three ways.[32] First, we attempt to determine the literal meaning of the inconsistent message. Second, we try increasing our level of concentration and search for any overlooked clues that will help us clarify the message. Third, we might withdraw from our interaction with the sending party. The upshot of this research is that inconsistency between verbal and nonverbal messages is very disruptive to a relationship and to an interaction. Consequently a good critical listener needs to be aware of possible explanations for why the inconsistency exists.

Reasons for Inconsistent Messages.   People who send inconsistent messages seem to do so for a number of reasons.[33] The sender might not be clear as to his or her intent. If you don't really know what you want to accomplish by sending a message, it will be difficult for you to truly be consistent in all aspects of your message. Think about it. If you have a fight with a sibling or close friend, your first meeting after the fight is probably going to be filled with inconsistent messages. Part of you wants to apologize; part of you might want to continue the disagreement. It will take a bit of give-and-take between you and the other party before you establish in your own mind what your exact purpose is.

A person might also have conflicting intentions in sending a message. Think about one of your favorite teachers. If that person has a reputation of being both tough and fun, it's possible that he or she sends out inconsistent messages at times. Keep in mind that these inconsistencies aren't signs of deception; they are signs of, to some extent, mixed motives.

Another reason messages might be inconsistent is that there is a disconnect between what is being said and what the individual actually means. At one level a perceptive listener will be able to detect the hesitation in the speaker's voice or see the slumped shoulders that indicate the individual's heart isn't behind the words. At another level some discrepancies are more difficult to detect because the other party is trying to deceive. Looking at a positive example, think about a time when you have attempted to keep a secret from someone you care about. It might have been about a surprise party or a really exciting gift. If the other person was very perceptive, he or she probably picked up signs of deception in your face, speech, voice, or body as you tried to conceal the truth.[34]

A fourth reason someone might display inconsistent messages is the information is unpleasant. Most of us will attempt to soften unpleasant news. One way we do so is to use softer, more supportive nonverbals. So the message might be bad, but we use nonverbal behavior to take part of the sting out of the message.

We also will use our nonverbal behavior to protect ourselves from being perceived in a negative light. The best example of this explanation of inconsistent messages is the experience of giving a speech. Most of us feel at least some level of anxiety when we get up in front of a class or meeting to deliver a speech. However, we also want to appear confident. Because we have the goal of appearing confident and the emotion of fear, we will more than likely send some inconsistent messages.

The types of listening covered up to this point have all focused on taking in information and processing it. However, listening can also be a pleasurable activity. The next type of listening addresses listening for pleasure.

Appreciative Listening

Wolvin and Coakley define **appreciative listening** as "listening for sensory stimulation or enjoyment."[35] According to another listening scholar, Anthony Clark, appreciative listening "occurs when a perceptive listener derives pleasure or satisfaction from the form, rhythm, and/or tone of aural stimuli."[36] It is worth our while to look at a couple of the elements to which Clark refers. Clark suggests that a perceptive listener is someone who is sensitive to the aesthetic elements of spoken and/or musical qualities. If you think about it, there are some voices that we appreciate more than others. Most of us find actor James Earl Jones's voice pleasant and rich, while we find the voice of comedian Bobcat Goldthwait irritating and painful at times as he screeches in high octaves.

The pleasure or satisfaction element refers to our physical or emotional response to sound. For example, think about the classic movie *Jurassic Park*. The sounds produced by the little dinosaurs were cute and nonthreatening, much like sounds we associate with baby animals of any kind. However, when the large dinosaurs came on the screen, the sounds they produced were intended to generate fear and anxiety, so they were loud and harsh. We also respond emotionally to other elements of sound such as form, the structure of the parts of a stimulus; rhythm, the flow of the stressed and unstressed parts of the stimulus; and tone, the quality of a voice or sound.

Appreciative listening then should help us become more enlightened and expand our minds as we learn to appreciate a wider variety of sounds. Appreciative listening is critical if we are going to expand our ability to understand and accept cultures other than the one in which we grew up. Every civilization and culture uses a language made up of varying sounds and produces musical sounds unique to that culture. Music is an important aspect of the civilization or culture because it is often an expression of spiritual joy.[37] Being good appreciative listeners requires us to keep an open mind to these expressions of joy.

> **THINK ON IT**
>
> How do you react when you hear music that doesn't conform to the eight-note scale many have learned in music appreciation class? Listen to some old music from Korea, Thailand, Kenya, or any other non-Western country. Compare that music to a Bach fugue. What are the specific differences you notice?

In addition to listening for pleasure and appreciation, we also listen to provide support to others. The next type of listening focuses on providing support when someone is in need.

Therapeutic Listening

The final type of listening Wolvin and Coakley discussed is therapeutic listening. We engage in **therapeutic listening** when we want to show support for someone who is troubled. All of us at one time or another need someone to "just listen," someone who will withhold the impulse to fix the situation or to give advice.

Wolvin and Coakley suggested that five skills are essential to therapeutic listening: (1) focusing attention, (2) demonstrating attending behaviors, (3) developing a supportive communication climate, (4) listening with empathy, and (5) responding appropriately. All of these skills keep the focus on the other person and away from the listener, who serves the function of supporter.

A tendency that many of us have is assuming that if someone tells us about a situation or problem, he or she is asking for our advice or wanting us to somehow "fix" whatever is going on. Many times this type of response is an artifact of the specific relationship. For example, parents often feel the need to fix the problems their children face. The special challenges of listening in relationships will be addressed more fully below and in Chapters 6 and 7.

A good therapeutic listener resists the urge to fix or give advice. As much as you might want to share your particular insight or wisdom with your friend, you should be sensitive enough to know that the other person needs nothing more from you than to be a listening ear. If you are truly sensitive and empathetic, you will recognize when your friend is asking for help.

To help us better understand the differences between supportive listening and other types of listening, we will look at a simple typology that illustrates the contrast. Bill Arnold adapted the work of Robert Carkhuff when he suggested that we engage in three types of listening that correspond to the color of traffic lights.[38] By taking a brief look at **Arnold's Typology of Listening,** we can get a clearer picture of how therapeutic listening differs from other, nonsupportive types of listening. The first of Arnold's three types is **red listening.** Red listening doesn't involve much listening. Red listeners tend to ignore the needs of the other person and instead focus on their own needs. So the red listener will acknowledge the other person in only the most cursory manner. The second of the Arnold listening categories is **yellow listening.** Yellow listening is characterized by a tendency to be judgmental and evaluate what is said. This type of listening is often accompanied by a "yes, but" or "let me tell you how to fix it" type of approach. With yellow listening, we listen to the message and respond from our perspective without really thinking about whether we truly address the needs of the other party. **Green listening** is true, supportive listening, the type that involves listening to the person from where he is, not where we want him to be. Green listening means you withhold judgment and don't unnecessarily shift away from the other person's concerns or needs. In essence, green listening is empathetic listening.

> **THINK ON IT**
>
> Can you come up with some examples of red, yellow, and green listening that you have experienced? How did you feel in each case?

Empathetic Listening

Therapeutic listening is an example of **empathetic listening.** Certainly being empathetic is an important part of listening. Michael Nichols, a family therapist, argued that empathy is the "essence of good listening," noting that it is "part intuition and part effort, it is the stuff of human connection."[39] He went on to say that "listening is the art by which we use empathy to reach across the space between us. Passive attention doesn't work."[40] A bit later in his book *The Lost Art of Listening,* he said that listening often "takes a deliberate effort to suspend our own needs and reaction" and to control "the urge to interrupt or argue."[41] In this section we explore empathetic listening.

A Feeling Touch

Nolvia remembers the day she and her father met with the doctor after his accident. When the doctor told him that he would need a motorized wheelchair, Mr. Gutierrez began to cry. The doctor sat down in a chair, took Mr. Gutierrez's hand in hers, and looked him straight in the eye. In a soft but clear voice, Dr. Kyle told him the following: *Your mental ability is better than mine. However, your body has been damaged. I want you to be able to live a fulfilling life, see your children grow up, and become fully reengaged in life. I can't heal your body, but this chair will give you the ability to actually be with your children and watch their activities, not just stay in a bed and hear about them.* ■

Before we continue, it is important to establish that *empathy*—feeling "with" someone—is qualitatively different from *sympathy*—feeling "for" someone. Focusing on a receiver-based definition, we define *empathy* as a process by which we emotionally connect with others. When we empathize with someone, we use our perceptions of how that person feels to help us determine how we should respond. This definition implies we can identify and share emotions with others by being empathetic listeners.

Notice in Case Study 2.3 that the doctor is able to understand how Mr. Gutierrez feels and is consequently able to respond appropriately.

The history of focusing on empathetic listening can be traced to the work of Carl Rogers, a psychotherapist. Rogers is credited with developing a client-centered style of listening that he used in therapy and taught to a new generation of therapists. We paraphrase Neil Friedman's explanation of Rogers's approach to listening: The primary role of the listening response is to acknowledge a client's feelings and experiences and encourage her to build on and continue communicating them with the therapist. The therapist must go beyond simply repeating or paraphrasing a client's words. Words are not feelings. The listening therapist's responses are attempts to make concrete the thoughts, feelings, and experiences of the client so they are more recognizable to the client and they can aid in reaching the ultimate goal of the therapeutic encounter for the client.[42]

Empathy is important to listening in that it affects our responses to speakers. If you are highly empathetic, you are more likely to provide comforting responses to the speaker, whether it is a friend or stranger. Your response manifests itself in three possible ways.[43] For example, imagine for a moment that your best friend has just broken up with her significant other. On one level, you engage in **empathetic responsiveness.** Essentially what happens is that you take on the emotions being felt by your friend; you feel "with" her. She is sad and upset, so you begin feeling sad and upset too. After all, she's a good friend. Second, you might engage in **perspective taking.** Perspective taking refers to your ability to put yourself in your friend's shoes. Of course, this is easier to do if you, too, have been in a serious relationship. However, it

THINK ON IT

Think about how you react when someone shares confidences with you. Do you attempt to understand without judgment? Do you look for solutions to the other person's problem? Are you taking steps to be empathetic, or are you simply nodding?

is not necessary for you to actually have had the same or a similar experience. What is required is that you be able to *imagine* yourself in her place.

The last way you might manifest an empathic response is in terms of **sympathetic responsiveness.** This concept is considered a relatively new aspect of empathy. It reflects our traditional definition of sympathy, where we feel "for" someone else, that we mentioned earlier. When you engage in sympathetic responsiveness, you also feel other emotions that are in keeping with the situation. You might feel concern for her, while at the same time you are angry at the "evil" former significant other. So with empathetic responsiveness, you would feel sad and upset, reflecting her feelings of sadness and being upset at the breakup, but with sympathetic responsiveness, you would feel other related emotions that would reflect your "emotional concern" for your friend.[44] Of course, this example presents a situation with your friend being upset about a breakup. She could just as easily be happy over receiving an *A* on her chemistry exam or getting promoted at her job.

Factors Affecting Empathy. Empathy seems to be influenced by a number of factors. One of them is the **gender** of the individual. Men's and women's listening skills differ in several ways. How many of these differences are biological and how many are learned is still debated by researchers. In the area of empathy, we do know that as young as one year, boys and girls differ in how they react to someone who has supposedly injured himself: girls generally react with more empathy and greater distress than boys.[45]

Empathy and how empathetically responsive we are appears to be related to sociability as well. Even at six months, girls tend to display a more social nature than boys by initiating more social interactions, engaging in turn taking, and developing more expressive language, including broader vocabularies, earlier than boys. So at a very young age, your little girl cousin has many of the elements needed to be empathetic—a greater focus on nonverbals, broader language skills, and a disposition to respond to the hurt of others. One school of thought suggests that parents respond to these characteristics by expressing more positive emotions to their daughters as well as using a greater variety of emotional words. However, when interacting with their sons, mothers behave differently. For example, they often exaggerate the faces they make to their sons. In other words, when expressing surprise or fear, mothers exaggerate their nonverbals. As a result, mothers might make it more difficult for boys to learn the more subtle nonverbal cues. For whatever reason, as adults, men tend not to be as adept at picking up subtle emotional cues from others.

Another factor that influences empathy is **culture.** Of course, cultural differences play a large role in gender differences. Differences in emphases on cultural conformity; display rules (what emotions are appropriate for men and women to display or present to others); and socialization by parents, peers, and others can affect how we respond empathetically. For example, if you grow up in a family where conformity and rule following were both expected and enforced and where crying was frowned on, you might find it difficult not only to express your own emotions but also to listen as others express theirs. Think of expressing empathy as a skill that you just have not had much practice with. You might feel awkward and think, *What am I supposed to do?*

In terms of the larger cultural context, Western cultures such as the United States tend to share a cultural belief that women are more emotional than men.[46] So while there does appear to be at least a small biological difference in empathy and sociability of male and female infants, the culture you grow up in has a major effect on how you use empathy in your interactions with others. In Western cultures, women are more likely to express prosocial emotions such as empathy, happiness, and joy. In addition, it is acceptable for women to express emotions such as fear and sadness. If you are from a Western culture such as the United States, you know that men are not encouraged to express those types of emotions publicly. Men, in contrast, are more likely to express "powerful" emotions such as anger and pride.[47] As a result, when it comes to empathetic and sympathetic responsiveness, women in Western cultures appear to have an advantage in terms of both biology and cultural learning.

But do these differences hold true for men and women in non-Western cultures? Recent research by Agneta Fischer and Antony Manstead provide us with a partial answer to this question.[48] These researchers examined the data from approximately 3,000 surveys administered to men and women from 37 countries across five continents. Countries included in the survey were Botswana, Brazil, China, Finland, India, Israel, Malawi, New Zealand, Poland, and the United States. Their research focused on how men and women from these different cultures compared in their intensity, duration, and nonverbal expressions of their emotions. *Intensity* refers to the strength or level of an emotional response, *duration* refers to the overall time a respondent reported an emotion lasting, and *nonverbal expression* refers to the behavioral expression of an emotion (e.g., laughing, crying, yelling, withdrawing from others). The analysis found that, in general, women from *all* the countries surveyed reported more intense emotions, which were longer in duration. Survey responses also indicated that the women were more overtly expressive of their emotions.

However, before you begin adjusting your current view of men and women, you need to also be aware of the cultural differences that Fischer and Manstead found. For example, they discovered that the behaviors of men and women from individualistic cultures differed from those in collectivistic cultures. **Individualistic cultures,** such as the United States, emphasize individual expression, self-reliance, autonomy, and independence, which leads its members to value "being yourself" or "expressing yourself." As a result, social ties in individualistic cultures are looser than those in collectivistic cultures, such as China or Japan. **Collectivistic cultures** value meeting social and group norms and respecting others of the group. In keeping with these differences, the research indicated that gender-specific display rules were associated more with individualistic cultures than with collectivistic cultures. What this means is that women and men differed more in how they displayed their emotions (intensity, duration, overtness) if they were from an individualistic culture, while the sexes were more alike if they were from a collectivistic culture. Thus, the rules of our individualistic culture lead women to value emotional expressiveness more than men do, and they give women the freedom to be more expressive. In fact, it is a cultural expectation.

Coming back to our discussion of empathy, it appears, then, that women have an "empathetic edge." Any empathetic responsiveness they are born with is culturally reinforced, particularly in individualistic cultures. As a result, women have more practice at empathy, resulting in a better ability to respond empathetically to others. In the United States, both men and women view women as more empathetic listeners than men. Some evidence suggests that women listen more to relationship information over fact-based information and prefer discussing topics associated with relationships and personal experiences. Subsequently they are more likely to gain a listener's trust and be privy to more intimate self-disclosures.[49] As noted in Chapter 1, one of the bases of empathetic listening is knowledge and understanding of the other person.

This is not to say that men cannot or will not respond empathetically. As you will be learning later in the text, a number of other factors affect how empathetic we are with others, including how well we know them, how closely we can identify with them, and how skilled we are at establishing a supportive listening climate. In addition, we will be learning how our verbal and nonverbal skills affect others' perceptions of how empathetic we are. Whether male or female, it is a good idea to assess your "empatheticness," so you can determine if you need to hone this particular listening skill.[50]

Up to this point, we have focused on types of listening. Related to types of listening is the notion of levels of energy and intensity we need to use as we listen.

LEVELS OF LISTENING

Another aspect of being a competent communicator and listener is knowing how much listening effort you need to expend in any given context. As a listener, you find yourself in situations where you need to identify the purpose of the exchange and respond appropriately. At other times you need to engage in the very deepest of critical listening or empathetic listening. For example, greeting someone you meet in the hallway calls for a different level or intensity of listening than does listening carefully to a lecture on molecular biology or to a friend talk about an emotionally charged event. Erik Van Slyke, managing director of Solleva Group, identified six levels of listening that provide a guide for us to use as we determine how deeply we need to listen.[51]

The first level Van Slyke identified is **passive listening.** This type of listening is one in which we sit quietly while another person talks. However, sitting quietly doesn't mean we are engaged in the listening process. Passive listening has also been referred to as marginal listening because the receiver hears words but is easily distracted and allows his or her mind to wander.[52] If we are guilty of passive listening, more than likely, we are engaging in low-fidelity listening because we catch only a few phrases or words. We are aware that the other person is talking, but we don't expend enough energy to truly comprehend what the individual is saying. We probably all have to admit that we have on occasion engaged in this type of behavior. Unfortunately most of us believe that if someone sits quietly while we are talking, the other person must be listening. This is a mistake many speakers (and teachers) make.

Chances are all of us use passive listening when we engage in certain levels of multitasking. For example, when you listen to music while you drive, you are probably using passive listening. In this case this level of listening allows you to stay focused on what is important: driving safely. In contrast, if you attend a concert, you will use a deeper level of listening since you are at the event specifically for the music.

Van Slyke's second level of listening is responsive listening. He identified responsive listening as making acknowledgments, either verbal or nonverbal, that we are listening. We would prefer to call this **responding listening** because all we are doing is going through the motions of listening and making "listening noises" rather than truly engaging our listening brain. This type of listening behavior has the potential to damage a relationship because we remain disengaged as a communicator but send the false message that we are paying attention and listening. In truth, we probably aren't really listening at all to the other person. This level of listening is probably useful for only purely social situations such as exchanging greetings as we pass someone in the hall or other setting. Even in this situation, responding listening can lead to inappropriate responses. Have you ever said hello to someone and had him respond, "Fine, thank you"? This interaction is a classic example of responding listening. The listener relied on a social schema (or expectation) that says greetings follow this pattern or script:

Hello. How are you?

Fine, thank you. And you?

Fine, thanks.

Because the listener was using responding listening, he or she didn't actually hear what was said. If this happens in a greeting, typically no harm is done. However, if this problem occurs during an important discussion, much damage can be done. (Social schemata are discussed more fully in Chapter 3).

The third level of listening is selective listening. **Selective listening** occurs when we engage our brains and listen for only things that support what we believe, think, or endorse. In essence, it is listening with an agenda. Van Slyke suggested that this is the type of listening we use when we argue or debate. When we use this type of listening, we tend to exhibit the following behavior. When we hear something that catches our attention, we will interrupt and deliver an evaluative response in the form of a statement or question. According to Van Slyke, the rest of the time, we are only partially engaged or busy thinking about our responses and listening for those points where we can break in. Unfortunately we don't gather the information we really need to understand what the other person wants. Instead we remain focused on what we want. If we continue to use this type of listening behavior inappropriately, our efforts will make the situation worse because the other person will probably grow to resent us for our lack of awareness.

With certain modifications, however, aspects of selective listening can be useful in situations where we are trying to diagnose something and keep an open ear and open mind to what the individual is saying. For example, if we are engaged in a conversation with someone who seems to be rambling, we can listen for opportunities to get the person back on track while we attend to what he or she is saying and monitoring for any cues concerning how the information might be related to the purpose of the discussion. Caring health-care providers will engage in this type of listening as they try to diagnose what is wrong with a patient. This type of listening is called **attentive listening.** Van Slyke said that while attentive listening is listening with an agenda, it includes probing and inquisitiveness. More important, we engage our analytic mind as we attend to the other party's message. An attentive listener will respond with evaluative questions that guide the responses of the other person. For example, your instructor might ask a question that guides you into admitting you chose to go to a social event rather than study for a test. The following quotation gives us an example of the perception of attentive listening:

> *One of the most powerful tools at our disposal is the ability to listen. Not only does active listening make those around you feel vested in the conversation; it also provides you valuable time to process and prepare your comments.*[53]

While the author of the above remark mentioned "active" listening, what he was really referring to is attentive listening. Notice that the focus of the listening in the quote is the listener. Attentive listening, like the previous levels we have discussed, is from the perspective of the listener. It doesn't focus on what the other person needs or wants from us; instead it focuses on what we need from the other person. For example, the caring health-care provider needs information that pertains to the person's ailment, so she will listen for facts and data and ignore any emotional content. Unfortunately sometimes the very information we need is in the emotion.

The level at which we shift away from our own interests and turn to the needs of the other party is truly active listening. **Active listening** involves us using all of our listening capabilities. It is total sensory listening. What this means is that we listen with not only our ears but also our eyes and the rest of our senses. So we listen to the paralinguistic aspects of the message, we focus on the facial expressions and the body language, and we listen to the patterns of silence. We truly listen with an open mind that isn't hindered by our expectations or agenda.

Active listeners respond with reflective responses that provide feedback to the other party. A reflective response helps verify the listener's understanding of what the other person is saying and encourages that person to continue. An example of a reflective response can be seen in the following scenario.

CASE STUDY 2.4

Nolvia's Frustration

NOLVIA: I am having such a hard time getting my grandparents to understand what is expected of me by my teachers. They . . . Oh, I don't even know how to put it into words.

RADLEY: It sounds like you're kinda frustrated with how your grandparents are reacting to your going to college.

NOLVIA: That's not the half of it. They don't understand just how different things are for me than things were for them as young people in Honduras. They don't understand the pressure.

RADLEY: Oh boy, generational and cultural differences. Do you have any ideas about what you are going to do next? ■

If you really examine the above example, notice that Radley paraphrases what Nolvia is saying. This use of *paraphrasing* shows that he is truly listening to what she is saying as well as the affect, or feelings, she is expressing.

Reflective listening engenders confidence in the listener on the part of the speaker. Consequently reflective listening tends to boost the self-esteem of the listener because we have been willing as listeners to accept that the other person has particular feelings and ideas. In other words, we can accept the fact the other person has particular feelings, but we might not accept the justifications of those feelings from that person's perspective. According to Van Slyke, active listening "allows us to accept the message, but we do not have to understand or accept the messenger."[54]

The last level of listening identified by Van Slyke is **empathetic listening.** Like the type of listening by the same name we discussed earlier, this level of listening involves "listening with the intent to accept and understand the other person's frame of reference."[55] This level of listening requires us to suspend our personal reality and immerse ourselves in the other person's reality. As discussed in the section on empathetic listening, this immersion in the other person's perspective reflects a change in attitude about the purpose of listening. The purpose shifts from gathering information to understanding and accepting the other person's feelings. So as Carl Rogers suggested, we must separate the person from the problem and accept the value of the person.

SUMMARY

Clearly listening is much more than "just a single communication skill." Instead it is a multilevel skill that involves a great deal of awareness and sensitivity to the other parties in an interaction. As you think back about the types of listening discussed in this chapter, you will see that they are connected with the Listening MATERRS model presented in the Chapter 1. In discriminative listening your mind is awakened to and becomes aware of the stimulus. In comprehensive listening you translate or make sense of the message as well as recall it later. Critical listening allows you to evaluate the information, while appreciative listening allows you to respond to the pleasure aspects of a stimulus. To be responsive to people, we use therapeutic and empathetic listening. If we use the appropriate type of listening, we will stay connected with the other party.

In essence, to be truly effective listeners, we must make strategic choices about what type of listening is needed and what depth of listening is needed in every listening situation. Our decisions will be based on the situations we find ourselves in, our relationship with the other person, and our assessment of the needs of the other party.

CONCEPTS TO KNOW

Literal Comprehension
Critical Comprehension
    Denotative Meaning
    Connotative Meaning
Listening Fidelity
Multidimensional Listening

Types of Listening
    Discriminative Listening
    Comprehensive Listening
    Critical Listening
    Appreciative Listening
    Therapeutic Listening

Arnold's Typology of Listening
Speech Intelligibility
Speaker Affect
Reasons for Message Inconsistencies
Empathetic Listening
    Empathy
    Sympathy
    Empathetic Responsiveness
    Perspective Taking
    Sympathetic Responsiveness

Factors Affecting Empathy
Van Slyke's Levels of Listening
    Passive Listening
    Responding Listening
    Selective Listening
    Attentive Listening
    Empathetic Listening
Active Listening
    Reflective Listening Responses

DISCUSSION QUESTIONS

1. Table 2.1 presents the listening dimensions measured by four separate listening tests. What do they have in common? What are major differences? Which of the three multidimensional models do you feel is the best? Why?

2. In the chapter we discussed the importance of discriminative listening to survival. Have you had an experience when discriminative listening helped you avoid an accident? What are behaviors we engage in today that might interfere with this type of listening?

3. Think back on a time when someone's verbal message was inconsistent with her nonverbal. Which of the sources of message inconsistencies might explain the discrepancy between what was said and how it was said?

4. Do you agree that "women appear to have an empathetic edge"? Are women more empathetic, or do men just express empathy differently? How can men express caring and empathy in culturally acceptable ways? To women? To other men?

LISTENING ACTIVITIES

1. Listen to a recording of different dialects. You can listen to dialects from across the country and around the world at the following Web site: http://web.ku.edu/~idea/. Can you tell what the person is saying? Try listening to computer-generated voices. Check out the following resources or you can search the Internet for other voices: www.saffas-voice.co.uk/animated-voices.php; http://en.wikipedia.org/wiki/Speech_synthesis; www.cereproc.com/products/voices.

2. Play the audio (not video) of the speeches of political candidates or other famous speakers. (Try the following Web sites for a great selection: www.presidency.ucsb.edu; http://millercenter.org/scripps/archive/speeches.) What biases, prejudices, or attitudes do you hear evidenced in the words? Try doing the same while listening to news stories. Can you identify biases of the announcer or commenter? What about the network? Finally why do you think we asked that you listen to the audio without the video of the political speech?

3. Get into groups of five or six. Each group should write a script of a short interaction that a person might typically face (asking for directions, friend in crisis, little sister with hurt knee, meeting classmate for the first time). Spend about 10 minutes developing the script from greeting to farewell. Identify the topics discussed; then identify the appropriate type of listening to use. Be prepared to role-play your script, and be ready to discuss the type of listening as well as the depth of listening needed.

ENDNOTES

1. Yalcinkaya, Muluk, & Sahin, 2009, p. 1137
2. Swanson, 1997, p. 3
3. Beatty, 1999
4. Speaking and Listening Competencies, 1998
5. Graham, 2006
6. Binford, 1977

7. Brant & Powers, 1980
8. Powers & Lowery, 1984a & 1984b; Powers & Spitzberg, 1986; Powers & Love, 1989; Kopecky & Powers, 2002; Dugas, Powers, & Sawyer, 2003
9. Mulanax & Powers, 2001
10. Powers & Bodie, 2003; Fitch-Hauser & Powers, 2005; Fitch-Hauser, Powers, Hanson, & O'Brien, 2007
11. Mulanax & Powers, 2001, p. 70
12. Fitch-Hauser et al., 2007
13. Fitch-Hauser & Hughes, 1988
14. Brown & Carlsen, 1955
15. Educational Testing Service, 1979
16. Bostrom & Waldhart, 1983
17. Watson, Barker, & Roberts, 2000
18. Wolvin & Coakley, 1996
19. Wilkin, 1991; Lecanuet, Granier-Deferre, & Busnel, 1988
20. Hepper, Scott, & Shahidullah, 1993
21. Meher, Lambertz, Jusczyk, & Amiel-Tison, 1986
22. Kuhl, 1991
23. Evitts & Searl, 2006
24. Yorkston, Strand, & Kennedy, 1996
25. Hirai, 1999
26. Wolvin & Coakley, 1996, p. 211
27. Goss, 1982
28. Goss, 1982
29. Mehrabian, 1971
30. Timm & Schroeder, 2000
31. Leathers, 1997
32. Leathers, 1997
33. Leathers, 1997
34. Ekman, 1985
35. Wolvin & Coakley, 1996, p. 363
36. Clark, 1989, p. 4
37. Klein & Ackerman, 1995
38. Arnold, 1996; Carkhuff, 1969
39. Nichols, 1995, p. 10
40. Nichols, 1995, p. 62
41. Nichols, 1995, p. 62
42. Friedman, 2005, p. 222
43. Richendoller & Weaver, 1994
44. Emotional concern is discussed by Davis (1980, 1983) and Stiff et al. (1988).
45. Brody, 2000
46. Fischer & Manstead, 2000
47. Fischer & Manstead, 2000
48. Fischer & Manstead, 2000
49. Gender differences have been addressed by many researchers, including Bassili (1970), Solomon (1998), Richardson (1999), & Borisoff & Merrill (1991).
50. See Drollinger, Comer, & Warrington (2006) for a discussion of an empathy scale.
51. Van Slyke, 1999
52. Comer & Drollinger, 1999
53. Michel, 2006
54. Van Slyke, 1999, p. 108
55. Van Slyke, 1999, p. 108

REFERENCES

Arnold, W. E. (1996). Listening and the helping professions. In M. Purdy & D. Borisoff (eds.), *Listening in everyday life: A personal and professional approach* (267–284). Lanham, MD: University Press of America.

Beatty, J. (1999). Good listening. *Educational Theory, 49,* 281–298.

Bassili, J. (1970). Emotional recognition: The role of facial movement and the relative importance of the upper and lower areas of the face. *Journal of Personality and Social Psychology, 37,* 249–258.

Binford, F. E. (1977). *A study of interrelationships among different approaches to measuring listening comprehension.* Unpublished doctoral dissertation, University of Iowa.

Borisoff, D., & Merrill, L. (1991). Gender issues and listening. In Purdy, M., & Borisoff, D. (eds.), *Listening in everyday life: A personal and professional approach* (59–85). Lanham, MD: University Press of America.

Bostrom, R. N., & Waldhart, E. S. (1983). *The Kentucky comprehensive listening test.* Lexington: Kentucky Listening Research Center.

Brant, D. R., & Powers, W. G. (1980). An approach to developing communication competency in scientific and technical communicators. *Journal of Technical Writing and Communication, 10,* 213–221.

Brody, L. R. (2000). The socialization of gender differences in emotional expression: Display rules, infant temperament, and differentiation. In A. Fischer (ed.), *Gender and emotions: Social psychological perspectives* (24–47). Cambridge, UK: Cambridge University Press.

Brown, J. I., & Carlsen, G. R. (1955). *Brown-Carlsen listening comprehension test.* New York: Harcourt, Brace & World, Inc.

Carkhuff, R. (1960). *Helping and human relations.* New York: Holt, Reinhart & Winston.

Clark, A. J. (1989). *Appreciative listening.* Paper presented at the annual meeting of the International Listening Association, Atlanta, GA.

Comer, L. B., & Drollinger, T. (1999). Active empathetic listening and selling success: A conceptual framework. *Journal of Personal Selling and Sales Management, 19,* 15–29.

Davis, M. H. (1980). A multidimensional approach to the study of empathy. *JSAS Catalog of Selected Documents in Psychology, 10,* 85.

Davis, M. H. (1983). Measuring individual differences in empathy: Evidence for a multidimensional approach. *Journal of Personality and Social Psychology, 44,* 213–236.

Drollinger, T., Comer, L. B., & Warrington, P. T. (2006). Development and validation of the active empathetic listening scale. *Psychology & Marketing, 23,* 161–180.

Dugas, D., Powers, W. G., & Sawyer, C. R. (2003). *Extroversion versus similarity: An exploration of factors influencing communication accuracy of social cognitions.* Paper presented at the annual meeting of the National Communication Association, Miami Beach, FL.

Educational Testing Service. (1979). *STEP III Manual and Technical Report.* Menlo Park, CA: Addison-Wesley Publishing Company.

Ekman, P. (1985). *Telling lies: Clues to deceit in the marketplace, politics, and marriage.* New York: Norton.

Evitts, P. M., & Searl, J. (2006). Reaction time of normal listeners to laryngeal, alaryngeal, and synthetic speech. *Journal of Speech, Language, and Hearing Research, 49,* 1380–1390.

Fischer, A. H., & Manstead, A. S. R. (2000). The relation between gender and emotion in different cultures. In A. Fischer (ed.), *Gender and emotions: Social psychological perspectives* (71–96). Cambridge, UK: Cambridge University Press.

Fitch-Hauser, M., & Hughes, M. A. (1988). Defining the cognitive process of listening: A dream or reality? *Journal of the International Listening Association, 2,* 75–88.

Fitch-Hauser, M., & Powers, W. G. (2005, April). *Examining the relationship between listening fidelity and listening effectiveness variables.* Paper presented at the annual meeting of the International Listening Association, Minneapolis, MN.

Fitch-Hauser, M., Powers, W. G., O'Brien, K., & Hanson, S. (2007). Extending the conceptualization of listening fidelity. *International Journal of Listening, 21,* 81–91.

Friedman, N. (2005). Experiential listening. *Journal of Humanistic Psychology, 45,* 217–238.

Goss, B. (1982). Listening as information processing. *Communication Quarterly, 30,* 304–307.

Graham, S. (2006). Listening comprehension: The learners' perspective. *System, 34,* 165–182.

Hepper, P. G., Scott, D., & Shahidullah, S. (1993). Newborn and fetal response to maternal voice. *Journal of Reproductive and Infant Psychology, 11,* 147–153.

Hirai, A. (1999). The relationship between listening and reading rates of Japanese EFL learners. *Modern Language Journal, 83,* 367–384.

Klein, L., & Ackerman, D. (writers). (1995). *Mystery of the Senses. Hearing.* In L. Klein (producer/director) and P. Jones (series producer). *NOVA* miniseries. Boston: WGBH.

Kopecney, C. C., & Powers, W. G. (2002). Relational development and self-image: Communication accuracy. *Communication Research Report, 19,* 283–290.

Kuhl, P. K. (1991). Perception, cognition, and the ontogenetic and phylogenetic emergence of human speech. In S. Brauth, W. Hall, & R. Dooling (eds.), *Plasticity of development* (73–106). Cambridge, MA: MIT Press/Gradford Books.

Leathers, D. B. (1979). The impact of multichannel message inconsistency on verbal and nonverbal decoding behaviors. *Communication Monographs, 46,* 88–100.

Leathers, D. B. (1997). *Successful nonverbal communication* (3rd ed.). Boston: Allyn & Bacon.

Lecanuet, J. P., Granier-Deferre, C., & Busnel, M. (1988). Fetal cardiac and motor responses to octave-band noises as a function of central frequency, intensity and heart rate variability. *Early Human Development, 13,* 269–283.

Mehler, J., Lambertz, G., Jusczyk, P., & Amiel-Tison, D. (1986). Discrimination de la langue maternelle par le nouveau-né. *C. R. Academie des Sciences, 303,* Series III, 637–640.

Mehrabian, A. (1971). *Silent messages.* Belmont, CA: Wadsworth.

Michel, C. (2006). Hallmarks of enlightened leadership. *U.S. Naval Institute Proceedings, 132,* 96. Retrieved from Academic Search Premier database. (AN 22693052)

Mulanax, A., & Powers, W. G. (2001). Listening fidelity development and relationship to receiver apprehension and locus of control. *International Journal of Listening, 15,* 69–78.

Nichols, M. P. (1995). *The Lost Art of Listening*. New York: Guilford.

Powers, W. G., & Bodie, G. (2003). Listening fidelity: Seeking congruence between cognitions of the listener and the sender. *International Journal of Listening, 17*, 19–31.

Powers, W. G., & Love, D. (1989). Basic communication fidelity: An extension. *Communication Research Reports, 6*, 79–83.

Powers, W. G., & Lowry, D. N. (1984a). Basic communication fidelity: A fundamental approach. In R. N. Bostrom (ed.), *Competence in communication* (57–71). Beverly Hills: Sage.

Powers, W. G., & Lowry, D. N. (1984b). Basic communication fidelity and nationality: Group interaction perceptions. *Communication Research Reports, 1*, 48–53.

Powers, W. G., & Spitzberg, B. (1986). Basic communication fidelity and image management. *Communication Research Reports, 3*, 60–63.

Richardson, J. L. (1999). Women lead in style. *Transportations & Distribution, 40*, 78–82.

Richendoller, N. R., & Weaver, J. B. (1994). Exploring the links between personality and empathic response style. *Personality and Individual Differences, 17*, 303–311.

Solomon, C. M. (1998). Women are still undervalued: Bridge the parity gap. *Workforce, 77*, 78–86.

Speaking and Listening Competencies for College Students (1998). National Communication Association. Retrieved from www.natcom.org.

Stiff, J. B., Dillard, J. P., Somera, L., Kim, H., & Sleight, C. (1988). Empathy, communication, and prosocial behavior. *Communication Monographs, 55*, 198–213.

Swanson, C. (1997). *Who's listening in the classroom? A research paradigm*. Paper presented to the meeting of the International Listening Association, Sacramento, CA (ERIC Document Reproduction Service No. ED407659).

Timm, S., & Schroeder, B. (2000). Listening/nonverbal communication training. *International Journal of Listening, 14*, 109–128.

Van Slyke, E. (1999). *Listening to Conflict: Finding constructive solutions to workplace disputes*. New York: AMACOM.

Watson, K. W., Barker, L. L., & Roberts, C. V. (2000). *Watson-Barker listening test facilitator's guide*. Sautee, GA: Spectra Incorporated Publishers.

Wilkin, P. E. (1991). Prenatal and postnatal responses to music and sound stimuli: A clinical report. *Canadian Music Educator (research ed.), 33*, 223–232.

Wolvin, A., & Coakley, C. (1996). *Listening*. (5th ed.). Boston: McGraw-Hill.

Yalcinkaya, F., Muluk, N. B., & Sahin, S. (2009). Effects of listening ability on speaking, writing and reading skills of children who were suspected of auditory processing difficulty. *International Journal of Pediatric Otorhinolaryngology, 73*, 1137–1142.

Yorkston, K. M., Strand, E. A., & Kennedy, M. R. (1996). Comprehensibility of dysarthric speech. *Journal of Speech-Language Pathology, 5*, 55–66.

Listening and Information Processing

Carter's Dilemma

Say, Carter, why are you looking so bummed?

Hi, Ben. I just sat through a lecture by a guest speaker, and I seem to have forgotten everything. I know that my professor is going to ask test questions over the presentation, and I can't remember a thing. I sure thought I was paying attention.

What was the lecture about?

It had something to do with nanotechnology and the latest discoveries in that area. Going into the presentation, I didn't know what nanotechnology was, and I sure don't know now. I wish I'd read up on the topic before the lecture. Maybe then . . . ■

As the receiving aspect of communication, listening involves much more than simply receiving the messages sent by the sender. As you saw in the listening models in Chapter 1, it involves all of the complexity associated with receiving, interpreting, storing, and recalling information. By understanding how you take in information and process it into meaningful, usable, and even memorable information, you should be able to make strategic choices as a listener that will help you more accurately process incoming stimuli and come closer to high-fidelity listening.

As you remember from the basic listening model presented in Chapter 1, the first thing that must happen for listening to occur is that the message must be physically received. This step is physiological. The appropriate receptor center, whether it be audio, visual, or some other sensation, receives the signal. A series of electrochemical responses occur, sending information to your brain, and your brain registers the physical reception of the stimulus. However, as we have previously pointed out, just because you physically receive the signal doesn't mean that you consciously recognize or process the stimulus. You are surrounded by sights and sounds that you either ignore or simply don't notice. For example, think about your dorm room or your apartment. Chances are your roommates or other occupants of the dorm or complex are going about their own business. Whatever they are doing probably makes some noise. Unless the noise is exceptionally loud or unusual, you probably "tune it out" and don't let it interfere with your reading this chapter. In other words, you physically receive the sound, but you have learned not to listen to it. This example is an excellent way to point out that being an effective listener involves a large dose of choice by you, the listener. That is, listening begins when we make the conscious decision to pay attention to incoming information. This chapter will look at what happens to the information to which you choose to listen.

RECEIVING AND PROCESSING INFORMATION

As you read in the first chapter, listening, as defined by both the ILA and the NCA, is an active, conscious communication act. Much of this activity occurs within your information processing system. The model of intraperson processing (Figure 3.1) illustrates how you process information when you receive it. Clearly this discussion is biased toward listening and isn't intended as a comprehensive review of either information or cognitive processing. However, you will learn enough about these two areas to have a good understanding of the importance of the cognitive aspects

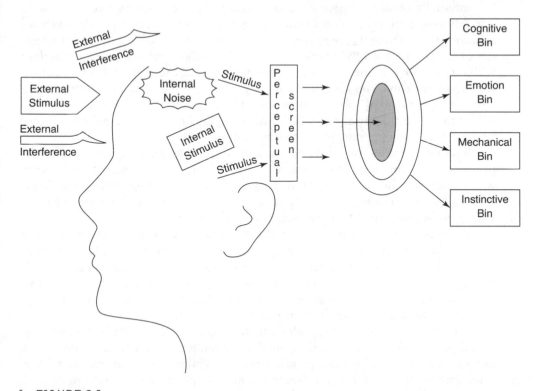

FIGURE 3.1
Intrapersonal Information Flow Model.

of the listening process. To help illustrate the internal listening process, we present the Intrapersonal Information Flow (IIF) model, which is adapted from an early model of intrapersonal processing developed by early-listening scholars Deborah Roach, Larry Barker, and Margaret Fitch-Hauser.[1] The IIF model illustrates the fundamental elements of cognitive processing that occur during the listening process. The model provides a visual illustration of what happens as information enters our conscious awareness, passes through our perceptions, and is perceived, used, or stored for future usage.

The model presents an overview of conscious and subconscious processing. The following discussion will examine each of the model's parts and focus on how they work together.

External stimuli are signs, signals, or any other stimuli transmitted by sources other than the receiver and picked up through the senses. In the listening process, the two senses most used are hearing and seeing. Stimuli, picked up subconsciously or consciously, become information that is transmitted to the central nervous system and the appropriate receptor centers in the brain.

External interference is noise that makes it difficult or impossible to perceive or identify external stimulus. Examples would include the temperature of a room, a train rumbling by, or a competing conversation. In other words, external interference is anything in the surroundings of an interaction that hinders you from focusing on the desired stimulus.

Internal stimuli are nerve impulses received by the brain as a result of your own physiological or emotional state. Hunger is an example of a *physical internal stimulus,* while thoughts are examples of a *cognitive internal stimulus,* and a feeling of joy is an *emotional internal stimulus.* Sometimes internal stimuli interfere with our listening. In the case study at the beginning of the chapter, Carter's confusion about the topic and his distress about not understanding are more than likely creating a great deal of internal distraction. This distraction then interferes with his ability to fully attend to the speaker's presentation. Any time internal stimuli prevent us from listening, they become internal noise.

Internal noises as stimuli within the person can take many forms. They might occur at a subconscious level, such as a vague feeling of discomfort that occurs when someone stands too close to us. They might also be at a more conscious level, such as being distracted in class when wondering whether you logged off from your bank account site before you left home this morning.

Reception is the neural reception of the stimulus. When you register the noise of the train rumbling by, whether you pay attention to it or not, you have received the sound. However, if that reception doesn't capture your attention, you will quickly dismiss the sound without registering its presence. For you to truly listen, you must recognize that you have received the stimulus. In essence, you have to choose to attend to the stimulus that you have received.

Perceptual screens are psychological filters that affect how you perceive the stimulus. Using the example of the train once again, we can illustrate how different experiences can affect how one perceives the sound. If you associate the sound of a train with something fun and adventuresome, you perceive the sound to be very nonthreatening or even pleasant. Also, if you live by a train track, you perceive the sound as something ordinary and probably don't waste any cognitive energy focusing on it. In other words, you ignore it. If you have had a bad experience with a train, such as knowing someone who has been involved in a train wreck, you might perceive the sound to be threatening. Perceptual filters can also take the form of stereotypes about people. This type of perceptual filter will be discussed more fully later in this chapter.

Once information gets into the system, you begin to sort it so it can be processed appropriately. According to the IIF model, information goes to one of four distinct areas. In the model these areas are depicted as four information bins: emotional, mechanical, instinctive, and cognitive.

The **emotional bin** includes attitudes, values, and beliefs that guide how you live your life. These three things form the predispositions used when responding to people, events, places, or objects. *Beliefs* are your "perceptions of the real world."[2] You act on these perceptions or observations as if they were true and real. Consequently these beliefs influence the way you perceive information as a listener and will influence the decisions you make about the information. *Attitudes* refer to your view of whether something is "good" or "bad."[3] Values differ. *Values* reflect your view of what "ought" to be.[4] Thus, your values form the core of the way you think things should be; beliefs reflect your views of the way things are, while attitudes signal how much or how little you like something. (It is also possible to have a neutral or ambiguous attitude if there are simultaneously elements you like and dislike about something or someone.) If, for example, you are concerned about global warming, that concern likely indicates that you *value* our environment and caring for it, that you *believe* global warming is a threat to the environment. As a result, you might develop a positive attitude toward alternative-fuel cars. Working together, these three constructs might lead you to write your congressional representative in support of a new bill giving tax breaks to people who buy such cars. The combination of values, attitudes, and beliefs provides the foundation of your emotional processes. As you can see in our global warming example, if you strongly support a position on an issue, your attitudes, values, and beliefs will affect how you listen to messages related to it. When you hear a message that supports your point of view, you will probably pay attention and participate in the interaction. On the other hand, when you hear a message that disagrees with your point of view, you might find yourself subject to internal stimuli (discussed above) that could interfere with your ability to fully listen. In such cases, you might spend your energy coming up with counterarguments or simply disagreeing rather than remaining open to actually listening to the message. If you find yourself doing that, remember that you can choose to bypass your biases and listen to messages that are contrary to your beliefs.

The **mechanical bin** of the IIF model addresses learned behaviors. Included in this type of processing are those everyday tasks that seem to take little cognitive effort on your part. Many of these tasks are behaviors that are habitual or everyday things that you do without really thinking about how to do them. For example, if you know how to play a piano, you don't have to think much about how to strike the keys. When you first learned how to drive, you consciously went through the process of identifying what you needed to do. However, after a few times of getting

THINK ON IT

Can you think of other tasks or behaviors that you engage in that would fall into the mechanical bin? What differentiates them from the other three areas we discuss?

behind the wheel, starting the car, fastening your seat belt, putting the car in gear, and so forth, you likely no longer really think about these aspects of the driving process. The knowledge has become automatic, almost encoded into your muscles. More recent research indicates that some of this processing might become programmed behavior or muscle memory.[5]

Nobel Prize–winner Eric Kandel found that repeated stimulation of sensory neurons in cells strengthened and created new synaptic connections that lead to long-term memory of appropriate reactions.[6] Even though Kandel looked at physical reactions, you can extrapolate from those results to other behaviors as well. For example, if you are accustomed to engaging in the same behaviors every time you are asked to listen to information, that response might become so automatic, or habitual, that you no longer engage the conscious aspects of cognitive functioning necessary for you to truly listen (that is, pay attention) to the information. If you are in a class where the professor presents everything in the same manner, such as breaking case studies down in the same way every class period, you might stop focusing on the content after the third or fourth time. We will revisit this concept when we look at the negative effect of schemata.

THINK ON IT

Think about classes you have taken. Can you identify anything about how the information is delivered that might affect your motivation to listen? Can you think of some strategies you can use to remain engaged in the conversation or lecture?

The **instinctive bin** is the third bin proposed by the IIF model. This function includes the physiological functioning of the human system. You don't have to think about how to sneeze; you just sneeze when your nose becomes irritated by some element such as pepper. The instinctive function also includes the functioning of the five senses through which you receive external stimuli. It is in this capacity that the instinctive function has an effect on listening.

The **cognitive bin** is associated with thought and the active processing of information. Included at this level are functions such as the interpretation and storage of information. Here we will briefly discuss three important factors that influence our cognitive processing: memory, priming, and framing. Later we will address schema formation, which also plays a significant role in cognitive processing and listening.

The type of memory that seems most relevant to listening is working memory.[7] **Working memory** can be defined as the *active* contents of memory. Working memory is the information base that you use as you listen. This content can help you listen better, or it can present challenges to the effectiveness of your listening. Laura Janusik suggested that working memory serves us in two important ways: the processing of information and information storage. These two functions are necessarily affected by the short-term and long-term feature of working memory.[8]

Short-term working memory has a direct effect on attending.[9] Using this aspect of memory, you move information from reception to cognitive interpretation. If you think back to the Listening MATERRS model presented in Chapter 1, you will find that short-term working memory helps you navigate between the awareness, translation, and evaluation functions as you process incoming mental stimuli. It also helps you incorporate the new information with what you already know by allowing you to retrieve appropriate information from your long-term memory. In essence then, short-term working memory becomes the recall link in the Listening MATERRS model. It is important to keep in mind that in working memory you will find information that you actively pay attention to as well as that which you either choose to ignore or simply don't recall. For example, if the incoming stimulus (either external or internal) is deemed unimportant, you dismiss it.

Part of a listener's challenge is that only a limited amount of information can be held in the focus of attention at any given time. If too much competing information is going on, such as when you send and receive text messages during lectures, you might lose critical information. However, if you decide the information might possibly be important, you either use it or send it on to other levels of memory. In situations where you don't pay attention to a thought or piece of information, you lose it very quickly. Have you ever had a thought that popped up, but before you had a chance to express it, it seemed to evaporate into thin air? Chances are that you delayed too long in attending to that piece of information.

The cognitive function also includes **long-term memory**. Your memories of language, events that have happened to you, the lessons you learn in school, and other information are all stored in your long-term memory. However, this aspect of working memory goes beyond the ability to recall, it also includes your ability to use that recalled information. So your logical reasoning capacities as well as your abilities to synthesize and analyze information and consequently assimilate information are all part of the cognitive function. It takes all of these activities for you to comprehend both the obvious and the more subtle meanings of events, messages, or feelings. To understand most incoming information, you need to be able to access the information you have stored in long-term memory.[10]

Exactly what information you access is, in part, affected by priming and framing. **Primes** are clues embedded in a message that signal how the information should be interpreted. For example, if someone says to you that he wants to discuss an opportunity, the word *opportunity* will influence how you interpret the message that follows. Your interpretation will be based on your knowledge of the term, your experiences with things labeled "opportunities," and your reaction to those experiences. The prime helps you decide what to focus on or attend to in the message. As seen in the previous example, the prime was a single word. However, it can also be a phrase or idea and may be visual as well as auditory.

Primes are part of how a message is framed. **Frames** function in two ways.[11] First, they are an aspect of how speakers compose their messages. At the same time, frames act as "cognitive structures that guide information processing."[12] Thus, the way in which a message is framed will promote a particular view, evaluation, solution, and so forth.[13] As you can see, how a message is framed affects individual perception. The effect of message framing has been examined in a number of areas, including news presentation and health communication. One area of health communication research addresses the effectiveness of gain-framed and loss-framed messages. Psychologist Alexander Rothman and his colleagues wrote, "*Gain-framed statements* can refer to both good things that will happen and the bad things that will not happen, whereas *loss-framed statements* can refer to bad things that will happen and good things that will not happen."[14] A simple example illustrates the difference between these two types of framing: "If you floss, you will enjoy fresh, minty breath" is a gain-framed statement, while "If you don't floss, you will have bad breath" is a loss-framed statement.[15] Findings from this research indicate that presenting the same information with slight differences in wording has a profound effect on how the listeners respond. In general, people exposed to a gain-framed message tend to be less willing to risk the bad outcome (in the above example, bad breath).[16] So frames, or how the message is worded, can affect how you process an incoming message by leading you to focus on specific information or by enhancing the importance of a particular part of a message.[17]

Along with priming and framing, how you receive, access, and store information in your memory is also affected by your use of schemata and scripts. Schemata and scripts are often thought of as patterns of information that you have learned to expect.

While we have discussed your emotional, mechanical, instinctive, and cognitive bins separately, it is important to realize that they work with each other as you process information and stimuli. For example, information is typically processed simultaneously, such as when you jump when a spider drops down from a ceiling. This instinctive response will be affected by how much you fear spiders.

As you look at the model of how we receive, screen, and process information, you can see what occurs internally as you listen. It is important to note that when this model is placed into the framework of interpersonal interactions, it helps you understand why listening is truly a complex process. Not only are you going through the process, so are all of the other parties involved in an interaction. To help explain further what happens internally when you listen, we next address the effect of schemata on the listening process.

SCHEMATA AND INFORMATION PROCESSING

One way to more clearly understand how listening and information processing are tied together is to learn more about how information is perceived and processed. Drawing on research from communication, psychology, and related areas, we use schema theory to help unravel the mystery of what happens as you make sense of the messages you receive as a listener.[18] More specifically, we will examine the effect of schemata on attending, perceiving, and recalling information. However, before we address these areas, you need to first understand what a schema is. A **schema** is a cognitive structure consisting of representations of some defined area (e.g., person, place, thing). These structures contain general knowledge, including expectations about relationships among attributes, examples, and expectations about how those attributes function. This knowledge helps you identify what a stimulus is as well as make sense of it. In essence, you develop scripts or templates that you use to understand the world around you. **Scripts** address the sequence of actions associated with a particular event.[19]

> **THINK ON IT**
>
> Do you believe it is possible for infants to develop a schema prior to birth? If so, what type of schema might they develop? If not, when do you think early schemata develop, and what form might they take?

Schemata and scripts start developing at an incredibly young age. In fact, some researchers feel that we can develop schemata even before we are born and certainly while still infants.[20] One of the early ways we experience schemata is in our expectations for how the information is "supposed to be" presented. For example, if your professor were to say, "Once upon a time," you would have little difficulty in taking up the thread of the story. You would almost automatically continue with information about a damsel in distress who has a wicked stepmother or other evil relative and who is ultimately rescued by a handsome prince. You can fill in the rest of the story because you use schematic processing, or an information processing system using schema(ta). As a child, your schema for this type of story was developed as you heard stories, such as *Cinderella,* that use this plot line. Our fairy-tale example reflects one of the many types of schemata that we can develop. When you think of such stories, *Cinderella* likely reflects what you typically think of as a script. However, we also use scripts for events that occur in our everyday life. For example, you have a script for the sequence of events that occurs when you go to your typical college class (i.e., find your seat, get your books/materials ready, silence your mobile phone, stop talking when the professor begins speaking). Schemata and scripts are drawn from our experiences, and the stronger those experiences and the more frequently we repeat them, the stronger and more established those schemata and scripts tend to be. If you know several people in college who are really into computers and are rather geeky, you might develop a schema for IT people that you take with you when you begin working after graduation. (This schema might also be reinforced by media portrayals.) Thus, when you experience information being structured in the same way, see events occurring in the same way, or interact with groups of people in the same way repeatedly, you begin to establish and strengthen your schemata.

As you have seen in the *Cinderella* example, you use your schema for narratives to help you first identify what the subject is—a fairy tale. In addition, you will fill in the story with expectations about what is "supposed to be" in the story. In this capacity schemata and scripts also function as maps for perceiving incoming information.[21] Not only do they influence what you pay attention to but they also act as large units of knowledge that help organize what you "know" about the world around you. In essence, they guide you in determining what information is worthy of attention and that which can be ignored.

Schemata and Attending

As we saw in the previous discussion, once you decide to attend to something, your schema for that thing triggers a set of expectations for the incoming information. Our discussion also demonstrated that many of our social interactions are based in narratives. Consequently how you handle narrative information will have a profound effect on how you listen, beginning with whether you truly pay attention to what the other person is saying. Seminal research by Roger Schank and Robert Abelson suggests that narrative information that evokes one of the story lines in your story bank can lead you to rely on a script rather than paying attention to the details of the incoming information.[22] So if you recognize the "baseball game won by a walk-off home run" script, you might focus more on what *you* want to say about your favorite baseball team or player than you do on the actual message. Another possibility can occur when you recognize what the story is about. With this recognition, you are steered toward listening to specific aspects of the story, particularly those that are really important to you. In essence, the schema helps you prioritize information so you focus your energy on that which is most important to you.

Schemata and Perceiving

Schemata affect not only what we attend to and how but also the way information is perceived. They do this, in part, by directing our attention to particular aspects of incoming messages. Working in conjunction with priming and framing, schemata help us track information as it comes in and provide a basis for predicting what will be said next. We will examine several ways in which schemata affect our perceptions, including our expectations for how information should be structured or organized; the effect of our attitudes, values, and beliefs on schemata; how we handle contradictory information; and the influence of several common social schemata.

Structural Expectations and Schemata As seen in our fairy-tale example, one of our expectations is that information is supposed to be structured or organized in a pattern that is appropriate to and in keeping with the triggered schema.[23] Just as you put together a puzzle by fitting the pieces together, you fit parts of a message with its other parts until you have something that makes sense to you. There are times when we are faced with an incomplete story. In such cases, you can use a schema to help you fill in the blanks of the missing information. Because this is often done unconsciously, it is not unusual for you to "remember" details that you filled in as if they were true and real.[24] For example, most of you have an established morning routine. If part of that routine is carrying coffee with you to class, you "remember" picking up the travel mug that morning when in reality you didn't. You convince yourself that you left the mug on the bus because you have a clear memory of picking it up on the way out the door. If so, you will be quite surprised when you return home and discover that your memory of leaving the house with coffee in hand was inaccurate.

Effect of Values on Schemata We introduced attitudes, beliefs, and values earlier in the chapter so won't review them again here. Suffice it to say, another way that schema affects how you perceive information focuses on the importance that you associate with it. The more incoming information is associated with schemata that are linked to strong values, beliefs, or attitudes you hold, the more motivated you will be to focus your attention on it, and as you will see in the next section, it can affect what information you choose to move from short-term to long-term memory.

Schemata do affect how messages are processed, particularly when the information contradicts your expectations. People can respond to **contradictory information** in one of several ways. They can discount or suspend the information, or they can reevaluate their schema and change it. *Discounting information* means that you basically ignore it. For example, you might convince yourself that the information is unimportant, that your friend had a good reason for being late, and so on. *Suspended information* is left in a type of cognitive limbo. It is significant enough for you to make note of, but you might not be sure what to do with it. In such cases you might *tag* the piece of information or the experience. However, one tag will rarely lead someone to adjust or *reevaluate a schema.* Generally speaking, the stronger the schema, the more tags will be needed to change it. Thus, if you have a schema of your best friend as a warm and caring person, he or she will likely have to engage in a number of negative events or

THINK ON IT

Have you ever changed an established schema? Did you change it after tagging one significant piece of information, or did it change as the result of tagging several separate pieces of information?

actions before you will reconfigure your schema to include the contradictory information. Tagging information that is out of sync with a schema is quite common. We also can tag information and use it when we are developing new schemata. As you remember from our earlier discussion, it can take repeated encounters to establish a working schema. It is important to note that there are occasions where it might take only one event to form or adjust a strong schema (e.g., you witness a scene of great courage or you find out your significant other was having an affair).

Types of Schema   Schemata also affect the way we perceive people, relationships, and events. These schemata are called **social schemata** and are expectations about how the social world operates. These schemata include how we organize our knowledge about people, self, social roles, and events. Other names associated with this type of schema are prototypes, stereotypes, and scripts.

People schemata affect how we perceive individuals.[25] We often use these schemata to help us categorize people so we can better understand them or make decisions about their credibility. One aspect of people schemata is personality. If you think about it, when you meet someone for the first time, you often classify that person as an introvert or extrovert (I-E). You then use this assessment to make assumptions about that person based on the expectations triggered by your use of your I-E schema. If you feel that extroversion is a positive personality trait, you will perceive individuals classified as extroverts in a positive manner and consequently be more willing to listen to them.

Research has shown that listeners also form impressions about and evaluate people using physical attributes, such as age, racial and ethnic backgrounds, physical appearance, and even their voices.[26] For example, a great deal of research has indicated that regional dialects and foreign accents greatly affect the perceptions of a speaker's status, intelligence, wealth, competence, friendliness, and kindness.[27] Many of the schemata based on these elements fall in the category of stereotypes. *Stereotypes* as schemata contain value-laden attitudes and beliefs. So a listener hearing a speaker with an Asian accent may well rate the speaker on dimensions such as leadership and social status based solely on the stereotypes the accent elicits in the listener's schema bank.

The above example illustrates another important aspect of people schemata. When you meet or hear someone for the first time, you tend to assess that person based on your experiences with others whom you feel are similar to him or her. Unfortunately when you have little or no experience with a particular group, your stereotypes are often based on what you hear other people say or media presentation of that group. If your only exposure to Buddhism is dramatic depictions of monks in martial arts movies, your schema about that group will reflect what you see in those movies and have little to do with the real values of followers of that religion. Consequently when you encounter a real Buddhist monk, your internal and external reaction to that individual will probably reflect the expectations established by that fiction-based schema. Likewise, if you grow up in households where certain groups are either revered or vilified, your stereotypes will more than likely reflect those values and attitudes.

Context also influences how you perceive an individual. Calling on your **event schemata** (expectations governing what we expect events to be like), you make assessments about the appropriateness of someone's behavior. For example, if you go to a boxing match and hear someone in the crowd yell, "knock him out," you don't think much about what the person has said. After all, that type of comment is expected in that setting. However, if you are walking down a sidewalk in your favorite shopping area and hear the same phrase yelled out, you will probably start looking around in alarm and think that something is wrong. As you can see, schemata are used to decode messages.

Gender schema is a subcategory of people schema. Gender schemata are cognitive representations of traits, attitudes, behaviors, occupations, and other information associated with maleness and femaleness.[28] These schemata, like all other schemata, affect how you interpret information and make inferences and predictions. It is interesting to note your gender schemata seem to influence your assessment of a person, particularly in situations when you know little about him or her as an individual.[29] Gender schemata are culturally defined.[30] However, this doesn't mean that the individual is simply a passive recipient of societal expectations about gender roles. More recent thinking suggests that we actively participate in the process of the social construction of gender roles. So as you look around and see that more than 50 percent of the members of your class are females, you will think that the women in the class value education and will be pursuing careers upon graduation. In fact, not so long ago, people joked about women going to college in pursuit of a MRS. degree. College was treated as a dating service, where women met future husbands; careers were something that happened on the way to having a family. While many of you (male and female) will meet your future spouses while at college, few people today would think your primary purpose for attending school was to gain a spouse.

Occupational schemata are yet another type of people schema. These schemata might work alongside your gender schemata. For example, you might think that firefighters are supposed to be men or that kindergarten teachers are supposed to be women. However, the reality of both of those occupations is that both men and women choose to enter them. Other elements of occupation schemata include the trustworthiness of the people holding the position, the types of duties expected, and the amount of money associated with the job. Examining trustworthiness, a 2005 survey conducted in Great Britain revealed that the five most trusted occupations are doctors, teachers, professors, judges, and clergy, in that order.[31] A similar study in 2006 conducted by the *Australian Reader's Digest* reported that Australia's five most trusted professions are ambulance officers, firefighters, mothers, nurses, and pilots. Doctors and pharmacists come in sixth and seventh.[32] In the United States, a 2008 Gallup poll identified nurses, pharmacists, physicians, police officers, and engineers as the top five most trusted occupations.[33]

The differences in the results of these polls indicate that where we live or the culture in which we live has an effect on the schemata we hold. Although we don't always think of Great Britain, Australia, and the United States as being different cultures, we have only to look at one element of the occupation schema, trust, to find cultural differences.

Culture and Schema When the theory of schema was first introduced in 1932 by Fredrick Bartlett, he very clearly articulated that culture affects schema in two ways. First, it affects the content and structure of any schema we form, which in turn influences how we use schemata to make sense of information, events, people, and other things we encounter. One way to illustrate this is to look at the folklore of any culture. For example, by listening to the traditional folk tales of many Native American tribes, we can identify a reverence for nature and the belief that we coexist with all creatures. This reverence is part of the cultural schema of how people treat the land and animals as well as how they would interpret certain events. For example, a Native American schooled in the traditions of the culture might watch a show about hunting deer from the perspective of thankfulness that Mother Earth provides for her children, while a non–Native American who grew up in a culture that values hunting for the experience and the trophy might focus on the number of points on the antlers of the deer. Although these perspectives are very different, they are simply ways of perceiving the world based on environment and culture. A good listener will take these cultural differences into account when interpreting incoming information from the two individuals.

As we noted earlier, your expectations about a culture are based on your exposure to it. That exposure can be direct or indirect. One group of researchers testing the effects of cultural exposure on schema building used an indirect method, teaching elementary school students a unit on a culture different from their own (e.g., Spain, China). When the students were tested over their own culture and the other culture, their responses to the questions about the new culture clearly reflected the effect of the instructional unit.[34] This finding suggests that the instructional unit on culture helped the students establish a schema for that particular culture and that they used the schema to understand and remember the information. Of course, direct experience, such as interacting with individuals from another culture or traveling to other areas or countries, can affect individual schemata as well.

When you hear cultural information or see visual evidence of cultural or ethnic background, you will more than likely use that information to process verbal and nonverbal messages.[35] As the example of the Buddhist monk earlier in the chapter illustrates, your perceptions of individuals are based on what you believe or think you know about a group. Any cultural bias, good or bad, will affect how you perceive the credibility of a person and how you translate information from that source. Many years ago, Professor Fitch-Hauser, who grew up in Texas, acquired a pen pal in Australia. The first letter from her new Australian friend, Broni, asked about Indians and cowboys in Texas. Broni's schema about Texas, or any Western state in the United States, was largely based on the television shows and movies that she had seen. She was very surprised to learn that her new friend lived in a town and went to a school very similar to hers.

> **THINK ON IT**
>
> Schemata established via direct means often tend to be stronger than those established indirectly. Following 9/11, many people experienced profound changes to their schemata of the Middle East, Arab-Americans, and terrorists and terrorism. Can you think of a time when an indirect exposure or experience significantly affected a schema you hold?

Schemata and Memory

In addition to influencing what you attend to and how you perceive many types of information as a listener, schemata also affect the memory stage of listening by helping us identify information that should be stored or forgotten, organize information in our memories, and aid us in recalling information.

Memory Storage and Recall Schemata help you decide when a message is complete and can be stored in memory or when you need to keep a category open until you gain sufficient information to formulate a working schema. They help you decide what information is important and what is not, and they help you determine what should be transferred from short-term to long-term memory.

In essence, the very way you perceive the information affects how you store and recall any message. Schema-consistent information fits the expected categories of a schema. Most research has shown that schema-consistent information is more readily and accurately remembered over time, while schema-inconsistent information tends to fade from memory.[36] More recent research suggests that schema-inconsistent memory might be resistant to decay if the receiver is required to recall the inconsistent information several times over a relatively brief period of time or if the schema-inconsistent information is extremely different from the expected. A category of information that does succumb to decay, however, is schema-irrelevant information, or information that has no relationship to the schema itself. Information that the professor of your class had pasta Alfredo for lunch would probably be irrelevant to your schema and, therefore, not worthy of taking up space in your memory.[37]

Suspended information, information that doesn't readily fit a schema, is often held in memory until either you get enough information to form the foundation of a new schema or you can link it to one of your existing categories. Remember Carter in the Case Study at the start of the chapter? He doesn't remember what the speaker said because he doesn't have a foundation of knowledge about the subject, nanotechnology. As he continues his studies, he will build a foundation that will allow him to integrate increasingly complex concepts into his knowledge structures.

Finally contradictory information can be held as a tagged memory until a sufficient number of tags lead you to adjust or change your existing schema. Previous research indicates that information that is inconsistent with or contradicts schemata tends to be forgotten more quickly than that which is schema consistent.[38] When this is factored in along with the overall strength of a schema, you can see how difficult it can be for a single tag to lead to a change in a schema. It might be easier for us to discount the information in such cases.

Memory and Organization In addition to schemata focusing your attention on information that is consistent or inconsistent with expectations, they also help organize information in memory in such a way that it can be recalled. For example, research shows that information about people (people schema) is stored in a different category than information about objects.[39] When storing information about people, you often call on stereotypes and categorize them by race and sex.[40] In addition, schemata associated with important values, beliefs, and attitudes tend to be ranked higher, and this ranking makes them easier to retrieve and, thus, more available to us when processing incoming information.

Finally our schema-based expectations also undergird how we organize information. For example, as we described earlier, you expect certain elements to be present in a narrative. As you listen to the story, you store elements of it in the appropriate categories. For example, if your friend says that a group went to the beach and rented a place, you will probably store the information in the following manner: {A group of friends (you might remember the names)} {vacationed on a beach} {rented a place}. You will break the information down into logical units, separating people from actions and places. When you recall the information, you might recall that your friends (you would say their names) rented a condo on the beach. Using your schema, you know that people who rent places don't stay in hotels; they rent either a house or some type of condominium. So when you reconstruct the story, you reconstruct it based on your schema and add the element of the condo.

This illustration also points to a potential source of ***schema-based distortions*** to our memories. In our earlier example of the missing coffee mug, we pointed out that when information is missing from an original narrative, your memories tend to fill in the missing data.[41] There might not be much of a consequence for forgetting your coffee mug (except perhaps being groggy in class), but misremembering information can play a more serious role in other aspects of life. For example, let's say you are the witness to a bank robbery. You overhear the robber demanding money. When later being interviewed by police, you might "remember" a weapon being used to threaten the bank employees. Visualizing a weapon would be consistent with most schemata about bank robberies. Consequently you "remember" that detail even though it was not part of the actual robbery.[42]

It is safe to say that schemata have an effect on human memory. They affect what we remember as well as how well we remember. As a listener, you can use schemata to focus your attention on the important elements of incoming messages. You can also examine your preconceptions about a person, event, or any other type of information to determine if schemata are distorting information as you reconstruct it.

SCHEMATA AND LISTENING

As the discussion about the effect of schema has indicated, the way we process information has a strong effect on us as listeners. Schemata contain knowledge about a subject, script, or person. They affect how you process information, and they guide your behavior.[43] As we conclude this chapter, we believe it is important to note that schema theory is only one theory of information processing; there are others. Individuals interested in human information processing can find a rich collection of theories and research in the cognitive psychological literature. We chose to discuss schema because of the breadth and depth of the theory. Schema theory helps explain what listeners do with information in four ways.[44] First, schema theory clearly shows that human information processing is dynamic. In other words, listeners actively seek to make connections in their minds. Schemata help prioritize information based on what is relevant or irrelevant for the purpose at hand. Consequently listeners use schemata to decide whether to assign importance (relevance) to incoming information and actually attend to that message. In addition, listeners will incorporate new material they encounter into their information banks if they deem the information important and relevant. The connections listeners make between new information and their existing schemata are influenced by all of their life experiences. This conclusion makes sense if you consider that your schemata are also dynamic and are adjusted as you experience and learn new things.

The second way that schema theory explains what happens to information during the listening process is to account for the effect of culture on how listeners structure schemata and subsequently interpret information. As listeners make connections between pieces of information, they are guided by the values, worldviews, and assumptions of the cultures in which they grew up. This suggests that listeners need to be aware of their own cultural values while keeping an open mind to the cultural values of others. Being open to the cultural values of others helps listeners more accurately understand what the speaker is saying and intending.

The third way that schemata affect listening is by providing a means to incorporate the context of the listening event. Schemata help listeners make sense of the world around them. Sometimes making sense of a situation is very easy because an interaction or event goes the way the schematic script says it should go. However, often things happen in such a way that listeners have to search for ways to interpret what is happening. This occurs when listeners find themselves in situations that call into question their existing beliefs (i.e., their version of truth or their expectations about the way things are supposed to be). A decade after 9/11, many of us still struggle to find some way of understanding the terror and shock of those events. Similarly many people have difficulty processing the idea of thousands of people not having access to food and water or not having the opportunity to get out of harm's way following Hurricane Katrina. And think about how you felt seeing video of oil pouring into the Gulf of Mexico and listening to reports of the damage that oil was doing to the beaches and ecosystems of the Gulf states. Events such as these force many listeners to reshape their schemata as they process the events and the messages.

The fourth way that schemata affect listening is assisting in the understanding of conversations and listener perceptions. As noted above, part of the effect of conversations comes in the transmission of cultural values. Conversations reveal the frames, story themes, and the words used to explain the world around us.

SUMMARY

Research into how individuals process information and the effect of schemata on information processing and memory continues. Each new discovery helps us better understand the link between the way we perceive, process, store, and recall information and the communication act of listening. Our perceptions color our listening behavior, and one of the principle components of our perceptions is our lifetime collection of schemata. As you have seen in this chapter, any number of factors can influence how we process information. In the next chapter, we explore a number of personality-based individual differences that affect how we process information and that can affect the schemata we form.

CONCEPTS TO KNOW

Interpersonal Information Flow Model
    External Stimuli
    External Interference
    Internal Stimuli
    Internal Noise

Reception
Perceptual Screens
Emotional Bin
Values, Beliefs, Attitudes
Mechanical Bin

Instinctive Bin
Cognitive Bin
Working Memory
Primes Framing
Schemata
  Scripts
  Tagging
  Discounting Information
  Suspending Information

Reevaluating Schemata
Social Schema
People Schema
Stereotypes
Event Schema
Gender Schema
Occupational Schema
Culture Schema
Memory Distortion

DISCUSSION QUESTIONS

1. Going back to Chapter 1, how would our information processing model be integrated within or contribute to the WFH model of listening?
2. Our information processing includes several prominent concepts (e.g., external and internal stimuli). However, no model can account for every potential input. Can you think of any additional aspects of communication that could or should be included in our model?
3. In this chapter we discussed several common schemata (e.g., people, event, gender). Can you think of any other common schemata that likely affect people's listening processes?
4. Make a list of five particularly strong schemata that you hold (e.g., dislike smoking). How are they associated with your values? Your beliefs and attitudes? How might these schemata affect your ability to listen effectively (and fairly) to others when interacting on these topics?

LISTENING ACTIVITIES

1. Write a brief summary of what you know about the following groups. Include what type of exposure you have had to each group (e.g., personal experience, read about them, saw them on television). Identify your biases. How likely is it that these biases will affect how you listen to someone in each category?

Girl Scouts	Professors
Boy Scouts	Firefighters
Asians	Pilots
New York City residents	Medical doctors
Christians	Buddhists
Dutch	Irish
South Africans	Brazilians

2. In groups of three to five individuals, using your summaries from the previous activity, compare your responses to others in your class. What similarities and differences do you find? What underlies or is the source of the similarities you hold? The differences you have?
3. Review two to three of your favorite advertisements. What type of schemata are they trying to invoke? What related values and attitudes are triggered?

ADDITIONAL READINGS

Albarracín, D., Johnson, B. T., Zanna, M. P., & Kumkale, G. T. (2005). *The handbook of attitudes.* Mahwah, NJ: Erlbaum.

Flavell, J., Miller, P., & Miller, S. (2002). *Cognitive development* (4th ed.). Upper Saddle River, NJ: Prentice-Hall.

Johnson, B. T., Maio, G. R., & Smith-McLallen, A. (2005). Communication and attitude change: Causes, processes, and effects. In D. Albarracín, B. T. Johnson, & M. P. Zanna (eds.), *The handbook of attitudes* (617–669). Mahwah, NJ: Erlbaum.

Slugoski, B. R., & Hilton, D. J. (2001). Conversation. In W. P. Robinson & H. Giles (eds.), *The new handbook of language and social psychology*. Chichester, UK: Wiley.

ENDNOTES

1. Roach, Barker, & Fitch-Hauser, 1987
2. Goss, 1982
3. Breckler & Wiggins, 1992; Cacioppo & Petty, 1996; Eagly & Chaiken, 1995
4. Breckler & Wiggins, 1992; Cacioppo & Petty, 1996; Eagly & Chaiken, 1995
5. Kandel, 2004
6. Kandel, 2004
7. Baddely, 1986, 2003; Janusik, 2007
8. Ericsson & Kintsch, 1995
9. Janusik, 2007, p. 142
10. Was & Woltz, 2007
11. Hoffner & Ye, 2009
12. Hoffner & Ye, 2009, p. 189
13. Entman, 1993; Kahneman & Tversky, 1984, 1986; Vishwanath, 2009
14. Rothman, Bartels, Wlaschin, & Salovey, 2006, p. S202
15. See Rothman et al. (2006) for other examples of gain-framed and loss-framed health messages.
16. Rothman et al. (2006) provide a nice summary of the effects of gain-framed and loss-framed health messages.
17. D'Angelo, 2002
18. Beals, 1998; Dahlin, 2001; Erwin, 1992; Fitch-Hauser, 1984; Mazzocco, Green, & Brock, 2007; Memelink & Hommel, 2006
19. Shank & Abelson, 1977; Woll, 2001
20. See, for example, Karmiloff-Smith (1995).
21. Fitch-Hauser, 1984
22. Schank & Abelson, 1995

23. Freeman & Martin, 2004
24. Fitch-Hauser, 1984
25. Cantor & Mischel, 1977; Hosoda, Sonte-Romero, & Walter, 2007
26. Hosoda et al., 2007
27. See Hosoda et al. (2007) for a good summary of research on this topic.
28. Bem, 1983; Frawley, 2008; Liben & Signorella, 1980; Martin & Halverson, 1981, 1983
29. Chang & Hitchon, 2004
30. Bem, 1987
31. Doctors, 2008
32. Australia's most trusted, 2006
33. Said, 2009
34. Erwin, 1992
35. Brown, Smiley, Day, Townsend, & Lawton, 1977
36. Chang & Hitchon, 2008; Frawley, 2008; Rice & Okun, 1994
37. Tuckey & Brewer, 2003
38. Tuckey & Brewer, 2003
39. Kuethe, 1964
40. Chang & Hitcheon, 2004; Frawley, 2008; Taylor, Fiske, Etcoff, & Ruderman, 1978
41. See Fitch-Hauser (1984).
42. Research into eyewitness accounts and testimony supports this example. See, for example, the body of research conducted by Elizabeth Loftus and her colleagues.
43. Frawley, 2008
44. For a discussion on schema, see Beals (1998).

REFERENCES

Australia's Most Trusted 2006. Reader's Digest Interactive. Retrieved from www.readersdigest.com.au.

Baddeley, A. D. (1986). *Working memory.* New York: Oxford University Press.

Baddeley, A. D. (2003). Working memory and language: An overview. *Journal of Communication Disorders, 36,* 189–208.

Beals, D. (1998). Reappropriating schema: Conceptions of development from Bartlett and Bakhtin. *Mind, Culture, and Activity, 5,* 3–24.

Bem, S. (1983). Gender schema theory and its implications for child development: Raising gender-aschematic children in a gender-schematic society. *Signs, 8,* 598–616.

Bem, S. (1987). Gender schema theory and the romantic tradition. In P. Shaver & C. Hendrick (eds.), *Review of Personality and Social Psychology* (vol. 7, 251–271). Newbury Park, CA: Sage.

Breckler, S. J., & Wiggins, E. C. (1992). On defining attitude and attitude theory: Once more with feeling. In A. R. Pratkanis, S. J. Breckler, & A. C. Greenwald (eds.), *Attitude structure and function* (407–427). Hillsdale, NJ: Erlbaum.

Brown, A., Smiley, S., Day, J., Townsend, M., & Lawton, S. (1977). Intrusion of a thematic idea in children's comprehension and retention of stories. *Child Development, 48,* 1454–1466.

Cacioppo, J. T., & Petty, R. E. (1996). *Attitudes and persuasion: Classic and contemporary approaches.* Boulder, CO: Westview Press.

Cantor, M., & Mischel, W. (1977). Traits as prototypes: Effects on recognition memory. *Journal of Personality and Social Psychology, 35,* 38–48.

Chang, C., & Hitchon, J. C. B. (2004). When does gender count? Further insights into gender schematic processing of female candidates' political advertisements. *Sex Roles, 51,* 197–208.

Dahlin, B. (2001). Critique of the schema concept. *Scandinavian Journal of Educational Research, 45,* 287–300.

D'Angelo, P. (2002). News framing as a multiparadigmatic research program: A response to Entman. *Journal of Communication, 52,* 570–888.

Doctors still top the poll as most trusted profession. (2008, March 5). Ipsos. Retrieved from www.ipsos-mori.com/researchpublications/researcharchive/poll.aspx?oItemId=232.

Eagly, A., & Chaiken, S. (1995). Attitude strength, attitude structure and resistance to change. In R. Petty and J. Kosnik (eds.), *Attitude Strength* (413–432). Mahwah, NJ: Erlbaum.

Entman, R. M. (1993). Framing: Toward clarification of a fractured paradigm. *Journal of Communication, 43,* 51–58.

Ericsson, K. A., & Kintsch, W. (1995). Long-term working memory. *Psychological Review, 102,* 211–245.

Erwin, B. (1992). *The effect of culturally related schemata and instruction using thematic units on comprehension.* Paper presented at the Fourteenth World Congress on Reading, Maui, HI.

Fitch-Hauser, M. (1984). Message structure and recall. In R. Bostrom (ed.), *Communication Yearbook 8* (378–392). Beverly Hills: Sage.

Frawley, T. J. (2008). Gender schema and prejudicial recall: How children misremember, fabricate, and distort gendered picture book information. *Journal of Research in Childhood Education, 22,* 291–303.

Freeman, A., & Martin, D. (2004). A psychosocial approach for conceptualizing schematic development. *Cognition and Psychotherapy* (2nd ed.) (221–256). New York: Springer.

Goss, B. (1982). *Processing communication.* Belmont, CA: Wadsworth.

Hoffner, C., & Ye, J. (2009). Young adults' responses to news about sunscreen and skin cancer: The role of framing and social comparison. *Health Communication, 24,* 189–198.

Hosoda, M., Stone-Romero, E., & Walter, J. (2007). Listeners' cognitive and affective reactions to English speakers with standard American English and Asian accents. *Perceptual and Motor Skills, 104,* 307–326.

Janicik, F., & Larrick, R. (2005). Social network schemas and the learning of incomplete networks. *Journal of Personality and Social Psychology, 88,* 348–365.

Janusik, L. A. (2007). Building listening theory: The validation of the conversational listening span. *Communication Studies, 58,* 139–156.

Kahneman, D., & Tversky, A. (1984). Choice, values and frames. *The American Psychologist, 39,* 341–350.

Kahneman, D., & Tversky, A. (1986). Rational choices and the framing of decisions. *Journal of Business, 59,* (4, Part 2: The behavioral foundations of economic theory), S251–S278.

Kandel, E. (2004, May). The storage and persistence of memory. Address delivered at the Symposia on Brain and Mind Functioning, New York, Columbia University. Retrieved from http://c250.columbia.edu/c250_now/symposia/brain_and_mind.html.

Karmiloff-Smith, A. (1995). Annotation: The extraordinary cognitive journey from fetus through infancy. *Journal of Child Psychology, 36,* 1293–1313.

Kuethe, J. (1964). Pervasive influence of social schemata. *Journal of Abnormal and Social Psychology, 68,* 248–254.

Liben, L., & Signorella, M. (1980). Gender-related schemata and constructive memory in children. *Child Development, 51,* 11–18.

Martin, C., & Halaverson, C. (1981). A schematic processing model of sex typing and stereotyping in children. *Child Development, 52,* 1119–1134.

Martin, C. L., & Halverson, C. F. (1983). The effects of sex-typing schemas on young children's memory. *Child Development, 54,* 563–74.

Mazzocco, P. J., Green, M. C., & Brock, T. C. (2007). The effects of a prior story-bank on the processing of a related narrative. *Media Psychology, 10,* 64–90.

Memelink, J., & Hommel, B. (2006). Tailoring perception and action to the task at hand. *European Journal of Cognitive Psychology, 18,* 579–592.

Rice, E., & Okun, M. (1994). Older readers' processing of medical information that contradicts their beliefs. *Journal of Gerontology, 49,* 119–128.

Roach, D., Barker, L., & Fitch-Hauser, M. (1987). Origins, evolution, and development of a systems-based model of intrapersonal communication. *Information and Behavior, 2,* 197–215.

Rothman, A. J., Bartels, R. D., Wlaschin, J., & Salovey, P. (2006). The strategic use of gain- and loss-framed messages to promote healthy behavior: How theory can inform practice. *Journal of Communication, 56,* S202–S220.

Said, L. (2009, December 9). Honesty and ethics poll finds Congress's image tarnished. Gallup. Retrieved from www.gallup.com.

Schank, R. C., & Abelson, R. P. (1977). *Scripts, plans, goals and understanding.* Hillsdale, NJ: Lawrence Erlbaum Associates.

Schank, R. C., & Abelson, R. P. (1995). Knowledge and memory: The real story. In R. S. Wyler (ed.), *Knowledge and memory: The real story* (1–85). Hillsdale, NJ: Lawrence Erlbaum.

Taylor, S., Fiske, S. T., & Ruderman, A. (1978, July). Categorical and contextual bases of person memory and stereotyping. *Journal of Personality and Social Psychology, 36,* 778–793.

Tuckey, M. R., & Brewer, N. (2003). How schemas affect eyewitness memory over repeated retrieval attempts. *Applied Cognitive Psychology, 17,* 785–800.

Vishwanath, A. (2009). From belief-importance to intention: The impact of framing on technology adoption. *Communication Monographs, 76,* 177–206.

Was, C. A., & Woltz, D. J. (2007). Reexamining the relationship between working memory and comprehension: The role of available long-term memory. *Journal of Memory and Language, 56,* 86–102.

Woll, S. (2001). *Everyday thinking: Memory, reasoning, and judgment in the real world.* Mahway, NJ: Lawrence Erlbaum Associates.

Individual Differences in Listening Processes

Different Strokes for Different Folks

NaMii Kim walked into class and slumped into a chair next to Ben.

BEN: *You look beat. Anything you would like to talk about?*

NaMII: *No, I'm fine.*

BEN: *Are you sure? I might be able to help.*

NaMII: *I'm really fine.* NaMii thinks, I wish Ben would leave me alone. I've got to figure out what to do about my grandmother.

BEN: *Hey, I was just trying to be nice.* Ben thinks, I thought we were becoming real friends. Friends help each other out.

A few minutes later, Nolvia walks into the room and sits next to Ben.

BEN: *Are you ready for your presentation today? Personally, I can't wait. I love public speaking.*

NOLVIA: *You are warped. Who actually wants to give a speech?*

BEN: *Well, I'd rather give a speech than work in a small group any day. No offense.*

NOLVIA: She laughs. *None taken.*

BEN: *I still can't believe you chose to do a group project instead of an individual one in your Interior Design class. How's it going, anyway?*

NOLVIA: She grimaces. *Slow. My classmate Sharee and I can't seem to get our act together. She is driving me crazy. I just don't understand what the problem is. I've never had a problem working in a group before.* ■

As you have learned over the previous three chapters, how you listen can be affected by a number of things, including your attitude when listening, your motivation to listen, the context of the listening setting, and of course, individual differences. Chapter 2 looked at types of listening, and Chapter 3 examined how cognitive processes related to schemata can affect our processing of incoming messages. In this chapter we look at how individual differences can affect how we listen.

WHY STUDY INDIVIDUAL DIFFERENCES?

To put it simply, we don't know as much as we should about how physical and psychological differences among people might (or might not) affect their listening processes and listening ability.[1] While early listening scholars were more interested in defining listening and identifying listening skills, research over the past 20 years has increasingly explored the role of individual differences.[2] One reason for this growing interest is that a number of personality and psychological constructs appear to be biologically based. Study in this area led to the rise of a new approach to studying communication: **communibiology**.[3] Many of the researchers studying this area argue that "personality and communication are inherently intertwined."[4] They believe that our communication behaviors are, in part, influenced by biology.

At the heart of this debate is the question of how much of our listening ability comes from our temperament or personality (nature) and how much is learned (nurture). Communibiologists argue that there is a robust body of research in areas such as neurobiology, psychobiology, psychological temperament, and personality suggesting that some aspects of our personality (those believed to be genetically driven) do affect how we interact with others. For example, Michael Beatty and James McCroskey study the relationship between interpersonal communication and temperament.[5] They note that a variety of communicative attributes have been associated with "inherited neurobiological processes" such as temperament (e.g., communicator style, empathy, extraversion). Researchers in temperament and personality often discuss the relationship among temperament type, personality, and social behavior, including communication preferences, miscommunication, and conflict.[6]

EXPLORING PERSONALITY TRAITS

For our purposes we first need to understand what makes up personality. Researchers often divide personality into two broad categories: temperament and personality. Temperament refers to personality traits we might possess. **Traits** are "enduring personal qualities or attributes that influence behavior across situations."[7] The underlying assumption of the study of temperament is that our personality traits should "meaningfully differentiate" us from others. In other words, people with different traits, such as introverts and extraverts, should systematically differ from one another.

Arnold Buss and Richard Plomin's theory of personality distinguishes temperament in terms of broad personality dispositions.[8] **Temperament** is generally considered that part of the personality that is "inborn." Essentially, then, temperamental traits form the biological basis of our personalities and is believed to be inheritable.[9] In other words, there's a good chance your temperament is derived in part from one or both of your parents, your grandparents, and so forth. It's one of the reasons that people might say, "You're just like your mother (or aunt, or uncle, or grandfather)." Temperament is also believed to be quite stable.[10] Thus, your introverted five-year-old cousin is likely to grow up to be an introverted 20-year-old.

Traits are also believed to be motivational in nature. Again, this does not mean that you are genetically programmed to behave in a certain way. It does, however, suggest that you might be predisposed to act (or not act) in a certain way. In addition, some traits such as communication and receiver apprehension appear to have a

> **TABLE 4.1**
>
> **Comparing Personality Traits and States**
>
> | Traits | States |
> | --- | --- |
> | Inborn/Inherited | Learned |
> | Stable | Adaptive |
> | Stylistic-driven | Content-driven |
> | Is a predisposition | Is situational |

broader influence on your behaviors than others. In general, temperament addresses the expressive behavior that a person brings to a role or situation (e.g., introverted, extraverted, empathetic).[11] For example, in our case study at the beginning of this chapter, Ben might be an extravert, someone who is generally outgoing and animated when meeting new people. Yet his temperament does not predetermine that he's going to be happy and outgoing with every new person he meets. In fact, as you saw, he wasn't overly happy with NaMii's response to his friendly overtures.

Personality States versus Traits

Obviously your interactions with your parents, siblings, cousins, and friends influence your behavior. Your personality reflects these influences. Thus, your personality is also a product of your social environment, the people and environment you come in contact with. Researchers often use the term *character* or ***state*** when discussing the effect that the external environment has on us.[12] For example, your general temperament traits can often be discerned shortly after birth (e.g., happy baby, grumpy baby), while your personality state develops as you grow into adulthood. Personality states, then, are those parts of your personality that are shaped by your experiences with your environment and the people within it.

A full discussion of the communibiological approach is beyond the scope of this book. What is important to keep in mind is that temperament traits are considered to be relatively stable over the course of your life and they are generally consistent across situations. Thus, temperamental traits may influence (but not determine) how you communicate with others. Table 4.1 summarizes the differences between temperament and personality.

Our traits and states have obvious implications for the elements of the Listening MATERRS model. Individual differences can affect how you translate, evaluate, and respond to a message. The remainder of this chapter explores several individual differences that can also significantly influence our listening: personality type, listening style preference, communication apprehension, receiver apprehension, and cognitive complexity.

PERSONALITY TYPE

The interest in personality and temperament has been significantly influenced by the development and introduction of the Myers-Briggs Type Indicator® (MBTI).[13] Even today, the MBTI is one of the best-known and most used personality inventories.[14]

Its developers, the mother-daughter team of Isabel Myers and Katherine Briggs, believe that many of the differences we see in people have to do with the "the way people prefer to use their minds."[15] The descriptions associated with the Myers-Briggs typology reflect the underlying cognitive or mental functions associated with each of the four areas comprising the MBTI.[16]

Undoubtedly some of you have had the opportunity to take the Myers-Briggs Type Indicator®. For those of you who have not, the measure centers around four bipolar preferences: extraversion/introversion, thinking/feeling, sensing/intuiting, and judging/perceiving. It is important to keep in mind that these distinctions are on a continuum. So for example, you could be a strong thinker, a strong feeler, or fall somewhere in between. Myers and Briggs believe that our preferences indicate two very important things about us. First, they reveal how we perceive or view things around us. Second, they draw attention to how we evaluate or draw conclusions about these perceptions.

Ultimately your preferences in these four areas reflect the communication patterns and behaviors you use with others as well as the tools you use to accomplish personal goals.[17] We next look at each of the four dimensions and discuss their relationships to listening.

> **LEARN ABOUT YOURSELF**
>
> Are you interested in knowing your own personality type? While the Myers-Briggs Type Indicator® can only be administered by professionals, David Keirsey has developed a shortened version that you can take and score yourself. It is available in his 1998 book, *Please Understand Me II,* published by Prometheus Nemesis Book Company. A truncated version is offered online at his Web site: www.keirsey.com.

Extraversion or Introversion

The easiest way to think about extraversion and introversion is to think of it as a source of personal energy.[18] Individuals who are strong extraverts tend to be outgoing, action oriented, and social. They enjoy spending time with others and find it easy to communicate with them. Extraverts become "energized" through their contact with others and might experience a "power drain" if they experience too much quiet or seclusion. Thus, the friend who is an "Energizer Bunny" at parties and is animated when working in groups is likely a strong extravert. On the other end of the continuum are introverts. These people prefer solitary pursuits. They generally find working in groups or being in crowds tiring. They experience a power drain if they socialize with others for too long. Essentially introverts need time alone to recharge their mental batteries. In addition, they need time for contemplation and thought. Please note, however, that this does not necessarily mean that introverts avoid working in groups or dislike parties. As a friend of ours once said, "Introverts are not party poopers, but they often get pooped by the party."

When communicating with others, extraverts have been described as "quick to speak and slow to listen," while introverts are "quick to listen and slow to speak."[19] This distinction is important for several reasons. For example, extraverts tend to unload their feelings as they feel them, while introverts tend to bottle their emotions up. Eventually, however, the introvert will have to let those emotions out, and they might do so quite explosively.

Another important communication difference between introverts and extraverts is that extraverts have a tendency to work out or solve problems out loud. If you tend to talk out loud to yourself when you are thinking a problem through, then you are likely an extravert. Strong introverts tend to do just the opposite. Remember, they like to contemplate things, so they tend to "think before they speak." As a result, they will mull over and process information until they reach a decision; then they are ready to discuss it. These differences can lead to communication misunderstandings in a couple of ways. It's easy to see that introverts and extraverts can operate very differently when responding to a message. For example, introverts will tend to want additional time to translate and evaluate information.

In our Case Study at the beginning of the chapter, Ben is trying to draw NaMii into a conversation about what is bothering her. However, NaMii resists. Thus, Ben, the extravert, is trying to get NaMii to discuss the issue, while NaMii, the introvert, refuses. Ben might interpret or translate her behavior as a sign of avoidance and feel hurt by what he perceives to be NaMii's unwillingness to open up to him. On the other hand, NaMii is thinking long and hard on her problem. As an introvert, she feels the need to think more deeply about the problem before she is comfortable discussing it. Contrast NaMii and Nolvia in our Case Study. Nolvia is certainly more extraverted than NaMii. She immediately voices her discontent with her classmate to Ben.

Miscommunication between introverts and extraverts can occur in other ways as well. For example, if during the remodel on the Goleman home, Mrs. Goleman was musing (aloud) on the type of door she wanted, her contractor, an introvert, might take her comments as a definite decision. The Goleman's could find themselves living with a sliding glass door to their patio instead of the French doors Mrs. Goleman actually wanted. As seen here, you need to keep in mind the effect these communication differences can have on your interactions when working with others who score differently than you on the introvert-extravert continuum.

Sensing or Intuiting

This dimension is particularly important to how you perceive and learn things. It has been described as the method by which people become "aware of things, people, events or ideas [including] information gathering, the seeking of sensation or of inspiration, and the selection of the stimulus to be attended to."[20]

Sensors tend to be quite practical and pragmatic. As a result, they are more interested in the "here and now" and are less interested in addressing hypothetical futures. Sensors trust their own senses and personal experiences, relying on their senses and experiences to aid them in assessing their perceptions. It's no surprise then that sensors tend to develop strong observational skills and are generally quite good at retaining and recalling details.[21] In fact, sensors are particularly known for being detail oriented.

Intuitors, in contrast, are more abstract in their thinking. As a result, they tend to be more imaginative than practical. They place greater trust in their intuition and imagination than in their senses. In other words, they will sometimes rely on a personal insight or a "hunch" when deciding a course of action rather than searching out facts or evidence as the sensor would. However, the downside is that intuitors are often not as good as sensors in focusing on current events or

THINK ON IT

Based on the description of sensors and intuitors, who might have a better working memory? Long-term memory? How might this affect their ability to recall information?

paying attention to details. On a positive note, intuitors have a better ability to address potential futures or courses of action.[22]

David Keirsey, author of *Please Understand Me,* argued that this dimension is a primary source of communication problems.[23] Usually when working on a project, sensors and intuitors will tend to be interested in different things. For example, imagine that Sharee and Nolvia have been working on their joint Interior Design project for about a month. Sharee is currently focusing on how they can adapt the William Morris style into the next phase of the project, the living room, while Nolvia is choosing the final accessories for the sunroom, the current phase of the project. Thus, Sharee, the intuitor, is focusing on the "big" picture and planning the next stage of the project, while Nolvia, the sensor, is focusing on the details necessary to complete the current stage of the project. When drawing on each other's strengths, intuitors and sensors can accomplish great things. Intuitors have the vision, while sensors have the follow-through. However, these same qualities can cause communication difficulties. For example, Nolvia can become frustrated with Sharee when Sharee continually tries to shift their conversation away from deciding the final details of the sunroom to possibilities for decorating the living room. What sensors and intuitors are interested in, how they approach problems, and what they perceive to be immediate and important, can differ substantially. Such differences can affect a number of listening levels, including awareness and recall.

Thinking or Feeling

This dimension or function addresses how people make decisions about what they have perceived. Thus, it includes "decision-making, evaluation, choice, and the selection of the response after perceiving the stimulus."[24] Not surprisingly, it has important implications for Evaluation, the fourth element in the Listening MATERRS model.

Rationality is at the core of this dimension of the MBTI. However, thinkers and feelers employ "rationality" in very different ways. For example, thinkers have strong analytic skills. They like focusing on the technical aspects of problems. In addition, they value logic, truthfulness, and criticism as well as objectivity, justice, and fairness. When making decisions, they analyze things in terms of causes and effects, and logic guides their behaviors and actions.[25]

Feelers differ markedly from thinkers. Feelers have a higher need for affiliation or belonging. As a result, they value sympathy, empathy, and harmony. When making decisions, feelers are more subjective, weighing the relative merits of alternatives.[26] One reason for this is that feelers rely on "attending to what matters to others" and "an understanding of people."[27] Thus, they tend to consider what the human effect of their decision will be. When working with others, feelers value tactfulness because it is related to being sympathetic and empathetic, two qualities feelers also value quite highly. This communication behavior also reflects a feeler's need for maintaining harmony with others.

Needless to say, thinkers and feelers value very different things. Thinkers will listen for causes and effects as well as for facts and evidence they believe will assist them in making a logical, objective, and fair decision. In addition, when engaging in discussions, thinkers stress truthfulness and criticism, two aspects they value highly. However, this tendency can cause them problems when working with feelers, who value tactfulness and harmony. Feelers often do not understand why a thinker is being, what appears to them, very blunt and critical. At the same time, a feeler's need for inclusion can sometimes lead to miscommunication. In a quest to maintain harmony with others, they might use ambiguous, vague, or euphemistic language, which allows greater listener discretion when interpreting incoming messages but can leave thinkers frustrated.

As noted above, feelers pay more attention to the human element of a message. They focus on relationships and are usually quite aware of the values and attitudes of others. Feelers listen for information to help them determine the best alternative, not in terms of objectivity, but in terms of its human cost. Finally in discussions with thinkers, feelers might not understand that they need to provide evidence to support their claims. It is not enough for Ben to say, "You don't care about me," when speaking to his thinker girlfriend, Susan. Ben needs to provide Susan with specific reasons, (e.g., "You work all the time" or "You've canceled our last three dates"). Logical arguments with clear support will carry more weight and be more convincing for Susan when listening to Ben.

Judgment or Perception

This final dimension addresses how we use time. Judgers value time and using it effectively. As a result, it is not unusual for them to push others for decisions. In addition, effectively using time includes organizing and planning a schedule. Judgers who experience a lack of structure in their daily lives might actually experience a great deal of stress. For example, when taking a class where there is a lot of free-wheeling discussion, Judgers might feel uncomfortable. They prefer classes with a clear agenda. In other words, they like classes where the instructor writes a key word outline on the board so they can clearly follow what is being discussed. Judgers also value work before play and subsequently are often seen as having a strong work ethic. For example, judgers will want to complete a project before taking time out of their day to go have "fun." If Ben tells his girlfriend, Susan, that he'll be happy to go out on Saturday night *if* he finishes his English homework, he might be a judger.

Perceivers are curious, flexible, and like keeping their options open. However, perceivers quickly learn that keeping their options open can sometimes mean a delay in making decisions and/or completing projects. It is this aspect of a perceiver's personality that often will drive judgers crazy. They don't understand why perceivers aren't like them (i.e., looking for closure by making a final decision). However, perceivers often hold off on decisions because they are searching for new or additional information. Finally perceivers view structure very differently than judgers. Too much structure prevents them from being spontaneous and doesn't allow them to integrate play or periods of relaxation throughout their day (e.g., e-mail friends, surf the net, take a short walk). As a result, perceivers experience stress when faced with too much structure in their daily lives. Perceivers dislike living a scheduled life because it prevents them from acting on new opportunities.

Differences in this personality dimension can affect our lives significantly. For example, when communicating with others, both perceivers and judgers will be focusing on gathering additional information and ideas. However, judgers will focus on information that helps them to reach the closure they desire, while perceivers will interpret the same information as just another step along the way to making a decision. Thus, how judgers and perceivers listen and what they attend to can differ markedly.

Understanding our judging-perceiving personality type can be important to job satisfaction. In a true-life example, Suzanne, a friend of one of the authors, graduated with a master's in business. She took a good-paying position with a respected firm in town. The job required her to manage her time constantly; there were lots of meetings with vendors and employees. Subsequently she had little personal free time at work. Within six months, she dreaded every morning and even called in sick to avoid having to go to work. Suzanne was a perceiver working at a job that would have been better suited for someone who is a judger. Eventually Suzanne quit her job and started her own business, which allowed her great personal flexibility. Today she is a successful small-business owner.

THINK ON IT

Have differences in personality affected your communication with others? What happened? How might knowledge about personality differences help you in future communication with others?

Whether an extravert or introvert, sensor or intuitor, thinker or feeler, or judger or perceiver, our personality type can significantly affect our personal and professional interactions with others. If we understand ourselves and others, we will be able to communicate better. Going back to our Case Study above, if Ben had understood that he was an extravert and that NaMii was an introvert, he would have had better insight into the best method of listening and communicating with her, and he would probably not have gotten offended by her lack of disclosure.

In Table 4.2 we summarize important attributes associated with each type. Now that you know more about these personality differences, review the different aspects of our Listening MATERRS model. How might these differences manifest themselves and affect each of the elements in the model? As we will see in the remainder of the chapter, these types are related to other individual differences, including listening style preference and empathy.

▶ **TABLE 4.2**

Summary of the MBTI Types

Extravert:	*Introvert:*
Outgoing; speaks then thinks; sociable; likes groups	Private; thinks before speaking; reflective; prefers working alone
Sensor:	*Intuitor:*
Focuses on details; factual; practical; realistic; present focused	Focuses on the big picture; theoretical; becomes bored with facts or details; future focused
Thinker:	*Feeler:*
Task oriented; logical; objective; analytical; detached; values truthfulness	People oriented; values harmony, empathy, and tactfulness
Judger:	*Perceiver:*
Well organized; prefers structure; likes clear deadlines	Flexible; spontaneous; dislikes deadlines

LISTENING STYLE PREFERENCE

As we noted earlier, the context or situation can affect both how we listen and how we respond. For example, when listening to your two-year-old sister, you might be more patient trying to understand what she is saying. In contrast, you might become frustrated with an IT instructor who doesn't provide a clear and precise explanation of the differences between Windows 7 and Vista. Although we know listening situations place different demands on us, evidence suggests that, as in many other areas of our lives, we are creatures of habit. Our listening habits are reflected in personal preferences, in how we approach a communication situation, and in how we listen to incoming information.[28] While listening scholars have studied and written about the individual nature of listening for quite some time, it was not until relatively recently that researchers Kittie Watson and Larry Barker identified specific individual listening style preferences.[29] A short time later, Watson and Barker, along with listening scholar James Weaver, developed the Listening Styles Profile (LSP-16), a measurement designed to identify our individual preferences. Specifically, Watson, Barker, and Weaver identified four listening styles or individual preferences: people, action, content, and time. Before we review each of these types, take a moment to learn about your own listening preferences by completing the original LSP-16 scale.

Listener Preference Profile—16

Using the following key, please answer the questions by filling in the appropriate circle on the following answer sheet.

    A = Never
    B = Infrequently
    C = Sometimes
    D = Frequently
    F = Always

1. I focus my attention on the other person's feelings when listening to him or her.
2. When listening to others, I quickly notice if they are pleased or disappointed.
3. I become involved when listening to the problems of others.
4. I nod my head and/or use eye contact to show interest in what others are saying.
5. I am frustrated when others don't present their ideas in an orderly, efficient way.
6. When listening to others, I focus on any inconsistencies and/or errors in what's being said.
7. I jump ahead and/or finish thoughts of speakers.
8. I am impatient with people who ramble during conversations.
9. I prefer to listen to technical information.
10. I prefer to hear facts and evidence, so I can personally evaluate them.
11. I like the challenge of listening to complex information.
12. I ask questions to probe for additional information.
13. When hurried, I let the others know that I have a limited amount of time to listen.
14. I begin a discussion by telling others how long I have to meet.
15. I interrupt others when I feel time pressure.
16. I look at my watch or clocks in the room when I have limited time to listen to others.

(continued)

Listening Preference Profile Response Sheet

Please circle the most appropriate response when answering each item:

1.	Never	Infrequently	Sometimes	Frequently	Always
2.	Never	Infrequently	Sometimes	Frequently	Always
3.	Never	Infrequently	Sometimes	Frequently	Always
4.	Never	Infrequently	Sometimes	Frequently	Always
5.	Never	Infrequently	Sometimes	Frequently	Always
6.	Never	Infrequently	Sometimes	Frequently	Always
7.	Never	Infrequently	Sometimes	Frequently	Always
8.	Never	Infrequently	Sometimes	Frequently	Always
9.	Never	Infrequently	Sometimes	Frequently	Always
10.	Never	Infrequently	Sometimes	Frequently	Always
11.	Never	Infrequently	Sometimes	Frequently	Always
12.	Never	Infrequently	Sometimes	Frequently	Always
13.	Never	Infrequently	Sometimes	Frequently	Always
14.	Never	Infrequently	Sometimes	Frequently	Always
15.	Never	Infrequently	Sometimes	Frequently	Always
16.	Never	Infrequently	Sometimes	Frequently	Always

Calculate Your Score

Place a check mark beside each item that you rated as Frequently or Always. (Some lines may be left blank). Total the number of checks for each column. Your total can range from 0 to 4.

1.	5.	9.	13.
2.	6.	10.	14.
3.	7.	11.	15.
4.	8.	12.	16.
People-oriented Section Score:	Action-oriented Section Score:	Content-oriented Section Score:	Time-oriented Section Score:

Reprinted with permission: Watson, Barker, & Weaver, 1995.

People Listening

Not surprisingly people listeners tend to focus on their relationships with others. People listeners are good at identifying the moods of others. At the same time, the moods of others might "rub off" on them. From a scholarly viewpoint, this means they might internalize the emotional states of others.[30] Ultimately people listeners pay particular attention to speakers' emotional states. Are they happy? Upset? Sad? People listeners will generally let speakers know they are interested in and concerned about their emotional state.

Looking back at the Myers-Briggs Type Indicator®, you probably are not surprised to discover that feeling has been associated with this people listening style.[31] As we learned, feelers are more interested in the human dimension of a decision rather than the technical aspect of problems.[32] Other studies have found this listening style positively associated with empathy, sympathy, and conversational sensitivity.[33]

Action Listening

Action listeners focus less on personal relationships and more on errors and inconsistencies within an incoming message. They also focus on information related to the task they are working on. For example, Nolvia is also a representative in the Student Government Association (SGA). If she is engaging in action listening, she is more likely to note that the description of expenditures for a concert do not add up to the amount that was discussed earlier. In addition, these listeners "prefer logical, organized speakers and direct, to-the-point messages."[34] Action listeners tend to engage in several listening behaviors that can affect message reception and evaluation. For example, when listening to messages, they often listen in "bullet point" or "outline form."[35] These tendencies can lead action listeners to jump to conclusions because they have not fully listened to the speaker. In addition, action listeners can become frustrated when they do not fully understand the message, when the message isn't as well organized as they would like, or when the speaker provides excessive details.

Action listening has been found to be associated with the Myers-Briggs types thinking, sensing, and judging.[36] As we discussed, thinkers are rational, logical, and have strong analytic skills, abilities necessary for critiquing messages.[37] Sensors are detailed oriented, which is reflected in our previously mentioned SGA example. Nolvia's ability to catch the inaccuracy in the SGA budget reflects a sensor's fondness for details. Finally judgers want to use time effectively. As we learned above, action listeners dislike disorganized presentations, which would likely be seen as a waste of time.

Content Listening

When listening to others, content listeners tend to "welcome complex and challenging information, listen to facts before forming judgments and opinions, or favor listening to technical information."[38] They are like action listeners in that they also analyze incoming messages; however, what they pay attention to differs significantly. Content listeners are more interested in how speakers support their claims. As a result, it is not unusual for content listeners to ask speakers to expand on ideas or to provide additional support for their claims.[39] One of the strengths of content listeners is that they will listen to a message in its entirety before forming a conclusion. Like action listening, content listening has been associated with a preference for the Myers-Briggs type thinking.[40] Just as thinkers prefer to be logical, objective, and fair, so do content listeners.

Time Listening

Time listeners generally prefer "hurried interactions" and have been described as engaging in "communicative time management."[41] Most descriptions of time listeners focus on specific behaviors.[42] For example, it is not unusual for them to check their watches or have clocks prominently displayed in their workplaces. When listening to others, they might interrupt the speaker to hurry the conversation along or they might tell the speaker how much time they have available for listening. It is also not unusual for them to discourage speakers they perceive to be wordy or rambling.

"Now tell me about yourself in a ten second sound bite."

Research suggests that time listening is associated with thinking, the dimension that addresses how we make decisions. As we saw above, feelers focus on the effect decisions have on the people involved, while thinkers are more interested in the technical aspects of a problem. It is believed that feelers are more willing to take the time needed to understand the human dimension of a problem. Thinkers, in contrast, might acknowledge the human cost but only as one aspect of the greater issue being addressed. Going back to our SGA example from above, if the SGA is considering approving student activity funding for the Gay, Lesbian, and Transgendered Student Association, the feelers in the group might want to spend more time discussing the response the decision will get from students, parents, and alumni. Thinkers will acknowledge this aspect of the decision. However, the public reaction is only one issue of many they will need to address when making the final decision.

> **THINK ON IT**
>
> Looking back at our Case Study, can you determine which listening styles Ben, NaMii, and Nolvia prefer?

EMPATHY

We introduced empathy in our discussion of empathetic listening in Chapter 2. As you learned then, empathy is an important aspect of relational listening. It is also central to building relationships with others. In Chapter 2 we discussed the differences between empathetic responsiveness (the ability to feel "with" others) and sympathetic responsiveness (feeling "for" someone). We expand on these concepts below.

Sociability

Empathetic response style does appear to vary with personality type. One area in which people appear to differ is in relation to their **sociability**. People who are highly sociable are adept at expressing sympathetic responses to others and believe it is important to try to engage in perspective taking (seeing things from others' point of view). In contrast, individuals who are more egocentric generally do not demonstrate signs of either empathetic or sympathetic responsiveness.[43] You express both types of responsiveness verbally and nonverbally. Listeners high in empathy are often quite skilled at picking up on cross-cues (when a person's words and nonverbals conflict with each other). As seen above, Ben easily determined that NaMii was upset about something. Individuals high in empathy rarely need such obvious cues, as presented in our Case Study, to determine someone is not fine. They are the ones who can often tell something is not right, even when the other person is doing her best to hide the fact. In other words, they are very good at picking up on subtle, nonverbal cues. One reason empathy and sociability are believed to occur together is that highly empathetic individuals also tend to be highly sociable. Sociability encourages you to interact with others and is believed to provide empathetic individuals with numerous opportunities to hone their verbal and nonverbal skills. Thus, sociability has implications for all elements of the Listening MATERRS model, but especially awareness, translation, and response.

This sociability difference might also help explain why some people differ in empathetic perspective taking. As you might recall from Chapter 2, empathetic perspective taking refers to your ability to place yourself in someone else's shoes, to understand things from his perspective. For example, while investigating individual listening style, James Weaver and Michelle Kirtley found that people with high people listening style scores—those who express a strong interest in listening/hearing about the relationships and emotions of others—tended to have higher *sympathetic responsiveness* scores but lower *empathetic* responsiveness scores.[44] Weaver and Kirtley suggest that one reason for this empathetic split is that people listeners are trying to control their emotions so they can be prepared to offer assistance or help in some active way. These listeners might feel that if they identify too closely with the other person, it might impair their ability to be helpful.

In comparison, those scoring high in action and time listening tended to score lower in empathetic responsiveness. This said, it does not mean that action and time listeners are unfeeling toward others but instead that they are more businesslike in their approach to listening. Dealing with others on an emotional level takes time and energy; just think of the last time you helped a friend weather a personal crisis.

High content listeners, in contrast, are unique in that they appear to have the ability to deal with someone who is emotionally upset without experiencing emotional contagion; that is, like strong people listeners, they remain in control of their emotions (i.e., they don't experience high levels of empathetic responsiveness). However, their propensity to remain objective when listening suggests that they might be able to more effectively evaluate the information being presented by others.

Conversational Sensitivity

People who are more empathetic also tend to be more conversationally sensitive.[45] **Conversational sensitivity** refers to how attentive and responsive you are to your conversation partners. People who are highly sensitive are particularly good at picking up cues during social interactions. For example, if you are high in conversational sensitivity, you will tend to enjoy conversing with others more than your friends who are low in conversational sensitivity. Let's assume for a moment that

Ben is high in conversational sensitivity. If the conversations in our Case Study continued, Ben would probably be the one who not only notices that NaMii continues to appear anxious but also retain or remember more about the conversation. If Nolvia is less conversationally sensitive, she will not only remember less but likely take the conversation at face value and miss some of the implied dynamics that occur during the conversation. For example, she will likely be less aware of nonverbal cues, which, as we noted above, often tell us a lot about the emotional state of the speaker. It is not surprising that individuals who score as high people listeners are more likely to be conversationally sensitive and that persons who tend to be more caring are more apt to be effective listeners.[46]

As you can see, empathy is composed of several components that are in turn linked to other emotion-related concepts. The next individual difference we discuss, emotional intelligence, is also related to empathy but focuses more on your awareness of specific emotions and your knowledge of how they can affect your interactions.

Emotional Intelligence

Individuals who are conversationally sensitive are likely to have a higher emotional IQ. Actually known as emotional intelligence, or EI, trait-emotional intelligence is a relatively new concept introduced by John Mayer and Peter Salovey.[47] The theory is quite popular with researchers in a variety of areas, including management, psychology, communication, and counseling. There is some disagreement among researchers about if and how we should distinguish between trait-EI (inborn/natural emotional intelligence) and ability-EI (learned emotional intelligence).[48] No matter the viewpoint (inborn or learned), EI has important implications for how we listen and communicate with others.

> **LEARN ABOUT YOURSELF**
>
> Dr. Petrides directs the London Psychometric Laboratory in the Department of Psychology at University College London. It is home to the trait-emotional intelligence research program. He has made several versions of his Emotional Intelligence Scale available to the public. If you are interested in learning about your own EI, you can visit his Web site at www.psychometriclab.com.

Salovey and his colleagues describe **emotional intelligence** as "the ability to perceive and express emotions, to understand and use them, and to manage them to foster personal growth."[49] They contend that emotions can inform your decision-making in four basic ways. First, *EI helps you to identify or perceive emotions,* your own as well as the emotions of others. They argue that this perception, also known as **emotional awareness,** can go beyond people to encompass all kinds of things, including your pets, the arts, and your home, as well as other objects or events. For example, Radley's parents are avid folk art collectors. When a neighbor asked them why they bought a particular piece, they said, "It's a fun piece, and we love the colors." With this dimension of EI, it's important that we have the ability to identify the emotions involved, both yours and others'.

Second, *emotion can be used to facilitate thought.* Salovey and others believe that emotions can help you focus your attention and process information more rationally.[50] Thus, your emotions can assist you in solving personal problems, can be used to encourage creativity at work, and can lead to more flexible and adaptive communication with others. For example, in our Case Study, if NaMii believes she has offended Ben, she might assess her options for making up with him (apologize, defend her actions) by how she thinks Ben will respond (angrily, sympathetically).

Third, it is important for you to ***understand emotions***. Of course, you use emotions to communicate concern or excitement to others. While this dimension seems straightforward, it is at the core of empathy. However, Salovey and his colleagues note that this function of EI includes both the ability to understand emotional information and the ability to understand how our emotions can change or morph over the course of a relationship. If you have had the opportunity to take an interpersonal or relational communication course, you are aware that relationships are dynamic (constantly changing and evolving). The emotions you experience over the course of the relationship will necessarily vary in both type (e.g., attraction, friendship, love, disappointment, hate) and intensity (e.g., weak to strong). What sets this aspect of EI apart is the emphasis on how emotions affect the changes that occur over the course of a relationship. It addresses (and emphasizes) the great variety of emotional or feeling states people can experience.[51] Going back to our earlier example, if Ben and Susan break up, they might be very angry with each other at first, but over time they might actually forgive one another and either get back together or become friends.

The final dimension of EI addresses how you ***manage emotion***. An important part of this dimension is simply being open to feelings, both your own and others'. For example, you have to be willing to recognize when you are sad but also when you make someone else sad. Another aspect of this dimension involves being able to regulate your feelings and assist others in doing the same. When you've had a bad day, you can use any number of strategies to cheer yourself up. Some people head for the movies. Others will call a friend and talk things through. Still others will eat chocolate. All of these strategies help you manage your emotions. You can do similar things for the other people in your lives. Oftentimes you can simply provide a willing ear and listen with an open attitude. Your friends appreciate and rightly expect you to be attentive listeners in both good times and bad. People who are particularly adept in this area of EI always seem to know just what to say and when to say it, so you end up feeling inspired or happier. Finally Salovey and his colleagues argue that this aspect of EI leads to self-actualization (i.e., personal understanding and growth). Essentially the more you know about and understand emotions, the better you understand yourself and the better you can communicate with others.

EI is essential to the listening process because it highlights the importance of emotions when interacting and listening to others. As you can see, you need to be aware of your own emotions and how they can affect or color your listening. For example, in our earlier example of Nolvia and Sharee's design project, it is understandable that Nolvia would be angry with Sharee for being late to work on their project and leaving her to meet a project deadline alone. However, when Sharee does arrive, Nolvia's anger might prevent her from fully listening to her reason for being late. Nolvia might also not want to hear anything Sharee has to say about the project as they complete the final touches together. In this case, Nolvia would be displaying low EI competency because she would not recognize how her anger is getting in the way of finishing the project.

If, on the other hand, Nolvia can see that Sharee is upset and she acknowledges that fact (as well as the fact she is none too happy herself), she can use this knowledge and what she knows about Sharee to make judgments about which section of the project would be best for her to work on. For example, should Sharee be working on editing, a detail-oriented job? Or would it be better for her to do something more global such as choosing artwork? It depends on how Nolvia thinks Sharee's emotions will affect her work. Will her task distract her from her emotions, or will her emotions be too distracting for detail work? Of course, she can and should apply the same emotional evaluation to herself.

Here we have only briefly introduced the topic of emotional intelligence. As you can see, it is related to our model of listening in several ways. How aware are you of your own and others' emotions? And how might you translate and evaluate them? Of course, it can affect how you respond as well. It is easy to see its application to interpersonal communication and, as seen in the example above, that it also has organizational and business applications. Later in the text, when we address relational and organizational listening, we will readdress this topic.

COMMUNICATION APPREHENSION

Another area of individual differences addresses the anxiety or apprehension you experience when communicating with others. It is important to realize excessive apprehension can affect how effectively and appropriately you communicate with others. Ideally you should be higher in approach predispositions and lower in avoidance predispositions. **Approach predispositions** refer to communication behaviors that lead you to interact comfortably with others, while **avoidance predispositions** make you feel uncomfortable. Communication and receiver apprehension fall into the latter category. When you are comfortable both in expressing yourself to others and in receiving information from them, you are likely more skilled at identifying and adapting to cues from others and generally will have and display greater poise and composure when dealing with them.[52] As a result, you are more likely to achieve your personal and professional goals.

Communication apprehension refers to the anxiety we feel when communicating with others. It has been associated with general social anxiety.[53] While we can talk about general communication apprehension, which might occur across situations, communication researchers also discriminate between the types of apprehension we feel in different communication contexts, such as interpersonal, small group, meeting, and public speaking.[54] Communication apprehension has a variety of sources.[55] First, some people experience a **generalized anxiety.** This type of feeling is often considered trait or personality based. The public speaker who engages in negative thinking—"I can't do this. I'm going to faint."—would be said to be expressing a trait-based predisposition or motivation (to avoid public speaking whenever possible). Other scholars suggest that we can also learn apprehensive behavior. Thus, Nolvia's attitude toward public speaking might be due to a bad experience (e.g., she blanked when giving a speech on Kipling to her high school English class). She is experiencing **conditioned anxiety,** most likely manifesting itself as sweaty palms, hyperventilation, or nausea.

Recent research suggests that communication apprehension is heritable.[56] This genetic predisposition and its apparent association with general social anxiety means that some people tend to feel more anxiety as they enter into a communication situation. Their anxiety leads them to focus a great deal of attention on how others will judge their communication competence. The problem is that, even when people have the motivation and the necessary skills to communicate with others, anxiety can still get in the way. Imagine a baseball player at the World Series. The very fact that he's playing in the World Series suggests that he has a lot of skill and knowledge about how to be a good baseball player. Presumably anyone who would ever make it to the World Series would be highly motivated to do a good job, (i.e., turn in a skilled performance). Have you ever seen a professional athlete in the World Series, Super Bowl, Olympics, or other major event do a bad job? Why did that happen? Simply put, a lot of anxiety can interfere with a performance, even when there is a lot of ability, skill, motivation, and knowledge. Unfortunately communication apprehension has been associated with reduced communicative abilities or skills.

Individuals experiencing high levels of CA (communication apprehension) often have difficulty achieving personal and professional goals. For example, the high-CA person and the low-CA person will differ in terms of their **social relations** and **conversational skills** as well as in **nonverbal leakage**.[57] In terms of overall social skills, individuals with low CA tend to be less shy, making it easier for them to establish friendships. In addition, they are more likely to date a variety of people, to take on group leadership positions, and to be less conformist. In contrast, those high in CA tend to view themselves as less attractive, are more likely to avoid blind dates, and have greater difficulty in developing friendships. They also have poorer conversational skills, as evidenced by a greater number of nonfluencies (e.g., "um," "you know"), longer silences, and increased speech repetitions. They are often unskilled at initiating or controlling conversations and can find it difficult to interrupt others. Finally high CAs tend to have more nonverbal leakage. Think of the behaviors anxious people engage in. Thus, for example, NaMii appears stiff and tense, looks away, fidgets, and might physically distance herself from others. You can often recognize anxious individuals by the vibes they give off.

Communication apprehension would intuitively appear related to how you listen, and research supports this connection. As noted earlier, high levels of anxiety interfere with your ability to perform any task, and listening is no different. Often when you become too focused on your "communicative performance," you forget or ignore the importance of listening to others. Even when you do try to listen, your anxiety can affect your ability to translate, evaluate, or recall a message.

Other types of anxiety have been studied as well. We cover one additional type of anxiety, informational reception apprehension, when we discuss conversation and conflict in Chapter 5. Drawn from early work in receiver apprehension, informational reception apprehension affects our ability to receive information, including processing, interpreting, and dealing with an information-rich environment.[58] Now we turn to our final individual difference: cognitive complexity.

COGNITIVE COMPLEXITY

Cognitive complexity is important because it affects how we process information and how we form schemata. As you learned in Chapter 3, information processing and schemata are important in determining how we perceive and interpret incoming messages. Whether a personality trait or not, cognitive complexity has been identified as underlying a variety of communication-related skills and abilities affecting our perception as well as our message generation and reception.[59] In addition, research suggests that listening comprehension is related to people's cognitive complexity. Thus, it is important for us to examine the effect individual differences in cognitive complexity might have on how we communicate with others.

Cognitive complexity addresses how you perceive the incoming message, organize it, and use it to interpret the communication event. When looking at differences in cognitive complexity, we look at the number of constructs you are able to use or develop.[60] For example, individuals who are lower in cognitive complexity might describe Ben as a white male, majoring in media studies, who has one brother and one sister, while someone who is more cognitively complex might describe Ben as all of these things as well as funny, friendly, and gregarious. As you can see, one way that individuals differ in cognitive complexity is that they are better able to identify a number of descriptors (also called elements or constructs) to apply to Ben Goleman. The ability to provide complex, detailed descriptions is often a sign someone is more cognitively complex. In addition, those high in complexity will often use more abstract descriptions. In our previous example, the first description is very concrete—white, male, with siblings—while the more complex description provides greater detail using more abstract terminology.

Keep in mind, however, that cognitive complexity is not necessarily related to how smart someone is. It is more of an expert-novice distinction.[61] People who are experts have more abstract and better-developed cognitive schemata. Subsequently they will have more links among the elements composing their schemata (in this case, of Ben), and the ways in which they mentally organize those elements will be more complex.[62] However, someone who is cognitively complex about cats might be less so about dogs or computers or plumbing. Just as you are not experts on every topic, you are not cognitively complex in every area (or domain). Applied to how you interact with others, cognitive complexity provides you with a way of differentiating people in terms of their "social information-processing capacity."[63] Thus, you might be cognitively complex in your interpersonal relationships. Just as with other areas of expertise, interpersonal cognitive complexity is based on knowledge, interactions, and experience with others. The resulting schemata can affect your communication in several ways. For example, cognitive complexity is believed to be associated with social perceptions skills, including empathetic perspective taking.[64] It follows, then, that if you are more cognitively complex, you might be better able to understand how someone, such as a friend, is feeling.[65]

Cognitive complexity can affect your interpersonal interactions in other ways as well. People who tend to engage in **polarization** are believed to be less cognitively complex. For example, they tend to see people in bipolar dimensions: smart/stupid, mean/nice, and so forth. Not surprisingly this limited perception colors how they view others. Individuals who are more complex will move beyond the concrete and begin to focus greater attention on more abstract levels of information, such as psychological data and how it fits in with their concrete data: confident, secure, happy, and so on. At this level you would begin assigning causes or reasons for why Ben does a particular thing (e.g., snap at us, help with Habitat for Humanity). The ability to do this is called **person-centeredness.** Cognitively complex individuals are more likely to be person-centered, tailoring their messages to match the people they are interacting with. People who are less complex might have more trouble doing this, especially with those they do not know very well. As a result, they might have greater difficulty differentiating among people or seeing each person as a unique individual.

As noted earlier, cognitive complexity affects a variety of social perception skills, which in turn are related to our listening skills and abilities.[66] For example, those who are cognitively complex have a larger, better-defined cognitive system through which to interpret others' actions. As a result, they not only have a greater ability to generate several different motives or reasons for the behavior but also are better at generating multiple costs or benefits tied to those actions.

In addition, cognitively complex individuals are better able to reconcile incoming information that does not fit or conform to their schema for a person or place. For example, let's assume for a moment that Tamarah tends to be quiet and does not say much during class discussions in her Public Speaking course. Ben, who's in the class with her, might develop an initial schema of her that is founded on communication apprehension. How confident will Ben think she will be? Will he think she will make an *A* or a *C* on her speech? When Tamarah gives her first major speech, she astounds Ben (and probably a lot of her classmates) by delivering a confident, well-supported, dynamic presentation. Now Ben has to adjust his original schema of Tamarah. If Ben is low in complexity, he might engage in polarization and simply replace one schema (she's shy or apprehensive) with another (she's outgoing or not communication apprehensive). However, if he is more cognitively complex, he will differentiate between the two situations (class discussion and speech making) and how Tamarah acts in each.

Looking back at our listening model, you can see that cognitive complexity is related to awareness, translation, retention, and response. There is some debate among researchers about whether cognitive complexity is motivational (traitlike) or situational (statelike). Generally speaking, researchers are divided on the question of whether cognitive complexity is a personality trait.[67] Those who argue against it being a personality trait contend that it is not motivational in nature, that it doesn't predispose us to act in a particular way.

However, we agree with scholars who have linked it to schema development and information processing; it is not so much related to intelligence as it is related to the level of expertise we have in a particular area (e.g., a best friend, a classmate, an instructor, wine, mushrooms, cats, dogs).

THINK ON IT

Looking back at the discussion of emotional intelligence, how might EI be related to high versus low cognitive complexity?

BUILD YOUR SKILLS

You can actually work at developing your cognitive complexity. So how can you go about broadening the topics or domains in which you are cognitively complex? Be curious. Expose yourself to new ideas. Read books and newspapers. Research topics online. Watch or listen to programs that give you more than a 30-second spot of coverage on a topic. Ask your friends questions. The more you know, the more developed your schemata become, and the more cognitively complex you will be.

SUMMARY

As we finish our review of individual differences, there are several things we should consider. While these individual differences in listening have been associated with several personality and temperament traits, how much do differences actually direct your listening behavior? Watson and Barker, the scholars who researched listening style preferences, argue that we adapt our listening style to fit a situation. However, as you saw above, the different listening styles have been associated with concepts that are generally considered traits. It is true that most of these associations are small or moderate in nature. However, they do suggest that there might be a link between our listening preferences and personality. Thus, we conclude this chapter asking a question that we posed at its beginning: Is it nature or is it nurture? What has the greatest effect on our listening abilities and skills? What do you think? What do your classmates think?

CONCEPTS TO KNOW

Communibiology
Personality
    Temperament
    State versus Trait
MBTI Types
    Introversion and Extroversion
    Sensing and Intuiting
    Feeling and Thinking
    Perceiving and Judging
Listening Style Preference
    People
    Action
    Content
    Time
Empathy
    Empathetic Responsiveness

    Sympathetic Responsiveness
    Sociability
Conversational Sensitivity
Emotional Intelligence
Emotional Awareness
Communication Apprehension
    Approach and Avoidance
    Generalized Anxiety
    Conditioned Anxiety
    Social Relations
    Conversational Skills
    Nonverbal Leakage
Cognitive Complexity
    Polarization
    Person-centeredness

DISCUSSION QUESTIONS

1. It has been argued that while we can adapt our listening style to a variety of contexts, under stress or high cognitive load, we might rely on a favored type. Do you think this is true? Do you think we tend to listen in a particular style no matter the context? Why?
2. We all experience communication anxiety. What types of situations tend to make you feel the most anxious? How does your anxiety affect your listening ability? What techniques can you use to help lessen your anxiety? Improve your listening?
3. On what topics or with what individuals would you say that you are cognitively complex or not? Why or why not?

LISTENING ACTIVITIES

1. For thirty seconds each class member should write down as many alternative words or synonyms as they can for the color purple. Next, class members should gather into small groups based on their sex (depending on the class size, either one large group of men and one large group for women or two to

three small groups). In a five-minute period, groups should first combine their individual brainstorming efforts then try to come up with even more terms. Which individuals listed the greatest number of words? Who provided the most sophisticated list? What does this suggest about their cognitive complexity on this topic?

2. After reading the different descriptions of the MBTI, write down which type you believe you are. Next, have two to three friends or family members read the descriptions. See if they agree with your personal assessment. If available, complete the Keirsey Temperament Sorter or the Myers-Briggs test and see if you and your friends are correct.

ADDITIONAL READINGS

Beatty, M. J., McCroskey, J. C., & Valencic, K. M. (2001). *The biology of communication: A communibiological perspective.* Cresskill, NJ: Hampton.

Fischer, A. H. (ed.). (2000). *Gender and emotion: Social psychological perspectives.* Cambridge, UK: Cambridge University Press.

Matthews, G., Zeidner, M., & Roberts, R. D. (2002). *Emotional intelligence: Science and myth.* Cambridge, MA: MIT Press.

Petrides, K. V., Furnham, A., & Mavroveli, S. (2007). Trait emotional intelligence: Moving forward in the field of EI. In G. Matthews, M. Zeidner, & R. Roberts (eds.), *Emotional intelligence: Knowns and unknowns* (series in affective science). Oxford: Oxford University Press.

Snyder, C. R., & Lopez, S. J. (eds.). (2002). *Handbook of positive psychology.* New York: Oxford University Press.

END NOTES

1. Bostrom, 1990
2. Bodie, & Villaume, 2003; Chesebro, 1999; McCroskey, Daly, Martin, & Beatty, 1998; Shestowsky, Wegener, & Fabrigar, 1998; Sorrentino, Bobocel, Gitta, Olson, & Hewitt, 1988; Weaver, Watson, & Barker, 1996; Worthington, 2003
3. McCroskey et al., 1998
4. Daly & Bippus, 1998
5. Beatty & McCroskey, 1998
6. See also Bates (1989), Bouchard (1993), & Snidman (2004); Myers & McCaulley (1985); Keirsey (1998); & Worthington (2003).
7. Gerrig & Zimbardo, 2002
8. Buss & Plomin, 1975
9. See Strelau, 1998, p. 35
10. See Strelau, 1991
11. Buss & Plomin, 1975, p. 7
12. For a more in-depth discussion of the terms *trait* and *state* and their relationship to measurement, see Daly & Bippus, 1998.
13. Keirsey, 1998
14. Thompson & Ackerman, 1994
15. Myers & McCaulley, 1985
16. Myers & Myers, 1980, p. 1
17. Keirsey, 1998, p. 26
18. Myers & McCaulley, 1985, p. 13
19. Keirsey, 1998, p. 331
20. Myers & McCaulley, 1985, p. 12
21. Myers & McCaulley, 1985, p. 12
22. McCaulley, 1990
23. Keirsey, 1998
24. Myers & McCaulley, 1985, p. 12
25. McCaulley, 1990, p. 183
26. McCaulley, 1990, p. 183
27. Myers & McCaulley, 1985, p. 12–13
28. Watson & Barker, 1992; Watson, Barker, & Weaver, 1995
29. Watson & Barker, 1992; Watson et al., 1995
30. Barker & Watson, 2000
31. Worthington, 2003
32. Myers & McCaulley, 1985
33. Weaver & Kirtley, 1995; Chesebro, 1999
34. Worthington, 2003
35. Barker & Watson, 2000
36. Worthington, 2003
37. Myers & McCaulley, 1985
38. Keyton & Rhodes, 1994, p. 59
39. Barker & Watson, 2000, p. 27
40. Worthington, 2003
41. Sargent, Fitch-Hauser, & Weaver, 1997; Worthington, 2001
42. Barker & Watson, 2000
43. Richendoller & Weaver, 1994
44. Weaver & Kirtley, 1995
45. Daly, Vangelisti, & Daoughton, 1987

46. Chesebro, 1999; Brommelje, Houston, & Smither, 2003
47. Salovey & Mayer, 1990; Mayer & Salovey, 1997; Petrides & Furnham, 2000, 2001
48. Van Der Zee & Wabeke, 2004
49. Salovey, Mayer, Caruso, & Lopes, 2003, p. 251
50. Salovey et al., 2003, p. 253
51. Smith, Ciarrochi, & Heaven, 2008
52. Dillon & McKenzie, 1998
53. Beatty, Heisel, Hall, Levine, & LaFrance, 2002
54. McCroskey, Beatty, Kearney, & Plax, 1985
55. McCroskey et al., 1998
56. Beatty, McCroskey, & Heisel, 1998; Shimotsu & Mottett, 2009; Wahba & McCroskey, 2005; Wrench, Brogan, McCroskey, & Jowi, 2008

57. McCroskey et al., 1998
58. Wheeless, 1975; Wheeless & Schrodt, 2001; Wheeless, Eddleman-Spears, Magness, & Preiss, 2005
59. Burleson & Caplan, 1998
60. Beatty & Payne, 1981
61. Burleson & Caplan, 1998
62. See Burleson & Caplan, 1998; Daly, Bell, Glenn & Lawrence, 1985; Ericsson & Smith, 1991; Fiske & Taylor, 1991; Hoffman, 1992
63. Burleson & Caplan, 1998
64. Burleson & Caplan, 1998
65. Beatty & Payne, 1981
66. Burleson, 1987
67. Burleson & Caplan, 1998

REFERENCES

Barker, L., & Watson, K. (2000). *Listen up*. New York: St. Martin's Press.

Bates, J. E. (1989). Concepts and measures of temperament. In G. A. Kohnstamm, J. E. Bates, & M. K. Rothbart (Eds.), APA Style has the abbreviation for Editor as (Ed. or Eds.), while the abbreviation for edition is (ed.) see page 108 in latest APA style manual. *Temperament in childhood* (3–26). New York: Wiley.

Beatty, M. J., Heisel, A. D., Hall, A. E., Levine, T. R., & LaFrance, B. H. (2002). What can we learn from the study of twins about genetic and environmental influences on interpersonal affiliation, aggressiveness, and social anxiety? A meta-analytic study. *Communication Monographs, 69*, 1–18.

Beatty, M. J., & McCroskey, J. C. (1998). Interpersonal communication as temperamental expression: A communibiological paradigm. In J. C. McCroskey, J. A. Daly, M. M. Martin, & M. J. Beatty (eds.), *Communication and Personality* (41–67). Cresskill, NJ: Hampton Press.

Beatty, M. J., McCroskey, J. C., & Heisel, A. D. (1998). Communication apprehension as temperamental expression: A communibiological paradigm. *Communication Monographs, 65*, 197–219.

Beatty, M. J., & Payne, S. K. (1981). Receiver apprehension and cognitive complexity. *Western Journal of Speech Communication, 45*, 363–369.

Bodie, G., & Villaume, W. A. (2003). Aspects of receiving information: The relationship between listening preferences, communication apprehension, receiver apprehension, and communicator style. *International Journal of Listening, 17*, 47–67.

Bostrom, R. N. (1990). *Listening behavior: Measurement and application*. New York: Guilford.

Bouchard, T. J. (1993). Genetic and environmental influence on adult personality: Evaluating the evidence. In J. Hettema & I. J. Deary (eds.), *Foundations of personality* (15–44). Norwell, MA: Kluwer Academic.

Brommelje, R., Houston, J. M., & Smither, R. (2003). Personality characteristics of effective listeners: A five-factor perspective. *International Journal of Listening, 17*, 32–46.

Burleson, B. R. (1987). Cognitive complexity. In J. C. McCroskey & J. A. Daly (eds.), *Personality and interpersonal communication* (305–349). Newbury Park, CA: Sage.

Burleson, B. R., & Caplan, S. E. (1998). Cognitive complexity. In J. C. McCroskey, J. A. Daly, M. M. Martin, & M. J. Beatty (eds.), *Communication and personality* (41–67). Cresskill, NJ: Hampton Press.

Buss, A. H., & Plomin, R. (1975). *A temperament theory of personality development*. New York: John Wiley & Sons.

Chesebro, J. L. (1999). The relationship between listening styles and conversational sensitivity. *Communication Research Reports, 16*, 233–238.

Daly, J. A., Bell, R. A., Glenn, P. J., & Lawrence, S. (1985). Conceptualizing conversational complexity. *Human Communication Research, 12*, 30–53.

Daly, J. A., & Bippus, A. (1998). Personality and interpersonal communication: Issues and directions. In J. C. McCroskey, J. A. Daly, M. M. Martin, & M. J. Beatty (eds.), *Communication and personality: Trait perspectives* (1–40). Cresskill, NJ: Hampton.

Daly, J. A., Vangelisti, A. L., & Daoughton, S. M. (1987). The nature and correlates of conversational sensitivity. *Human Communication Research, 14,* 167–202.

Dillon, R. K., & McKenzie, N. J. (1998). The influence of ethnicity on listening, communication competence, approach, and avoidance. *International Journal of Listening, 12,* 160–171.

Ericsson, K. A., & Smith, J. (eds.). (1991). *Toward a general theory of expertise: Prospects and limits.* New York: Cambridge University Press.

Fiske, S. T., & Taylor, S. E. (1991). *Social cognition* (2nd ed.). NY: McGraw-Hill.

Gerrig, R.J. & Zimbardo, P. G. (2002. *Psychology and life (16th ed.).* Boston, MA: Allyn & Retrieved from http://www.psychologymatters.org/glossary.html Moved up from below (originally Psychology Matters citation) and changed in footnotes (#7).

Hoffman, R. R. (1992). *The psychology of expertise: Cognitive research and empirical findings.* New York: Springer-Verlag.

Kagan, J., & Snidman, N. (2004). *The long shadow of temperament.* Cambridge, MA: Belknap.

Keirsey, D. (1998). *Please understand me II.* Del Mar, CA: Prometheus Nemesis.

Keyton, J., & Rhodes, S. (1994). The effects of listener preference styles on identifying sexual harassment. *Journal of the International Listening Association, 8,* 50–79.

Mayer, J. D., & Salovey, P. (1997). What is emotional intelligence? In P. Salovey & D. Sluyter (eds.), *Emotional development and emotional intelligence: Implications for educators* (3–31). New York: Basic Books.

McCaulley, M. H. (1990). The Myers-Briggs type indicator: A measure for individuals and groups. *Measurement and Evaluation in Counseling and Development, 22,* 181–195.

McCroskey, J. C., Beatty, M. J., Kearney, P., & Plax, T. G. (1985). The content validity of the PRCA-24 as a measure of communication apprehension across communication contexts. *Communication Quarterly, 33,* 165–173.

McCroskey, J. C., Daly, J. A., Martin, M. M., & Beatty, M. J. (1998). *Communication and personality: Trait perspectives.* Cresskill, NJ: Hampton.

Myers, I. B., & McCaulley, M. H. (1985). *Manual: A guide to the development and use of the Myers-Briggs type indicator.* Palo Alto, CA: Consulting Psychologists Press.

Myers, I. B., & Myers, P. B. (1980). *Gifts differing.* Palo Alto, CA: Consulting Psychologists Press.

Petrides, K. V., & Furnham, A. (2000). Gender differences in measured and self-estimated trait emotional intelligence. *Sex Roles, 42,* 449–461.

Petrides, K. V., & Furnham, A. (2001). Trait emotional intelligence: Psychometric investigation with reference to established trait taxonomies. *European Journal of Personality, 15,* 425–448.

Richendoller, N. R., & Weaver, J. B. (1994). Exploring the links between personality and empathic response style. *Personality and Individual Differences, 17,* 303–311.

Salovey, P., & Mayer, J. D. (1990). Emotional intelligence. *Imagination, Cognition, and Personality, 9,* 185–211.

Salovey, P., Mayer, J. D., Caruso, D., & Lopes, P. N. (2003). In S. J. Lopez & C. R. Snyder (eds.), *Positive psychological assessment: A handbook of models and measures.* (251–265). Washington, D.C.: APA.

Sargent, S. L., Fitch-Hauser, M., & Weaver III, J. B. (1997). A listening styles profile of the type-A personality. *International Journal of Listening, 11,* 1–14.

Shestowsky, D., Wegener, D. T., & Fabrigar, L. R. (1998). Need for cognition and interpersonal influence: Individual differences in impact on dyadic decisions. *Journal of Personality and Social Psychology, 5,* 1317–1328.

Shimotsu, S., & Mottett, T. P. (2009). The relationships among perfectionism, communication apprehension, and temperament. *Communication Research Reports, 26,* 188–197.

Smith, L., Ciarrochi, J., & Heaven, P. C. L. (2008). The stability and change of trait emotional intelligence, conflict communication patterns, and relationship satisfaction: A one-year longitudinal study. *Personality & Individual Differences, 45,* 738–743.

Sorrentino, R. M., Bobocel, D. R., Gitta, M. Z., Olson, J. M., & Hewitt, E. C. (1988). Uncertainty orientation and persuasion: Individual differences in the effects of personal relevance on social judgments. *Journal of Personality and Social Psychology, 55,* 357–371.

Strelau, J. (1991). *Explorations in temperament.* New York: Plenum.

Strelau, J. (1998). *Temperament: A psychological perspective.* New York: Plenum.

Thompson, B., & Ackerman, C. (1994). Review of the Myers-Briggs type indicator. In J. Kapes, M. Mestie, & E. Whitfield (eds.), *A counselor's guide to career assessment instruments* (3rd ed.) (283–287). Alexandria, VA: American Counseling Association.

Van Der Zee, K., & Wabeke, R. (2004). Is trait-emotional intelligence simply or more than just a trait? *European Journal of Personality, 18,* 243–263.

Wahba, J. S., & McCroskey, J. C. (2005). Temperament and brain systems as predictors of assertive communication traits. *Communication Research Reports, 22,* 157–164.

Watson, K. W., & Barker, L. L. (1992). Comparison of the ETS national teacher examination listening model with models used in two standardized tests. *International Journal of Listening, 6,* 32–44.

Watson, K. W., Barker, L. L., & Weaver III, J. B. (1995). The listening styles profile (LS–16): Development and validation of an instrument to assess four listening styles. *International Journal of Listening, 9,* 1–13.

Weaver, III, J. B., & Kirtley, M. D. (1995). Listening styles and empathy. *Southern Journal of Speech Communication, 60,* 131–140.

Weaver III, J. B., Watson, K. W., & Barker, L. L. (1996). Individual differences in listening style: Do you hear what I hear? *Personality and Individual Differences, 20,* 381–387.

Wheeless, L. (1975). An investigation of receiver apprehension and social context dimension of communi-cation apprehension. *Communication Education, 24,* 261–268.

Wheeless, L. R., Eddleman-Spears, L., Magness, L. D., & Preiss, R. W. (2005). Informational reception apprehension and information from technology aversion: Development of a new construct. *Communication Quarterly, 53,* 143–158.

Wheeless, L. R. & Schrodt, P. (2001). An examination of cognitive foundations of informational reception apprehension: Political identification, religious affiliation, and family environment. *Communication Research Reports, 18,* 1–10.

Worthington, D. L. (2001). Exploring juror listening processes: The effect of listening style preference on juror decision making. *International Journal of Listening, 15,* 20–35.

Worthington, D. L. (2003). Exploring the relationship between listening style preference and personality. *International Journal of Listening, 17,* 68–87.

Wrench, J. S., Brogan, S. M., McCroskey, J. C., & Jowi, D. (2008). Social communication apprehension: The intersection of communication apprehension and social phobia. *Human Communication, 11,* 409–429.

Listening in the Conversational Context

Stressed Out

Hey, NaMii. Did you get the message I sent you? Will you be able to go with me to interview Dr. Wood, the family therapist?

Oh, hi, Tamarah. I was just about to text you back. What type of information are we trying to get? We have so many things going on right now that I'm having problems keeping some of it straight.

You seem to be a little stressed. Want to grab a cup of coffee and talk a bit? It'll make you feel better, and we can coordinate our part of the group project. I think I'll try a mochachino . . .

Thanks, Tamarah. I think I could use both the caffeine and the shoulder. Of course, getting at least one project organized won't hurt any either. ■

For most of us, engaging in a conversation is something we do daily. Seldom, unless the topic or situation is emotionally charged, do we think a great deal about the communication process that is going on. And we rarely, if ever, stop to think about the effect of listening on the conversation. In this chapter we look at listening as a critical element of conversations in general. Then we will look at two types of conversational situations that we regularly face: giving and receiving social support and handling conflict.

CONVERSATIONS AND INTERACTION

If you think of a conversation as simply two or more people talking, it is metaphorically equivalent to saying baseball is a game of two pitchers pitching. Without a batter to swing at the ball, there is no need for a pitcher. Similarly when you say something, our "pitch" is meaningless without someone else to "swing" or receive and respond to that message.

In fact, as you will see in the following discussion, without a meaningful listener, conversations tend to flounder and eventually grind to a halt.

Traditionally listeners have been considered part of the background of a conversation, meaning that a listener was simply considered a speaker in waiting.[1] As one communication scholar put it, when looking at a conversation, many researchers focus on the source or the effect, not the process, which includes listening.[2] Laura Janusik, a listening scholar, said that such a perspective ignores the transactional nature of conversations.[3] In the context of conversations, all parties are both a sender and a receiver, creating a transactional process where the listener both receives and responds.

David Bohm, a world-renowned physicist and modern-day Renaissance man, suggested that human relationships are essentially collaborative activities and a process of creation.[4] He also believes that in many listening instances we are blocked from fully understanding the other. Our need to protect ourselves and the meanings we create often gets in the way of our ability to truly understand one another. Bohm argued that ideally, when we communicate with others, we should engage in a collaborative dialogue. Such a dialogue is based on the cocreation of meaning. It necessarily entails an ability to truly listen to others without bias and without trying to influence others, with a willingness to move beyond our own beliefs. To do this, Bohm essentially argued that we embrace and acknowledge our blockages while fully giving our attention to what our conversational partner is saying. It is at this point, Bohm would say, we are truly communicating with one another.

In our Case Study at the beginning of the chapter, our characters leave us with the idea that they are going to have a real conversation. Tamarah recognizes and acknowledges NaMii's mood and understands how it could have an effect on what they are going to talk about as well as how they interact. Had Tamarah been more focused on her own message rather than recognizing how stressed NaMii felt, chances are a misunderstanding would have ensued.

Professors Janet Bavelas, Linda Coates, and Trudy Johnson from the University of Victoria in British Columbia, Canada, offered one explanation for why scholars have largely ignored the importance of the listener to a conversation. They believe the problem might be traced back to the Shannon-Weaver model of communication.[5] Chances are you learned about this model in a basic speech course. As you recall, this model presents the linear configuration presented in Figure 5.1. In this type of model, the receiver (listener) takes a back seat to the sender. As one scholar pointed out, the sender (speaker) has the front channel and the receiver (listener) takes the back channel.[6] From this perspective, the role of the listener is to respond minimally and in a noninterruptive manner until it is his or her turn to be the sender.

Clearly conversation is much more involved than the model indicates. Good listening is a critical part of any successful conversation. To support this assertion, we

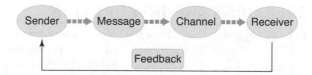

FIGURE 5.1
Shannon-Weaver Model of Communication.

have only to look at research examining what happens when a listener fails to fully participate in a conversation. This research has shown consistently that when appropriate listening behavior is removed, reduced, or eliminated, the performance of the sender as well as the quality of the communication suffer.[7] The findings of this body of research are quite interesting. For example, when listener feedback is reduced or absent, speakers tend to use more words.[8] However, more words do not necessarily make for greater understanding. Other research finds that listeners better understand a speaker's message when they are allowed to provide feedback. What's more, speakers are so sensitive to listener nonverbal behavior that they will restart a phrase if the listener looks away then looks back.[9] These research results support the conclusion that a conversation is a cooperative interaction between speakers and listeners.

Grice's Maxims

To help us understand this cooperative interaction, we can look at expectations we have for conversations. Noted researcher H. P. Grice proposed some conversational maxims based on the key principle that we engage in an interaction to get the maximum amount of information possible and that we expect the other party to cooperate in this effort. This expectation is called the **principle of cooperation.**[10] To get the information, we must focus on both the actual words of the message and any information implied in the comment. That is, as we listen to a conversational partner, we draw inferences based on what is said. These inferences help us complete the picture of what the speaker intends to convey.

In essence, Grice's maxims lay out a logic for what we expect from the cooperating partner when we participate in a conversation. As listeners, if we embrace these expectations, they will shape both what we listen for and the types of inferences we make. The first maxim is **quality.** This maxim suggests that we expect the other person to tell us the truth or at least what she believes to be the truth. The second is the maxim of **quantity,** which leads us to expect the speaker to give us useful information that we don't already know without overwhelming us with too much information. This maxim allows us to rely on our own storehouse of knowledge to interpret the speaker's comments. For example, if one of your friends tells you that studying for a test really paid off, he doesn't have to tell you he passed the test; you will assume that from his statement. If, on the other hand, you know someone who seems to constantly dominate the conversation, then he might be violating or breaking this unwritten rule of conversation.

The next two maxims address the interaction itself. The maxim of **relation** leads us to believe the information we get is going to be relevant to the purpose of the interaction as well as to the flow of the conversation. So we expect to get information that we don't already obviously know and that is relevant to the specific conversation. When this expectation is violated, it frequently leads to confusion or the feeling that we were being misled. Think about what happens when you are in a conversation and the other person inserts a statement that seems to be totally random. Doesn't it cause you to either wonder if the other party is in the same conversation that you are or to believe you have "zoned out" and missed something critical?

The final maxim, the maxim of **manner,** leads us to expect the speaker to be brief, orderly, and unambiguous. Unfortunately this maxim assumes that we share

THINK ON IT

Chances are you have met international students on your campus. How do your expectations and conversational behaviors differ when you talk with a nonnative speaker of your language?

the same level of ability and knowledge about the language we use to converse. If this assumption isn't correct, that is, we are talking with someone who isn't as well versed in our language, we tend to rely on tactfulness and politeness to help us cope with this turn of events.[11] For example, when you talk with a young child, you adjust your expectations of her ability to use the language in a sophisticated manner. Likewise, when you visit another country, you don't expect the residents to have the same ability in your language as you do.

Defining Conversation

So after all of this discussion, what is a conversation? We can define **conversation** as "an orderly jointly managed sequence of utterances produced by at least two participants who may or may not share similar goals in the interaction."[12] This definition stresses the importance of all parties in the interaction *working together to manage* the sequencing of the speakers' utterances. Doing so requires appropriate responding on the part of the listener(s), or receiver(s). That is, the listener must remain engaged in the interaction and respond either verbally or nonverbally in a manner that is appropriate for what was said. This definition excludes situations where people happen to be in the same space talking past each other. A scene from the movie *Rainman* illustrates this point. At one point in the movie, Charlie Babbitt, played by Tom Cruise, stops at a doctor's office to talk with the doctor about his autistic brother, Raymond, whom he has kidnapped from a home. In the waiting room, an older gentleman is holding forth about "going west." Though the waiting room is crowded with people, no one is responding to the man. He is simply talking, not conversing. On the other hand, Charlie and a nurse engage in an interaction in which the nurse tries to figure out what is wrong with Raymond. Both the nurse and Charlie respond to each other in a way that the flow of the interaction moves forward. Each participant in this example has a different goal: the nurse wants information about the patient, and Charlie wants to get his brother examined. Nevertheless, both parties respond appropriately to each other so they are truly engaged in a conversation.

Notice that our definition of conversation *does not* specify face-to-face or mouth-to-ear interactions. Thanks to modern communication technology, many of our conversations take the form of e-mails, instant messages, or text messages. Regardless of whether the conversation is in person or electronically mediated, as conversational listeners, we engage in a conversation specifically to interact with another party for some purpose. The ultimate result of the conversation truly is a product of the interaction itself.

Conversations as Cocreations

While conversations are one of the most ordinary of our communication events, they are also one of the most important. In fact, many scholars see conversations as fundamentally important to language, to communication, to being human.[13] Through conversations, we learn about our families, our friends, our coworkers. We solve problems and make both ordinary and significant decisions. It is what makes us social beings.

As noted in the previous section, many of us focus on the speaker when we think about a conversation. Think about the last conversation (or any conversation) you participated in. What do you remember? Chances are that you remember what you said and at least part of what the other person said. You probably don't remember or even think about your or the other person's listening behavior. Isn't it funny that we don't really think about the role of listening in conversation?

Well-known communication scholars Stephen Littlejohn and Kathy Domenici addressed this point by saying, "We normally think of conversation as an event in which people take turns talking. How would conversations change if we thought of them as taking turns at listening?"[14] They noted that while it is important to let conversational participants speak their minds, we need to think of conversations as dialogues or exchanges. When we take this perspective, listening, not talking, becomes the centerpiece of any conversation.

To illustrate more fully how important listening is to the flow and development of a conversation, we go back to Professors Bavelas, Coates, and Johnson and their research examining listeners as conarrators of an interaction.[15] While many studies have addressed this topic, the work by Bavelas and her colleagues differs because they examined actual conversations (instead of written descriptions), and their line of investigation raises a number of important points for us to consider.

First, they pointed out something that all of us know: not all listening responses are verbal or actual words. The researchers identified two kinds of listener responses. The first of these is **generic responses.** Generic responses include nonverbal actions such as nodding and vocalizations such as "mhm" or "uh-huh." Another term that has been used to describe this type of response is **back channel.** Generic or back-channel responses aren't specifically connected to what the speaker is saying. Instead they serve as markers that we are cognitively engaged in what the speaker is saying. So we might nod to indicate we are listening to the speaker, regardless of what the topic or emotional load of the narration is. If we give generic responses when we *aren't* cognitively engaged, we are merely making **listening noises** and essentially deceiving the speaker.

The second type of listener response identified by Bavelas, Coates, and Johnson is **specific responses.** As you can guess, these are responses that are directly tied to what the speaker is saying. Therefore, these responses should be appropriate for the content and emotional load of the speaker's narration. So a sad facial expression is appropriate feedback when we listen to a sad story and so forth. Interestingly some of these specific responses can even get incorporated into the speaker's narration. The conversation in Case Study 5.2 illustrates how this can happen:

CASE STUDY 5.2

Cocreating Conversation

TAMARAH: I went with my mom on one of her visits to a homeless shelter. You know she's a social worker.

BEN: Yuck! Was it depressing?

TAMARAH: Well, it wasn't as bad as I expected. The place was pretty clean, airy, and not nearly as loud as I thought it would be. And the kitchen was efficiently run. The cots were—

BEN: [interrupting] Probably crowded and not very comfortable.

TAMARAH: Not as bad as you would expect. All the cots were in a row, and they were pretty crowded. I sure wouldn't have found it comfortable. Anyway, I left there feeling very thankful. ■

Notice that Tamarah incorporates Ben's thoughts into her narration. She might or might not have intended to talk about the crowding or comfort. Later, when she tells the same story to another friend, she might again incorporate Ben's description of the sleeping area of the shelter into her story. Consequently the story will include both her experience and Ben's assumptions.

It is also important to remember that listeners don't always respond verbally and interrupt the speaker as Ben does in our example. Many of our responses are nonverbal. Research has shown that speakers are particularly sensitive to facial expressions and eye gaze.[16] If listeners engage in appropriate responses, whether verbal or nonverbal, conversations flow smoothly. For this to happen, both individuals must track the conversation closely.

When listeners are distracted, they tend to make fewer responses of any kind, particularly specific responses. In turn, when speakers notice how disengaged or distracted the listeners are, their narration suffers and they begin to use coping strategies. They could abruptly end the message, become less articulate, or feel the need to justify elements of the story.[17] Regardless of their coping strategy, their role as speaker is adversely affected, as is the overall interaction. Good conversations are clearly dependent on both the speaking and listening roles of the participants. In fact, listening in good conversations illustrates all of the primary elements of the WFH Listening MATERRS model: the interactants must be motivated to stay engaged, attend to each other, interpret the message, and provide appropriate responses.

> **THINK ON IT**
>
> Can you think of an example where your story about one of your experiences has incorporated someone else's thoughts or observations? If you can, what is it about the information that makes you remember the source? If you can't, does it make you wonder how your stories might have changed over time?

CONVERSATIONAL VARIABLES

The best conversations require a willingness to truly express our opinions, feelings, or ideas and a willingness to listen to the same from others. Susan Scott, author of the book *Fierce Conversations,* talked about the importance of "fierce" conversations, conversations that thrive on openness and debate, not anger and hostility. She believes that our successes and failures are built "one conversation at a time" and stressed that "the conversation *is* the relationship."[18] She argued that when our conversations slow or stop, our relationships are weakened. Conversations are proof that we are responsive to the others in our lives. However, to be responsive, to engage in fierce conversations, we have to be open to change.

You'll notice that we haven't said anything about being able to come to an agreement as being important. Sometimes we have to agree to disagree, but in these types of conversations, our goal is to understand the point of view of others and for them to understand ours. When we assess conversational listening, our assessments should include who the speaker is, what is said, and how it is said as well as the underlying reasons it was said. When we assess these elements, we get into the importance of considering the differences in the individuals participating in the conversation.

Individual Differences

As you recall, in Chapter 4 of this text, we talked about how individual differences affect how we listen. Not surprisingly individual differences can also affect our conversations with others. In this section we will briefly discuss how several individual differences affect conversational listening.

One way we differ is in terms of our **cognitive complexity,** or the number of personal constructs we use when evaluating messages or our conversational partners. The potential effect on conversational listening can be seen in the findings of early research in the area. This research established that those who are cognitively complex tend to be more accurate when processing information about others, are better able to imagine themselves in the other person's place, and tend to withhold judgment when forming impressions of others.[19] In contrast, people who are less complex are more likely to quickly form initial impressions and find it more difficult to change that impression. Thus, when they receive contradictory information (e.g., Ella's evil stepmother does something nice for Ella), they might choose to minimize or ignore it. From this research we can see how cognitive complexity can make us more flexible as listeners in social situations. Those who are cognitively complex should be more capable of keeping an open mind and responding in ways that are appropriate for the specific conversation. Unfortunately, however, a good listener, regardless of how cognitively complex, must continue to work on being a good listener. Being cognitively complex doesn't mean that we are always open-minded or take the high road in conversations. After all, all of us, even the cognitively complex, are human.

> **THINK ON IT**
>
> What might happen in conversations where Carter is highly cognitively complex and his friend Joe is not? What differences would occur in their conversations, especially those related to listening?

Linked to cognitive complexity is another individual trait: **individual receiver apprehension.** Individual receiver apprehension is more specialized that the general communication apprehension we discussed in Chapter 4. This is a type of anxiety that impairs our ability to manage information. Those who are high in this type of apprehension tend to experience anxiety and anger or antipathy when facing an interaction. These heightened emotions, in turn, have a negative effect on their willingness to receive or interpret incoming messages.[20] In other words, people who are highly receiver apprehensive don't want to listen. One reason they might not want to listen is that they also tend to be intellectually inflexible and fear having to comprehend complex or abstract information.[21]

Just as individuals who are highly complex are quite adaptable in social situations, so are high self-monitors. **Self-monitoring** occurs when we attempt to manage the impressions we leave with others. All of us do this to varying degrees. However, low self-monitors tend to be more consistent in the "face" they present to others. What this means is that they present a very similar "face" regardless of who is in the conversation or what the context might be. According to scholar Mark Snyder, low self-monitors are more likely to look at a situation and ask, "Who am I and how can I be me?" while the high self-monitor will ask, "Who does this situation want me to be, and how can I be that person?"[22] In their effort to adapt, they are more likely to use ambiguous language, particularly in situations where they do not agree but don't believe the situation or context really allows for

THINK ON IT

Looking back at Chapter 4, how might other individual differences affect our conversational interactions with others?

disagreement (e.g., dinner party, casual coffee with friends). In addition to understanding the effect of individual differences on your conversations, other variables can also affect your conversational listening.

Accommodation

Closely related to self-monitoring is **accommodation,** or how we adjust our communication behavior to the other party. While this theory was first developed to look at adjustments in speech behavior, more recent applications have wisely begun to look at receiving behavior as well.[23] Accommodation allows us to respond to the needs of the other party whether it be for privacy or empathy. In the Case Study at the beginning of the chapter, Tamarah is very perceptive of NaMii's mood and shifts her focus from doing the interview to providing support for NaMii. Like Tamarah, when we use accommodating listening behavior, we take into account the other party's uniqueness and social identity. This accommodation will include making adjustments in your delivery style as well as your nonverbal behavior. For example, if you were to engage in a conversation with NaMii's grandparents, you would take into consideration that they are Korean. As an adroit listener, you would accommodate your responding behavior so you showed respect for both their age and their culture. So you would keep your voice fairly quiet and your eye contact indirect, rather than direct.

As listeners, when we accommodate our conversational partner, we attempt to fit our responding behavior to that person. We would listen closely, put ourselves in the other person's perspective (be empathetic), and respond in a way that is respectful of the other person. Unfortunately we aren't always successful in our accommodation. Sometimes we will **underaccommodate,** or fail to appreciate, pay sufficient attention to, or simply be unwilling to take into account, the needs of the other party.[24] Think about talking with your grandparents and their friends. If you have a negative stereotype of older people, you might ignore their needs for you to talk more clearly, use terms they are unlikely to understand or would misinterpret (e.g., chillaxin, ballin, requestion), or fail to appreciate their experiences. It is very easy to dismiss (or zone out from) what the other person is saying when we haven't directly experienced the same thing. Not surprisingly intergenerational and intercultural communications seem particularly susceptible to underaccommodating because of this difference in experience.

On the other end of the spectrum is **overaccommodation.** Overaccommodating can best be characterized as talking down to or being condescending.[25] Examples of this type of behavior include using diminutives (e.g., "sweetie," "my dear," "little darling"), overly simplistic grammar, overenunciation, or excessively slow speech in combination with continual head nodding and excessive smiling and touching.[26] Unfortunately we once again find that this type of accommodation behavior seems to be common in intergenerational and intercultural conversations as well as in interability encounters. For example, we find this type of interaction in health-care settings when nurses talk in a patronizing way to patients.[27]

Once again, as listeners we need to be aware of any biases or stereotypes that might lead us to overaccommodate and be negative participants in an interaction. Another set of negative behaviors can be found in nonaccommodating behaviors. **Nonaccommodation** occurs when we engage in behavior that in some way either excludes the other party or makes them feel excluded.[28] Perhaps the easiest way to illustrate this type of conversational behavior is to look at some research that examines language use in male-dominated workplaces.[29] One study found the dominant male group excessively used sports metaphors and sexual innuendos. Not surprisingly women in this workplace felt excluded and sometimes offended. The resulting interactions between the two groups led to a cycle of behavior that was detrimental to the workplace (e.g., difficulty communicating, minimum communication, uncooperative group interactions). On a larger stage, we can see the failure to accommodate people who sound or look different from the group in the majority. You can see this in the news as you watch and listen to stories about ethnic strife around the globe. On your campus you might see nonaccommodation when some students interact with international students or students who choose to adopt a different style of dress, hair color, or body art, for example.

As a good conversational listener, you want to remember the importance of taking into account the background and needs of the other party so you can engage in a mutually beneficial interaction. Of course, the setting and purpose of the interaction will also have an effect on how the conversation progresses.

Conversational Context

One of the elements of conversation that we need to explore is the setting, or context where a conversation takes place. For example, if a conversation is taking place in a noisy setting, the dynamics of the conversation will be different than when the conversation is taking place in a quiet setting. As you would expect, conversations have difficulty succeeding in noisy settings.[30] You will remember from the discussion of our model, Listening MATERRS, we must first be able to attend to a stimulus in order to listen. In a noisy setting, picking up the conversation or the message can be either impossible or extremely challenging. If the setting is too difficult, the listener loses motivation to remain engaged. In addition, it is very difficult to respond appropriately in ways that will sustain a conversation.

> **THINK ON IT**
>
> Think of the last time you were sitting with a large group at a dinner party or restaurant. Who did you end up talking to? What were some of the topics of conversation? How do you think the context affected the conversation?

Research in this area shows that listeners tend to engage in certain coping behavior in very noisy settings. One of the strategies is to withdraw from the conversation. With this strategy, the listener might physically remain in the location but mentally seem to withdraw. More proactive approaches occur when listeners make comments about not being able to hear or attempt to change the topic. While telling the speaker that you can't hear is usually appropriate, changing the topic, on the other hand, might be perceived negatively. If nothing is done to help the listener hear better, that person will probably withdraw. No matter the approach that is used, if speakers are not responsive, listeners will ultimately tend to be nonresponsive or fail to take up the conversation. If they do respond, that response probably isn't going to be based on the speaker's comments.[31] Consequently the relationship with the conversational partner might be negatively affected: "You never listen to me!" "You have no idea how I feel!" "You didn't say anything when I mentioned it before!" It is not always the physical location that provides a context for listening; other factors such as the state of the relationship between the interactants also contribute to the context in which the conversation occurs.

Self-verification

As seen above, conversations tend to occur in the context of some type of relationship. The next two chapters will focus on listening in specific relationships; however, it is important to look at some general effects of the relationship on a conversation. Storytelling is an important part of our conversations with others. Chances are if Tamarah listens to NaMii's stories about living with her grandparents, she will learn a great deal about both NaMii and the Korean culture. In the exchange, Tamarah will experience something called self-verification.[32] **Self-verification** refers to how we as individuals construct our own social worlds. The social world we construct is based on perceptions of ourselves and includes our self-concept and self-esteem, and it helps us to support our beliefs about our ourselves (e.g., smart, funny, witty). For example, if you view yourself as funny, you are more likely to tell personal stories that reflect the funny things that you did or that happened to you in the past week. If you value work over play, then you are more likely to tell tales related to the work or projects you completed (or did not complete). Tamarah takes pride in her ability to help others (remember she works in public safety and takes emergency calls) as well as her cultural sensitivity. As the daughter of the tribal leader of the Choctaw Nation, she knows firsthand the challenges of living in two cultures. As she and NaMii talk and exchange stories, Tamarah will tell stories that reflect these beliefs about herself.

Storytelling and Identity

With our storytelling, we maintain and change our identities. A number of theorists in this area believe that personal storytelling is important to the development of self-identity, not just when we are children or young adults, but throughout our lives.[33] The previous example helps illustrate this. Like Tamarah, we seek personal confirmation of who we are through our stories.

THINK ON IT

Have you been listening to a story and been shocked or surprised by what the person said? Did you tell her you disagreed with her opinion/interpretation or with what she chose to do? What affected your decision to openly disagree (or not)?

How people respond to our stories is also important. Research in psychology suggests that *how* people respond to our storytelling can actually affect this self-confirmation or self-verification process. Self-verification is possible when our families, friends, and other significant individuals agree with our personal views.

As we have relayed throughout this text, listening is a dynamic process. The roles of speaker and listener are constantly changing during the ebb and flow of the conversation. As the roles change, listeners can agree or disagree with a story, which in turn affects the self-verification process. So when you tell the story about someone being rude to you, your listener might disagree with your interpretation. Because we tend to tell stories that support our self-view, we tend to find it problematic when others don't agree with our interpretations. Thus, if our friends and families outright disagree with our story, we might feel we have been disconfirmed.

Worse than disagreeing, another means of disconfirming a story is inattentive listening. Attentiveness is central to social interactions. We can tell when others are paying attention to our stories by the verbal "uh-huhs" or nonverbal eye contact and head nods. These attentional cues are also important for maintaining the flow of conversations and provide the means by which we let others know we understand and support (or don't support) what they say. Distracted listeners are generally not very good at providing these cues or signals.

Attentiveness affects our storytelling in other ways. For example, when we feel someone is really listening to us, our stories tend to be longer and more detailed. We also tend to be more expressive and more eloquent.[34] Essentially then, distracted listeners affect both the quantity and quality of our storytelling.[35]

It is interesting that while we might be seeking a responsive, supportive listener to validate our identity, we can deal with an attentive, disagreeing listener better than we can an inattentive listener. Attentive listeners, whether they agree or disagree with us, confirm that the experience or event that we are recounting is both understandable and worthy of attention. Both types of listeners provide us with the opportunity to elaborate on the story. Distracted listeners, however, aren't keeping up their end of the listening "bargain." If you think about the previous discussion of Grice's maxims, you know that when we face a nonlistening situation, we need to cut short our story or run the risk of violating these conversational norms.[36] Clearly the so-called listener finds no importance in what we are saying. When telling stories of personal verification, if we are faced with an inattentive listener, we are more likely to feel the person is disconfirming the part of our identity we seek to validate. Subsequently the way others listen to us, and the way we listen to them, has important implications for how we think about ourselves and how much we are willing to reveal about ourselves.

SOCIAL SUPPORT

Perhaps one of the most important functions of conversation is giving and receiving social support. When we receive sensitive social support, particularly emotional support, it tends to make us feel better and we can more effectively address our problems. It might even lead us to feel mentally and physically better.[37] Social support has been identified as one of the most desired and essential types of support we seek from our close relationship partners.[38] Individuals who personally value emotional support and are good at providing it tend to be more popular, have more satisfying relationships, are less lonely, and are less likely to be rejected by their peers.

As you can see, positive social support benefits both the sender and the receiver. The difficulty is often trying to determine how to provide such support. Research by Loretta Pecchioni and Kelby Halone shows that part of the answer depends on the type of relationship and the support that is required.[39]

Directive and Nondirective Social Support

To better understand how to give positive social support, we need to explore just what social support looks like. First, we can distinguish between two categories of support: directive and nondirective.[40] **Directive support** involves providing *unrequested* specific types of coping behaviors or solutions for the recipient of the support. If you tell someone to take three deep breaths to calm down, that is directive support. **Nondirective support** shifts the focus of control from the giver to the receiver. The recipient dictates the support provisions. If Radley were to ask your advice on how to handle a problem with a group member in his Health Communication class and you suggest he make an appointment to see his instructor, your suggestion is considered nondirective support because Radley specifically asked for the advice. Nondirective support tends to be more effective than directive support. The listening challenge is often in identifying when someone is asking for support. In Case Study 5.3, we look at an example that might sound familiar to you.

Chances are you have been involved in an exchange similar to the one presented in Case Study 5.3. An aware listener will know that the underlying paralanguage and nonverbal messages are as important, if not more important, than the actual words. At the point where we stopped in the example, Carter has a couple of options. He can say, "OK," accepting the face value of the message, and continue the social exchange; he can choose to leave; or he can drop the line of questioning. On the other hand, he can be sensitive to the entire message, notice that the emphasis on the last word, *fine*, indicates just the opposite, and offer social support. He can be empathetic, continue using reflexive listening, and say something such as, *"Are you sure? Did something happen at work last night that upset you? If you'd like to talk about it, I'm here to listen."* Saying this particular script might be a little uncomfortable for some. Another alternative would be for Carter to say and do something a bit less "touchy feely." He could ask if he could join her and sit down at the table and ask her about how work is going. Either response will give Tamarah the choice of whether to share her frustration and seek social support.

CASE STUDY 5.3

Listening for Tone

CARTER: Hey, Tamarah. How you doing?

TAMARAH: Oh, hello, Carter. I'm fine. How about you?

CARTER: Hmm, you don't sound like you're doing "fine." What's going on?

TAMARAH: Oh, nothing. Really, I'm fine. ■

Additional Attributes of Social Support

As seen above, effective social support tends to be nondirective as well as invisible.[41] That is, the recipient isn't consciously aware that support is being given and, therefore, doesn't feel any negative consequences of being the recipient. Negative consequences include feeling obligated to the support giver, losing self-esteem, drawing more attention to the problem, and feeling inadequate.[42] One way we see negative social support is in the form of overprotectiveness. If you think about your family, for instance, you might remember times when your parents or older siblings were overly protective. Chances are you didn't appreciate their very visible support. However, in retrospect, you can probably also think of times when you received support but were unaware of that support because it just fit into the naturalness of the event or was in some other way very unobtrusive. Some possible examples would include your roommate, without your asking him to do so, going to the library or to another friend's home when you are planning on having a study group over the night before a big exam or a partner taking care of everyday household chores such as mowing the lawn so you aren't distracted by them.

Effective support is also reciprocal.[43] Reciprocity is especially important in intimate relationships. Both people need to feel supported by the other. When one person feels he or she is doing the majority of the supporting in the relationship, resentment and conflict tend to build and undermine the relationship.

Professor Brant Burleson provides several suggestions for how we can respond as supportive conversational listeners.[44] The suggestions are listed in Table 5.1.

As you recall from previous discussions, social support is using supportive communication to help others make sense of what they are experiencing. Clearly, being supportive or receiving support is important for all of us. However, research shows that to be effective, ***social support must be well timed.***[45] Up to this

> **THINK ON IT**
>
> Can you think of a time when you tried to be supportive or help someone and that person got angry or showed resentment? What elements of negative social support can you identify in that event? Using your 20/20 hindsight, what could you have done differently?

TABLE 5.1

Positive Social Support Behaviors

- Express your understanding of the situation and the other's feelings (but avoid saying, "I know exactly what you're going through"—every situation and every person is different).
- Convey your interest in listening.
- Use open-ended questions.
- Encourage the other to talk or explain the situation or her feelings, to "tell her story" (as much as the person desires or is willing to disclose).
- Clearly express your desire to help.
- Express positive regard or affection. (Remember, one reason people seek emotional support is that their self-esteem was threatened or invalidated.)
- Express concern and active interest in the situation.
- Show that you are available for the person.
- Express your support ("I've got your back; I'm behind you all the way").

CASE STUDY 5.4

A Long Day

Mrs. Gutierrez: What a day this has been. My feet hurt, my head hurts, and all of the new regulations affecting pharmacies on top of the impending merger are about to drive me nuts.

Nolvia: Oh, Ma, I'm so sorry you are feeling stressed. Is there anything I can do for you? Why don't I run a bubble bath? That always makes me feel better. And don't worry about dinner; I have some time before my study meeting. I'll stir something up and make certain the kids and Papa are taken care of. Just go relax.

Mrs. Gutierrez: Thank you, dear, but no. I have everything laid out to cook pollo con papas, and you know how your dad loves that. Plus, I think the tamalitos are ready. ∎

point, we have talked about the importance of effective social support. However, it is important to point out that not all of us want social support all of the time. There are times when we can be upset, but we don't seek social support. If, or when, we seek support is determined by several factors, such as our perceptions of our relationship with the other person and his or her views of what has upset us. Other factors can include our personalities (some people simply don't feel the need for lots of social support) and our views of the risks and benefits of seeking support (e.g., your friend might make fun of you).[46] Whether or not the timing is right seems to be dependent on how willing the partners are to engage in direct communication and listen to both the spoken message as well as the nonverbal message.

As an example, let's look at the following scenario between Nolvia and her mother in Case Study 5.4.

At first glance, you probably think that Nolvia's considerate offer is just what Mrs. Gutierrez needs to decompress from her very stressful day. However, a closer examination might show that Nolvia is actually adding to her mother's stress level. Remember, for social support to be effective, good communication is necessary. One lesson that we can learn from the example is to listen to the entire message before jumping to conclusions. Notice that Nolvia quickly offers social support for her mother. However, she forgets to listen to the entire message. As a good listener, she should have used her inquiry or responding skills (remember Listening MATERRS) to get more information. Notice that her idea of social support is to offer solutions, not to listen more deeply. As a mother and a wife, Mrs. Gutierrez might feel the need to provide care for her children and husband. And she certainly wouldn't want to interfere with Nolvia's study group.

THINK ON IT

Review our discussion of red, yellow, and green listening in Chapter 2. What type of listening is Nolvia using? What advice would you offer her the next time her mother has a long, stressful day?

Identifying Negative Social Support

The problem is that, even with the best of intentions, we often find ourselves engaging in behaviors that are not supportive of our friends and families. One scholar who

---

> ### TABLE 5.2
>
> ### Negative Social Support Behaviors
>
> - Be wary of giving advice. (It should be desired, be sound, and have the ability to actually solve the problem with few significant disadvantages.)
> - Avoid platitudes. ("It will all work out.") Maybe it will but when someone is in the middle of a crisis, he likely won't feel that way.
> - Don't tell people they should stop crying. Everyone releases emotions differently.
> - Avoid telling people that what they are feeling (or saying) is wrong, embarrassing, and so forth.
> - Don't minimize what people are feeling. ("It's not such a big deal.")
> - Avoid making the support seeker "bad" or responsible for the problem. ("Well, you didn't lock your car; no wonder your CDs were all stolen.")
> - Don't tell others how they should be feeling or that they should forget about the problem or ignore their feelings.

---

spent a good portion of his career studying social support, empathy, and related social interaction skills is Brant Burleson. Professor Burleson identified several types of messages we should avoid.[47] Most of the following examples, if engaged in, will make someone sense that his feelings are unwelcome. The list in Table 5.2 illustrates ways people *don't* show social support.

As you can see, social support attempts that include advice giving and downplaying feelings expressed by others are often perceived as ineffective.[48] Drawing from Chapter 2, you know that these types of responses fall into the yellow category of listening. That is, they acknowledge the speaker but in some way downplay the person's concerns. Other times our attempts to provide social support actually lead the other person to be more dependent.[49] For example, if we constantly jump to help others rather than giving them the option of helping themselves, we might empower a sense of helplessness rather than actually helping the person. Professor Fitch-Hauser's mother is wheelchair bound. However, she rolls herself around the facility in which she lives. The caregivers in that facility encourage her to do as much for herself as possible, rather than doing everything for her. This allows her to feel some sense of independence and pride in knowing she isn't helpless. This in turn contributes to her self-esteem. In addition, the response also keeps the focus off her fragile physical condition and on the more positive aspect of being able to partially take care of herself.

So how does this information translate into your world? Think about your various relationships. Do you have a friend who seems to constantly turn to you for solutions to problems? Notice the question doesn't ask you for *advice;* instead it focuses on asking you for *solutions.* In this type of case, if you constantly provide solutions for the other person, it disempowers that person from taking responsibility for his or her actions.

Now let's reexamine the interaction between Nolvia and Mrs. Gutierrez in Case Study 5.4. In her attempts to be both a good daughter and a supportive family member, Nolvia isn't giving her mother the gift of listening. Instead she is trying to "fix" the problem. Isn't it possible that Mrs. Gutierrez just needs to let off a little steam to a willing ear? If Nolvia had used reflexive responding skills and said something such as, "You sound like you've had a hard day. What can I do to help?" or "Today must have been pretty rough. Want to have a glass of tea and chat a while?" she would have invited her mother to accept support in the form of either action or being listened to.

Problem- and Emotion-focused Support

Previously we talked about directive and nondirective social support. Two other types of support that we need to discuss are **problem-focused support** and **emotion-focused support**. Sometimes we seek support to solve a problem (e.g., you flunked the last exam, your dog keeps jumping the fence), while other times we seek emotional support (e.g., your significant other just dumped you, your dog was hit by a car). According to Professor Burleson, emotional support "includes helping distressed others work through their upset by listening to, empathizing with, legitimizing, and actively exploring their feelings."[50] **Emotional support** is particularly important given that the stress and emotional pain often "stem from the invalidation of the self, either directly (e.g., rejection by a valued other), or indirectly (e.g., failing at something connected to one's self-concept)."[51]

In addition, emotional support for others is one of the primary means we use for showing others we care and are interested in and committed to them. Thus, it is a means of showing compassion and love. As a result, social support is a relationally significant behavior.[52] In fact, a number of researchers suggested that social support skills are fundamental to social competence at all ages (childhood through adulthood) and can affect our ability to have close, personal relationships, such as friendships and dating relationships, marriage, and quality parent-child relationships.[53]

One of the biggest problems we face as conversational listeners and support-givers is that we often feel pressure to speak. Simply being quiet and allowing the other person to have his or her say is difficult. Thus, one of the most important conversational listening lessons we can learn is to refrain from speaking and simply listen. The fact is not everything we think needs to be said. This statement is especially true in the realm of social support. Whether providing emotional or problem-focused support, listening provides the key to giving the type and amount of support that is being sought.

Meeting Social Support Needs

How we feel about the social support we receive is also affected by several things. One of the most important is whether the support we receive matches the support we feel we need. In other words, if you are seeking emotional support, but the person you are talking to is giving you problem-focused support, you are likely going to be dissatisfied with the support you receive. In addition, we tend to want a certain level or amount of support; we don't want too much or too little.[54] For example, you might complain to your parents about a teacher at school but would be mortified if they took it upon themselves to call him or her. As you can see, support-givers can be in a bit of a bind. How can we tell what type of support someone wants or how much support to give her? The problem can sometimes be made worse when those seeking support are indirect or ambiguous about their needs. When this occurs, we might not recognize that assistance is being sought.

Central to support-giving of any type is listening. In an ideal world, we could immediately tell the type of support a person wanted, or he would tell us, "Hey, I need you to help me solve this problem," or "I just need someone to let me talk out my frustration." Unfortunately people are seldom this direct.

Thus, as support-givers, we sometimes rely on those indirect and ambiguous cues mentioned earlier. We have to pay attention to both verbal and nonverbal behaviors that can help us determine who actually wants support and what type of support they are most likely seeking. Communication scholar April Trees studied these nonverbal and verbal behaviors. Focusing on conversations between young adults (ages 17 to 29) and their mothers, Trees found that emotional disclosures (e.g., "I'm really upset," "This is driving me crazy") at the beginning of a conversation were a sign that these adults were seeking social support, either emotional or problem focused. When we hear emotional disclosures that are more in depth or stronger than those normally given, it might be a cue that the person we are talking with is upset or stressed and in need of support. Trees' work also indicates that people might start off with emotional disclosures no matter the type of social support they ultimately are seeking. So as listeners it's important to be aware that emotional disclosures are not necessarily a sign that a person is just seeking emotional support. In terms of nonverbal behaviors, Trees reported that few of her study participants appeared to strategically use nonverbal cues when seeking social support. However, mothers in her study tended to be good at determining when their children were seeking problem-focused support. A louder voice combined with less movement (e.g., kinesics and proxemics) apparently suggested to moms that their children were having problems that they needed advice or help with. Most of us believe that people have less control over their nonverbal behaviors, which might be one reason we cue into them as an indicator of stress.

Seeking and providing social support is one of the primary communication goals we engage in during our daily conversations. However, we also face times when misunderstandings and miscommunications can occur. Occasionally these miscommunications can result in conflict.

CONFLICT

Conflict can be defined as "the interaction of interdependent people who perceive incompatible desires, goals, personal comforts or communication preferences, and the possibility of interference from others as a result of this incompatibility."[55] Conflict can occur at any time and any place, and it will always present a challenge to us as listeners. Listening during conflict can be quite difficult, in part because it is emotionally defined, addresses our identity, and affects our relationships.[56]

We also know that conflict can cost a lot. On a personal level, we lose sleep or can't eat. You might not speak to your brother for a week, missing the opportunity to say happy 21st birthday. You might dismiss what your teacher has to say and so do

© Mike Baldwin/Cornered

"What's important is that we found some common ground. Let's try not to get bogged down over who found it first."

poorly on an exam or assignment. You might break up with your significant other, losing a close confidant. In the workplace, employees leave and new ones must be trained.

In essence, where there are people, there is the potential for conflict: at home, in computer chat rooms, at school, on freeways, or at the office. Regardless of the location and circumstances, there seem to be a number of **sources of conflict**.[57] For example, we differ in the following:

- Judgments of what constitutes good evidence (e.g., Is global warming real or just a weather blip in the history of the world?)
- Personal interests (e.g., who gets the dog in the divorce)
- Beliefs about how something should be done (e.g., flip a coin to decide the winner or have a playoff)
- Role expectations (e.g., beliefs in what a role entails or power imbalances from the roles)
- Communication (e.g., how something is said, how it is interpreted)
- Values (e.g., what is most important to us: spending money on cancer research or reducing carbon emissions)
- Views of relationships (e.g., lack of trust, respect, or honesty; don't feel listened to)

Any of these sources might lead to disagreements, and it's not uncommon for multiple sources to be involved. In addition, what you perceive to be the source of conflict might not fit the other person's perceptions at all. Thus, when addressing any conflict, we have to keep in mind our perceptions of the conflict as well as the actual underlying issues related to the dispute. We also need to keep in mind how the other person perceives the conflict and manages conflict. Getting stuck on who said what and taking ownership of particular ideas, as seen in the cartoon here, is simply counterproductive. So how can you show others you are willing to engage in productive conflict resolution?

Handling Angry People

Good listening skills form the basis for being able to successfully handle the angry person. Introduced by Jeff Bannon, the **Bannon Four Stage Conflict Process** is one means of approaching this type of situation.[58]

First, *you should inquire,* using your active-listening skills to fully focus on the other person's concerns. For example, you might say, "You seem to be upset that you couldn't have Saturday off. Is there something going on we need to know about?" (It's important to let the other party do the talking once you begin exploring the person's concerns.) Second, you should empathize by connecting with the other person on his or her emotional level. This is particularly important in an emotionally charged situation, such as when you are dealing with someone who is angry or experiencing other very strong emotions. As a part of his second stage, Bannon suggested *expressing empathy,* using a two-step model. Step one goes something like this: "I _____ your _____." The blanks can be filled in with words to make phrases such as "I understand your frustration," "I appreciate your concern" and other similar words. This type of statement helps the other know you are attempting to connect with him and better understand his frustration. In the second step of this stage, Bannon suggested using phrases such as "I, too, _____." This blank will be filled in with words that let the other person know that you feel or have felt the same type of emotion (e.g., "I've also missed a family reunion because I couldn't get off from work").

In the third stage, Bannon suggested *asking for permission.* Ask if the other person wants more information; don't just assume that you should automatically give him further explanations. By asking, you give the other person some control over the interaction, and it reduces the chance that you will engage in unwanted problem solving. For example, a question that you would use in a situation such as this is "What information would be helpful?" Be sure to listen carefully to the answer so your response will be appropriate and allow you to move on to the last step.

Finally you should both *explain and offer choices.* If you get a yes in the third stage, you can continue the other person's positive involvement by explaining the situation and offering options from which the other party can select. While Bannon's suggestions won't resolve all your conflicts, they will aid you in many of the common conflicts you face.

Conflict and Culture

Finally a critical component in how we perceive and manage conflict seems to be cultural background. Research done in the United States indicates people from diverse backgrounds will react to conflict differently.[59] Some examples of this include findings that when compared to Americans of European decent, African Americans seem to prefer a highly affect-laden conflict style, while Asian Americans seem to prefer avoiding conflict or turning to a trusted third party and seeking mediation.[60] Further research has indicated that Native Americans take a restrained approach to conflict and often turn to tribal elders to help settle the conflict.[61] From this description, you can see that NaMii and Tamarah, who come from Asian and Native American backgrounds, respectively, probably have some commonality in their approaches to managing conflict. As listeners, we need to be sensitive to these different approaches when we either find ourselves in a conflict situation with someone with a different cultural background or are called upon to mediate such a conflict.

In any context one of the keys to successfully managing conflict is being a good listener. When you find yourself in a conflict, remember to listen to the other parties' perspectives, use rational arguments, value contributions from all parties, and try to understand points of view other than your own.[62] Trying to do all of this might sound like a tall order and it is. Of course, it is impossible to understand other points of view if you aren't listening carefully. This suggests that you focus on what the speaker is saying and keep quiet until he or she is finished. It is also a good idea to paraphrase what you heard before you state your perspectives. This shows the other party that you have indeed remained attentive to what was said. Chances are you have experienced a conflict in which all of these suggestions have been ignored. How might the exchange have been different if you and the other party had followed these guidelines?

It is unrealistic for us to think all conflict is going to be resolved. However, with skill, care, and good listening, we can often arrive at solutions that will resolve at least part of the issues in dispute. If the unresolved issues are really important, you might want to go through the process again, focusing on the unresolved issues. The feeling we are being heard is central to conflict resolution. At the same time, close listening to the other person will help us to better understand the underlying causes of the disagreement, another central element of resolving conflict.

SUMMARY

This chapter began with an example of a conversation between two friends. In that Case Study, we can find elements of conversation that we talked about in this chapter: sensitivity to the other person, appropriate responding, and interaction within the context of a relationship. Listening is an essential element of any conversation. Whether we are engaged in a conflict or a pleasant social exchange, without listening, there is no conversation. Here is a summary of the main points covered in this chapter:

- Conversations are interactions. To have an interaction, there must be listening.
- Meanings in a conversation are cocreated by the participants.
- Conversations are based on the principle of cooperation.

- Conversations thrive on openness.
- Sensitive conversationalists are aware of individual and cultural differences and make appropriate accommodations.
- Good conversationalists provide social support for their partners.
- Conversations take place within the context of a relationship.
- Conflict resolution calls for well-developed conversational and listening skills.

One of the main points made in the chapter is that conversations take place in the context of a relationship. The next two chapters will focus on listening in the relationships of our lives: family, friends, and romantic partners.

CONCEPTS TO KNOW

Grice's Maxims
   Principle of Cooperation
   Four Maxims
Cocreating Conversations
   Generic Responses
   Back Channel
   Listening Noises
   Specific Responses
Individual Differences
   Cognitive Complexity
   Receiver Apprehension
   Self-monitoring
Accommodation
   Underaccommodation

Overaccommodation
Nonaccommodation
Context
Self-verification
Directive and Nondirective Social Support
Positive and Negative Social Support
   Behaviors
Problem- and Emotion-focused Support
Conflict
Sources of Conflict
Bannon's Four Stage Process
Conflict and Culture

DISCUSSION QUESTIONS

1. Do you feel you are guilty of regularly violating one or more of Grice's four maxims? How do you think the violations affect your interactions with others? Which one do you think you violate the most? Why? Describe two to three things you can do to better meet this maxim. Which do you notice other people violating most frequently? Why do you think this maxim stands out for you?

2. Would you rather be high in cognitive complexity or be a high self-monitor? Why? What are some communicative consequences of each?

3. Do you think the amount and type of social support given is influenced by gender? Why or why not? If so, in what ways do you think it varies?

4. This chapter discusses how conflict and conversation differ across cultures. Would you consider male and female to be different cultures? If so, in what ways would conflict and conversation vary between these two cultures?

LISTENING ACTIVITIES

1. With the participants' approval, audio- or videotape a short conversation. It might be between you and a friend, two friends talking over a cup of coffee, or even a short discussion in the classroom. As you listen to the conversation, how do you see/hear Grice's maxims exemplified? How do they help contribute to the flow of the conversation? People often break rules when trying to make a point (e.g., sarcasm, irony). Were there any rules broken? If so, which ones? Did the other person realize a rule was being broken? How did a broken rule affect the conversation?

2. Using the same conversation from the exercise above or a short conversation from a movie or television show, explore how the conversation was cocreated. First, note everything, verbals and nonverbals, that the speaker did to better get his or her point across. Next, listen to the same conversation from the

listener's perspective. What did the listener appear to do to assist the speaker? Were there any behaviors by the speaker or listener that might have negatively affected their conversation? Based on what you've read in this chapter, what could they do differently to improve their conversation experience?

3. How can you use Bannon's stages of conflict resolution? Try the following role-playing exercise. First, write a brief description of a conflict you are dealing with. Get into a group of three. You can role-play the other party while one of your classmates plays you. The third person will coach each of you in how to incorporate these strategies into your interaction. So if the coach hears you making a judgmental statement, he or she will point out the behavior and coach you through the process of incorporating good conflict-resolution behavior.

ADDITIONAL READINGS

Deutsch, M., Coleman, P. T., & Marcus, E. C. (Eds.). (2006). *The handbook of conflict resolution: Theory and practice*. San Francisco: Jossey-Bass.

Fine, D. (2005). *The fine art of small talk*. New York: Hyperion.

Molder, H., & Potter, J. (Eds.). (2005). *Conversation and cognition*. New York: Cambridge University Press.

Oetzel, J. G., & Ting-Toomey, S. (Eds.). (2006). *The Sage handbook of conflict communication: Integrating theory, research, and practice*. Thousand Oaks, CA: Sage.

Rabie, M. (1994). *Conflict resolution and ethnicity*. Westport, CT: Praeger.

Tannen, D. (2005). *Conversational style: Analyzing talk among friends*. New York: Oxford University Press.

Wooffitt, R. (2005). *Conversation analysis and discourse analysis: A comparative and critical introduction*. Thousand Oaks, CA: Sage.

ENDNOTES

1. Bavelas, Coates, & Johnson, 2000
2. Rubin, 1990
3. Janusik, 2007
4. Bohm, 2006
5. Bavelas et al., 2000
6. Yngve, 1970, 2004
7. See Bavelas et al. (2000) for a good summary of research in this area.
8. Krauss & Wienheimer, 1966; Krauss, Garlock, Bricker, & McMahon, 1977; see also Manusov & Patterson, 2006
9. Goodwin, 1981; Kraut, Lewis, & Swezey, 1982; see also Manusov & Patterson, 2006
10. Grice, 1957
11. Brown & Levinson, 1987
12. Slugoski & Hilton, 2001, p. 194
13. Clark & Wilkes-Gibbs, 1986; Schegloff, 1995; Shotter, 1993; Shotter & Gergen, 1994; Stewart, 2006
14. Littlejohn & Domenici, 2001, p. 35
15. Bavelas et al., 2000
16. Bavelas & Chovil, 1997; Bavelas et al., 2000; Goodwin, 1981
17. Bavelas et al., 2000
18. Scott (2004) (pp. 5–6) credits poet and author David Whyte with the original quote.
19. For a review, see Allen (2002).
20. Wheeless, Eddleman-Spears, Magness, & Preiss, 2005
21. Schrodt & Wheeless, 2001; Schrodt, Wheeless, & Ptacek, 2000; Wheeless & Schrodt, 2001
22. Snyder, 1974, 1979
23. Giles, 2008
24. Giles, 2008
25. Giles, 2008
26. Ryan, Hummert, & Boich, 1995
27. Williams, Kemper, & Hummert, 2003
28. Giles, 2008
29. Boggs & Giles, 1999
30. McKellin, Shahin, Hodgson, Jamieson, & Pichora-Fuller, 2007
31. McKellen et al., 2007
32. Pasupathi & Rich, 2005
33. McAdams, 1993; Pasupathi, 2001; Thorne, 2000
34. Bevelas et al., 2000; Dickinson & Givon, 1995; Pasupathi, Stallworth, & Murdoch, 1998; Tatar, 1998
35. Pasupathi & Rich, 2005, p. 1057
36. Bevelas et al., 2000; Grice, 1957
37. For a brief review, see Burleson (2003)
38. Xu & Burleson, 2001
39. Pecchioni & Halone, 2001
40. Fisher, 1997; Fisher, La Greca, Greco Arfken, & Schneiderman, 1997; Harber Schneider, Everard, & Fisher, 2005
41. Bolger & Amarel, 2007; Bolger, Zukerman, & Kessler, 2000; Rafaeli & Gleason, 2009
42. Rafaeli & Gleason, 2009
43. Rafaeli & Gleason, 2009
44. Burleson, 2003, p. 566–567
45. Rafaeli & Gleason, 2009
46. See, for example, Collins & Feeney (2000); Cutrona, Suhr, & MacFarlane (1990); Goldsmith & Parks (1990).
47. Burleson, 2003, p. 567–568
48. Rafaeli & Gleason, 2009
49. Bass, Tausig, & Noelker, 1988–1989
50. Burleson, 2003
51. Burleson, 2003
52. Burleson, 1990
53. Asher, Parker, & Walker, 1996; Burleson, Kunkel, Samter, & Werking, 1996; Burleson, Kunkel, & Birch, 1994; Cunningham & Barbee, 2000; Stevenson, Maton, & Teti, 1999

54. Cutrona, Cohen, & Igram, 1990; Cutrona, 1996; Horowitz et al., 2001
55. Folger, Poole, & Stutman, 2008, p. 5
56. Bodtker & Jameson, 2001
57. Isenhart & Spangle, 2000
58. Bannon, 2003
59. Bresnahan, Donohue, Shearman, & Guan, 2009
60. Hecht, Jackson, & Ribeau, 2003; Ting-Toomey & Chung, 2005
61. Ting-Toomey & Chung, 2005
62. Simonsen & Klispch, 2001

REFERENCES

Allen, M. (2002). A synthesis and extension of constructivist comforting research. In M. Allen, R. W. Preiss, B. M. Gayle, & Nancy Burrell (Eds.), *Interpersonal communication research: Advances through meta-analysis* (pp. 227–246). Mahwah, NJ: Lawrence Erlbaum.

Asher, S. R., Parker, J. G., & Walker, D. L. (1996). Distinguishing friendship from acceptance: Implications for intervention and assessment. In W. M. Bukowski, A. F. Newcomb, & W. W. Hartup (Eds.), *The company they keep: Friendship in childhood and adolescence* (pp. 366–405). New York: Cambridge University Press.

Bannon, J. (2003, October). Anger at work: Whether it's others' or your own, here's how to deal with it. *Training & Development*. Retrieved from http://findarticles.com/p/articles/mi_m0MNT/is_10_57/ai_108787970/.

Bass, D. M., Tausig, M. B., & Noelker, L. S. (1988–1989). Elder impairment, social support and caregiver strain: A framework for understanding support's effects. *Journal of Applied Social Sciences, 13,* 80–115.

Bavelas, J. B., & Chovil, N. (1997). Faces in dialogue. In J. A. Russell & J. M. Fernandez-Dols (Eds.), *The psychology of facial expression* (pp. 334–348). Cambridge: Cambridge University Press.

Bavelas, J. B., Coates, L., & Johnson, T. (2000). Listeners as co-narrators. *Journal of Personality and Social Psychology, 79,* 941–952.

Bodtker, A. M., & Jameson, J. K. (2001). Emotion in conflict formation and its transformation: Application to organizational conflict management. *International Journal of Conflict Management, 12,* 259–275.

Boggs, C., & Giles, H. (1999). The canary in the cage: The nonaccomodation cycle in the gendered workplace. *International Journal of Applied Linguistics, 22,* 223–245.

Bohm, D. (2006). *On dialogue.* London: Routledge.

Bolger, N., & Amarel, D. (2007). Effects of social support visibility on adjustment to stress: Experimental evidence. *Journal of Personality and Social Psychology, 92,* 458–475.

Bolger, N., Zuckerman, A., and Kessler, R. C. (2000). Invisible support and adjustment to stress. *Journal of Personality and Social Psychology, 79,* 953–961.

Bresnahan, M. J., Donohue, W. A., Shearman, S. M., & Guan, X. (2009). Research note: Two measures of conflict orientation. *Conflict Resolution Quarterly, 26,* 365–379.

Brown, P., & Levinson, S. C. (1987). *Politeness: Some universals in language usage.* Cambridge, UK: Cambridge University Press.

Burleson, B. R. (1990). Comforting as everyday social support: Relational consequences of supportive behaviors. In S. Duck (Ed.), *Personal relationships and social support* (pp. 63–104). Beverly Hills: Sage.

Burleson, B. R. (2003). The experience and effects of emotional support: What the study of cultural and gender differences can tell us about close relationships, emotion, and interpersonal communication. *Personal Relationships, 10,* 1–23.

Burleson, B. R., Kunkel, A. W., & Birch, J. D. (1994). Thoughts about talk in romantic relationships: Similarity makes for attraction (and happiness, too). *Communication Quarterly, 42,* 259–273.

Burleson, B. R., Kunkel, A. W., Samter, W., & Werking, K. J. (1996). Men's and women's evaluations of communication skills in personal relationships: When sex differences make a difference—and when they don't. *Journal of Social and Personal Relationships, 13,* 201–224.

Clark, H. H., & Wilkes-Gibbs, D. (1986). Referring as a collaborative process. *Cognition, 22,* 1–39.

Collins, N. L., & Feeney, B. C. (2000). A safe haven: Support-seeking and caregiving processes in intimate relationships. *Journal of Personality and Social Psychology, 78,* 1053–1073.

Cunningham, M. R., & Barbee, A. P. (2000). Social support. In C. Hendrick & S. S. Hendrick (Eds.), *Close relationships: A sourcebook* (pp. 272–285). Thousand Oaks, CA: Sage.

Cutrona, C. E. (1996). *Social support in couples; Marriage as a resource in times of stress.* Thousand Oaks, CA: Sage.

Cutrona, C. E., Cohen, B. B., & Igram, S. (1990). Contextual determinants of perceived social support. *Journal of Personal and Social Relationships, 7,* 553–562.

Cutrona, C. E., Suhr, J. A., & MacFarlane, R. (1990). Interpersonal transactions and the psychological sense of support. In S. Duck & R. Silver (Eds.), *Personal relationships and social support* (pp. 30–45). London: Sage.

Dickinson, C., & Givon, T. (1995). Memory and conversation: Toward an experimental paradigm. In T. Givon (Ed.), *Conversation: Cognitive, communicative, and social perspectives* (pp. 91–132). Amsterdam: John Benjamin.

Fisher, E. B., Jr., (1997). Two approaches to social support in smoking cessation: Commodity model and nondirective support. *Addictive Behaviors, 22,* 818–833.

Fisher, E. B., Jr., La Greca, A. M., Greco, P., Arfken, C., & Schneiderman, N. (1997). Directive and nondirective support in diabetes management. *International Journal of Behavioral Medicine, 4,* 131–144.

Folger, J. P., Poole, M. S., & Stutman, R. K. (2008). *Working through conflict: Strategies for relationships, groups, and organizations* (6th ed.). Boston: Allyn & Bacon.

Giles, H. (2008). Accommodating translational research. *Journal of Applied Communication Research, 36,* 121–127.

Goldsmith, D., & Parks, M. (1990). Communication strategies for managing the risks of seeking social support. In S. Duck (Ed., with R. Silver), *Personal relationships and social support* (pp. 104–121). London: Sage.

Goodwin, C. (1981). *Conversational organization: Interactions between speakers and hearers.* New York: Academic.

Grice, H. P. (1957). Meaning. *Philosophical Review, 66,* 377–388.

Harber, K. D., Schneider, J. K., Everard, K., & Fisher, E. (2005). Nondirective support, directive support, and morale. *Journal of Social and Clinical Psychology, 24,* 691–722.

Hecht, M. L., Jackson, R. L., & Ribeau, S. (2003). *African American communication: Exploring identity and culture* (2nd ed.). Mahwah, NJ: Lawrence Erlbaum.

Horowitz, L. M., Krasnoperova, E. N., Tatar, D. G., Hansen, M. B., Person, E. A., Galvin, K. L., & Nelson, K. L. (2001). The way to console may depend on the goal: Experimental studies of social support. *Journal of Experimental Social Psychology, 37,* 49–61.

Isenhart, M. W., & Spangle, M. (2000). *Collaborative approaches to resolving conflict.* Thousand Oaks, CA: Sage.

Janusik, L. A. (2007). Building listening theory: The validation of the conversational listening span. *Communication Studies, 58,* 139–156.

Krauss, R., Garlock, C., Bricker, P., & McMahon, L. (1977). The role of audible and visible back-channel responses in interpersonal communication. *Journal of Personality and Social Psychology, 35,* 523–529.

Krauss, R. M., & Wienheimer, S. (1966). Concurrent feedback, confirmation, and the encoding of references in verbal communication. *Journal of Personality and Social Psychology, 4,* 343–346.

Kraut, R., Lewis, S., & Swezey, L. W. (1982). Listener responsiveness and the coordination of conversation. *Journal of Personality and Social Psychology, 43,* 718–731.

Littlejohn, S. W., & Domenici, K. (2001). *Engaging communication in conflict.* Thousand Oaks, CA: Sage.

Manusov, V., & Patterson, M. L. (2006). *The Sage handbook of nonverbal communication.* Thousand Oaks, CA: Sage.

McAdams, D. P. (1993). *The stories we live by: Personal myths and the making of the self.* New York: Guilford.

McKellin, W. H., Shahin, K., Hodgson M., Jamieson, J., & Pichora-Fuller, K. (2007). Pragmatics of conversation and communication in noisy settings. *Journal of Pragmatics, 39,* 2159–2184.

Pasupathi, M. (2001). The social construction of the personal past and its implications for adult development. *Psychological Bulletin, 127,* 651–672.

Pasupathi, M., & Rich, B. (2005). Inattentive listening undermines self-verification in personal storytelling. *Journal of Personality, 73,* 1051–1085.

Pasupathi, M., Stallworth, L. M., & Murdoch, K. (1998). How what we tell becomes what we know: Listener effects on speakers' long-term memory for events. *Discourse Processes, 26,* 1–25.

Pecchioni & Halone, 2001. Relational listening: A grounded theoretical model. *Communication Research Reports, 14,* 59–71.

Rafaeli, E., & Gleason, M. E. J. (2009). Skilled support within intimate relationships. *Journal of Family Theory & Review, 1,* 20–37.

Rubin, R. B. (1990). Communication competence. In G. Phillips & J. T. Wood (Eds.), *Speech communication:*

Essays to commemorate the 75th anniversary of the Speech Communication Association (pp. 94–129). Carbondale, IL: Southern Illinois University Press.

Ryan, E. B., Hummert, M. L., & Boich, L. (1995). Communication predicaments of aging: Patronizing behavior toward older adults. *Journal of Language and Social Psychology, 13,* 144–166.

Schegloff, E. A. (1995). Discourse as an international achievement III: The omnirelevance of action. *Research on Language and Social Interaction, 28,* 185–211.

Schrodt, P., & Wheeless, L. R. (2001). Aggressive communication and informational reception apprehension: The influence of listening anxiety and intellectual inflexibility on trait argumentativeness and verbal aggressiveness. *Communication Quarterly, 49,* 53–69.

Schrodt, P., Wheeless, L. R., & Ptacek, K. M. (2000). Informational reception apprehension, educational motivation, and achievement. *Communication Quarterly, 48,* 60–73.

Scott, S. (2004). *Fierce conversations.* New York: Berkeley.

Shotter, J. (1993). *Conversational realities: Constructing life through language.* Beverly Hills: Sage.

Shotter, J., & Gergen, K. (1994). Social construction: Knowledge, self, others, and continuing the conversation. In S. Deetz (Ed.), *Communication Yearbook 17* (pp. 3–33). Thousand Oaks, CA: Sage.

Simonsen, A., & Klispch, K. (2001, December). Conflict with class. *Parks & Recreation,* 77–79.

Slugoski, B. R., & Hilton, D. J. (2001). Conversation. In W. P. Robinson & H. Giles (Eds.), *The new handbook of language and social psychology* (pp. 193–219). New York: John Wiley & Sons.

Snyder, M. (1974). Self-monitoring of expressive behavior. *Journal of Personality and Social Psychology, 30,* 526–537.

Snyder, M. (1979). Self-monitoring process. In L. Berkowitz (Ed.), *Advances in Experimental Social Psychology* (vol. 12, pp. 85–128). New York: Academic.

Stevenson, W., Maton, K. I., & Teti, D. M. (1999). Social support, relationship quality, and well-being among pregnant adolescents. *Journal of Adolescence, 22,* 109–121.

Stewart, J. (2006). Communication and interpersonal communicating. In J. Stewart (Ed.), *Bridges not walls* (9th ed., pp. 16–41). New York: McGraw-Hill.

Tatar, D. (1998). *Social and personal consequences of a preoccupied listener.* Unpublished dissertation, Stanford University, Stanford, CA.

Thorne, A. (2000). Personal memory telling and personality development. *Personality and Social Psychology Review, 4,* 45–56.

Ting-Toomey, S., & Chung, L.C. (2005). *Understanding intercultural communication.* Los Angeles: Roxbury.

Wheeless, L. R., Eddleman-Spears, L., Magness, L. D., & Preiss, R. W. (2005). Informational reception apprehension and information from technology aversion: Development of a new construct. *Communication Quarterly, 53,* 143–158.

Wheeless, L. R., & Schrodt, P. (2001). An examination of cognitive foundations of informational reception apprehension: Political identification, religious affiliation, and family environment. *Communication Research Reports, 18,* 1–10.

Williams, K., Kemper, S., & Hummert, M. L. (2003). Improving nursing home communication: An intervention to reduce elderspeak. *The Gerontologist, 43,* 242–247.

Xu, Y., & Burleson, B. R. (2001). Effects of sex, culture, and support type on perceptions of spousal social support: An assessment of the "support gap" hypothesis in early marriage. *Human Communication Research, 27,* 535–566.

Yngve, V. H. (1970). On getting a word in edgewise. *Papers from the Sixth Regional Meeting, Chicago Linguistic Society* (pp. 567–578). Chicago: Chicago Linguistic Society.

Yngve, V. H. (2004). The conduct of hard-science research. In V. H. Yngve & Z. Wasik (Eds.), *Hard-science linguistics* (pp. 342–367). London: Continuum International.

Listening and Relationship Building

The Family Context

All in the Family

Carter, you are so lucky, that your sisters are older and have moved away. My sisters are driving me crazy. They call me all the time and complain about our parents. Personally, I don't see how my mom and dad deal with having two teenage girls in the house. They seem to either be talking and giggling or whining. And when I give them advice about whatever they're complaining about, they ignore me. Man, I hope my little brother doesn't get that way when he gets a little older.

Wow, Radley, you sound pretty frustrated. I always thought you were lucky to be the oldest and have siblings at home. I kind of felt like an only child when I was growing up since my youngest sister is 15 years older than me. You and your family always seem to be so close.

Well, I guess we really are. Even though both Mom and Dad are really busy, they have always stressed the importance of having family time to talk and listen to one another. Even the "brats" seem to set aside their adolescent nonsense and listen. You know, I even kind of like them then.

Radley, you'd better not let them hear you call them "brats." ◼

LISTENING IN RELATIONSHIPS

Listening is a critical element in successful relationships. We feel this so strongly that we devote two chapters to the subject. This chapter will focus on family relationships, and the next one, on friends and romantic partners. Certainly there are similarities in listening needs in any type of relationship. However, as you will see, some of the listening demands placed on you will vary as you interact with others on different relational levels. For example, think about how you listen to your best friend, your significant other, your teacher or adviser, your parents, or your cousin. Don't you listen to all of them just a little bit differently? Don't you expect them to listen to you in different ways?

All humans depend on relationships. In fact, one of the most fundamental of human needs is to connect with others, to establish and maintain human relationships.[1] As infants, our parents and other family members were our first introduction to relationships. The attitudes expressed by our families and the experiences we share with them profoundly influence us: our self-concept and self-esteem, how we listen and express ourselves, and ultimately how we view and build our own relationships. Relationship history develops over time and over our life span. The first and most important relationships we have begin with our families.

One of the most challenging aspects of looking at listening in the family context is the very shape of families today. Many of us grew up with a mental picture of a family that we picked up from television. That mental picture, whether it be like the Cleavers of the 1950s or the Simpsons from today, probably includes a married, heterosexual couple with both biological parents present. Chances are, however, fewer than 50 percent of you come from that type of family.[2] More current shows are portraying a different picture of a family. For example, the television show *Two and a Half Men* features a boy being raised by his divorced father and playboy uncle. Many children today are being raised by a single parent, are in shared-custody arrangements, are part of blended families, or are being raised by grandparents or other relatives. Dads are increasingly choosing to stay home and take on primary parenting roles. In addition, it is more acceptable for single parents and gay and lesbian couples to adopt or have biological children in their own family unit.

> **THINK ON IT**
>
> Think about your own family. How many members does it have? How old are you? Your parents? Siblings? Grandparents? What about your ethnic background and culture? How do you think your family makeup affects the relationships and communication within your family?

The age factor in families also varies from the existing stereotype. What do you think of when you think of a family? Our guess is that you will envision parents who are about 20 to 25 years older than their children and grandparents who are 40 to 50 years older than the grandchildren. In 2002 the average age of a first-time grandparent was 47, the lowest in history.[3] Depending on when children are born, the age distance between generations can run from 15 to 40 years. Needless to say, the abilities and contributions of grandparents and other relatives to family life can be affected by their age.[4]

Finally cultural and ethnic background affects family functions and communication. Who does what, who has power (or doesn't), and nonverbal expressiveness are just a few things that are affected by the culture, society, and family we are born into. For example, the characters featured in the cases at the beginning of each chapter come from different backgrounds. Consequently their family communication is likely to be different. Nolvia is Honduran and her grandparents play a very important part in her family. NaMii is Korean and since her father is the eldest son, his parents live with them. Tamarah is Native American, Ben is Jewish, and so forth. Much like the "characters" who are part of your lives, each of them faces slightly different family concerns. However, regardless of the family makeup or background, it is safe for us to say that the family in which we grow up as well as other adults who are important to us have a profound effect on our listening behavior.

WHY STUDY LISTENING IN FAMILIES?

Of the many communication behaviors advocated by family communication experts, listening is the most common.[5] One of the problems, however, is that most of our parents were not taught good listening skills. If we're lucky, we end up in a family that values and teaches good listening, such as Radley's in the Case Study at the beginning of this chapter. If we aren't so lucky, we have to spend a lot more time learning the basics on our own, often through our mistakes.

The importance of the communication in our families to us can't be overemphasized. A family's communication patterns can influence information processing in children (e.g., political views, media use), behaviors (e.g., conflict styles and behaviors, self-disclosure), and psychosocial tendencies (e.g., anxiety, self-concept, relational satisfaction, communication apprehension).[6] To illustrate the importance of the effect of family communication patterns, think of your family as your first "communication classroom."[7] A number of family-related variables affect how we develop and use social and communication skills with our friends and peers. How we learn to talk and listen to one another, how we discuss and argue, and how we give and receive affection are all profoundly influenced by our family relationships. The communication skills we practice as children with family and peers enable us to successfully adjust later in life.[8]

> **THINK ON IT**
>
> How was communication handled in your family? Did you feel free to express your concerns? Do you feel family members listened to you? Did you listen to family members?

People who are skilled communicators tend to enjoy a number of positive psychosocial outcomes. For example, they tend to be less lonely, be more accepted by their peers, have better relationships, and generally be more sociable. Other positive social behaviors include being friendly; having greater impulse control; being more person-centered when communicating; and having a greater tendency to be more helpful, share more, and comfort others. In addition, communication and social competence appear to be linked.[9] Socially skilled children are better able to regulate their own and to "read" others' emotions and nonverbals, to strategically choose the best communicative means of reaching personal and social goals (e.g., persuasion, compromising), and balance personal goals while maintaining positive relationships with others.[10]

To gain a better understanding of the role listening plays in family communication and how it is related to these positive outcomes, we first look at several general family communication factors; then we study the effect of family stories and family conflict on our attitudes and behaviors toward listening. We wrap up the chapter with an examination of the communication between parents and children and factors affecting our communication with older adults.

FAMILY COMMUNICATION FEATURES

As we established in the previous chapter, listening is a critical component of any context in which a conversation occurs. For us to understand the role and effect of listening in family relationships, we first need a basic understanding of how families are structured and how elements of that structure can affect family conversations.

How a family functions has a huge effect on the quality of family life. Good communication often sets successful families apart from the rest. According to many scholars, the family is one of the most important contexts in which we learn important social skills.[11] Some even suggest that we learn how to shape and interpret messages from the communication patterns we learn at home.[12]

Family Orientation Schemata

To illustrate just how family can affect your future listening and communication behavior, we need to examine factors that affect our schemata and look at how schema theory applies to family communication. In Chapter 3 you learned about the effect of schemata on how you take in, perceive, process, and store information. The schema that you learn from the communication patterns in your family influences whether you value listening and are willing to listen in a relationship. **Family communication schemata** have been defined as "knowledge structures that represent the external world of the family and provide a basis for interpreting what other family members say and do."[13] These schemata may well influence our interactions in *all* our future relationships.[14] Researchers Ascan Koerner and Mary Ann Fitzpatrick feel that these schemata are originally shaped by how parents communicate with each other and their children. They also feel that the schemata are reflected in the communication behaviors as family members interact with each other.

Koerner and Fitzpatrick proposed that families have one of two orientations to, or schemata, about communication.[15] The first one is **conversation orientation.** Conversation orientation is the degree to which a family encourages its members to participate in unrestricted discussions about a wide variety of subjects. If your family has high conversation orientation, you grew up interacting frequently and embraced open and direct conversations regardless of how controversial the topic may have been. On the other hand, if your family has low conversation orientation, you didn't feel particularly free to share your thoughts or opinions with other members of the family.

The second orientation that Koerner and Fitzpatrick propose is **conformity orientation.** Conformity orientation is the extent to which a family stresses the importance of having homogenous attitudes, values, and beliefs. If your family is high in conformity orientation, it stresses the importance of hierarchy and clear rules. Parents enforce the rules and don't tolerate deviation from family norms and expectations. This type of family tends to avoid conflict. Low-conformity-orientation families encourage the diversity of thought and opinion. They also encourage children to ask questions and challenge family rules. That is, they tend to encourage healthy conflict management as well as freedom to negotiate house rules.[16]

As you think about the family orientations we just covered, you can begin to see how family communication patterns can have great effect on your development as a communicator and listener. Families that promote open interaction on a variety of topics tend to create an environment that encourages active listening and critical thinking.[17] On the other hand, research indicates that children from high-conversation-conformity families tend to have more listening anxiety and intellectual inflexibility.[18]

THINK ON IT

What type of conversation orientation and conformity orientation did your family exhibit when you were growing up? How does it differ from that of some of your friends? How do you think it has affected your interactions with others?

While our family backgrounds set the stage for our listening behavior, we have the choice of whether we want to perpetuate the pattern and follow the same communication scripts. In the following sections, we will talk about three aspects of family communication we feel influence what type of communication orientation a family has: talk, confirmation, and self-disclosure.

Family Talks

Talking goes beyond saying, "I love you," to include direct conversations about our family relationships. As we noted in the previous chapter, conversations are part of what makes us social animals. The sharing of daily events, addressing problems that arise, and comparing perceptions are important for developing a relationship. It is through talk that people are connected. Think about the Case Study at the beginning of the chapter. Radley feels connected to his siblings because they talk regularly. Carter, whose sisters are much older and left home while he was a child, feels less connected with them. The true difference is that Carter and his sisters had less opportunity to talk than do Radley and his sisters. However, talk is at best only half of the equation. Feeling loved and accepted are two goals that are closely tied to family conversations. Notice that Radley, even in his frustration with his adolescent sisters, recognized the power of listening to the talk in his family. He clearly feels love and acceptance. When family members listen, they establish high conversation orientation or an atmosphere that encourages family talk time. This in turn, as you read in the previous section, establishes listening as an important and valued skill.

Research validates this conclusion. One dimension of family communication is family strength.[19] **Strong families** are characterized by the following:

- Commitment to the family and well-being of its members
- Positive communication and the ability to engage in constructive conflict management
- Regular expression and confirmation of affection among family members
- Enjoyment of quality time together
- A feeling of spiritual well-being
- Ability to effectively manage stress and crisis situations

As you read the list, you can see that both talk and listening are critical to several of these characteristics. For example, in order to have positive communication and expression and confirmation of affection, both talking and listening must occur.

Research into strong families reflects a further connection with the relationship between family talk and family schema. One study found that strong stepfamilies engaged in more everyday talk, openness, and family problem solving than did families struggling to blend.[20] Other studies have found that families who value expressiveness were more likely to be cohesive and adaptable. On the other hand, families with a schema of structural traditionalism and conflict avoidance tend to be less cohesive and adaptable.[21] Overall, research supports the conclusion that families' attitudes toward talk, or expressiveness, are an important aspect of the family schema. Of course, when a family supports talk, we assume that the positive attitude toward expressiveness includes the supportive element of listening. It is partially through listening that we provide confirmation to others.

Confirmation

Confirming messages are one of the important ways in which the identities we seek to construct are maintained. These messages imply an acceptance of and by others. However, messages are not always verbal. We can engage in confirmation nonverbally, as when we include others in our conversations. Ignoring people, talking about them as if they were not there, or excluding them from conversations (verbally or nonverbally) are just a few of the ways we can send disconfirming messages. When we get disconfirming messages, we assume we aren't being listened to, and when we send nonconfirming messages, we are sending messages that we aren't willing to listen.

Whether we are prone to sending confirming or disconfirming messages seems to be part of the family communication schema. For example, husbands and wives seem to use many of the same nonverbal behaviors when they convey negative emotions toward something the other spouse is saying.[22] This commonality for the type of **back-channel messages** (nonverbal messages) being sent would indicate that the family (or at least the parents) has developed a schema for how to react in such situations.

We can also find support for the inclusion of confirmation in family schema by looking at behaviors associated with family communication patterns. In families with high conformity orientation, parents often set the pattern of withdrawing confirmation and affection when the child fails to conform to the expected family standards.[23] In contrast, families low in conformity and high in conversation tend to be much more forthcoming with positive confirmation.

> **THINK ON IT**
>
> Who do you look toward for confirmation? Who looks toward you for confirmation? Can you identify any patterns in confirmation behavior in your family?

Many messages we rely on for confirmation are responses to various levels of intimacy. For example, if you are very close to someone, you will probably use a pleasant voice when talking with him as well as have a more pleasant facial expression. In addition, you will probably also confirm the relationship and your feelings for the person by using personal nicknames and increasing the level of verbal intimacy.[24] On the other hand, when the level of intimacy is less, as when you are talking with someone you don't know well or are in the midst of a conflict, you may compensate by leaning forward and increasing attention, almost as if you are trying to resolve the loss of connection with the other person. The level of intimacy will be determined by the levels of affection, trust, involvement, similarity, and familiarity you feel toward the other person.[25] For most of us, our most intimate relationships are with family members. When those we care for and depend on, our families, send us confirming messages, we tend to feel more confident and listened to. We also tend to be more comfortable with self-disclosure.

Self-disclosure

By now, you have an understanding of the importance of self-disclosure in our lives. However, self-disclosure takes on an even greater importance in families. It is in families that we first come to trust others and to open up to them, to tell them something personal or private. As young children we may not have fully realized that we were engaging in self-disclosure. However, as we grow older, we come to realize the implications of disclosing to family (and friends).

Keeping in mind that families construct the social reality of children, it's easy to see how the pattern for self-disclosure practiced by your family affects your willingness to share your thoughts, background, and feelings with others.[26] Families high in communication orientation encourage open discussion, including self-disclosure.

It is interesting to note that self-disclosure in parent-child relationships suggests that the amount and nature of disclosure differs among family members. Think about your own life. Do you tell some things to your mom and other things to your dad or a sibling? Not surprisingly the parent who is seen as the most nurturing and supportive tends to receive greater disclosure. In addition, parents are often very good at reading their children's nonverbals. They can tell when children are pretending to be upset or scared and when they actually are. In such cases nonverbals lead to a parent inviting self-disclosure from a child. Higher levels of disclosure tend to occur more often in dyads.[27] It can be difficult for families with multiple children to have alone time with one child. It might be even less likely to happen in blended families. Trust (and liking) leads to self-disclosure, and the time we spend together is necessary to building trust and developing liking. Research in family communication suggests it can take blended families (e.g., stepfamilies) more than five years to develop a solid foundation of positive social relationships.[28]

Marriage and family therapist Glenn Boyd wrote, "listening changes the relationship."[29] The truth of this statement is most evident when we look at the effect of how family members react to disclosure. When our family members listen to us, we are more likely to engage in self-disclosure. Feeling listened to provides us with a sense of being rewarded for our openness. So families that show they are interested in each other's feelings and emotions, and who want to know what's going on in each other's lives, are more likely to disclose. Once again we can see the positive effect of a high-conversation–low-conformity family.

Similar patterns of disclosure are seen across all types of families: stepfamilies, single-parent or two-parent biological families.[30] How we disclose is more often related to the family structure or system. Does your family sit down together at meals? Without the television on? Do you take family vacations together? Is there an expectation that you share what went on in your day? One family we know tends to take an evening walk together almost every day. During that time, with few interruptions, they are able to catch up on each other's day and stay connected with one another. The walk is family listening time.

Of course, the value of self-disclosure occurs only when we attempt to be honest and accurate in our disclosures. Such disclosure brings people together. However, not everyone is so honest. Some individuals attempt to manipulate or control us by engaging in pseudo self-disclosure. At other times, individuals choose not to self-disclose because they believe it might hurt the other's feelings. For

THINK ON IT

Looking at your own family members, do you disclose some information to your mom and other information to a sibling? Or a grandparent? How and why does your disclosure differ?

example, if your little brother takes up the tuba and is really awful at it, you may be rather circumspect in your comments so you don't discourage him. As a perceptive family listener, you will know when to be direct and when to be kind.

THE ROLE OF FAMILY STORIES

Another important element of family communication is family stories. In a recent e-mail, family communication scholar Jody Koenig Kellas outlined the importance of storytelling to family life. She wrote, "Stories and storytelling are one of the primary ways that families and family members make sense of everyday, as well as difficult, events, create a sense of individual and group identity, remember, connect generations, and establish guidelines for family behavior. With so many important functions, storytelling is a significant but still understudied communicative process for the family."[31]

Family stories are also one of the ways that we become family. Listen closely to your own family stories. As listeners, we are often unaware of the influence that stories have on us and our family life. Our understanding of what family is (and isn't) and what family members do (and don't do) are embedded in the stories we hear. So stories are one of the many contexts where listening is central to family life. Hearing about your grandmother's wedding day catastrophe, your aunt's lottery win, the cousin who was told she would never have children but did, implicitly and explicitly inform our views of what it means to be a family.

Establishing Family Schemata and Scripts

Family stories are one means of establishing and/or reinforcing family scripts or schemata. As you learned in Chapter 3, **scripts** (i.e., expectations, beliefs, norms) help us assign meaning to an interaction and act as a guide to behavior. When scripts are "broken" or violated by one family member, other family members may see that break as a threat to family stability and attempt to bring that family member back into line.[32] Just as with other schemata, family communication schemata provide a basis for interpreting the communication and actions of other family members. They also tend to establish how members of a family communicate, as you learned earlier in this chapter. When family members have a common family communication schema, they are more likely to agree on other dimensions of family life.[33] For example, family members may be more likely to agree on the dimension of **expressiveness,** the level to which family members (including children) are encouraged to express viewpoints, ideas, and emotions. The family communication schema will also have an effect on the types of stories family members tell. Since stories reflect the family values and norms, the family schema will also reflect what is emphasized in the stories.

Another aspect of family schema is **structural traditionalism,** which is how much family members embrace conventional notions of marriage and family life (i.e., parents have the ability/authority to get children to conform to family life). While the structure of the family doesn't affect listening, the rigidity of the value

> **THINK ON IT**
>
> What commonalities can you find between structural traditionalism and avoidance and conversation and conformity orientation?

reflects how willing family members are to listen to points of view that challenge their beliefs. For example, if someone feels that a family is only two heterosexual people legally connected to each other by the laws of the land (marriage license), they are unlikely to consider other perspectives on family. They may also feel that children should be strictly subservient to parental control and, therefore, not encourage children to express themselves.

Yet another aspect of family schema is avoidance. **Avoidance** addresses how much family members will avoid conflict (e.g., avoid engaging in an unapproved behavior; avoid certain topics of conversation). Additional research in this area by Paul Schrodt suggests that families that are more expressive and willing to address issues of contention (i.e., willing to engage in some conflict, address uncomfortable topics) tend to have stronger emotional family bonds.[34] More important, from a listening perspective, this indicates such families encourage listening to dissenting voices.

Regardless of the schema, you will hear the related values reflected in the stories that a family tells, particularly those that are told repeatedly. As a member of a family, you learn a great deal about who you are, what is expected of you, and how you should behave from these stories.

Professors Sunwolf and Lawrence Frey, who have written extensively about the role of storytelling in our lives, agree with Professor Kellas's comment on the relationship between storytelling and personal identity. They argued that "Storytelling is a tool for the construction of shared identities and communities."[35] As we grow up listening to the tales told by our families, our lives are influenced in many ways: our self-concept is shaped, our notion of individual choice (both ability and range) is developed, our perception of our individual power is formed, and our view of community (and our place in it) is molded. This is one reason Sunwolf and Frey believe that we are socialized via the stories we hear (by our family, friends, teachers, religious leaders).

THINK ON IT

What type of stories have you heard in your family? What do they tell you about yourself? Your family? Your culture? Their beliefs, attitudes, and values? What is valued? (And just as important, what is not?)

It is also through narratives that our culture makes itself known. The attributes that are important to your family (and your culture) are often expressed in the stories you hear. For example, many of the stories told by the Landreth side of Professor Worthington's family stress individual sacrifice for the family. Her great-grandmother's family moved from downtown to outside the big city of Atlanta (at the turn of the 20th century) because the doctor said her brother (one of 16 siblings) needed fresh, country air to cure him of "consumption." Stories told by the Owens side of her family often stress hard work, frugality, and religious conviction. Professor Fitch-Hauser's stories are quite different. She is both Korean and adopted, and her family's stories often emphasize family as residing in the heart, not based on biological ties. They also emphasize the importance of making one's own mark in the world, independent of family history. Other stories emphasize the character-building aspect of the struggle to fit in and the importance of accepting others, regardless of their ethnic backgrounds, physical abilities, or appearance.

As we noted earlier, family stories are one of the primary ways we communicate family identity. Previous research has found family storytelling to be related to overall family satisfaction and family functioning.[36] It is through family stories we

learn the norms, values, and goals of our family, and subsequently stories then help establish the standards for
family relationships. Other research has found that families differ in their level of storytelling engagement, turn-
taking, perspective-taking, and coherence.[37] **Engagement**
refers to both the overall responsiveness and liveliness of
other family members (verbal and nonverbal) during the
telling of the story as well as the level of warmth embed-

> **THINK ON IT**
>
> Engage your family in a storytelling session.
> (If possible, audiotape it.) Analyze the
> session in terms of engagement, turn-taking,
> perspective, and coherence. How does your
> family work together to tell stories?

ded within the story. **Turn-taking** is discussed more in depth elsewhere in the text,
but here it refers to not only turns of talk but also how dynamic and/or polite family members are when they listen. **Perspective-taking** refers to family members'
ability to confirm the perspectives of other family members and to take those
perspectives and experiences into account while telling a story. Finally **coherence**
is related to family members' ability to work together during the joint telling of a
story to be able to integrate it into a larger whole.

Some families are more prone to storytelling than others. If you want to learn
more about your family, try the following:

- Generally ask open-ended questions (e.g., Where were you born? What was
  your favorite birthday celebration? What was your favorite class, teacher, or
  friend in school?).
- Of course, listen. Interest is often the key to getting a person to feel more at
  ease and willing to share her stories with you.
- Try getting a storytelling session going around a holiday or other family
  event. You often have relatives there who are not part of your everyday life.
- Record family stories and provide copies for relatives living away from home.
  They could have something to add to the stories as well.

Our personal propensity for storytelling, the family schemata we hold, the
family orientations we share are all learned behaviors. While we interact with
many family members, our parents (or those holding parental roles) tend to be
among the most influential. The next section examines the influence of parents on
our communication and listening attitudes and skills.

PARENTS AS COMMUNICATION TEACHERS

Learning Conversational Rules

In the previous chapter, we discussed the relationship between Grice's maxims of
conversation and listening. Parent/guardian–child conversations are where most
children learn these rules. For example, children as young as two can follow some
aspects of the cooperative principle, and kindergarteners are amazingly good at
identifying utterances that violate Grice's maxims (i.e., quantity, quality, manner,
relation).[38] When small children do violate a maxim, they often do not respond
(quantity) or don't understand the communication well enough to respond appropriately (relation).[39] Some research suggests mothers and fathers respond differently to these rule violations.[40] For example, fathers are more likely to point out
violations by using repetition to encourage an appropriate response or by modeling

correct responses. Both moms and dads use clarification to notify children of rule violations (often by making a statement or asking a question). However, mothers are more likely to not respond to a violation, most likely because of a greater concern for maintaining the conversation. For example, if a child responds off topic, mothers are more likely than fathers to change topics.

Since family interaction is our first communication learning laboratory, we learn about the rules of conversations from observing and interacting with our parents and other family members. As children, we learn much more than the semantics and syntax of the language spoken in the home. We also learn the most basic rules for how to carry on a conversation usually by the age of four.[41] As we learn the rules of conversation, we also learn the importance of listening and being listened to. These lessons come directly from what our parents say and the behaviors they model. An acquaintance told us a story about her young daughter who asked her to listen to something. Our friend, who was busy at the time, told her daughter to go ahead and tell her the story because "mommy is listening." Her daughter responded by going over to her mother, placing her hands on either side of her mother's face, turning it toward her, and saying, "Now you're listening." Clearly the mother had previously taught her daughter that she had to stop what she was doing and look at her mother to truly listen.

Learning Problem Solving

In addition to learning how to listen and communicate, family communication also sets the tone for how children learn to address problems and other life challenges. Recent research at Vanderbilt University indicates that children seem to learn more when their mothers listen.[42] Child psychologists Bethany Rittle-Johns, Megan Saylor, and Kathryn Swygerty found that children who have to explain the solution to a problem to their mothers have a much-improved ability to solve similar problems later on. In their study they asked each mom to listen to her child without providing assistance. Of the various methods they tested (e.g., having the child restate the answer, having the child explain the solution to themselves, or having the child explain the solution to their moms), the act of their mother's listening to the explanation was the one most effective in aiding the children's learning process. Explaining the reasoning behind the problem's solution to a parent (or someone else they know) not only appears to help children better understand the problem but also helps them apply what they learned to other situations.

Learning to Manage Emotions

Parents also influence how children learn to express and manage emotions. For example, through their parents, preschoolers learn about "the appropriate expression of emotions, possible reactions to others' positive and negative emotions, the nature of emotional expression, and the types of situations that are likely to elicit emotions."[43] Think about how you react to emotional situations. Chances are if you come from an emotionally expressive family, you, too, are expressive. Likewise, if your family is more restrained, you probably are too. If you learn to perceive emotional expressiveness as normal, you will probably be more comfortable listening to emotionally expressive messages.[44] On the other hand, if you come from a restrained family, you could be very uncomfortable listening to those expressive messages. Through our parents we learn what emotions can be expressed (or not) within the family and in specific contexts.[45] Think back to your early years or to conversations your parents had with a younger sibling. Did they verbally discuss an emotion and how it related to an event? If so, they were acting as an **emotion coach.** Parents who engage in this type of coaching actively discuss their children's emotions, helping them to distinguish between differing emotions and assisting them with their emotional skill building (i.e., identifying, experiencing, and regulating them).

Expressiveness (the ability and willingness to express emotions) is particularly important for parent-child relationships. Individual parental expressiveness appears to affect a variety of factors, such as a child's emotional expressiveness, social popularity and prosocial behaviors (e.g., helpfulness, empathy).[46] Children often carry these modeled behaviors of expressiveness into their relationships with friends and romantic partners. While children who are exposed to and learn about expressiveness may not necessarily be more emotionally expressive themselves, they are oftentimes considered more socially competent by their peers.[47] We can assume that this perceived competence is due to the ability to listen for emotional content and effect. These expressiveness styles are often reflected in their dating relationships.

Not all parents are comfortable with emotion coaching. These parents are sometimes called **dismissing parents** because in their efforts to be helpful and make their children feel better, they often ignore the children's emotions. In other more negative cases, parents can be dismissive, actually punishing the child for either showing or asking about emotions. Whatever the situation, dismissing parents deprive their children of the opportunity to reflect on themselves and their feelings. Unfortunately it also teaches a child that listening to emotions is unimportant. Conversations provide important coaching moments in which to address feelings and emotions and how to manage them. For example, moms who both talk about and spend time discussing emotions tend to have young children who are more "emotionally competent." While coaching and dismissing are often associated with handling a child's negative or "upset" emotions, learning to express affection is also very important.[48] It is one of the ways to gain positive attention from a parent. Children want and need positive interactions with their parents as well as attention to distress or pain. Greater understanding of emotions becomes important as children learn and develop an understanding of empathy and empathetic behaviors. Children from low-conformity families seem more able to develop the flexibility and spontaneity necessary to cope with relational maintenance messages. They learn early that listening to and accepting different feelings is important.[49]

If you reflect back to the Case Study at the beginning of the chapter, you can see from Radley's comments that his family is low conformity. From the research we have discussed, we can expect their norm of having family listening time will help the children be more socially successful.

Ultimately emotional communication is embedded in our interpersonal and social relationships and transactions.[50] Family interactions form the foundation for how we express emotions and cope with emotional issues.[51] In a sense, our emotional views are socially constructed and based on personal experiences and events as well as the stories that family members tell. Family stories often emphasize which behaviors (emotional and otherwise) are acceptable and which are not. These family interactions become a primary conduit by which we learn our "emotion scripts" and interpretive schemata.[52] Of course, you know by now that schemata "color our world," biasing how we approach relationships, interact with others, and interpret both our own and others' emotions. In addition, our emotional schemata predispose us to experience some emotions over others.[53] These schemata also affect our worldviews. For example, if we grow up in an emotional-expressive family, we likely view the world, and those in it, as empathetic and demonstrative. Finally our schemata can affect the meaning we attach to an emotional event, which in turn can affect our emotion-related behavior.[54] For example, if your experience with anger, or your anger schema, is such that anger is always negative, chances are you will become anxious when someone around you gets angry, rather than viewing it more objectively and exploring the causes.

Molding Children's Listening Behaviors

Of course, active listening is one of the most frequently suggested techniques for improving parent-child interactions (by both parents and children). Another suggestion focuses on *responsive style.* As we pointed out in our discussion of emotions, how parents respond to their children and teenagers helps them to name feelings, shows that it's OK to have those feelings, and provides a means of addressing them constructively. It is clear, then, that it is especially important for parents to be nonjudgmental in how they respond to their children, especially when emotions are involved. When parents are able to achieve these things, they become a resource person for their children.

Ideally parents will teach and model good listening behavior.[55] Whether you are a parent, a cousin, a brother, or an aunt, a review of advice on how to best raise good listeners tends to also depend on the adults' being positive models by being good listeners themselves. Look at the following **six suggestions for young children** and see if you agree with us.

Not surprisingly our first suggestion is to *avoid distractions.* Children don't listen (nor do adults) when distracted. Turn off the TV, iPod, or video games. Some experts argue children shouldn't even be allowed to "plug in" until the weekend. They believe that cutting down on the electronic "noise" in children's lives makes it easier for them to listen. We're realists. Most people won't go to this extreme. However, we do agree that cutting out the distractions during important conversations should be done.

Our second suggestion is to *be a good role model.* Asking a child to attend to what you have to say when you then turn around and tune them out doesn't encourage them to be good listeners. "Do as I say" and actually "Do it" when it comes to teaching and practicing good listening habits (like the daughter we described in the previous example who made her mom look her in the eye). What are good role model behaviors? Listening closely and without criticism is important for building trust. Avoid giving out too much advice, denying feelings, jumping to conclusions, or brushing children off, all of which send the message that they and their concerns aren't important to you. This means hearing children out. Allowing them to finish their thoughts is also important. Interruptions (except when needed for clarification) should be avoided. One means of achieving this end is to try sitting and having a pleasant conversation. These conversations help children to experience positive outcomes to listening. You might also try reading out loud. This piece of advice is primarily aimed at preschoolers. Getting them to listen to stories encourages them to focus. As they begin to learn to read, you can become the one who listens carefully and attentively.

Our third suggestion is to *be direct.* Avoid making statements in the form of a question. "Wouldn't you like to go study now?" It sounds like an option or choice is being offered when in reality it is not.

Next, we suggest *asking children to paraphrase* (or write it down). Whether orally or written, good listening requires the ability to analyze and summarize information. Practice will help them learn this important listening skill. Here is a tip: avoid yelling across the room, down the hall, or out the door. Tell them you need their attention for a specified amount of time (e.g., five minutes). Clearly make eye contact (even if you have to sit down or kneel to make this happen), tell them what you need, then ask for the all-important paraphrase.

One suggestion you might not think of is to *allow children to look away.* Yes, we just said you should make eye contact when *telling* something to a child. However, recent research by a group of developmental psychologists suggests that when we ask small children to answer questions, we should allow them to look away while answering, in a manner to *aid* their concentration (e.g., not watching TV). Gaze aversion is often a sign that the child is taking time to formulate a response.[56] Actually giving children a bit more time to answer the question (in other words, not interrupting their thinking) can be beneficial if you want to improve the accuracy of their responses. It appears that the human face is "stimulating" to small children, which results in its taking up additional cognitive processing "time and space."

Finally *reward good behavior.* Children (and adults) like praise. So letting them know they've done a good job of listening is an important means of encouraging future good listening habits.

Unfortunately there will be times when a child has to face the music. If a child repeatedly doesn't listen, then he shouldn't depend on you constantly repeating yourself. If you tell him you're leaving for the mall at 1:00 p.m., with or without him, then do it. Leave. Next time we bet he'll be ready. Chances are you can think of some examples of how your parents used some of these suggestions as you were growing up.

Why Parents "Don't Listen"

Listening is the foundation of authentic communication, representing a basic human need. In fact, listening has long been identified as a key component in parent-teen relationships. Given its importance, it's not surprising that one of the most common adolescent and teenage complaints is that their parents don't listen to them.[57] (Isn't it interesting that the same complaint is expressed by parents about their teens?) As we have noted throughout this text, listening is one of the primary ways that we show others that we believe them to be a valued, worthwhile person.

It shows respect for their opinions (even if we don't agree), that we care about them as individuals, and that we respect them as individuals. Thus, a supportive family listening environment is important. When parents listen respectfully to their children, they are more likely to have children who will return the favor. Of course, there are a number of reasons listening can be difficult in parent-child relationships. Here are just a few, along with suggestions for improvement.[58]

Role Definition   Parents can sometimes think that to be successful parents, their children must espouse the same views and values that they have. When they don't, it can become difficult for parents to fully listen. In addition, parents often see the parent-child relationships as asymmetrical (one up/one down). However, the best listening occurs when we treat the other person as an equal partner in the listening process. This commonsense conclusion is supported by recent research that indicates that open communication behavior on the part of mothers promotes reciprocal communication from their children. This same research also suggests that the quality of discussion during a conflict is important to a child's mental health and ability to internalize problems.[59]

Confusion over Acceptance   The best listening occurs when we accept people just the way they are and accept their views (this doesn't mean we have to agree). Sometimes parents think that if they truly listen, they will necessarily have to accept their children's views. This is not the case. It does mean that parents have to understand both the content and the underlying emotions involved. So parents can empathize with the need to maintain solid friendships but still disagree with having a friend stay overnight during the school week. Ideally parents will fully listen to their children even when they know in the first few minutes what the child is requesting is an unfeasible idea (e.g., it costs too much, the child isn't old enough). Such moments provide great opportunities for understanding what's important to and what's going on in a teenager's life.

Inability to Accept Criticism   Some parents see disagreements as attacks on their parenting skills. They can become defensive when their teenagers offer even constructive criticism. Parents who are aware they are not perfect, especially those with a good sense of humor, are usually accepting of their teenagers' comments and criticisms. In fact, such comments from teenagers are often a test, one that tests their ability to point out parenting (or personal) flaws and still be loved and accepted by their parents.

Lack of Time   It's a busy world for both parents and teens. Finding opportunities to interact and engage one another can be difficult. Unfortunately watching television or simply eating together are activities that many researchers believe *do not* constitute "quality" time.[60] An important strategy, however, is to acknowledge when we are too busy to listen. Impatience and distraction are often evidenced in our nonverbals, leading the speaker to feel devalued and less likely to want to enter into future conversations. Set a time when each person can listen closely, and keep that promise. Turn off the mobile phone and the TV and move away from the computer. Such actions clearly signal that we respect and are willing to listening to the other person. For example, one parent we know who has a television in her home office turns it off (not just muted) whenever one of her children comes in to speak with her. This simple gesture is a clear signal to her children that she is truly focused on them.

Some family communication specialists suggest that weekly family meetings are one way to build in quality listening time. At these meetings, accomplishments as well as concerns are addressed. Other spontaneous moments can be used more effectively as listening moments (e.g., cleaning the kitchen, running errands together). Finally when possible, it's great for parents and children to set regular one-on-one appointments with each other: Saturday lunch with Mom, Wednesday night dinner with Dad, and so forth. As young adults, you can take the initiative and offer to take Mom or Dad to lunch—even a fast-food place—at an off time (to reduce noise and distractions). The point is to make opportunities to share your lives with each other.

Willingness to Listen   This is an attitudinal issue. Sometimes it seems that parents and teenagers work at cross-purposes. When one is ready to listen, the other isn't ready to talk. Recognizing and taking the opportunities to actively engage each other is crucial for quality family listening. Adolescents who come from families that encourage expressing both negative and positive feelings are more likely to maintain close relationships with their parents.[61] Like all of us, adolescents and teens want and need to share their joys, problems, and concerns. However, how they ultimately share that information is often dependent on the relationships they have with both their parents and their peers. If they feel that their parents aren't willing to listen, they are more likely to begin excluding them in favor of friends. In fact, during their prime teenage years, peers will trump parents in most cases.

Perspective and Parent-Teen Interactions   Of particular interest is how parents and children, particularly teenagers, view the lines of communication between them.[62] Chances are that you and your parents had slightly different perspectives about just how freely you could communicate while you were going through your adolescent years. An important study by pioneer listening scholars Carolyn Coakley and Andy Wolvin found that parents tend to see the lines of communication as open or very open, while teens see them as open or somewhat open.[63]

This finding supports our conclusion that there are perceptual differences between each group's views of this aspect of their relationship. It is interesting to note parents and teenagers tended to agree about their assessment of the parents' listening skills. Parents tended to rate themselves as "good" listeners, and their teens tended to also view them as good listeners. In contrast, parents were more likely to rate their teens as excellent listeners, while teens generally rated themselves as average listeners. Of note, the majority of topics of discussion between parents and their teens focused on the teen (e.g., college, social activities, grades, career plans). What doesn't get discussed? Sex. Both parents and teenagers listed sex-related topics as the ones causing them the greatest discomfort. We're pretty certain this finding doesn't surprise any of you. However, recent research indicates that the willingness of families to talk about sensitive subjects as well as how they go about this communication is based on the communication climate in the family.[64] For example, parents who have an open style of communication with their adolescents and are able to express their own values, beliefs, and expectations are more likely to delay the onset of sexual activity as well as risky behavior on the part of their child.[65]

This finding also suggests that in addition to being an open listener, a parent can present information in ways that will make it more listenable. By tailoring information to the individual adolescent's physical, emotional, and psychological level of development as well as taking into account the social environment (i.e., peer pressure), parents can present sensitive information to fit the specific needs of the child.[66]

Of course, as you grow older, personal privacy becomes more important. Not surprisingly adolescents and teens tend to have fewer interactions with their parents and more with friends and peers. While peers eventually take the place of parents as the primary receiver of self-disclosure (and listening), it is important that parents continue to be available to listen. There are real consequences if they aren't. For example, teenage girls who believed their parents or guardians were unavailable or unwilling to listen to them tended to score higher on eating-disorder measurements (e.g., drive for thinness, bulimia, interpersonal distrust). Thus, family interaction patterns appear to contribute to the psychological and behavioral traits associated with eating disorders.[67] Unfortunately not all communication between parent and child is happy. As with all relationships, this one, too, is subject to conflict.

PARENT-CHILD CONFLICT

We touched on important aspects of conflict and conversation in the previous chapter. Here we explore attributes specific to family life. An important aspect of family life is how the family unit handles conflict. It is no surprise that most of us first come into contact with conflict (and conflict management) within our own families. We observe how others in the family engage in conflict, including conflict strategies. Of course, family conflict has both tangible and intangible elements.[68] **Tangible conflict** elements focus on specifics of the conflict, such as what time curfew should be. **Intangible conflict** elements address issues such as what makes your family unique (to yourself and to others) and what binds you together (besides blood, marriage, or choice). It can include your level of inclusion or exclusion in the family (e.g., the golden child versus the black sheep). Thus, an issue of curfew might actually be one of autonomy and authority. Family disputes can affect individual personal and social identity (i.e., both in and out of the family).

As we discussed earlier in the chapter, family communication climate will have an effect on how you handle conflict. For example, adolescents from families with higher levels of positive family expressiveness tend to have better family relationships (i.e., less conflict, better communication, less trouble addressing family problems).[69] If your family has a high conformity orientation, chances are that conflict is discouraged, whereas if your family is conversation oriented, you are encouraged

to express yourself and view conflict as an opportunity to both express and learn.[70] This difference between positive and negative expressiveness is important for understanding family conflict. Ultimately how your family handles conflict tends to predict how you will handle conflict in your personal and romantic relationships.[71]

Finally one significant area of conflict that affects conflict schema formation for children and adolescents is interparental conflict.[72] In such cases children often blame themselves for the conflict and, thus, experience a great deal of emotional distress.[73] Much of this distress can be allayed by parents talking with the child, listening to his or her concerns, and providing reassurance that the child is blameless in the conflict.[74]

Given the high saliency, emotional arousal, and personal relevancy, it's no wonder that children (even very young children) quickly form schemata for parental arguments. Children exposed to constructive conflict generally feel less threatened and have fewer negative emotions and will believe that the conflict will be effectively resolved. They also tend to feel that the conflict won't negatively affect them or their families. Family conflict schemata are also affected by consistency. The more consistent parents are in how they express and resolve conflict, the stronger a schema will likely become. Children of these parents often develop strong expectations for how conflict "plays itself out." If parents, however, rarely argue or have inconsistent patterns of conflict behavior, then their children's conflict schemata tend to be less developed, often leading these children to focus greater attention on conflict events.

Once developed, these schemata are frequently activated when we enter intimate relationships. Children who witness hostile, negative conflict may respond to peers and dating partners with fear and avoidance or may be aggressive or coercive to get the upper hand first.[75] These latter behaviors are more likely to occur if children believe they are successful means of goal attainment.

Good listening habits aren't going to stop the inevitable arguments that parents and children experience. However, family therapist Michael Nichols suggested that responsive listening is one means of handling parent-child conflicts.[76] His technique was designed to provide children with greater opportunity to express themselves while reducing the odds of a major meltdown. His method relies on mutual respect, cooperation, and empathy. He believes that when parents begin to "argue back" with their kids, they are being drawn down to their children's level, in many cases unnecessarily. He feels that good listening skills can end many disagreements before they actually get started. Some of his primary suggestions for handling parent-child conflict are outlined below.

First, he suggested that parents *get the right attitude*. Parents need to understand that **conversations are about listening,** not arguing or establishing who's right or in authority. They have to be committed not only to encouraging their children to speak their minds but also to making sure they understand what their children actually *mean*. Oftentimes parents don't recognize that they don't "get it," resulting in additional misunderstandings and conflict. He also noted that *parents are in charge.* Nichols believes that taking on the role of listening is a purposive, active event, one that puts parents in charge. He argued that as long as parents keep this in mind, when their children start yelling, "I hate you," they can respond more actively (and more calmly) (e.g., "You really didn't like what I said, did you?"). Such responses place ownership of the statements. The children's outbursts remain their own, but at the same time, the parents acknowledge the reaction to what triggered the outburst.

Third, he argued that it's OK to *postpone decision-making.* It's OK for parents to make a considered decision. This gives children the feeling that they are being listened to while giving parents the opportunity to actually consider all sides of the issue. An immediate "no" is very likely to trigger an immediate argument.

> **THINK ON IT**
>
> Identify a parent-child relationship that you can observe. (Perhaps you have nieces and nephews.) Think about the interactions you observed. Did you see any of Dr. Nichols's suggestions at work? If so, what was the effect on the conversation? If not, how did the participants in the interaction ultimately react?

Of course, this assumes that a parent will be open-minded enough to actually see the issue or problem from the child's point of view. Careful, thoughtful decisions often lead to compromises.

Nichols also believes it's important to *keep it simple.* Parents don't always need to provide long, reasoned-out justifications for their actions. Long justifications can invite debate. If crossing the street against the light is unsafe, a child does not need a detailed explanation about traffic patterns. A simple, "No, it's not safe," should suffice. Finally he reminded parents that *children grow up,* and their listening needs change as they grow and mature. As you know, small children accept parental authority more readily than do adolescents and teenagers. Nichols believes that paying a lot of attention to the needs and wants of adolescents and teenagers is an important means of staying connected. As noted earlier, children who feel their parents are willing to listen are more likely to talk to them. Again, parents can reject a child's point of view, but parents have to listen, or they'll never hear that viewpoint.

SIBLING RELATIONSHIPS

An important family group that we have ignored up to now is siblings. While it has been described as "the most enduring and egalitarian connection of all family relationships," it has received much less attention in the communication literature than parent-child relationships.[77] The odds are that most of you reading this book have at least one brother or sister. Even if you are an only child, understanding sibling relationships will help you to better understand your friends and, perhaps, future romantic partners. For those of you with brothers and sisters, you understand how sibling relationships pervade your life. As children, the effect of these relationships might not have been as apparent. In your early years, you probably didn't view your siblings as providing much more than companionship and emotional support (when you weren't fighting with each other). You might have been a babysitter for a younger sibling, occasionally worked together to manage your parents, and helped each other out in specific situations (e.g., ride to a party, loaning money), but you probably didn't view them as an important source of social support. In fact, you still might not view them as an important source of social support. However, research in this area suggests that as we age, particularly in late adolescence and early adulthood, our relationships with our siblings change, leading us to grow emotionally closer.[78]

The emotional closeness you feel with your siblings is based on "shared experiences, trust, concern, and enjoyment of the relationship."[79] Emotional closeness may be expressed in affectionate communication and communication-based emotional support, both of which have been related to concepts such as relational satisfaction, relational closeness, and self-disclosure. In addition, individuals who are highly affectionate communicators tend to be more outgoing and have higher self-esteem.[80] In general, if you and your siblings are affectionate and emotionally supportive of each other, the odds are that your commitment to each other will remain stable throughout your lives.[81] This commitment is related, in part, to the loyalty that you feel toward one another, and loyalty is related to your feelings of family obligation. Thus, even if you really dislike your sister's husband, you'll still get together for major holidays and other family events. You won't allow your dislike to overcome your loyalty to your sister. Similarly, even if you disapprove of some of the things your sister does (e.g., quitting that perfectly good job to start her own business), if you're committed to each other, you will still be loyal and likely supportive (even as you voice your disapproval and disbelief).

Sibling commitment is also related to sibling intimacy. Close sibling relationships are based as much on friendship as on blood or marriage ties. Self-disclosure or confiding is related to closer sibling relationships. And as we have discussed a number of times already, listening is an important part of the foundation that makes us feel comfortable disclosing. We have some young (tween) friends who are very close siblings. In age they are about a year apart. It has been very interesting to watch them grow up and develop a close brother-sister relationship. The most noteworthy aspect of their bond is that they seem to be each other's best friend. They are supportive of each other and confer with one another when making important decisions. Their family encourages open communication, so we suspect this close relationship will last through the challenges of adolescence and into adulthood.

Sibling relationships can become even more significant as we age. For example, approximately 80 percent of older adults living today have living siblings.[82] In addition, while we will experience ups and downs in our sibling relationships, most of us will maintain some level of contact with our brothers and sisters. Our sibling relationships provide a means of maintaining and sharing our common background, the uniqueness of our family life. In addition, sibling relationships tend to be the longest relationships of our lives. Reminiscing about family roots helps us to remember and reinforce those things that make families unique. They also provide a network for personal support and ears to listen.

COMMUNICATING WITH OLDER ADULTS

As children age, so do parents. In later stages of life, adult children (and their parents) face changing roles. Listening is central to these changed relationships as well.[83] Good listening becomes important to identifying, recognizing, and enacting the social support that older family members need. If parents don't feel their children listen to them, then they are less likely to approach them in times of real need. Older parents need our time, just as much as we needed theirs when we were young. Taking the time to truly listen to aging parents can open up avenues of kinship and love that can surprise and gratify us. However, just as when we were young, our parents need to feel that they are more important to us than our business or other social relationships.

As adults age, they also face specific listening needs based on changes in physiology. The one immediately related to listening is a **loss of hearing acuity**. Even small hearing losses result in increased difficulties in understanding speech in our daily lives.[84] These difficulties are multiplied in situations where there are multiple talkers or sudden topic changes. The question for researchers is how much of this common problem can be attributed to hearing problems and how much should be attributed to cognitive declines. Understanding the source has profound implications on how hearing-related problems can be or should be addressed. Recent research in audiology suggests two important things.[85] First, when listening is viewed as information processing, then hearing loss can profoundly affect our normal flow of information. Second, with some limitations, we appear to have the ability to "tune" our hearing. This tuning function can occur when expectations for a particular noise (i.e., frequency) have been triggered. So if someone tells us the cat has a particularly low rumble of a purr, we'll tune in to that frequency to better hear it. This ability also can be triggered by context. In particularly noisy environments (or when age-related hearing loss occurs), we tune our entire hearing system (perception, memory, and so on) to help us to "fill in" the information that is being lost (via noise or poor hearing). Such cases also affect our processing resources, another issue that can affect our ability to listen. Not surprisingly if we have difficulty in hearing, we are less likely to contribute to an interaction.

Related to hearing, another common belief is that our memory worsens as we age. Research into age-related changes in memory has helped pinpoint some of the attributes that lead to this common belief (and experience).[86] Important to listening is that, as we age, we tend to have more problems with our working memory. In general, there is a reduced capacity in our processing speed. As you recall, working memory involves both storage of and processing of information. It seems that as we age, our processing resources become more limited.[87] One of the reasons for this is it appears that older adults have more difficulty in "clearing" their working memory of irrelevant information. However, an important question we should ask is how much memory is adequate. Just because memory studies of older adults (usually past age 50) show age-related deficits (when compared to 20-year-olds) does not mean their memory is "broken" or that they are working with a memory "deficit." It does, however, suggest that young adults likely have memories that work at a much higher capacity than really needed for everyday functioning. Thus, downward changes in adult memory are more aggravating than anything else.

Finally many older adults, and even younger adults, don't want to acknowledge to themselves or to others that they are experiencing hearing problems. While this is often done to protect their self-image, recent research in communication suggests that hiding a hearing loss or disability can actually have the opposite effect.[88] In fact, older adults, and especially younger individuals, with hearing problems who acknowledged the problem tended to be viewed more favorably, despite hearing-related communication difficulties.

SUMMARY

As we have suggested throughout this chapter, families need quality communication to enhance and maintain healthy family function.[89] Quality communication means that true conversations occur where the involved family members take turns talking and listening. Effective communication enables families to balance cohesiveness and adaptability. Clear and open communication among family members brings families closer together, enhances member personal identity and well-being, and leads to better social and coping skills.[90] As we have seen in this chapter, quality listening is an important element of quality family communication, helping to bring families closer together, contributing to family member personal identity and well-being, and enhancing social and individual coping skills.[91]

Perhaps as important as any other contribution that family communication makes to the development of the children are the foundations it establishes for future interaction. The communication lessons we learn from our families help us develop schemata about interpersonal communication in general and how to engage in relational maintenance behavior with our friends.[92] The next chapter will focus on friendship and romantic relationships.

CONCEPTS TO KNOW

Family Orientation Schemata
    Conversation Orientation
    Conformity Orientation
Family Strength
Confirmation
Back-channel
Family Schema and Scripts
    Structural Traditionalism
    Avoidance
Family Stories
    Engagement
    Perspective-taking
    Coherence

Managing Emotions
    Emotion Coaching
    Dismissing Parents
Parental Responsive Style
Six Tips for Listening
    to Children
Why Parents Don't Listen
Handling Parent-Child Conflict
    Tangible Conflict
    Intangible Conflict
    Tips for Parents
Hearing Acuity

DISCUSSION QUESTIONS

1. How are structural traditionalism and avoidance related to conversation and conformity orientation?
2. Think of the stories that are frequently told by family members. What do those stories tell others about your family, how it handles conflict, views about family structure, and so forth?
3. Therapist Michael Nichols offered a number of suggestions for parents. Of his suggestions, which do you think is the most important? Why?

4. Have you noticed changes in how your parents listen to you over time? If so, how has their listening changed? What do you think led to this change?
5. Looking at the discussion of the importance of storytelling to family life and culture, how do you believe it can contribute to sibling relationships?

LISTENING ACTIVITIES

1. The next time you visit with your family, keep a diary of your interactions. Identify positive and negative listening behaviors that we've discussed in this chapter. Of the behaviors you've identified, do you personally tend to engage in them or not? If you engage in negative behaviors, choose one and develop a plan for substituting a positive listening behavior in its place. Next, set your plan in motion. Track your success over a five-day period. Do you think you are improving? Why or why not? If not, what do you think can be done to help you further improve your listening?
2. Conduct an Internet search to help you identify three common hearing problems (besides being legally deaf). What are common treatments? Is there anything you can do to avoid developing the hearing problem you identified?

ADDITIONAL READINGS

Braithwaite, D. O., & Baxter, L. A. (Eds.). (2006). *Engaging theories in family communication: Multiple perspectives* (pp. 35–49). Thousand Oaks, CA: Sage.

Dailey, R. M., & Le Poire, B. A. (Eds.). (2006). *Applied interpersonal communication matters: Family, health, and community relations.* New York: Peter Lang Publishing.

Fitzpatrick, M. A., & Caughlin, J. P. (2002). Interpersonal communication in family relationships. In M. L. Knapp & J. A. Daly (Eds.), *Handbook of interpersonal communication* (3rd ed., pp. 726–777). Thousand Oaks, CA: Sage.

Nichols, W. C. (2000). *Handbook of family development and intervention.* New York: Wiley.

Tuner, L. H., & West., R. (2006). *Perspectives on family communication* (3rd ed.). New York: McGraw-Hill.

Vangelisti, A. L. (Ed.). (2009). *Feeling hurt in close relationships.* New York: Cambridge University Press.

ENDNOTES

1. Baumeister & Leary, 1995
2. Coontz, 1997; U.S. Census Bureau, 2010
3. AARP, 2002
4. For a comprehensive review, see Johnson, Bengtson, Coleman, & Kirkwood (2005)
5. Coakley & Wolvin, 1997
6. Schrodt, Witt, & Messersmith, 2008
7. Wilkinson, 2003
8. Rubin, Bukowski, & Parker, 1998
9. Odom & McConnell, 1992
10. Burleson, Delia, & Applegate, 1995; Mills & Rubin, 1993; Rubin & Rose-Krasnor, 1992
11. Braithwaite & Baxter, 2005; Koerner & Fitzpatrick, 2002; Ledbetter & Schrodt, 2008
12. Ledbetter & Schrodt, 2008
13. Fitzpatrick & Ritchie, 1994, p. 276
14. Ledbetter, 2009
15. Koerner & Fitzpatrick, 2002
16. Ledbetter & Schrodt, 2008
17. Ledbetter & Schrodt, 2008
18. Ledbetter & Schrodt, 2008
19. DeFrain & Asay, 2007; DeFrain & Stinnett, 2002
20. Golish, 2003
21. Schrodt, 2005, 2009
22. Doohan, 2007
23. See Schrodt et al. (2008) for a meta-analysis of family communication pattern research.
24. Guerrero, Jones, & Burgoon, 2000
25. Mikkelson & Hesse, 2009
26. Schrodt et al., 2008
27. Galvin, Bylund, & Brommel, 2004
28. Galvin & Cooper, 1990, as cited in Galvin et al., 2004
29. Boyd, 2003, p. 354
30. Caughlin, 2003; Caughlin, Golish, Olson, Sargent, Cook, & Petronio, 2000
31. Kellas, 2008
32. Byng-Hall, 1988
33. Fitzpatrick & Ritchie, 1994
34. Schrodt, 2005
35. Sunwolf & Frey, 2001, p. 122
36. Kellas, 2005
37. Kellas & Trees, 2005
38. Ackerman, 1981; Eskritt, Whalen, & Lee, 2008; Pellegrini, Brody, & Stoneman, 1987; Shatz, 1983
39. Pellegrini et al., 1987
40. Pellegrini et al., 1987
41. Eskritt et al., 2008
42. Rittle-Johnson, Saylor, & Swygert, 2008
43. Denham & Kochanoff, 2002. See also Eisenberg, Fabes, Carlo, & Karbon (1992); Izard (1991)
44. Gentzler, Contreras-Grau, Kerns, & Weimer, 2005
45. See Denham & Kochanoff (2002) for a review of literature related to parental emotional coaching.
46. Gottman, Katz, & Hoover, 1996; Halberstadt, Crisp, & Eaton, 1999; Halberstadt, Fox, & Jones, 1993
47. Gottman et al., 1996; Orrego & Rodriguez, 2001
48. Dunn, Brown, & Beardsal, 1991
49. Ledbetter, 2009
50. Saarni & Buckley, 2002
51. Saarni & Buckley, 2002, p. 235. See also Gentzler et al. (2005)
52. Saarni, 1999; Saarni & Buckley, 2002
53. Malatesta, 1990
54. Saarni & Buckley, 2002, p. 235
55. Church, 2001; Miller, 2001; Woods, 2001
56. Phelps, Doherty-Sneddon, & Warnock, 2006
57. See Coakley & Wolvin (1997) for a review of parent-teen listening/communication
58. See Coakley & Wolvin (1997) for a review of parent-teen listening/communication and additional suggestions
59. Brown, Fitzgerald, Shipman, & Schneider, 2007a

60. Brecher & Brecher, 1987, as cited in Wolvin & Coakley, 1997
61. Gentzler et al., 2005
62. Coakley & Wolvin, 1997
63. Coakley & Wolvin, 1997
64. Eisenberg, Sieving, Bearinger, Swain, & Resnick, 2006; Brown, Fitzgerald, Shipman, & Schneider, 2007b
65. Eisenberg et al., 2006
66. Eisenberg et al., 2006
67. Larson, 1991
68. Taylor, 2002
69. Capaldi, Forgatch, & Crosby, 1994; Flannery, Montemayor, & Eberly, 1994
70. Barbato, Graham, Perse, 2003
71. Reese-Weber & Marchand, 2002
72. Grych & Cardoza-Fernandes, 2001
73. See Brown et al. (2007a) for a discussion.
74. Brown et al., 2007a
75. Grych & Cardoza-Fernandes, 2001, p. 172
76. Nichols, 2005
77. Fowler, 2009
78. Fowler, 2009; Floyd, 1996; Goetting, 1986. See also Conger, Bryant, & Brennon, 2004
79. Lee, Mancini, & Maxwell, 1990, p. 433; Folwell, Chung, Nussbaum, Sparks-Bethea, & Grant, 1997
80. Floyd, 2002
81. Rittenour, Myers, & Brann, 2007
82. McKay & Caverly, 2004
83. Ross & Glenn, 1996
84. Schneider, Daneman, & Pichora-Fuller, 2002
85. Schneider et al., 2002
86. See Maylor (2005) for a short, in-depth review on age-related changes in memory
87. Verhaeghen, Marcoen, & Goossens, 1993
88. Ryan, Anas, & Vuckovich, 2007
89. Coakley & Wolvin, 1997, p. 95; Olson & Gorall, 2003
90. Galvin & Brommel, 2000; Nelson & Lott, 1990
91. Noller & Callan, 1991; Riesch & Forsyth, 2007
92. Ledbettter, 2009

REFERENCES

Ackerman, B. (1981). When is a question not answered? The understanding of young children utterances violating or conforming to the rules of conversational sequencing. *Journal of Experimental Child Psychology, 31,* 487–507.

American Association of Retired Persons. (2002). The grandparent study 2002 report. Retrieved from http://assets.aarp.org/rgcenter/general/gp_2002.pdf.

Barbato, C. A., Graham, E. E., & Perse, E. M. (2003). Communicating in the family: An examination of the relationship of family communication climate and interpersonal communication motives. *Journal of Family Communication, 3,* 123–148.

Baumeister, R. F., & Leary, M. R. (1995). The need to belong: Desire for interpersonal attachments as fundamental human motivation. *Psychological Bulletin, 117,* 497–529.

Boyd, G. E. (2003). Pastoral conversation: Relational listening and open-ended questions. *Pastoral Psychology, 51,* 345–360.

Braithwaite, D. O., & Baxter, L. A. (Eds.) (2005). *Family communication: Multiple perspectives.* Thousand Oaks, CA: Sage.

Brown, A. M., Fitzgerald, M. M., Shipman, K., & Schneider, R. (2007a). Children's expectations of parent-child communication following interparental conflict: Do parents talk to children about conflict? *Journal of Family Violence, 22,* 407–412.

Brown, A. M., Fitzgerald, M. M., Shipman, K., & Schneider, R. (2007b). Parents' communication with adolescents about sexual behavior: A missed opportunity for prevention? *Journal of Family Violence, 35,* 893–902.

Burleson, B. R., Delia, J. G., & Applegate, J. L. (1995). The socialization of person-centered communication: Parents' contributions to their children's social-cognitive and communication skills. In M. A. Fitzpatrick & A. Vangelisti (Eds.), *Explaining family interactions* (pp. 34–76). Thousand Oaks, CA: Sage.

Byng-Hall, J. (1988). Scripts and legends in families and family therapy. *Family Processes, 27,* 167–179.

Capaldi, D. M., Forgatch, M. S., & Crosby, L. (1994). Affective expression in family problem-solving discussions with adolescent boys: The association with family structure and function. *Journal of Adolescent Research, 9,* 28–49.

Caughlin, J. P. (2003). Family communication standards: What counts as excellent family communication and how are such standards associated with family satisfaction? *Human Communication Research, 29,* 5–40.

Caughlin, J. P., Golish, T. D., Olson, L. N., Sargent, J. E., Cook, J. S., & Petronio, S. (2000). Intrafamily secrets in various family configurations: A communication boundary management perspective. *Communication Studies, 51,* 116–134.

Church, E. B. (2001). Needing to be heard. *Scholastic Parent & Child, 9,* 31.

Coakley, C. G., & Wolvin, A. D. (1997). Listening in the parent-teen relationship. *International Journal of Listening, 1,* 88–126.

Conger, K. J., Bryant, C. M., & Brennon, J. M. (2004). The changing nature of adolescent sibling relationships: A theoretical framework for evaluating the role of relationship quality. In R. D. Conger, F. O. Lorenz, & K. A. S. Wickrama (Eds.), *Continuity and change in family relations: Theory, methods, and empirical findings* (pp. 319–344). Mahwah, NJ: LEA.

Coontz, S. (1997). *The way we really are: Coming to terms with America's changing families.* New York: Basic Books.

DeFrain, J., & Asay, S. (Eds.). (2007). *Strong families around the world: The family strengths perspective.* New York: Haworth.

DeFrain, J., & Stinnett, N. (2002). Family strengths. In J. J. Ponzetti, Jr. (Ed.) *International encyclopedia of marriage and family* (2nd ed.) (pp. 637–642). New York: Macmillan Reference Group.

Denham, S., & Kochanoff, A. T. (2002). Parental contributions to preschoolers' understanding of emotion. *Marriage and the Family Review, 34,* 311–343.

Doohan, E. (2007). Listening behaviors of married couples: An exploration of nonverbal presentation to a relational outsider. *International Journal of Listening, 21,* 24–41.

Dunn, J., Brown, J., & Beardsal, L. (1991). Family talk about feeling states and children's later understanding of others' emotions. *Developmental Psychology, 27,* 448–455.

Eisenberg, M. E., Sieving, R. E., Bearinger, L. H., Swain, C., & Resnick, M. D. (2006). Parents' communication with adolescents about sexual behavior: A missed opportunity for prevention? *Journal of Youth & Adolescence, 35,* 893–902.

Eisenberg, N., Fabes, R. A., Carlo, G., & Karbon, M. (1992). Emotional responsivity to others: Behavioral correlates and socialization antecedents. *New Directions for Child Development, 55,* (pp. 57–73). San Francisco: Jossey-Bass.

Eskritt, M., Whalen, J., & Lee, K. (2008). Preschoolers can recognize violations of the Gricean maxims. *British Journal of Developmental Psychology, 26,* 435–443.

Fitzpatrick, M. A., & Ritchie, L. D. (1994). Communication schemata within the family: Multiple perspectives on family interaction. *Human Communication Research, 20,* 275–301.

Flannery, D. J., Montemayor, R., & Eberly, M. B. (1994). The influence of parent negative emotional expression on adolescents' perceptions of their relationships with their parents. *Personal Relationships, 1,* 259–274.

Floyd, K. (1996). Communication closeness among siblings: An application of the gendered closeness perspective. *Communication Research Reports, 13,* 27–34.

Floyd, K. (2002). Human affection exchange: V. Attributes of the highly affectionate. *Communication Quarterly, 50,* 135–152.

Folwell, A. L., Chung, L. C., Nussbaum, J. F., Sparks-Bethea, L., & Grant, J. A. (1997). Differential accounts of closeness in older adult sibling relationships. *Journal of Social and Personal Relationships, 14,* 843–849.

Fowler, C. (2009). Motives for sibling communication across the lifespan. *Communication Quarterly, 57,* 51–66.

Galvin, K. M., & Brommel, B. J. (2000). *Family communication: Cohesion and change* (5th ed.). New York: Longman.

Galvin, K. M., Bylund, C. L., & Brommel, B. J. (2004). *Family communication: Cohesion and change* (6th. ed.). Boston: Allyn & Bacon.

Gentzler, A. L., Contreras-Grau, J. M., Kerns, K. A., & Weimer, B. L. (2005). Parent-child emotional communication and children's coping in middle childhood. *Social Development, 14,* 591–612.

Goetting, A. (1986). The developmental tasks of siblingship over the life cycle. *Journal of Marriage and the Family, 48,* 703–714.

Golish, T. D. (2003). Stepfamily communication strengths: Understanding the ties that blind. *Human Communication Research, 29,* 41–80.

Gottman, J. M., Katz, L. F., & Hooven, C. (1996). Parental meta-emotion philosophy and the emotional life of families: Theoretical models and preliminary data. *Journal of Family Psychology, 10,* 243–268.

Grych, J. H., & Cardoza-Fernandes, S. (2001). Understanding the impact of interparental conflict on children. In J. H. Grych & F. D. Fincham (Eds.), *Interparental conflict and child development,* (pp. 157–187). New York: Cambridge University Press.

Guerrero, L. K., Jones, S. M., & Burgoon, J. K. (2000). Responses to nonverbal intimacy change on romantic dyads: Effects of behavioral valence and expectancy violation. *Communication Monographs, 67,* 325–346.

Halberstadt, A. G., Crisp, V. W., & Eaton, K. L. (1999). Family expressiveness: A retrospective and new directions for research. In P. Philippot & R. S. Feldman (Eds.), *The social context of nonverbal behavior: Studies in emotion and social interaction* (pp. 109–155). New York: Cambridge University Press.

Halberstadt, A. G., Fox, N. A., & Jones, N. A. (1993). Do expressive mothers have expressive children? The role of socialization in children's affect expression. *Social Development, 2,* 48–65.

Izard, C. E. (1991). *The psychology of emotions.* New York: Plenum.

Johnson, M. L., Bengtson, V. L., Coleman, P. G., & Kirkwood, T. B. (Eds.). (2005). *The Cambridge handbook of age and ageing.* New York: Cambridge University Press.

Kellas, J. K. (2005). Family ties: Communicating identity through jointly told family stories. *Communication Monographs, 72,* 265–389.

Kellas, J. K. (2008, July 22). Call for papers: Special issue of the *Journal of Family Communication* on narrative and storytelling in the family. Posted on the Communication Research and Theory Network. [Electronic mailing list message]. CRTNET: Conferences & Calls #10473. Retrieved from www.natcom.org/CRTNET.

Kellas, J. K., & Trees, A. R. (2005). Interactional sense-making in joint storytelling. In V. Manusov (Ed.), *The sourcebook of nonverbal measures: Going beyond words* (pp. 281–294). Mahwah, NJ: Lawrence Erlbaum Associates.

Koerner, A. F., & Fitzpatrick, M.A. (2002). Toward a theory of family communication. *Communication Theory, 12,* 70–91.

Larson, B. J. (1991). Relationship of family communication patterns to eating disorders: Inventory scores in adolescent girls. *Journal of the American Dietetic Association, 91,* 1065–1067.

Ledbetter, A. M. (2009). Family communication patterns and relational maintenance behavior: Direct and mediated association with friendship closeness. *Human Communication Research, 35,* 130–147.

Ledbetter, A. M., & Schrodt, P. (2008). Family communication patterns and cognitive processing: Conversation and conformity orientations as predictors of informational reception apprehension. *Communication Studies, 59,* 388–401.

Lee, T. R., Mancini, J. A., & Maxwell, J. W. (1990). Sibling relationships in adulthood: Contact patterns and motivations. *Journal of Marriage and Family, 52,* 431–440.

Malatesta, C. (1990). The role of emotions in the development and organization of personality. In R. Thompson (Ed.), *Socioemotional development: Nebraska symposium on motivation* (Vol. 36, pp. 1-56). Lincoln, NE: University of Nebraska Press.

Maylor, E. A. (2005). Age-related changes in memory. In M. L. Johnson, V. L. Bengtson, P. G. Coleman, & T. B. L. Kirkwood (Eds.), *The Cambridge handbook of age and ageing* (pp. 200–208). Cambridge, UK: Cambridge University Press.

McKay, V. C., & Caverly, R. S. (2004). The nature of family relationships between and within generations: Relations between grandparents, grandchildren, and siblings in later life. In J. F. Nussbaum & J. Coupland (Eds.), *Handbook of communication and aging research* (2nd ed., pp. 251–271). Mahwah, NJ: LEA.

Mikkelson, A. C., & Hesse, C. (2009). Discussions of religion and relational messages: Differences between comfortable and uncomfortable interactions. *Southern Communication Journal, 74,* 40–56.

Miller, S. A. (2001). Listen to this! *Early Childhood Today, 16,* 32–33.

Mills, R. S. L., & Rubin, K. H. (1993). Parental ideas as influences on children's social competence. In S. Duck (Ed.), *Learning about relationships* (pp. 98–117). Newbury Park, CA: Sage.

Nelson, J. & Lott, L. (1990). *I'm on your side.* Rocklin, CA: Prima.

Nichols, M. P. (2005). *Stop arguing with your kids.* New York: Guilford.

Noller, P., & Callan, V. (1991) *The adolescent in the family.* New York: Routledge.

Odom, S. L., & McConnell, S. R. (1992). Improving social competence: An applied behavior analysis perspective. *Journal of Applied Behavior Analysis, 25,* 239–244.

Olson, D. H., & Gorall, D. M. (2003). Circumplex model of marital and family systems. In F. Walsh (ed.), *Normal family processes* (3rd ed., pp. 514–547). New York: Guilford.

Orrego, V. O., & Rodriguez, J. (2001). Family communication patterns and college adjustment: The effects of communication and conflictual independence on college students. *Journal of Family and Communication, 1,* 175–189.

Pellegrini, A. D., Brody, G. H., & Stoneman, Z. (1987). Children's conversation competence with their parents. *Discourse Processes, 10,* 93–106.

Phelps, F. G., Doherty-Sneddon, G., & Warnock, H. (2006). Helping children think: Gaze aversion and teaching. *British Journal of Developmental Psychology, 24,* 577–588.

Reese-Weber, M., & Marchand, J. F. (2002). Family and individual predictors of late adolescents' romantic relationships. *Journal of Youth and Adolescence, 31,* 197–206.

Riesch, S. K., & Forsyth, D. M. (2007). Preparing to parent the adolescent. *Journal of Child and Adolescent Psychiatric Nursing, 5,* 32–40.

Rittenour, C. E., Myers, S. A., & Brann, M. (2007). Commitment and emotional closeness in sibling relationship. *Southern Communication Journal, 72,* 169–183.

Rittle-Johnson, B., Saylor, M., & Swygert, K. (2008). Learning from explaining: Does it matter if Mom is listening? *Journal of Experimental Child Psychology, 100,* 215–224.

Ross, C., & Glenn, E. E. (1996). Listening between grown children and their parents. *International Listening Journal, 10,* 49–64.

Rubin, K. H., Bukowski, W., & Parker, J. G. (1998). Peer interactions, relationships, and groups. In N. Eisenberg (Ed.), *Handbook of child psychology: Social, emotional, and personality development.* (Vol. 3., pp. 7619–7700). New York: Wiley.

Rubin, K. H., & Rose-Krasnor, L. (1992). Interpersonal problem solving and social competence in children. In V. B. Van Hasselt & M. Hersen (Eds.), *Handbook of social development: A lifespan perspective* (pp. 283–323). New York: Plenum.

Ryan E. B., Anas A. P., & Vuckovitch, M. (2007). The effects of age, hearing loss, and communication difficulty on first impressions. *Communication Research Reports, 24,* 13–19.

Saarni, C. (1999). *The development of emotional competence.* New York: Guilford.

Saarni, C., & Buckley, M. (2002). Children's understanding of emotion communication in families. *Marriage & Family Review, 34,* 213–242.

Schneider, B. A., Daneman, M., & Pichora-Fuller, M. K. (2002). Listening in aging adults: From discourse comprehension to psychoacoustics. *Canadian Journal of Experimental Psychology, 56,* 139–152.

Schrodt, P. (2005). Family communication schemata and the circumplex model of family functioning. *Western Journal of Communication, 69,* 359–376.

Schrodt, P. (2009). Family strength and satisfaction as functions of family communication environments. *Communication Quarterly, 57,* 171–186.

Schrodt, P., Witt, P. L., & Messersmith, A. S. (2008). A meta-analytical review of family communication patterns and their associations with information processing, behavior, and psychosocial outcomes. *Communication Monographs, 75,* 248–269.

Shatz, M. (1983). Communion. In J. H. Flavell & E. Markman (Eds.), *Handbook of child psychology* (Vol. 3, pp. 841–890). New York: Wiley.

Sunwolf, & Frey, L. R. (2001). Storytelling: The power of narrative communication and interpretation. In W. P. Robinson & H. Giles (Eds.), *The new handbook of language and social psychology* (pp. 119–135). Sussex: Wiley.

Taylor, A. (2002). *The handbook of family dispute resolution.* San Francisco: Jossey-Bass.

U.S. Census Bureau. (2010). Families and living arrangements. Retrieved from www.census.gov/population/www/socdemo/hh-fam.html.

Verhaeghen, P., Marcoen, A., & Goossens, L. (1993). Facts and fiction about memory aging: A quantitative integration of research findings. *Journals of Gerontology: Psychological Sciences, 48,* 157–171.

Wilkinson, C. A. (2003). Expressing affection. In K. M. Galvin & P. J. Cooper (Eds.), *Making connections: Readings in relational communication,* (3rd ed., pp. 183–190). Los Angeles: Roxbury.

Woods, S. (2001, November). How to raise a good listener. *Family Life* (25).

Listening and Relationship Building

Friends and Romance

What Makes a Relationship?

We find the group gathered around a table at the coffee shop in the student union. They seem to be focused on the laptop in front of Nolvia.

I'm so happy you all like my idea of conducting a survey about what students are looking for in a relationship. It will help me in my survey research class and give us some original research that we can incorporate into our listening project. I've put in some standard demographic questions, but what specific

relationship and listening questions should we ask, Carter?

Well, I was thinking we could do a list of attributes and ask people to indicate the importance of them. You know, things like being honest, open, responsive—stuff like that.

Great! Let's start on those questions. Should we list the attributes and ask respondents to check the ones they feel are important? I guess we'd better specify what type of relationship too. ■

In the previous two chapters, we explored a number of factors associated with relationship building. In this chapter we expand on this discussion, focusing on two additional significant relationships: friendships and romantic partners. More specifically we will explore how the joys and pressures of being a friend (however casual or romantic that friendship might be) affect listening. We will also discuss ways you can be a better listening friend or partner.

MAKING AND BECOMING FRIENDS

Chances are when the students in the case at the beginning of this chapter tabulate their survey results, they will find people most desire warmth and kindness, expressiveness and openness, and a sense of humor in their relationships no matter the type (e.g., intimate or casual, same- and opposite-sex friends).[1] If so, their research will reflect the findings of academic researchers who report that we value **intrinsic** attributes more than traditional *external* qualities (e.g., good looks, money, social status). These characteristics reflect both the motivation and the ability on the part of our friends and lovers to provide us with social and emotional support.[2] We seem to value these traits even more in our romantic partners than our friends. In fact, these attributes are fundamental to establishing and maintaining *all* interpersonal relationships.[3]

Before we specifically address listening, we need to first briefly look at what we know about friends and the role they play in our lives. This background will lay the groundwork for seeing how and why we use different types and levels of listening as relationships progress.

Friendships are based on perceptions that each person is an equal and that the feelings of friendship are reciprocated. That is, you both feel close to one another, and you don't feel the relationship is forced (e.g., you are friends by choice, not because your moms are best friends).[4] Perhaps most important, friendships are founded on the interpersonal skills of the individuals involved.[5] In general, we are more fully engaged when interacting with our friends than when interacting with peers or strangers. Even as children, we tend to show greater prosocial behaviors (sharing snacks, toys) and engage in more positive communication behaviors (eye contact, smiling, talking, laughing) with our friends than with acquaintances.[6] Some researchers suggest these friendship behaviors have other positive effects. For example, our problem-solving and memory skills are enhanced when working on tasks with friends rather than acquaintances.[7] All of this begs the question, "How do we develop friendships?"

Early Friendships—Early and Middle Childhood

As early as age four, we begin to use the word *friend*. At this age, however, we often mean "friend" in terms of the level of familiarity we have with a peer.[8] So the more time a four-year-old spends with someone, the more likely the word *friend* will be used to identify that child (of course, this label is often reinforced by family). Friendships are important across our life spans. Children and adults with few or no friends are more likely to have adjustment problems (e.g., dropping out of school, drug and alcohol abuse, thoughts of suicide, depression, anxiety).[9] Thus, friendship is positively associated with increased health and both mental and physical wellness.

Friendships generally possess three fundamental characteristics: voluntariness, equality, and reciprocity. In other words, we *voluntarily* enter into a friendship with someone we see and treat (and expect them to see and treat us) as an *equal,* where we expect the relationship to be returned or *reciprocated.*[10] However, as we age, our expectations of what it means to be a friend and the functions our friendships serve change.[11] As we grow out of early childhood, our friends are no longer defined by proximity or who is available to play.

Unlike very young children, older children (five to eight years) begin to develop a broader, and narrower, view of friendship. Friendship becomes more closely associated with supportive or helping behaviors. For example, friends *help* with homework, help with doing tasks, and provide emotional support.[12] Children also become more skilled at entering into ongoing games or activities and sharing and generally don't insult or behave aggressively. As you would expect from this discussion, friendship listening skills begin to develop more fully at this time. For example, assume that Carter's sister Sylvia is a socially competent nine-year-old. Chances are she will listen and attend to the activities of a group that is already engaged in play prior to joining it. By doing so, she can determine what is the best means of "inserting" herself into the game in a smooth and ideally nondisruptive manner.

We will also notice if we observe Sylvia that she is beginning to develop same-sex friendships. It is at this same time we see gender differences beginning to emerge. For example, girls tend to play in smaller groups or dyads, while boys often prefer larger groups. This finding has, in part, led researchers to describe girls' friendships as "exclusive and dyadic," and boys' friendships as "inclusive and group-oriented."[13] Gender differences in play also begin to appear at this age. Girls focus greater attention on collaborative conversation making than do boys. Girls will also be more likely to "express agreement, acknowledge what a previous speaker has said, show concern for turn taking, and refrain from interruptions."[14] If you think back to the Listening MATERRS model, you will see that girls seem to be actively developing good responding listening skills during this period of their lives.

In contrast, boys express greater competitiveness than girls of this age. So as a youngster, Carter probably focused his conversations and behaviors on establishing a social hierarchy with those with whom he interacted.[15] This tendency for boys to have "fewer close friendships and to experience lower levels of intimacy within these relationships" is likely related to peer group culture.[16] It is important to note, however, that while different, boys also develop close, same-sex friends as sources of social support.[17] The understanding, acceptance, trust, and respect boys gain from these close relationships help build confidence and self-esteem and help buffer them against outside peer pressure.[18]

THINK ON IT

Researchers don't explicitly address how these differences in development may affect listening behaviors. How might the differences in how girls and boys play together affect how they learn to listen to one another? Do you believe listening behaviors will differ? If so, how?

In several chapters of this book, we talk about the importance of emotional intelligence (IQ). Emotional IQ seems to develop in middle childhood (eight to 12 years) as children develop an understanding of emotional communication. Specifically they seem to develop competence in accurately understanding and labeling emotions as well as regulating or managing their emotions (i.e., how well a child manages intensely felt emotions).[19] At this stage, to be viewed as socially competent by their peers, children must learn how to express emotion but do so in a somewhat regulated way (i.e., avoiding temper tantrums, uncontrolled crying, hitting, and so forth). These important skills are often distinguishing characteristics of popular children. Thus, popular children are better at recognizing what is expected in a certain situation as well as when the emotional reaction is out of proportion to the situation.[20] So a more emotionally mature child (and probably a more popular child) recognizes that expressing sadness over a broken toy is acceptable but throwing a temper tantrum about the loss isn't. Another way of looking at this is to recognize that the child is beginning to develop skills in sorting through the nuances of a social situation.

The example in Case Study 7.2 illustrates the effect of emotional intelligence as well as gender differences.

CASE STUDY 7.2

Ben's Story

I remember once when my family went to a neighborhood party at the local park for a picnic. My older sister, who was about eight, wanted the two of us to go down the slide together. While she tried to figure out a way for that to happen, I pushed her out of the way and climbed up the steps to the top of the slide. I just wanted to go down the slide and didn't really care whether she went or not. Funny thing was that she didn't get mad; she just got sad about us not doing something together. Some of the other children invited her to join them in some game they were playing. They didn't ask me. I don't think it was because I was too young; I think it was because I was being a brat. In retrospect, the difference might have been that I was acting like a typical, competitive boy and she was more emotionally mature.

Not surprisingly many communication skills develop during childhood. As seen in this Case Study, we learn what it means to be a friend as well as the communication and listening skills needed to sustain such a relationship. In addition to developing communication-related skills, most of us also emotionally mature. These skills are important to later friendships, romances, and commitments to others.

Adolescent Friendships

With friendships come obligations. For adolescents, friendship obligations typically include loyalty, trust, and emotional support.[21] However, as noted earlier, friendships are dynamic, and as you go from early to late adolescence, your relational orientations and friendship dynamics undergo a number of changes.[22] First, you begin to appreciate the differences between yourself and your friends. For example, as young children, you might tease a less-skilled friend, but you understand and are more accepting of varying skill levels in late adolescence. For example, imagine that NaMii tells the group that she played soccer from the time she was five until she was 13. Unfortunately she wasn't very good as a small child and some of the other children teased her for being a klutz. By the time she entered her teens, the teasing had become less hurtful.

By late adolescence, you also become more attuned to the importance of effectively handling conflict to maintaining and sustaining your friendships. While having similar values and interests is still important, you become more cognizant of the values and beliefs you share (or don't share). Of course, listening to others is the primary way adolescents learn about the similarities and differences they share with others. As we have noted throughout the text, a willingness to listen to others' self-disclosures is fundamental to supporting and maintaining all relationships. Adolescence is the time where you truly begin to see and, it is hoped, understand the importance of listening to maintaining relationships. It is also at this time that you mature to the point where you realize that you have a responsibility as a listener in a relationship.

Early research by listening scholars Andy Wolvin, Carolyn Coakley, and Kelby Halone found that prior to adolescence, children failed to express any responsibility for listening, essentially leaving it up to the speaker. However, most adolescents acknowledge that they have a role in listening.[23]

It is important to note that your level of self-esteem can "color your friendship world." One recent study suggests that high-self-esteem adolescents are better able to address conflict with their friends and move on. However, those with low self-esteem tend to engage in avoidance while remaining mentally fixated on the problem.[24] Remaining fixated on a problem can result in a number of negative listening behaviors. For example, you keep thinking of what you "should have said," thus missing what is currently being discussed. It is common for unresolved feelings to interfere with how you perceive, interpret, or translate later communication. Thus, when your friend asks about how your date went, you interpret the statement as sarcasm indicating that you really didn't have a date or as an attempt to make fun of the person with whom you went out.

Adult Friendships

Friendships play a number of important roles as we become adults. Our friends help us make career decisions, assess our romantic relationships, and negotiate changing self-perceptions.[25] One of the primary ways we maintain our friendships is through "everyday" talk.[26] While women tend to focus on personal topics more than men do, the conversation itself strengthens and reinforces our relationships with our friends. Such conversations are evidence of both the existence and the importance of the friendship.[27] As we established in Chapter 5, listening is essential to a good conversation.

People also use several **explicit strategies to maintain relationships.** However, the strategy varies depending on the nature and stage of the relationship.[28] Among the many strategies we can use are *openness* (as evidenced by self-disclosure), *assurance* (as exemplified by supportiveness), *joint activities* (spending time together), *positivity* (working to keep exchanges pleasant), and *avoidance* (avoiding talking about specific issues or avoiding the person). Of these strategies, openness, assurance, and joint activities tend to most closely apply to friendships, while positivity and avoidance are used more frequently in romantic and family relationships. Self-disclosure, as it occurs in everyday conversations, is a primary implicit relationship maintenance strategy for friends. Supportiveness is also generally viewed as a given in friendships. Friendships provide us with social support (e.g., comfort, assistance in solving problems) and instrumental support (e.g., providing a ride). Perhaps one of the more important means of maintaining friendships is simply doing things together. Engaging in joint activities with your friends means that you are immediately available to engage in self-disclosure and to provide support, ultimately helping to sustain that relationship.

As you can see from the discussion above, listening is fundamental to the strategies we use to maintain relationships. Talking with friends can also be good for your relationships. Previous research indicates that spending time with common friends also helps maintain our romantic relationships, especially marriages. One way this works is that our friendships provide an outlet for expressing feelings toward and about our romantic partners.[29] Friendships appear to be particularly important for married women. Through their friendships, married women have an avenue for expressing anger, frustration, or other similar emotions. Expressing these emotions helps diffuse them, with the side effect of increasing marital stability and commitment.[30]

Our romantic relationships can actually have a negative effect on friendships. Interpersonal communication scholar Chris Segrin notes that when we enter into committed relationships, particularly marriage, we often "cut back" on our social network of friends.[31] However, if our partner dies or we get divorced, we'll need close friends to help us weather the ensuing life changes. Thus, making new friends and maintaining old friendships can be good for our mental health so we'll have someone to listen to us in both good times and bad.

LISTENING IN INTIMATE RELATIONSHIPS

As often happens, some friendships take on an added dimension: romance. In this section we address the role of listening in developing serious intimate relationships. We begin with dating, or initiating romantic relationships, then move to developing and maintaining relationships, followed by listening in committed relationships.

Dating/Initiating Romantic Relationships

One of the first sites for listening in dating is in the context of an opening line.[32] Opening lines offer, and are interpreted by the listener, as an invitation to get to know one another more fully. It is interesting that several listener characteristics can affect how opening lines are received and interpreted. For example, men and women appear to evaluate opening lines differently. Men tend to respond to opening lines more positively than women do. In fact, it is not unusual for women to feel threatened when listening to opening lines. In other words, women can feel threatened when men attempt to initiate relational contact via an opening line (whether it was a good one or a bad one). In fact, women are more likely to report trying to avoid or withdraw from the interaction.[33] Male listeners, in contrast, generally do not feel as threatened by opening lines. Many men indicate they are happy to be receiving any type of opening line, whether it is a good-quality one or even an obnoxious one. The fact that they receive an opening line at all appears to positively dispose men toward relating with the sender (i.e., they're flattered). This response can be mediated by a person's willingness to listen.

> **THINK ON IT**
>
> What's the best and worst opening lines you've received? Compare your examples to others in your class. What distinguishes good openings from bad openings? How did you (and your classmates) react when receiving a good opening versus a bad one? What was the effect on your listening?

However, individuals who are higher in "readiness to listen" appear to be less threatened by opening lines, particularly if it was a good-quality opening line. For example, men who scored as highly ready to listen were more likely to positively respond to a good-quality opening line than men who were scored as low or moderate in readiness to listen. While women in general appear somewhat leery of opening lines, it appears that those higher in readiness to listen found them less threatening than women low in readiness to listen. So if you're looking for advice on opening lines, research suggests avoiding many of the opening line clichés (e.g., "Do you come here often?") and instead be direct (e.g., "I'd like to meet you"). This technique appears to be preferred by both men and women.[34]

While many of us think that getting the first date is the hard part of dating, previous research suggests that communication is the most common dating problem.[35]

Just as in our other relationships, we use scripts to guide us, whether asking someone out on a first date or guiding our behaviors and expectations while on a date. It's no surprise that a lot of listening goes on during a date. However, there is a lot of speaking as well. Our attempts at conversation as we search for common interests are considered part of the script for dating.[36]

Underlying these "get to know you" dating moments is Grice's concept of reciprocity. As we discussed in the conversation chapter, a conversation occurs only if there is an exchange of information or a real interaction. We also have an expectation that if we reveal something personal to someone else, that person will, at some time, share something equally personal. However, if one conversational partner feels that he or she has to carry the communication load during a date, or if one person discloses too much personal information too fast, there might not be a second date.

Just as in other parts of our lives, we tend to have well-developed scripts for key events in our dating lives (e.g., being asked out, first dates, relationship development and termination).[37] These scripts appear to be commonly held by most members of mainstream North American culture. Of course, just because our dating scripts have much in common does not mean that every person carries exactly the same dating script around in his or her head.

Recent research suggests that when the expectations set up by our scripts do not match up with those of our relationship partner, we often view the relationship less positively. The more similar the scripts, the easier it becomes for individuals who are dating to predict each other's future behavior.[38] So if you like someone but your interactions seem to be unusually awkward, it could be that you're operating from different dating scripts. At such times, direct communication about your expectations is the most likely route for maintaining and further developing the relationship.[39]

Developing and Maintaining Romantic Relationships

Assuming that all goes well, the odds are that you will eventually find one of these initial dates developing into a more serious relationship. Once it is fully developed, you then have to engage in relational maintenance. What does **relational maintenance** mean? Well, it depends on whom you ask. Researchers who study this area of relationships variously define it as keeping a relationship in existence, keeping it at its current level of development, maintaining relational satisfaction, and/or keeping a relationship in repair (i.e., addressing problematic issues).[40] We tend to take a broad view of relational maintenance, believing that in order to have relational satisfaction, partners must work to keep the relationship at a mutually satisfactory level. This necessitates relationship repair, including handling conflict (which we discussed in Chapter 5 and will discuss again later in this chapter).

While some individuals are quite direct in their approach to escalating a relationship (e.g., "I'd like to date you," "Let's go steady," "Want to move in together?" "Will you marry me?"), many individuals prefer a more indirect route.[41] The indirect route includes a variety of techniques and strategies, including increasing the

"You're the first guy I've met who really listens and blah, blah, blah..."

amount of time spent communicating or in contact with the other person, verbal and nonverbal expressions of affection (e.g., expressing interest in your values and goals, expressing love, compliments, doing favors, giving gifts, revealing more personal information, seeking or giving support). Needless to say, careful listening to these and similar cues lets us know that the other person wishes to escalate (i.e., make more serious) the relationship, giving you the opportunity to respond in a way you wish (i.e., welcoming or distancing). If you are the one hoping to make the relationship more serious, then listening becomes the means by which you can more accurately assess both the state of the relationship and the other's view of it. Many of the same techniques used to escalate a relationship can be and are used to test or assess the current state of the relationship. Thus, the rest of this section focuses on "involved daters."[42]

Involved daters are "emotionally involved in a reciprocal love relationship with one person."[43] In contrast, **casual daters** are dating any number of individuals. Research suggests that communication issues become more salient as we become more involved in the relationship. For example, nonverbal communication becomes more important and is focused on to a greater degree by both partners in more serious dating relationships. As a result, there appear to be fewer cross-cues (verbal and nonverbal messages that don't match) between involved relationship partners, likely leading to reports of increased relational satisfaction. Thus, as individuals become more vested in a relationship, it appears that they work harder on their communication messages, especially making sure that verbal and nonverbal modes of communication are congruent. Why are these findings important? They can help us listen more effectively and efficiently. Incongruities between channels make it more difficult to decode and process information. As a result, we may miss part of the message or misinterpret it.

Relationship scholars Kathryn Dindia and Lindsay Timmerman noted that "relationships do not maintain themselves."[44] Communicative interactions are the foundation of our relationships. Dindia and Timmerman argued that there are several **relationship functions** that help maintain our relationships; among them are *maintaining interaction, maintaining liking* and *maintaining intimacy, conflict* *resolution,* and *emotional support.* These functions are most frequently expressed through the time we spend together and the activities we share.[45] However, relationship partners can't be together 24/7. "Talk," whether general conversations or catching up with one another at the end of the day, is one of the most important relationship maintenance strategies we engage in. In fact, those "end of the day" or "while we were separated" conversations appear to be one of the important ways that relational partners define their "togetherness." The same research has found these catching-up conversations to be positively related to relational satisfaction.[46]

These conversations become a means of addressing relational discontinuity (i.e., time apart). These moments are important sharing times and often include moments of empathy, self-disclosure, and social support, all of which require excellent listening skills and are fundamental to maintaining satisfying relationships. They are also likely related to another important aspect of relationships maintenance: liking.

At its simplest level, it makes sense that we should like the person we are in a relationship with. It is important, however, that expressions of liking (affection) are verbally and nonverbally expressed by both parties in a relationship. **Verbal assurances** stress our commitment to the other, showing our love and demonstrating our faithfulness.[47] Some research suggests that the longer (and more serious) our relationships become, the more frequently we engage in assurances. Relational satisfaction, commitment, and liking appear to be related to relational assurances.[48] In other words, we like to hear them. We also appreciate partners who are positive, cheerful, and overall engage in prosocial communication (i.e., avoid criticism, engage in conflict avoidance).[49] In fact, these types of conversations are often the foundation of the next type of relationship we discuss: committed couples.

Committed Couples

In their early work *Marriage and the Social Construction of Reality,* Peter Berger and Hansfried Kellner wrote, "The reality of the world is sustained through conversation with significant others."[50] Whether a spouse or committed partner, individuals in close relationships are important sources of feedback in our interactions with the social world.

Through marriage and marriagelike relationships (e.g., sustained, long-term, cohabitation), we experience our most intimate adult relationship, one that serves as our primary source of affection and support.[51] Central to this type of close relationship is intimacy, a sense of being close to and connected to the other person.[52] This feeling of closeness develops through our communication with our partners.[53] The process of intimacy is based on self-disclosure and partner responsiveness. *Responsiveness* occurs as you respond to your partner's disclosure in a way that validates the other person and shows caring and understanding. Intimacy develops through reciprocal responsive communication. As you know, listening is fundamental to responsiveness. A key aspect of developing feelings of closeness is your perception of your partner's responsiveness. When you perceive your partner to be responsive, you feel more valued by the listener. Responsiveness also encourages additional disclosure, helping to further establish a close, intimate relationship. This listening process is "dynamic and fluid, with each person taking on the role of speaker and listener."[54] Thus, feelings of intimacy are moderated by our perceptions and evaluations of how the other responds to our disclosures. This appears to apply particularly to disclosures of emotions.[55]

Relatively few studies have examined the relationships between communication and relational intimacy, especially sexual intimacy.[56] However, research in this area does suggest that self-disclosure and personalized communication (e.g., "we" language, pet names) does appear to be related to maintaining liking and maintaining intimacy. Scholars Deborah Borisoff and Dan Hahn suggested that intimate relationships are founded on self-disclosure, interdependence, trust, reciprocated commitment, and quality communication.

Borisoff and Hahn were particularly interested in listening differences of men and women. They believe that men and women differ in what they listen to as well as how they express their listening behavior and suggest that these differences can be a source of relational problems. For example, they suggested that when women share their problems and experiences, the process of the conversation itself is viewed as a means of expressing empathetic communication. Men, in contrast, are often more utilitarian in their approach to a conversation. They see the conversation as the opportunity to solve a problem. Thus, a woman may be seeking understanding, while the man in her life sets out to provide (sometimes unwanted) advice.[57] Both individuals may end up feeling hurt or exasperated, wondering why the other doesn't listen.

> **THINK ON IT:**
>
> Do agree with Borishoff and Hahn? Do you believe that men and women listen differently? What experiences lead you to draw this conclusion?

Professors Borisoff and Hahn have two primary suggestions for improving listening in close relationships. First, you have to *accept and validate your partner's contributions* to the relationship. They wrote, "Accepting others and encouraging their self-expression reflects a true gift of love."[58] This is most possible when we are able to look at the world through our partners' eyes, see the world from their perspective. Second, you need to *understand how your partner listens.* Professors Borisoff and Hahn also believe that while men and women might hear the same message, how it is interpreted (i.e., how they listen to it) can be quite different. Awareness of this difference could help you better understand your partner's response to a listening moment.

Self-disclosure (by both individuals) and partner responsiveness are strongly related to feelings of intimacy by both husbands and wives. However, they seem to be particularly important to women. In other words, wives' ratings of relationship closeness and intimacy seem to focus on "feeling understood, validated, accepted, and cared for" by their spouses. Reflecting the importance of responsiveness, women tend to be more communicatively responsive than men. Men, in contrast, experience greater relationship intimacy with increased self-disclosure. As you can see, men and women emphasize different parts of the communication process, affecting what and how they listen to one another.

However, both men and women value the feeling of *mutual commitment.* According to some researchers, mutuality of commitment is a key element we look for in our close relationships.[59] We want partners who feel the same way about the relationship and have the same expectations. A recent study examined how romantic partners communicate their commitment to each other.[60] The study generated

928 communication behaviors, which were collapsed into the following 10 commitment indicators:

1. providing affection
2. providing support
3. maintaining integrity
4. sharing companionship
5. making an effort to communicate regularly
6. showing respect
7. creating a relational future
8. creating a positive relational atmosphere
9. working on relationship problems together
10. reassuring one's commitment[61]

Typically the greater the level of mutuality of commitment, the more committed partners use the 10 commitment indicators.[62]

Marital Satisfaction

In addition to mutuality of commitment, self-disclosure is also important to the success of marital (or marriagelike) relationships. (We describe relationships in this section as marriages because much of the research has focused on married couples. However, much of this research can be applied to other marriagelike relationships.) Early research by Mary Ann Fitzpatrick found self-disclosure to be correlated to marital satisfaction. Related to self-disclosure are debriefing conversations.[63] As we discussed earlier, debriefing conversations are also important to building a sense of intimacy. Discussing daily routines, how one's day went, and so forth can then lead to topics that are more important and perhaps touch couples' lives more deeply.

For these conversations to enhance the relationship, the partners must listen to each other and show they are listening. Marriage therapist John Gottman claims that he can predict within five minutes whether a couple will remain together. One of the behaviors he looks at is the way the couple listens. If one or both of them stonewalls (i.e., continually avoids listening to the other one), particularly with unpleasant messages, chances are the relationship will fail.[64] However, when partners are responsive to each other, verbally and nonverbally signaling they are listening, the chances of relationship survival are much greater.

Thus, husbands and wives who regularly self-disclose and listen to one another appear to be happier, with some limitations. For example, if one partner has a high amount of negative feelings and regularly discloses those feelings, it can lead to lower marital satisfaction. Like many things in life, too much of a good thing can be detrimental. Essentially people can listen to only a certain amount of negativity before becoming overloaded, as seen in the following example. In a recent conversation, one of our friends asked his mother why she and his father had divorced. His mother told him that his father had gone through a period where he was really dissatisfied with his job. He would come home every day and spend much of his time (sometimes hours) talking about how the job was driving him crazy and how much he disliked it. His mother said that it got to the point where she was making excuses to work late because she could not take listening to it day in and day out anymore. With his wife's encouragement, our friend's father eventually sought counseling. The counselor understood the need to vent. However, he also understood the negative effect it could have on others. The counselor recommended that the father complain about his job for only 30 minutes when he first got home. Eventually the job situation improved, but the continual negative talk and disclosures put the marriage on shaky ground, setting it on a downward spiral, from which it never recovered.

As seen in this example, self-disclosure follows rules similar to that of Grice's maxim of quantity. However, there are times when we also need to evaluate the content and the quantity of our self-disclosure. Sharing some information can actually hurt a relationship. Does one spouse tell another about an affair or simply vow to never let it happen again? What would the knowledge do to the relationship? While this is certainly an ethical question and responses will vary based on personal backgrounds and beliefs, the fact is that such a self-disclosure will have profound implications for the relationship of those involved. Thus, one of the things we have to consider when self-disclosing is boundary management. *Boundary management* refers to the decisions we make about what information and feelings we will share with others and our awareness of the potential cost of sharing that information. Our boundary management decisions are generally tied to other relationship rules (e.g., family background, family status, gender, traditions). Previous research in this area suggests that we are most satisfied with our relationships when moderate amounts of self-disclosure are provided. If there is too little disclosure, we may feel the other person doesn't trust or love us, but when there is too much, we may be overwhelmed or feel manipulated.

> **THINK ON IT:**
>
> Have you ever felt someone was manipulating you in a relationship? What happened? Do you feel that your listening was affected? If so, how?

Authors Harold Bloomfield and Robert Cooper believe that "one of the reasons that love wanes is neglect, and one of the principal kinds of neglect is the inability to listen well."[65] As you can see from our discussion in this section, listening increases validation and makes your partner feel appreciated. Through listening, you gain greater empathy and understanding of your partner, which can make him or her feel more valued and loved.

Previous research indicates that positive and responsive listening tends to be "more characteristic of happily married than of unhappily married couples."[66] It is also associated with greater marital satisfaction. Positive and responsive listening is characterized by emotionally positive facial expressions, frequent eye contact, backchannel vocalizations (e.g., mm-hmm). To the extent such behaviors are missing, we will judge listening to be more neutral or negative (with negative nonverbal expressions).[67]

COUPLES IN CONFLICT

All relationships face their ups and downs, conflicts and conciliations. The fact is it can be difficult for us to respond in a positive, prosocial way to someone when we are in conflict. In many cases the responses we provide are more constructive than those that we initially thought of or those that we really wanted to say.[68] While much of the early research in marital functioning focused on studying and solving marriage problems, today there is a growing focus on identifying the positive communication and interactions necessary to maintain marriages (and other committed permanent bonds). How couples maintain positive regard and intimate connections is just as important, if not more so, as understanding how couples handle conflict.[69] Linda Roberts and Danielle Greenberg, researchers in family studies, believe that relational harmony depends on how well each partner engages in positive behaviors and communication during their interactions together. They suggest that when relational partners regularly engage in behaviors that encourage relational closeness, those behaviors help to establish and maintain "the climate of security, trust, and acceptance that characterize well-functioning relationships."[70] However, when relational partners ignore or neglect this important aspect of their relationship, greater hostility and more negative conflicts can result. Essentially, positive emotional expressions are reassuring for the other partner, even when in the middle of an argument, while negatively expressed behaviors create greater problems.[71]

Related research suggests that decreases in expressions of affection and partner responsiveness distinguish couples who eventually divorce from those who remain married.[72] Certainly one important way we provide responsiveness is through listening. This research suggests that active listening is one of the means by which we can provide this type of relational support and emotional responsiveness.

Relational research has also found that when we or our partners engage in intimacy avoidance, marital dissatisfaction can increase. **Intimacy avoidance** occurs when our partners avoid or withdraw from us when we try to confide in them. In other words, they don't want us to self-disclose to them; they are avoiding having to listen to us. If you remember in our discussion of self-disclosure and conversation, reciprocity is an important component of both. If we try to avoid receiving disclosures, we don't have to provide them, and it lessens the closeness and understanding we have with our partners. This can be quite important, given that previous research suggests that greater levels of self-disclosure occur between married spouses than in our relationships with our closest friends.[73]

Professors Roberts and Greenberg explored a number of behaviors that are associated with emotional supportiveness and caregiving.[74] These behaviors include direct expressions of caring or indirect vulnerable disclosures. For example, **direct expressions of caring** (either verbal or nonverbal) may be expressions of love, affection, and concern. **Validation** occurs when we engage in behaviors that enhance our partners' self-esteem and show we accept and have confidence in them. *Active understanding* is evidenced by behaviors, such as paraphrasing, which show we are available, empathetic, and understanding of the other person's feelings. Other intimacy processes such as *open-ended questions* encourage our partners to provide greater disclosure, while *general sharing* refers more to the factual sharing and disclosing of information. If these behaviors sound familiar, it's because they are good responding and empathy-building behaviors discussed earlier in this book. **Indirect vulnerable disclosures** are often expressions that signal the need for emotional support and understanding. For example, the wife of one couple participating in a study by Roberts and Greenberg expressed concern for her weight. An appropriate response

THINK ON IT:

Looking at a current or previous relationship, what are things that you did to help your partner feel validated? Why did you do them? How did it affect the relationship? Was your partner aware you were trying to help him or her feel validated? What effect do you think it had on your relationship?

from the husband would directly (e.g., "You sound like you want to start a diet," "Why do you think you've gained weight?") or indirectly (e.g., confirming nod of the head, squeeze her hand) address her concern. Such responses signal active listening, caregiving, and emotional validation. Silence, as actually occurred in this case, was inappropriate. In fact, the wife eventually became angry with her husband because he was not providing the expected emotional support.

Related to listening processes, couples in distressed (unhappy) marriages and relationships tend to have problems decoding nonverbal communication of their spouses. This **decoding deficit** appears to be specific to that relationship. The couples don't appear to have the same problem decoding the nonverbals of other individuals. Strangers observing a conflict between individuals in an unhappy relationship tend to be better at decoding the nonverbals than the individuals actually in the distressed relationship.[75] Needless to say, an important aspect of listening is being able to decode and interpret a message. Couples who are having marital problems apparently get a double whammy. Not only are they having problems but their problems make it more difficult for them to communicate with each other. This communication difficulty is further compounded by the fact couples are generally quite confident in their interpretation of the spouse's message.[76] Researchers believe that one reason for this overconfidence lies within the nature of the relationship itself: the partners know each other so well (or think they do).[77]

Distressed couples also exhibit other related communication problems. For example, they interrupt more, tend to criticize and complain more, and are more likely to provide negative solutions (e.g., "It's hopeless," "Just forget it").[78] They are also less likely to self-disclose, to offer acceptance or empathy, and to make eye contact with or smile at their partners.[79] In fact, nonverbal behaviors appear to truly set happy couples apart from unhappy couples.[80] Previous research indicates that the ratio of positive to negative behavior (30:1) distinguishes happy couples from unhappy couples (4:1).[81] Distressed couples are also less able to engage in problem description, have poorer active listening skills, and have difficulty in creating constructive solutions to problems.

The overall state of the marriage can be quite important to how messages and behavior are interpreted. Individuals in distressed marriages are more likely to assign negative connotations to ambiguous communication and behavior, while people in happy marriages will use a more positive lens for interpreting those same behaviors and communications.[82] The focus on the positive likely has a better chance of successfully resolving conflict. Unfortunately distressed couples also are more likely to respond negatively, so while reciprocity occurs, it sets off a negative spiral, often resulting in an escalation of the conflict.[83] Not surprisingly this pattern of behavior not only reduces marital satisfaction but also has been associated with increased rates of divorce.[84] One of the contributors to these conflicts is social perception.

Social perception addresses "what one attends to or the impressions one forms of another."[85] Distressed couples often have significant differences in how they describe relationship events, reflecting the effect of cognitive schemata and personal biases. For example, a distressed spouse is more likely to attribute a marital problem to something inherently related to the other (e.g., personality attributes such as laziness) rather than to extrinsic causes (e.g., stressed out from work). In contrast, happily married couples tend to view their partners more positively, even than their partners view themselves. In addition, they are more likely to give their partners the benefit of the doubt. Giving another the benefit of the doubt when assessing events increases the likelihood of focusing on behaviors that confirm our perceptions of our spouses and makes it much easier for us to respond positively when in conflict.[86]

Listening Responses to Conflict

Relational dissatisfaction and conflict are givens in close relationships. How we respond to these moments is most important to relational repair. If we are to engage in constructive conflict, we need to *avoid* a variety of negative behaviors, including "defensiveness, criticism, contempt, avoiding the issue, mindreading[, and] making negative attributions toward the partner."[87] Avoiding blame, ensuring we understand the other's perspective (via paraphrasing), and avoiding personal attacks (by focusing on the annoying behavior) generally will increase our overall satisfaction with our relationships.[88] Relationship scholar Tara Emmers-Sommer summarized the research in this area: "Overall, the prescription [is] simple: Be nice to your partner to maintain your relationship, if you transgress, engage in prosocial, communicative behaviors to repair the relationship."[89]

The relationship between speaking and listening is particularly apparent in marital conflict. How the listening partner responds to the speaking partner can affect whether a conflict increases or decreases in intensity. For example, when observing other relationships, you may have noticed that when one partner feels ignored, he or she may talk more loudly or continue to pick on the same minor point repeatedly. Thus, a speaker who feels he or she isn't receiving the appropriate quantity or quality of listening response may escalate the argument to get some type of response (even negative) from the listener. The fact is withholding listening responses or "freezing someone out" is a poor response to conflict.

In addition, as we mentioned earlier, the ratio of positive to negative behaviors is related to overall marital satisfaction and marital stability.[90] In general, marital stability can be maintained when there are five positive behaviors to each negative behavior. Thus, the balance between positive and negative marital behaviors becomes important for maintaining a marriage. As outlined below, poor communication, including poor listening, are related to increased negativity and greater marital instability.

Communication Patterns

Research in conflict suggests that there are distinct differences in the communication and conflict patterns of distressed and nondistressed couples.[91] Table 7.1 presents types of conflict communication based on hostile speaking behavior and withdrawn

TABLE 7.1		
Typology of Marital Conflict Styles		
	Regulated Listening	Nonregulated Listening
Regulated Speaking	Conflict Engagers	Avoiders
Nonregulated Speaking	Hostile	Hostile Detached

listening behavior. In the table **regulation** and **nonregulation** refer to the ratio of positive to negative behaviors that a couple exhibits over time.[92] Thus, a nonregulated couple would have a higher ratio of negative to positive behaviors, while a regulated couple would exhibit more positive behaviors than negative behaviors. Examples of negative speaking behaviors include verbally attacking each other, including belittling, blaming, and contemptuousness.[93] **Conflict withdrawal** is often characterized by negative listening behaviors such as physically turning away from the other person, changing the topic, and avoiding backchannel behaviors (e.g., head nods, verbal encouragements to continue speaking).[94]

Couples that engage in nonregulated behaviors tend to be more unhappy with their relationships. They express more negative and fewer positive emotions, are more stubborn, withdraw more, and are more defensive.[95]

Thus, people who are **conflict engagers** are more likely to express regard for their significant others by directly addressing potentially contentious issues, listening closely, and responding appropriately. As a consequence, they actually will express more negative emotions than avoiders. However, conflict engagers also express more positive behavior as well. **Avoiders**, in contrast, are more likely to withdraw from listening, likely because the act of really listening carries with it the expectation of a response.

Hostile and hostile-detached couples also differ from one another. Hostile couples engage in fewer negative and more positive behaviors than hostile-detached couples. Some research suggests that hostile and hostile-detached couples tend to be the most unstable and prone to divorce.[96] **Hostile-detached** couples are the most likely to experience problems when attempting to coparent a child. Their disengagement with and hostility toward one another appears to spill over in their relationships with their children and can ultimately influence their children's own interpersonal interactions. Withdrawal, in the face of hostility, exemplifies a type of emotional disregulation, behavior that can negatively affect children's interactions with peers and other individuals, if they model their parents' conflict behaviors.

Culture and Commitment

Intercultural relationships can face a number of difficulties as related to the expectations of each romantic partner. Thus, interracial and interethnic couples have to work hard at understanding and recognizing how cultural differences can affect their relational maintenance beliefs and behaviors, especially those related to communication and listening.[97] For example, while Americans often focus on fairness and equity in each partner's contributions to the relationship, Koreans do not. Because equity is much less important to them, Koreans are more likely to take for granted that their marriage partner will remain in the relationship. As a result, they do not track the types of commitments or obligations that an American couple would. In addition, Koreans may feel less need to express and/or acknowledge displays of affection and commitment.

Cultural differences in self-disclosure can also occur. While we have stressed the importance of self-disclosure to listening and relationships, our examples often reflect our individualistic cultural orientation. Self-disclosure in individualistic cultures often will emphasize individual accomplishments, abilities, and characteristics. In collectivistic cultures, a more interdependent view of self-disclosure emerges such that restraint and harmony are emphasized and likely leads to differences in both the quantity and the quality of individual self-disclosure.[98]

SUMMARY

One of the most important elements of our lives is the relationships that we use to define who and what we are. As we have seen in this chapter, our listening skills grow as we age and mature. With effective communication and listening skills, we are better able to establish friendships and enter into long-term, committed relationships. We are also better able to both elicit and provide the social support needed to validate our own and others' self-views. Over the previous two chapters, we have examined the influence of listening and listening processes on the most important relationships we will form over the course of our lives. However, as we have discussed earlier in the text, listening occurs in context. The next four chapters of the book explore four common listening contexts: education, organizations, health, and the law.

CONCEPTS TO KNOW

Friend
Friendship Characteristics
    Voluntariness
    Equality
    Reciprocity
Helping Behavior
Strategies to Maintain Relationships
    Openness
    Assurance
    Joint Activities
    Positivity
    Avoidance
Involved Daters
Casual Daters
Relationship Functions
    Maintaining Interactions
    Maintaining Liking
    Maintaining Intimacy
    Conflict Resolution
    Emotional Support
Cross-cues

Verbal Assurances
Responsiveness
Boundary Management
Mutual Commitment
Intimacy Avoidance
Direct Expressions of Caring
Validation
    Active Understanding
    Open Questions
    General Sharing
Indirect Vulnerable Disclosures
Decoding Deficit
Social Perception
Marital Conflict Styles
    Regulation/Nonregulation
    Conflict Withdrawal
    Conflict Engager
    Avoider
    Hostile Couple
    Hostile-detached Couple

DISCUSSION QUESTIONS

1. Make a list of the many qualities you like about your best friend or friends. Compare your list to those of the people sitting around you. How is the importance of listening seen in your list? How many things on your list would be considered an intrinsic quality? An extrinsic quality? What does

your list tell you about what you and others value in your friendships?

2. Some people find it easy to make friends, while others find it more difficult. What qualities lead someone to be described as "friendly"? How are those qualities related to listening? What advice or tips would you give to someone who finds it difficult to make friends?

LISTENING ACTIVITIES

1. As a communication consultant, you've been asked to develop a survey to help individuals identify their "best" friends. Develop 10 items. What type of questions did you put on the questionnaire? Why? Compare your survey to others' in your class. What similarities and differences do you observe? Would you use the same questions if you were trying to identify a romantic partner?

2. Soap operas seem to thrive on conflict. Over the course of a week, pick a soap opera and observe the interactions of a primary couple on the show. What are some of the qualities of committed couples that you observed? Do their interactions reflect real life? What you've learned in this chapter? In other areas of the text? What effect might soap operas have on the schemata and scripts children or adolescences develop about dating relationships? How couples communicate and listen to one another?

3. Earlier in the chapter, we discussed the ethical dilemmas committed couples often face. Do you believe that if one member of a couple has an affair, he or she should tell the partner? Do you know someone who has received news such as this? How did it affect the relationship? If the couple remained committed, how do you think it affected their relationship? Their conflict communication patterns? Their listening?

3. Interview a committed couple in your life. It may be your parents, grandparents, an aunt and uncle, or good friends. How did they meet? What drew them together? What qualities did they admire about each other when they first met? Who escalated the relationship and how? How does what you learned reflect the discussion of communication and relationship development presented in this chapter?

4. In a group of three to four people, imagine that you have been asked to develop a conflict management workshop for committed couples. What tips would you offer and why? As a class, compare your tips. Are they similar or different? What would the class top five or six tips be? Each group should develop a two- to three-minute skit to present one of the tips to the class.

ADDITIONAL READINGS

Duck, S. W., & McMahan, D. T. (2009). *The basics of communication: A relational perspective*. Thousand Oaks, CA: Sage.

Galvin, K. M. (2010). *Making connections: Readings in relational communication* (5th ed.). New York: Oxford University Press.

Guerrero, L. K., Andersen, P. A., & Afifi, W. A. (2007). *Close encounters: Communication in relationships* (2nd ed.). Thousand Oaks, CA: Sage.

Guerrero, L. K., & Floyd, K. (2005). *Nonverbal communication in close relationships*. Mahwah, NJ: LEA.

Kirkpatrick, D. C., Duck, S., & Foley, M. K. (Ed.). (2006). *The processes of constructing and managing difficult interaction*. Mahwah, NJ: LEA/Routledge.

Rogers, L. E., & Escudero, V. (Eds.). (2004). *Relational communication: An interactional perspective to the study of process and form*. Mahwah, NJ: LEA.

Yingling, J. (2004). *A lifetime of communication: Transformation through relational dialogues*. Mahwah, NJ: LEA.

ENDNOTES

1. Sprecher & Regan, 2002
2. Sprecher & Regan, 2002
3. Sprecher & Regan, 2002
4. Hartup & Abecassis, 2002
5. Asher et al., 1996; Guerrero, 1997
6. Fehr, 1996; Halpern, 1997; Planalp & Benson, 1992
7. Anderson & Ronnberg, 1997; Newcomb & Brady, 1982
8. Hartup, 1983

9. For reviews, see Fehr (1996) and Ladd (1999)
10. Samter, 2003
11. Samter, 2003
12. For a review, see Samter, 2003
13. Samter, 2003, p. 642
14. Samter, 2003, p. 642
15. Berdnt, 1981a, 1981b; Thorne, 1986
16. Chu, 2005, p. 7
17. Chu, 2005
18. Chu, 2005
19. Gertner et al., 1994
20. Ianotti, 1985
21. Azmitia, Ittel, & Radmacher, 2005
22. Azmitia et al., 2005
23. Wolvin, Coakley, & Halone, 1995
24. Azmitia et al., 2005
25. Rawlins, 1992
26. Duck, 1994
27. Fehr, 2000
28. Canary & Stafford, 1994
29. Bell et al., 1987; Dindia & Baxter, 1987; Stafford & Canary, 1991
30. Oliker, 1989
31. Segrin, 2006
32. Cline & Clark, 1994
33. Cline & Clark, 1994
34. Kleinke, 1981
35. McGinty, Knox, & Zusman, 2003
36. Berger & Bell, 1988; Miell & Duck, 1986; Pryor & Merluzzi, 1985
37. See Homberg & MacKenzie (2002) for a review
38. These claims are based on early research by Homberg & MacKenzie (2002). These researchers are continuing their line of research in this area
39. Homberg & MacKenzie, 2002
40. See Dindia & Canary (1993) for a review
41. Dindia & Timmerman, 2003
42. McGinty, Knox, & Zusman, 2003
43. McGinty et al., 2003, p. 68
44. Dindia & Timmerman, 2003, p. 705
45. See Dindia and Timmerman (2003) for a review
46. Vangelisti & Banski, 1993
47. Dindia & Timmerman, 2003, p. 707
48. Stafford, 2003; Stafford & Canary, 1991
49. Canary & Stafford, 1994; Dindia & Baxter, 1987
50. As quoted in Neff & Karney, 2002, p. 32
51. Laurenceau, Feldman, & Rovine, 2005; Levinger & Huston, 1990
52. Laurenceau et al., 2005
53. Perlman & Fehr, 1987
54. Laurenceau et al., 2005
55. Laurenceau, Feldman, & Pietromonaco, 1998
56. See Dindia & Timmerman (2003), p. 708, for a brief review; cf., Borisoff & Hann (1992)
57. Tannen, 1990
58. Borisoff & Hahn, 1992, p. 35
59. Knobloch & Solomon, 2003; Weigel, 2008
60. Weigel & Ballard-Reisch, 2002
61. As reported by Weigel, 2008, p. 26
62. Weigel, 2008
63. Fitzpatrick, 1987
64. Gottman & Silver, 1999
65. Bloomfield & Cooper, 1995, p. 93
66. Pasupathi, Carstensen, Levenson, & Gottman, 1999
67. Gottman, 1989, as cited in Pasupathi et al., 1999
68. Yovetich & Rusbult, 1994
69. Roberts & Greenberg, 2002
70. Roberts & Greenberg, 2002, p. 121
71. Pasupathi et al., 1999
72. Huston, Caughlin, Houts, Smith, & George, 2001
73. Tschann, 1988; Kito, 2005
74. Roberts & Greenberg, 2002
75. Gottman & Porterfield, 1981; Noller, 1981
76. Noller & Venardos, 1986
77. Sillar & Scott, 1983
78. See Kelly, Fincham, & Beach (2003) for a review of the literature
79. See Kelly et al. (2003) for a review of the literature
80. Gottman et al., 1977; Smith, Vivian, & O'Leary, 1990
81. Birchler, Weiss, & Vincent, 1975; Fincham, Bradbury, Arias, Byrne, & Karney, 1997
82. Noller & Fitzpatrick, 1993
83. Gottman, 1994
84. Gottman, 1994
85. Kelly et al., 2003
86. See Kelly et al. (2003) for a review.
87. Gottman, 1994, as described by Emmers-Sommer, 2003
88. Gottman, 1994
89. Emmers-Sommer, 2003, p. 199
90. Gottman & Levenson, 1992
91. See, for example, Christensen & Heavey (1990); Fitzpatrick & Indvik (1982); Gottman (1993, 1994); Kurdek (1995)
92. Gottman & Levenson, 1992
93. Brown & Smith, 1992, Gottman, 1993
94. Christenseen & Heavey, 1990; Gottman, 1993
95. Gottman & Levenson, 1992
96. Gottman, 1993, 1994
97. Yum & Canary, 2003
98. Markus & Kitayama, 1991

REFERENCES

Anderson, J., & Ronnberg, J. (1997). Cued memory collaboration: Effects of friendship and type of retrieval cue. *European Journal of Cognitive Psychology, 9,* 273–287.

Asher, S. R., Parker, J. G., & Walker, D. L. (1996). Distinguishing friendship from acceptance: Implications for intervention and assessment. In W. M. Bukowski, A. F. Newcomb, & W. W. Hartup (Eds.), *The company they keep: Friendship in childhood and adolescence* (pp. 366–405). New York: Cambridge University Press.

Azmitia, M., Ittel, A., & Radmacher, K. (2005). Narratives of friendship and self in adolescence. In N. Way, J. V. Hamm (Eds.), *New directions for child and adolescent development* (no. 107, pp. 23–39). San Francisco: Jossey-Bass.

Bell, R. A., Daly, J. A., & Gonzalez, C. (1987). Affinity-maintenance in marriage and its relationship to women's marital satisfaction. *Journal of Marriage and the Family, 49,* 445–454.

Berger, C. R., & Bell, R. A. (1988). Plans and the initiation of social relationship. *Human Communication Research, 14,* 217–235.

Berndt, T. J. (1981a). Age changes and changes over time in prosocial intentions and behavior between friends. *Developmental Psychology, 17,* 408–416.

Berndt, T. J. (1981b). Effects of friendship on prosocial intentions and behavior. *Child Development, 52,* 636–643.

Birchler, G. R., Weiss, R. L., & Vincent, J. P. (1975). Multimethod analysis of social reinforcement exchange between martially distressed and nondistressed spouse and stranger dyads. *Journal of Personality and Social Psychology, 31,* 349–360.

Bloomfield, H. H., & Cooper, R. K. (1995, July). Take five to make love last. *Prevention* (90–97).

Borisoff, D., & Hahn, D. F. (1992). Dimensions of intimacy: The interrelationships between gender and listening. *Journal of the International Listening Association, 6,* 23–41.

Brown, P. C., & Smith, T. W. (1992). Social influence, marriage, and the heart: Cardiovascular consequences of interpersonal control in husbands and wives. *Health Psychology, 11,* 88–96.

Canary, D. J., & Stafford, L. (1994). Maintaining relationships through strategic and routine interaction. In D. J. Canary & L. Stafford (Eds.), *Communication and relational maintenance* (pp. 3–22). San Diego: Academic Press.

Christensen, A., & Heavey, C. L. (1990). Gender and social structure in the demand/withdraw pattern of marital conflict. *Journal of Personality and Social Psychology, 59,* 73–81.

Chu, J. Y. (2005). Adolescent boys' friendships and peer group culture. In N. Way, J. V. Hamm (Eds.), *New directions for child and adolescent development* (no. 107, pp. 7–22). San Francisco: Jossey-Bass.

Cline, R. J. W., & Clark, A. J. (1994). "I've fallen for you like a blind roofer": Some effects of listener characteristics on interpreting opening lines. *International Journal of Listening, 8,* 80–97.

Dindia, K., & Baxter, L. (1987). Strategies for maintaining and repairing marital relationships. *Journal of Social and Personal Relationships, 4,* 143–158.

Dindia, K., & Canary, D. J. (1993). Definitions and theoretical perspectives on maintaining relationships. *Journal of Social and Personal Relationships, 10,* 163–173.

Dindia, K., & Timmerman, L. (2003). Accomplishing romantic relationships. In J. O. Greene & B. R. Burleson (Eds.), *Handbook of communication and social interaction skills* (pp. 685–721). Mahwah, NJ: Lawrence Erlbaum Associates.

Doohan, E. (2007). Listening behaviors of married couples: An exploration of nonverbal presentation to a relational outsider. *International Journal of Listening, 21,* 24–41.

Duck, S. (1994). Steady as (s)he goes: Relational maintenance as a shared meaning system. In D. J. Canary & L. Stafford (Eds.), *Communication and relational maintenance* (pp. 45–60). San Diego: Academic Press.

Emmers-Sommer, T. M. (2003). When partners falter: Repair after a transgression. In D. J. Canary & M. Dainton (Eds.), *Maintaining relationships through communication* (pp. 185–205). Mahwah, NJ: Lawrence Erlbaum Associates.

Fehr, B. (1996). *Friendship processes.* Thousand Oaks, CA: Sage.

Fehr, B. (2000). The life cycle of friendship. In C. Hendrick & S. Hendrick (Eds.), *Close relationships: A sourcebook* (pp. 71–82). Thousand Oaks, CA: Sage.

Fincham, F. D., Bradbury, T. N., Arias, I., Byrne, C. A., & Karney, B. R. (1997). Marital violence, marital distress, and attributions. *Journal of Family Violence, 11,* 367–372.

Fitzpatrick, M. A., & Indvik, J. (1982). The instrumental and expressive domains of marital communication. *Human Communication Research, 8,* 195–213.

Gertner, B. L., Rice, M. L., & Hadley, P. A. (1994). Influence of communicative competence on peer preferences in a preschool classroom. *Journal of Speech and Hearing Research, 37,* 913–923.

Goffman, E. (1967). *Interaction ritual: Essays on face-to-face behavior.* New York: Pantheon.

Gottman, J. M. (1993). The roles of conflict engagement, escalation, and avoidance in marital interaction: A longitudinal view of five types of couples. *Journal of Consulting and Clinical Psychology, 67,* 6–15.

Gottman, J. M. (1994). *What predicts divorce.* Hillsdale, NJ: Lawrence Erlbaum Associates.

Gottman, J. M., & Levenson, R. W. (1992). Marital processes predictive of later dissolution: Behavior, physiology, and health. *Journal of Personality and Social Psychology, 63,* 221–233.

Gottman, J. M., Markman, H., & Notarius, C. (1977). The topography of marital conflict: A sequential analysis of verbal and nonverbal behavior. *Journal of Marriage and the Family, 39,* 461–477.

Gottman, J. M., & Porterfield, A. L. (1981). Communicative competence in the nonverbal behavior of married couples. *Journal of Marriage and the Family, 43,* 187–198.

Gottman, J. M., & Silver, N. (1999) *The seven principles for making marriage work.* New York: Crown Publishers.

Guerrero, L. K. (1997). Nonverbal involvement across interactions with same-sex friends, opposite-sex friends, and romantic partners: Consistency or change? *Journal of Social and Personal Relationships, 14,* 31–58.

Halpern, J. J. (1997). Elements of a script for friendship in transactions. *Journal of Conflict Resolution, 41,* 835–868.

Hartup, W. W. (1993). Adolescents and their friends. In B. Laursen (Ed.), *Close friendships in adolescence* (pp. 3–21). San Francisco: Jossey-Bass.

Hartup, W. W., & Abecassis, M. (2002). Friends and enemies. In P. K. Smith & C. H. Hart (Eds.), *Handbook of childhood social development* (pp. 286–306). Maiden, MA: Blackwell.

Hormberg, D., & MacKenzie, S. (2002). So far, so good: Scripts for romantic relationship development as predictors of relational well-being. *Journal of Social and Personal Relationships, 19,* 777–796.

Huston, T. L., Caughlin, J. P., Houts, R. M., Smith, S. E., & George, L. J. (2001). The connubial crucible: Newlywed years as predictors of marital delight, distress and divorce. *Journal of Personality and Social Psychology, 80,* 237–252.

Iannotti, R. J. (1985). Assessments of prosocial behavior in preschool children. *Developmental Psychology, 21,* 46–55.

Kelly, A. B., Fincham, F. D., & Beach, S. R. H. (2003). Communication skills in couples: A review and discussion of emerging perspectives. In J. O. Greene & B R. Burleson (Eds.), *Handbook of communication and social interaction skills* (pp. 723–751). Mahwah, NJ: LEA.

Kito, M. (2005). Self-disclosure in romantic relationships and friendships among American and Japanese college students. *Journal of Social Psychology, 145,* 127–140.

Kleinke, C. L. (1981). How not to pick up a woman. *Psychology Today, 15,* 18–19.

Knobloch, L. K., & Solomon, D. H. (1999). Measuring the sources and content of relational uncertainty. *Communication Studies, 50,* 261–278.

Kurdek, L. A. (1995). Predicting change in marital satisfaction from husbands' and wives' conflict resolution styles. *Journal of Marriage and the Family, 57,* 153–164.

Ladd, G. W. (1999). Peer relationships and social competence during early and middle childhood. *Annual Review of Psychology, 50,* 333–359.

Laurenceau, J-P., Feldman, B. L., Pietromonaco, P. R. (1998). Intimacy as an interpersonal process: The importance of self-disclosure, and perceived partner responsiveness in interpersonal exchanges. *Journal of Personality and Social Psychology, 74,* 1238–1251.

Laurenceau, J-P., Feldman, B. L., & Rovine, M. J. (2005). The interpersonal process model of intimacy in marriage: A daily-diary and multilevel modeling approach. *Journal of Family Psychology, 19,* 314–323.

Levinger, G., & Huston, T. L. (1990). The social psychology of marriage. In T. Bradbury & F. Fincham (Eds.), *The psychology of marriage* (pp. 19–58). New York: Guilford.

Markus, H. R., & Kitayama, S. (1991). Culture and the self: Implications for cognition, emotion, and motivation. *Psychological Review, 98,* 224–253.

McGinty, K., Knox, D., & Zusman, M. E. (2003). Nonverbal and verbal communication in "involved" and "casual" relationships among college students. *College Student Journal, 37,* 68–71.

Miell, D. E., & Duck, S. (1986). Strategies in developing friendships. In V. J. Derlega & B. A. Winstead (Eds.), *Friends and social interaction* (pp. 129–143). New York: Springer-Verlag.

Neff, L. A., & Karney, B. R. (2002). Self-evaluation motives in close relationships: A model of global enhancement and specific verification. In P. Noller and J. A. Feeney (Eds.), *Understanding marriage* (pp. 32–58).Cambridge, UK: Cambridge University Press.

Newcomb, A. F., & Brady, J. E. (1982). Mutuality in boys' friendship relations. *Child Development, 53,* 392–395.

Noller, P. (1981). Gender and marital adjustment level differences in decoding messages from spouses and strangers. *Journal of Personality and Social Psychology, 41,* 272–278.

Noller, P., & Fitzpatrick, M. A. (1993). *Communication in Family Relationships.* Englewood Cliffs, NJ: Prentice Hall.

Noller, P., & Venardos, C. (1986). Communication awareness in married couples. *Journal of Social and Personal Relationships, 3,* 31–42.

Oliker, S. J. (1989). *Best friends and marriage: Exchange among women.* Berkeley: University of California Press.

Pasupathi, M., Carstensen, L. L., Levenson, R. W., & Gottman, J. M. (1999). Responsive listening in long-married couples: A psycholinguistic perspective. *Journal of Nonverbal Behavior, 23,* 173–193.

Perlman, D., & Fehr, B. (1987). The development of intimate relationships. In D. Perlman & S. W. Duck (Eds.), *Intimate relationships: Development, dynamics, and deterioration* (pp. 13–42). Beverly Hills: Sage.

Planalp, S., & Benson, A. (1992). Friends' and acquaintances' conversations I: Perceived differences. *Journal of Social and Personal Relationships, 9,* 483–506.

Pryor, J. B., & Merluzzi, T. V. (1985). The role of expertise in processing social interaction scripts. *Journal of Experimental Social Psychology, 21,* 362–379.

Rawlins, W. K. (1992). Young adult friendships. In W. K. Rawlins (Ed.), *Friendship matters: Communication, dialectics, and the life course* (pp. 103–123). New York: Aldine de Gruyter.

Roberts, L. J., & Greenberg, D. R. (2002). Observational "window" to intimacy processes in marriage. In P. Noller and J. A. Feeney (Eds.), *Understanding marriage* (pp. 118–149). Cambridge, UK: Cambridge University Press.

Samter, W. (2003). Friendship interaction skills across the life span. In J. O. Greene & B. R. Burleson (Eds.), *Handbook of communication social interaction* (pp. 637–684). Mahwah, NJ: Lawrence Erlbaum Associates.

Segrin, C. (2006, April 24). Loneliness takes its toll. *USA Today,* 8D.

Sillars, A. L., & Scott, M. D. (1983). Interpersonal perception between intimates: An integrative review. *Human Communication Research, 10,* 153–176.

Smith, D. A., Vivian, D., & O'Leary, K. D. (1990). Longitudinal prediction of marital discord from premarital expressions of affect. *Journal of Consulting and Clinical Psychology, 58,* 790–798.

Sprecher, S., & Regan, P. C. (2002). Liking some things (in some people) more than others: Partner preferences in romantic relationships and friendships. *Journal of Social and Personal Relationships, 19,* 463–481.

Stafford, L. (2003). Maintaining romantic relationships: A summary and analysis of one research program. In D. J. Canary & M. Dainton (Eds.), *Maintaining relationships through communication* (pp. 51–77). Mahwah, NJ: Lawrence Erlbaum Associates.

Stafford, L., & Canary, D. J. (1991). Maintenance strategies and romantic relationship type, gender and relational characteristics. *Journal of Social and Personal Relationships, 8,* 217–242.

Tannen, D. (1990). *You just don't understand: Women and men in conversation.* New York: HarperCollins.

Thorne, B. (1986). Girls and boys together . . . but mostly apart: Gender arrangements in elementary school. In W. W. Hartup & Z. Rubin (Eds.), *Relationships and development* (pp. 167–184). Hillsdale, NJ: Erlbaum.

Tschann, J. M. (1988). Self-disclosure in adult friendship: Gender and marital status differences. *Journal of Social and Personal Relationships, 5,* 65–81.

Vangelisti, A. L., & Banski, M. A. (1993). Couples' debriefing conversations. *Family Relations, 42,* 149–157.

Weigel, D. J. (2008). The concept of family: An analysis of laypeople's views of family. *Journal of Family Issues, 29,* 1426–1447.

Weigel, D. J., & Ballard-Reisch, D. S. (2002). *Journal of Social & Personal Relationships, 19,* 403–424.

Wolvin, A., Coakley, C., & Halone, K. (1995). A preliminary look at listening development across the lifespan. *International Journal of Listening, 9,* 62–83.

Yovetich, N. A., & Rusbult, C. E. (1994). Accommodative behavior in close relationships: Exploring transformation of motivation. *Journal of Experimental Social Psychology, 30,* 138–164.

Yum, Y., & Canary, D. J. (2003). Maintaining relationships in Korea and the United States: Features of Korean culture that affect relational maintenance beliefs and behaviors. In D. J. Canary & M. Dainton (Eds.), *Maintaining relationships through communication* (pp. 277–296). Mahwah, NJ: Lawrence Erlbaum Associates.

Listening in Context

Education

Classroom Listening

Tamarah, I'm glad to see you could make our meeting. We didn't know if you would be able to get off work, and we really need your input about the listening skit.

Hey, Carter. Fortunately I was able to get a little time off. Good thing too. I have so much going on in the listening class and my other classes. Have you been working on your part of our skit?

Well, not as much as I should have. But you know, all of that information Professor Merritt talked about the other day about the amount of time we spend listening has gotten me thinking about setting our skit in a classroom. Remember that study by Imhof said that students listen for about 60 percent of instructional time? Of course, she didn't include college students, but I started thinking that we could set our skit in the classroom and show what happens when students don't listen.

Well, it will at least give us a starting point. Remember we also talked about some other research that shows how college students spend their time. Maybe we could track a typical student's day rather than just the classroom. Oh, look. Here comes Nolvia. Over here, Nolvia! Wow! You look excited.

I just came from my literature class. We've been struggling through *Beowulf* for a week, and I think I'm finally beginning to understand it. I've really had problems with the Old English sounds, you know; it's just like a foreign language. Anyway, today we watched a movie version. I could actually understand what the actors were saying. I wonder if we can put something in our skit about listening difficulty and other languages. ■

INTRODUCTION

As college and university students, you have reached a point in your life where you are assuming greater personal accountability in all aspects of your lives, including academic listening. At this point, you are expected to be independent learners and to take responsibility for your learning. For good or ill, you choose to begin writing a paper two weeks in advance, or the night before. You can decide whether you want to read an assignment the night before going to class or spend the evening out with your friends. The bottom line is all of your choices about how you approach school will have an effect on how you listen. As we cover the material in this chapter, remember you ultimately bear at least half of the responsibility for your communication with your instructor, and in spite of whether you like or dislike the way the instructor teaches, you bear the full responsibility for your learning.

Throughout this text you have read about the importance of listening in achieving a successful personal life. As children, teens, and young adults, school is one of the places where you spend significant portions of your time. As you know, speaking and listening are the primary methods by which you acquire knowledge. However, the educational aspects of listening begin long before you start school. Think, for example, about how you acquired language. Your parents and other family members encouraged you to talk to them. As they coaxed you to say certain words and names, you listened to the sounds until the day you were able to actually form them. Listening, then, is the first of the communication skills that a child develops. It is fundamental to speaking, reading, and writing.[1] Thus, we learn to listen then speak, speak then read, and read then write.

In spite of the fact you learned to listen very early in your life, teachers often complain that students never seem to listen. To put the previous statement into perspective, you spend just less than seven hours communicating at school, and approximately 25 percent of that time, or 1.75 hours, is spent listening in the classroom.[2]

And while as students the amount of time you listen in the classroom has increased yearly, few, if any of you, have received any listening training.[3] Sadly, despite the importance of listening to learning, few schools have standalone courses that teach students listening skills, and few classes (including communication classes) incorporate units on listening into their course schedules.[4]

Strong listening skills can affect your overall success in college. Previous studies suggest that listening skill has a greater effect on college success and student retention than reading skills or academic aptitude.[5] In addition, students who are trained listeners often make higher grades.[6]

The good news for you is that your institution and instructor believe listening is important. The class you are taking provides you with the opportunity to hone your listening skills in the classroom and a variety of other contexts.

THINK ON IT

Looking back at your previous classes, what listening lessons have you received? Sometimes you may not recognize it as training that can help you listen. Did you practice how to recognize main points during a speech? Did you take any courses that provided note-taking training?

THINK ON IT

Before you read the next section, on academic listening, make a list of the ways you believe conversational listening and academic listening differ. Then read the section and see how your list compares to ours.

ACADEMIC LISTENING

Most students take the listening skills used with daily conversations and simply apply them to the academic context. However, as you will see, listening in the educational context differs substantially from our normal, everyday listening. You can be a great listener but lack fundamental skills and so do poorly in a class. On the other hand, you could be a poor listener in the classroom but able to compensate by reading the text and following written directions. Academic listening is related to and affected by a number of factors, including motivation, learning style, and teaching method. Academic listening affects how you and your teachers communicate and how you communicate with your classmates.

Margarete Imhof, a noted listening scholar, suggested that effective academic listeners should be able to integrate information from numerous sources, manage their attitudes and motivation, focus attention, activate and modify cognitive schemata, and use metacognitive strategies to encode and retain information.[7] While you probably do all of these things to some extent in everyday listening, they are critical to being good academic listeners.

John Flowerdew, a senior lecturer at City University of Hong Kong, has researched academic listening extensively. Compare your responses to the previous *Think on It* box with the differences in academic and conversational listening Flowerdew identified and that are presented in Table 8.1.

TABLE 8.1

Comparing Elements of Conversational and Academic Listening

	Conversational Listening	Academic Listening
Determining Relevancy	*Somewhat important.* Individuals jump from topic to topic	*Very important.* Understanding of relevancy important to note-taking, main purpose of lecture, and so forth
Background Knowledge	*General.* Not expected to be specialist in all areas/topics under discussion	*More specialized.* Generally expected to have prepared for class or have background in subject matter
Turn-taking	*Essential.*	*Only when required/allowed.*
Level of Implied Meaning	*High.* Necessary for complete understanding; greater interpersonal meaning present	*Low.* Focus is on information transfer
Concentration	*Varies.* Depends on context or situation	*High.* Necessary to comprehend large amounts/long periods of talk
Note-taking	*Unusual.*	*Usual/Expected.* Requires decoding, comprehending, identifying main points, determining when/what to record, writing quickly and clearly[8]
Information Integration	*Not necessary.*	*Necessary.* Integrate information from a variety of media (handouts, readings, video clips)

As you can see, academic listening is constrained in a number of ways. We will be discussing several of these differences (as well as others) as we continue this chapter.

INDIVIDUAL DIFFERENCES IN THE LEARNING EXPERIENCE

The first area of difference we will examine is individual differences, or how your own traits and responses to the learning situation affect your listening. These areas include relevancy, learning styles, emotional intelligence, and apprehension.

Relevancy

When you understand the importance of a topic to your personal life or needs, the topic has **personal relevancy.** Think back over classes you've taken. Wasn't it easier to listen to the instructor when you were interested in the topic? On the other hand, wasn't it more difficult to listen in classes you expected to be boring? And what about those classes that were a pleasant surprise because they violated your expectations and were much more interesting than you expected. In this situation chances are the instructor was able to peak your interest and make the topic relevant to you. Whether inspired by the instructor or the topic, creating links between what you are learning and personal interest is a great way to enhance your academic listening; the more meaningful the lesson, the more likely you will listen and retain the information in your long-term memory.[9]

Related to relevancy is **motivation.** You are the only person who can assess your motivation. In a listening situation, particularly an academic one, ask yourself, "Why am I here?" Few people seek to be bored or confused, and it is very easy to blame the instructor when we are. However, a motivated listener will be proactive by prepping for class and identifying reasons to listen. Reasons (or motivators) can range from intrinsic, "This will help me in my career," to extrinsic, "It's going to be on the next exam." It is not unusual for students to report that they find it easier to listen in their major-related courses and more difficult in other classes. So if your world isn't rocked by information about the Paleolithic period, find a reason to motivate yourself to listen to that lecture. Reasons can range from wanting to maintain a high GPA to using the information to wow your friends or critique the next dinosaur movie you see. Our interview with recent graduate Jordan Greenleaf emphasizes the importance of motivation.

Jordan Greenleaf
Communication Major/Women's
Basketball Player
Auburn University

I majored in Communication and minored in Sports Coaching. While I hope I can play basketball professionally for a few years, eventually I would like to be a college basketball coach or a sports

(continued)

commentator. I majored in Communication because I wanted to become a better communicator. While I've never been shy about talking to others, I knew I was not a very good listener. In fact, listening in the classroom was always difficult for me. My classes have taught me how to deal with distractions, such as friends trying to get my attention, a professor who has an accent or speaks too fast, as well as the challenge of listening effectively when the material is not immediately interesting. In basketball you have to stay focused or you'll miss an important pass or making a crucial basket. The same is true for listening in the classroom. Staying focused may be hard, but it's crucial to being successful!

Learning Style

Just as motivation affects our listening in the classroom, so can other individual differences. One in particular is learning style. Learning styles affect how we attend to messages in the classroom. Earlier in the book we talked about different individual listening style preferences (see Chapter 4). We also seem to have preferences about how we learn. Eugene Sadler-Smith, a professor of management development and organizational behavior, defined **learning style** as "an individual's propensity to choose or express a liking for a particular instructional technique or combination of techniques."[10] The three main learning styles identified in much research are auditory, visual, and kinesthetic.[11] Each of these styles represents ways of taking in and storing information. So an *auditory learner* prefers spoken information, while a *visual learner* wants to see, observe, and write down information. The *kinesthetic learner,* on the other hand, better absorbs information through demonstration or physical involvement with that information.[12] Research has shown that not only do we tend to find learning easier when we receive information in a manner that matches our learning preference but we also tend to have better comprehension and retention of the material.[13] Thus, fundamental to our learning style is how we take in information, process it, remember it, and apply it. As you can see, learning style and listening both address information processing. We will look more closely at one perspective on learning styles to better illustrate the relationship between listening and learning preferences.

David **Kolb's Experiential Learning Model** is likely the best known of the learning style models.[14] Kolb views learning as a *four-stage process* or cycle. He suggested we begin with our actual, concrete experiences, observe and reflect on these experiences, then integrate them into related schemata. The resulting cognitions are then used to process future experiences. The Kolb model is based on two primary dimensions. The first dimension includes **concrete experience** (sensing/feeling) and **abstract conceptualization** (thinking), while the second addresses our preference for **active experimentation** (doing) and **reflective observation** (watching). *Concrete experience* addresses our preference for relying on concrete facts. *Abstract conceptualization* or thinking focuses on our preference for relying on and using more abstract ways of processing information. *Active experimentation* identifies our need for hands-on learning (doing) versus a preference for learning via *reflective observation* (watching). As seen in Figure 8.1, these dimensions result in four learning styles: diverging, assimilating, converging, and accommodating.[15]

Converging Learners As you can see in the model, these learners have doing and thinking as their dominant learning abilities. If this is your learning style, you like

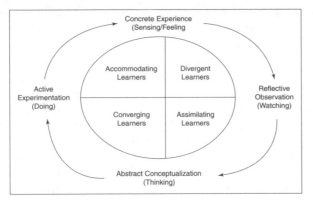

FIGURE 8.1
Kolb's Learning Process and Style Types.

to find practical applications for the ideas you learn. One of your strengths is problem solving. You probably also prefer to deal with technical problems rather than interpersonal issues. In the classroom you prefer experimenting with new information in the way of simulations or role-playing and focusing on those practical applications. If you are a converging learner, be mindful of your tendency as a listener to tune out when you fail to see the applicability of the information or when you think something is too touchy-feely or interpersonally based. If you are an MBTI thinker (remember our Myers-Briggs personality types from Chapter 4), then you may prefer this learning style. When listening, thinkers enjoy direct, clear messages. As a result, like the action listener (described in Chapter 4), when instructors get off topic, you might sit in class, wondering when they are going to get to the point instead of attending to the lecture or discussion.

Diverging Learners   If you are a diverging learner, you tend to prefer sensing/feeling and reflective observation. If this is your learning style, you like to be in situations that call for brainstorming or coming up with ideas from different points of view. Diverging learners tend to be imaginative and emotional and prefer working in groups. Consequently diverging learners are good at using their imagination. If you are a diverging learner, you are probably skilled at deconstructing events to better understand how the parts affect the whole. Thus, you may be particularly good at seeing all sides of an issue. At the same time, you are people oriented and likely enjoy learning about other people and cultures. You also learn best when personal relevancy is high. As a result, it is important for you to work at making personal connections to what is being taught. Otherwise, you will tune out.

One of your listening strengths is that you tend to keep an open mind while listening to different perspectives. This suggests that you would probably be open to receiving personalized feedback but tend to disregard feedback that is presented in an impersonal manner.[16]

Accommodating Learners   If you are an accommodating learner, your learning strengths combine sensing/feeling with doing. You would fall in the kinesthetic learning category that we talked about earlier. That is, you prefer to learn primarily via doing and experimentation. For example, when you get a new mobile phone, you probably simply sit down and start playing with it rather than reading the accompanying manual. So when you take a picture and cut off the subject's head, you learn what not to do in the future. More important, you also tend to apply what you learn from your mistakes to other situations you face. You enjoy new challenges, embrace change, like flexibility, and welcome risk taking. Chances are you also like to develop a plan then carry it out. Accommodating learners also have a tendency to act on their gut feelings rather than logic. Consequently as a listener, you could face several challenges. For example, when answering a teacher's question, you may be less able to provide a logical reason for how you arrived at your answer. In addition, your desire for change and challenges can result in your becoming bored in the classroom. You will likely need to focus on personal motivation and topic relevancy to stimulate your listening. For example, you could concentrate on future assignments and consider how the topic or material can help you complete them.

THINK ON IT

In Chapter 4 we introduced the four listening style preferences: people, action, content, and time. We have talked about a few ways they are related to learning styles. In what other ways may they be related? What about other individual differences we've introduced?

Assimilating Learners   Assimilating learners are particularly good at synthesizing material because their strengths as learners are thinking abstractly and reflecting on observations. If you are an assimilating learner, you like a wide range of information but want it in a concise, logical form. You may surprise your instructors with your ability to pull in material from previous classes or readings and integrate it into the topic under discussion. Not surprisingly you enjoy learning abstract information, such as theories and related processes. Like a content listener, you want information presented in a logically organized manner with well-supported examples. As a result, you are probably an excellent listener in traditional, lecture-format types of classes. However, in classes where there are a lot of group activities, your search for theory and continuity may cause you to feel frustrated. You may become impatient when you feel the lecture or discussion is getting off topic or experience stress when you are not given sufficient time to reflect on the information before taking action.

LEARN ABOUT YOURSELF

If you'd like to learn more about your own learning style, try visiting the following Web site: www.dentistry.bham.ac.uk/ecourse/kolb/testresults.asp. It provides you with a shortened version of Kolb's original scale.

Emotional Intelligence

Another individual difference that can affect your academic listening is emotional intelligence. As you recall from Chapter 4, emotional intelligence is "the ability to perceive and express emotions, to understand and use them, and to manage them to foster personal growth."[17] How you handle your emotions can influence how you approach assignments and how you work with your peers.[18] For example, one longitudinal study found that preschoolers who were better at delaying immediate gratification (waiting for a marshmallow), later tended to have higher SAT scores and be more interpersonally liked by teachers and peers.[19] Delaying gratification shows that you can deal with one important emotion: frustration. If you can manage frustration, you can likely manage other emotions as well. Being able to *recognize* your own feelings and the feelings of others, being able to *manage* your emotions, *motivate* yourself, and *handle relationships* all positively affect academic success.[20] For example, you will likely be able to recognize and cope with the frustration you feel when you don't understand an assignment, receive a poor grade, or deal with group members who aren't pulling their weight. Frustration can generate internal noise, which as you know can negatively affect listening ability.

Communication and Individual Receiver Apprehension

As you learned earlier in the text, **communication apprehension** is a generalized fear you experience when put into a particular communication situation. Students who experience communication apprehension can respond in several ways.[21] First, they can try to physically or psychologically withdraw from the situation. For example, they could write the bulk of a group paper to reduce or eliminate their presentation speaking time. When asked a question by their instructor, they could say, "I don't know." Although rare, some students will respond by overcommunicating. These are the students who seemingly dominate a group or class discussion, when in actuality they are apprehensive and essentially talking their way through their anxiety.

High communication apprehension can result in a variety of negative academic outcomes, including lower grades, negative attitudes toward school, and a greater likelihood of dropping out of school. In addition, these students often have fewer classroom friends and have difficulty asking their teachers for help.[22] Finally it is not unusual for someone suffering from high communication apprehension to be apprehensive in several communication areas.[23] Consequently they might be apprehensive when working both interpersonally and in groups, two contexts used extensively in the classroom. Not surprisingly the greater one's level of apprehension in an area (e.g., public speaking, groups, dyads), the more difficult it is to listen. People who suffer from apprehension seem to concentrate so much on what they are going to say and their feelings of incompetency that they lack the ability or motivation to focus on what others have to say.

One category of communication apprehension very related to listening is **receiver apprehension,** or feeling anxiety about being on the receiving end of the communication process. This fear is particularly problematic for listeners in the classroom. As you learned at the beginning of the chapter, the educational setting requires great amounts of academic listening. In the classroom receiver apprehension is more likely to occur when you are anxious about the course content (e.g., math frightens you) or by the teacher's behavior (e.g., you find him or her to be intimidating). Research indicates that receiver apprehension negatively affects listening and information processing and is associated with several negative outcomes, including the following:

- Getting lower test scores
- Holding negative attitudes toward the course and the instructor
- Being less motivated to learn
- Having lower perceptions of one's ability to learn[24]

The good news for you if you do suffer from any type of communication apprehension is that it doesn't have to be a barrier to listening. Those of you who are motivated enough can turn the effect anxiety has on listening into an opportunity.

Research by a number of scholars has indicated that teachers can have a great impact on how well students listen and can be particularly helpful for those who suffer from apprehension. You may know someone who is highly motivated but feels intimidated by the subject matter in a class. Usually these students feel stressed or anxious about learning the class material and can end up experiencing high levels of apprehension. Imagine that Nolvia told her group about her attempts to learn German. As the conversation progressed, she noted that the more she tried to hear and learn the language (e.g., studying daily, doing all the homework, even working with a tutor), the more anxious she became about the class. Fortunately having the right kind of teacher can help you if you are like Nolvia. A fairly recent study suggests that *teacher clarity* and *teacher immediacy* can help highly apprehensive students.[25] Clear, understandable presentations are easier to absorb and process. If you think about your experiences in the classroom, you have probably found that when the teacher used personally relevant examples, it generally made the material easier to incorporate into your schemata or knowledge bank about the subject matter. In contrast, you probably found teachers who talked too fast or used unfamiliar terms difficult to listen to and perhaps even found that you felt increased levels of apprehension.[26]

Part of the reason anxiety has a negative effect on listening is that it makes you feel disempowered or not in control of learning. Once again, your teacher can have an effect on your listening. Teacher immediacy behaviors (e.g., smiling, using humor, engaging in dynamic movement, using appropriate eye contact) have been associated with increased positive feelings about the teacher and the class, as well as increased perceptions of control over one's learning. Researchers argue that teacher clarity and teacher immediacy work together to decrease receiver apprehension in the classroom. Less apprehension leads to less anxiety in the classroom, which makes it easier for you to pay attention to both instructors and peers over the course of the class period.

How can you address your own receiver apprehension? While individual receiver apprehension can vary widely, we make two primary suggestions. First, try to **build motivation.** Carefully choosing classes that you are interested in or classes taught by instructors who are known for motivating their students can help you develop a positive outlook toward the class. Second, **be prepared.** Coming properly prepared for class is a major element of reducing anxiety. You can link what you're hearing to what you've learned outside of class. You'll also know what areas are confusing to you and can ask for further clarification when it is covered during class. The more you can prepare for a particular interaction, the greater your personal feeling of control. So thoroughly reading class materials, seeking out the instructor or classmates in the class to clarify concepts, searching out helpful Web sites, or hiring a tutor when necessary are just a few of the things you can do to enhance feelings of control. You may also find it helpful to choose an instructor who uses a teaching method that you prefer. We discuss various teaching methods in the following section.

Joanna B. Boyd
First-grade Teacher
Dean Road Elementary School
Auburn, Alabama

As an educator, I believe that listening skills play a vital part in student performance. If the student is not engaged in the learning process completely, they cannot fully grasp all of the concepts the teacher is trying to present. At the very beginning of the school year, when we begin setting our classroom rules, the students always put "being a great listener" at the top of the list.

Creating an atmosphere where students understand the importance of being a great listener is also essential to the learning process. I believe that to keep students engaged, you must provide hands-on activities for them to participate in throughout the day and offer opportunities for the students to share their own ideas. Students are very interested in what their peers think, and they can gain new ideas and broaden their vocabulary just by listening.

Technology is also a key component in helping to gain students' attention, and it helps to foster stronger listening skills. I integrate technology daily by providing a listening center for students to use. This center gives students the opportunity to improve their listening skills through various activities.

I feel that great listening skills create a strong foundation in every area of life, especially in the classroom.

Teaching Goals and Methods

You know from your own experience that instructional methods are as varied as teachers and students. The type of listening required varies with the teaching method. Some instructors will choose methods that they personally prefer, in keeping with their own learning preferences. Other teachers recognize and attempt to accommodate a variety of learning styles. Of course, the subject matter can sometimes dictate the method that is chosen. Kenneth Moore, in the book *Effective Instructional Strategies*, grouped teaching methods into three main areas: direct, indirect, and integrated.[27] Each type has distinct differences and affects classroom listening in unique ways. **Direct methods** often are teacher centered with the teacher acting as the primary information source and often involve lecturing, using class workbooks, and so forth. It's likely that many of your college introductory classes have used this method, especially if they were large classes. The goal of such classes is to provide a large amount of information in an efficient method. Not surprisingly these classes largely focus on comprehensive listening. In contrast, **indirect methods** tend to focus on showing. If your professor uses this method, he or she tends to act as a facilitator of learning. Classes that use case studies or other readings as springboards to developing knowledge and building skills likely use this method. The teacher will essentially jump start the discussion, making sure that the class or group understands the nature and purpose of the discussion, keeping the discussion on track, and ensuring everyone has the opportunity to participate. Many instructors integrate a variety of teaching methods. If your instructor uses this method, he or she likely expects a greater emphasis on critical listening.

Instructors who use **integrated methods** not only tell their students; they show them and give them access to learning on their own. While comprehensive listening is used at times, critical listening is the primary focus of this type of teaching. This method emphasizes self-directed learning. Of the three methods we discuss, this approach gives you the greatest control over your own learning.[28] It works best with students who are internally motivated and who accept that they are responsible for much of their own learning. For example, each year our university sponsors a robotics championship where groups of students are given buckets of parts and asked to solve a problem (e.g., a machine that could facilitate a repair to the Hubble Telescope, a robot that could collect particular molecules).[29] Even though all of the groups were given the same parts, no two groups develop the same robot or solve the problem in exactly the same way. Students take their technical know-how, do additional research (i.e., access to learning), and develop a number of fun, funky, and truly incredible robots.

Whatever the method, developing critical thinking skills is generally one of the main goals of teaching. In fact, it is one of the primary goals of education today and not just in the United States. Professors at University Putra Malaysia also stress the importance of listening to developing critical thinking skills for college students.[30] They noted that it is through communication skills (including listening) that students grow personally and academically. They argued that critical listening and critical thinking share a number of attributes, including assessing main ideas, differentiating between facts and opinions, and recognizing language problems (e.g., loaded language and logical fallacies).

THINK ON IT

Class discussion methods can take two forms: whole-class discussion and small-group discussion (e.g., small groups of four to six students discussing a topic, brainstorming ideas, completing an assigned task). Does active listening differ between large- and small-group discussions? If so, how? Does one type have distinctive advantages? Disadvantages? What have been your experiences with classroom discussion? How does the classroom environment affect class discussion?

LISTENING AND THE EDUCATIONAL "AUDIENCE"

There are a number of educational audiences: teachers, administrators, students, parents, alumni, and other community members. Addressing all of these audiences is beyond the scope of this text. In the pages that follow, we focus on your interactions with your instructors both in and out of the classroom. Lev Vygotsky, an early-learning theorist, suggested that our relationships with our teachers are fundamental to our learning.[31] As you discuss the importance of listening in your interpersonal and classroom interactions with your instructors, consider how they apply to Vygotsky's words.

Communicating Interpersonally: Teachers and Students

Emerson once said, "The secret of education lies in respecting the pupil." We would add to that another secret: respect for the teacher. As you learned earlier in this text, respect for one another is one of the foundations of good listening. We have also stressed remaining open-minded as a critical listening essential. Teachers

"You're listening to what you hear. I like that in a teacher."

and students who can establish such a foundation have the beginning of a strong learning relationship. There are several things you can do to be a better academic listener regardless of your personality, listening style, or the teaching method of your professor:

- Respect your instructor's role as a content specialist.
- Recognize and respect that you each have your own style.
- Prepare for any interaction with your instructors.
- Think before you speak.
- Be aware of your academic attributions.

We address each of these areas below.

Respect Your Instructor's Role as a Content Specialist   Showing respect tends to lessen any defensiveness and motivate both parties to listen more closely. We also find it's much easier to listen to others empathetically when we feel they also respect us as individuals.

Recognize and Respect That You Each Have Your Own Style   However, don't use that style as an excuse to be a poor listener. While you have your own learning and listening styles and your teachers use a variety of different teaching methods, you must accept responsibility for your own learning and adjust to the listening demands of the situation. By doing so, you will find it easier to motivate yourself to listen to those subjects that are not very interesting to you.

Prepare for Any Interaction with Your Instructors   If you schedule meetings with your instructors, plan out what needs to be discussed in advance by making note of your questions and concerns. This will keep your meeting on track and show that you understand how busy your professor is. All listeners appreciate clear, concise presentations of concerns on a busy day.

Think before You Speak   If a situation arises where you disagree with an instructor, lab assistant, or other school personnel, keep in mind that your choices about how you react can have long-term effects on future interactions with that person. Our biggest piece of advice is be respectful. While you often don't have control over what happens to you, you can choose how you react. If you view disagreements as a problem to be solved rather than a personal attack, it will be easier for you to focus on listening to the other party. How can you do this? Basically you should take time to objectively assess the situation. Did you study the wrong material? Misunderstand the wording on the exam question? You certainly have the right to discuss your concerns with your professors and you should. However, you need to be in a frame of mind where you are truly willing to listen, and you want to create an atmosphere where your professor will be open to your comments and concerns.

Be Aware of Your Academic Attributions   Attributions refer to our belief in underlying causes of an event or situation. When you talk to instructors about classes, they tend to assess your explanations of your academic success and failure. Your explanation can lead them to draw conclusions about your future performance in the class. Students tend to attribute performance to one of the following: effort, ability, luck, and task difficulty.[32] *Effort* ("I didn't study enough") and *ability* ("I'm not an economics person") are related to **internal attributions,** while *luck* ("I guessed right") and *task difficulty* ("This project is unreasonable") are related to **external attributions.** If you are attributing a grade to internal causes, then you are taking responsibility for the grade, while attributing it to external causes indicates you are avoiding responsibility. For most of us, these attributions can change from class to class. When they do so, they are called an *unstable attribution.* Thus, you might claim to be deaf to foreign languages, but really get it in your chemistry class. Some students, however, develop a pattern response based on one of these attribution areas to explain their success or failure in every class. As a listener, if you have *stable internal attribution,* you take responsibility for your listening behavior in all of your classes, not just the ones you like.

Two Attribution Dimensions

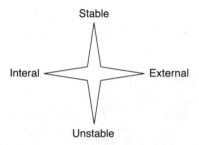

FIGURE 8.2
Attribution Dimensions.

Academic attributions are important because they affect your expectations of success, your view of your own ability, your emotional reactions (e.g., pride in an achievement, feelings of helplessness) to classroom situations, and your willingness to apply and self-regulate your academic efforts.[33] Good teachers generally will encourage you to take ownership of your successes by focusing on your personal efforts and abilities. You can demonstrate that ownership by engaging in good academic listening.

Communicating in the Classroom

Listening is an important component of a positive classroom learning environment; it contributes to your motivation to meet high expectations and to your academic success. The connection between students and teachers is the foundation of a positive **classroom climate.** Instructors who listen well are better able to understand their students' needs and preferences. By listening carefully and critically, teachers create a classroom climate that encourages student involvement.[34] For example, one colleague, after learning her students had an interest in cultural differences in persuasive discourse, responded by introducing her class to material on the civil rights movement.

The foundation of a positive classroom climate is skilled listening from both the teacher and the students. Students should feel comfortable expressing ideas, asking for clarification, and disagreeing with each other and their instructor. As Mary Renck Jalongo professor at Indiana University of Pennsylvania, wrote, "Listening, in the full sense of the word, is both interactive and constructive. It is *interactive* because good listeners are involved with the message; it is *constructive* because listeners build meaning from what they hear."[35] A supportive classroom climate allows teachers and students to achieve academic listening that is interactive and constructive. These instructors motivate students by providing a clear purpose for listening, modeling good listening and speaking behaviors (and expecting their students to do the same), reducing listening distractions, and promoting (and expecting) active listening in the classroom. As can be seen, you have much to contribute to a supportive classroom climate. When you no longer are part of a "listen and learn" classroom (i.e., straight lecture), your responsibilities for listening and contributing to the learning experience are expanded. You have increased opportunity to practice your listening skills (e.g., informational/discriminative listening, clarification of concepts, elaboration on ideas, critical analyses via discussions). We discuss four of the elements related to a positive classroom climate.

Teacher Self-disclosure   Previous research suggests that award-winning instructors engaged in moderate self-disclosure in their classes.[36] It is important that the self-disclosure be honest, relevant to course content, and/or used to clarify concepts under discussion. Thus, in his Public Relations class, Dr. Kim may discuss his experience working at Wilde Corporation as a public relations specialist. Such self-disclosure may lead students to feel more comfortable discussing their own work or group experiences. We also often find self-disclosure interesting or motivating. Subsequently we may listen more closely in class and develop a more positive attitude toward both the teacher and the course.

Teacher Immediacy   Generally speaking, verbal and nonverbal immediacy behaviors tend to reduce the psychological distance between teachers and their students. In other words, students will feel a more personal connection with their teachers. A number of behaviors contribute to teacher immediacy, including eye contact, movement and gestures, and vocal variety. Highly immediate teachers address students by name, are comfortable using humor, and employ relevant personal examples during class.

Student Engagement   One result of high teacher immediacy is student engagement. Student engagement is affected by a number of factors, including personal interest in the topic. However, teacher interest can be just as important. Teachers who are enthusiastic and interested in the topics they teach and who are willing to share that enthusiasm and interest with their students tend to be more effective in energizing the classroom.[37] When teachers can generate an atmosphere that connects and focuses student attention, they increase the chances that their students are actively listening in the classroom. High immediacy also provides students with the sense that their teacher enjoys teaching and cares for them. One outcome is that students who feel valued by their teachers may put more effort into their own learning. One leading scholar on immediacy, Virginia Richmond, argued that teacher immediacy positively affects students by leading them "to listen more, learn more, and have a more positive attitude about school."[38]

Classroom Management   Have any of you ever been in a class where the students seemed to be more in control of the class than the instructor? If so, you have a real understanding of the effect of classroom management on creating a positive classroom and learning environment. The good news is that classroom management issues are usually not a problem in the university classroom. Some of the primary issues in today's college classes are associated with mobile phones ringing, students talking, and surfing the Net in computer labs. You understand the implicit rules of the college classroom (e.g., be on time, listen/pay attention, take notes, discuss/participate, and do not study or work on other class materials). Of course, there are the explicit rules (what you can and cannot do), basic class procedures (how to contact your instructor and so forth), and stated standards (what it takes to make an *A*). All of these elements contribute directly to classroom management and classroom climate. Established rules, procedures, and standards guide not only our behaviors but our expectations about the class.

Listening and Taking Notes

While note-taking is a writing activity, to do it well takes effective listening skills. In this section we will address how you can use your listening skills to become a better note taker.

Mary O'Hair and colleagues found that more than 75 percent of the students they polled felt their notes were essentially useless when it came time to actually study.[39] A more recent study found students record less than 40 percent of what they hear.[40] Needless to say, incomplete and useless notes aren't very helpful when it comes to enhancing exam and other class grades. One reason notes might be worthless is that students are not fully attending to or processing the information they receive. For example, students may have difficulty discriminating between what is important and what is not. Listening and good note-taking are strongly connected. As O'Hair and her colleagues noted, "Meaningful notes result from carefully planned listening for structure and from fighting distractions."[41] They found a number of barriers to good note-taking.[42] These barriers include lectures that are boring because the pace is too slow or frustrating because the pace is too fast. In either case it is difficult to stay attentive and listen. Another set of barriers is internal and external distractions. As we discussed in Chapter Three, *internal noise* is your own thoughts and emotions that pop up in your mind during the lecture. *External interference,* of course, comes from the environment, such as noise in the halls. Your emotional or evaluative reactions can also derail your listening and subsequent note-taking. When you focus on judging either the speaker or the topic, it is difficult to take notes. Other times your listening and note-taking might be hurt by relying too much on only the oral presentation. Let's face it; some topics are easier to understand when we can see a good picture or diagram. Can you imagine a math, computer programming, or physiology class without some illustrations?

Building Your Note-taking Skill So what's a student to do? Like any skill, you can improve your note-taking listening ability with a bit of practice. Table 8.2 identifies some things you can do to improve your note-taking.

As you can see from the table, many of the ideas we have talked about in this book can be applied to helping you be a better note-taker. In assessing your attitudes, remember **motivation** is one key to good listening. It helps to develop a positive attitude and find a personal reason to focus your attention in class. Of course, motivation is closely related to awareness of both your attitudes and biases. You will be a better listener when you don't prejudge others, including the teacher, by focusing on content and keeping an open mind.

Another interesting strategy in Table 8.2 is to use the "predict then confirm strategy." This approach requires you to prepare in advance (e.g., read the text, previous notes) then make predictions of what is likely to be covered by generating questions over the lecture content. We think this is a great suggestion for two reasons. First, you will obviously come prepared to class. Second, your reading will likely be reinforced by what you hear. You can also ask for clarification as needed. One of our students who is very much a visual learner added to these suggestions,

THINK ON IT

Dr. Alan Shields, a retired professor of sociology at Auburn University, taught the very first class Professor Worthington attended as an undergraduate (Introduction to Sociology). As he introduced the students to the class, he gave a piece of advice that has remained with Professor Worthington to this day: "If you write down everything that I'm saying, you're not listening to me."

Think about how you take notes. Do you write down key words or phrases, or do you attempt to write down everything the instructor says? What do you think Dr. Shields meant? What does this statement tell us about listening and note-taking?

THINK ON IT

What types of techniques help or hinder your note-taking? Are they related to classroom climate? Motivation?

TABLE 8.2

Tips for Improving Classroom Listening and Note-taking[43]

Behavioral	Mental/Cognitive	Psychological
Intentionally focus attention	Activate appropriate schemata	Check attitudes and bias toward topic
Block out internal and external distractions	Identify prior knowledge about topic	Get emotionally ready to listen
Control energetic arousal	Use mental organizers to revise schema based on the incoming information	Monitor nonverbal input from speaker
Get physically ready to listen and take notes	Mentally summarize the key points of the lecture	Monitor your own listening
Ask questions to gain information needed to understand the topic	Use predict and confirm strategy	
Physically revise and complete notes after the lecture	Listen for organizing cues	
Practice note-taking for accuracy and discrimination ability		

noting that diagramming or outlining the reading not only helps her make predictions but enables her to make connections to what was covered in class. Her outlines also help her to quickly identify differences between what was introduced in the reading but *not* covered in class. When necessary she asks her teachers to highlight or identify the relationships between what was covered in lecture and what was presented in the book at the time that it was freshest in her mind. These types of questions also help place the information into her long-term memory.

Another key to taking good notes is to listen for **organizational lecture cues:**

- *Verbal signals* are used to help clarify the relationships between ideas ("The three main things to remember are . . ." "This concept can be divided into two broad themes . . .").
- *Transitional statements* signal the conversation is moving from one topic to another ("Now that we understand what an attitude is, let's look at how it differs from beliefs").
- *Summary statements* remind listeners of topics that have just been covered ("So now that we've covered attitudes, beliefs, and behaviors, let's move on to . . .").[44]

Research demonstrates that **organizational clarity** also contributes to student learning.[45] So listen for the pattern. The organizational pattern will help you process the information by providing natural breaks; allowing you to "chunk" the information and store it more easily in your short-term memory; and facilitating schema development, which assists you with long-term memory. Better-organized lectures help you determine what is important and streamline the note-taking process. As a result, your notes may be better in terms of quality and quantity. In other words, they might be better organized, and you might actually be able to record more material. Recording more class material (obviously quality notes are important) can increase your success on exams by increasing your overall recall of information.[46]

CULTURE AND DIVERSITY

No look at academic listening would be complete without a discussion about the impact of culture, diversity, and socialization in the classroom. This is particularly true when we consider those students who are listening in a language other than their native one. We will take a brief look at selected socialization-related factors then examine second-language factors.

Gender

All of us are socialized in gender roles. As you were growing up, you learned what girls and boys were *supposed* to do (i.e., established gender schemata). While the way you have been socialized is probably a bit different than the way we were because of generational differences, each of you are still taught certain beliefs about the way you are supposed to interact with the world. As we have noted elsewhere, your gender socialization can affect how you listen. It can also affect how you act and react in school. For example, previous research supports claims that males and females are treated quite differently in educational settings. These differences usually advantage boys and men over girls and women.[47] Specifically boys tend to get more attention (both positive and negative), detailed instructions, and praise for intellectual content than girls. Girls, on the other hand, usually have to wait longer for attention, which tends to be neutral or negative (especially if the girl is a minority student), and they are more often recognized for neatness and form. Another interesting difference can be found in where teachers place the locus of control (or cause) for poor performance. With boys, teachers tend to stress internal attributions such as lack of effort, while external causes for failure or poor performances are emphasized for girls (e.g., "That problem was particularly difficult," "It's hard to concentrate in a hot room").

While the above paragraph presents only a small sample of the differences in how boys and girls are treated in the classroom, you can see the beginnings of a pattern. Essentially the research indicates that males become empowered in the educational setting while women are encouraged to be passive listeners. In addition, the emphasis on an external locus of control suggests that female students may feel less responsibility for listening in the classroom. Men, in contrast, expect more from their teachers and are not afraid to ask for it (e.g., clarification of an instruction, expanding on a topic).

The research also indicates that the interpersonal interaction with the teacher will influence how students feel about a subject as well as their interest in studying it.[48] As you know by now, motivation is an important element of listening and learning. Thus, male students, who are often given preferential treatment in their communications with their instructors, might be more motivated to listen. The way they are treated may also help them to develop attitudes favoring accountability and ownership, features associated with academic success.[49]

Author and scholar Deborah Tannen suggested that men tend to be confrontative in their listening, while women listen collaboratively.[50] Thus, men will be more comfortable challenging the teacher's comments, engaging in classroom discussions, and verbally critiquing class readings. They will gravitate toward debate-type activities. These activities encourage, if not require, students to engage in critical listening. Women, in contrast, will be more comfortable responding while working in small groups, where they can provide the nonverbal feedback (smiles, head nods) they prefer and where they are better able to use clarification and other encouraging verbal cues. Thus, women often prefer classroom activities that emphasize relational listening. They also place greater importance on having the right answer, which suggests that they emphasize comprehensive listening more than their male classmates.

Socioeconomic Differences

Another area of socialization is socioeconomic background. In the classroom a disproportionate number of underachievers are from lower socioeconomic groups. Unfortunately these students, who are likely experiencing a number of economic and learning disadvantages, often get less support from their teachers than they need. Research suggests that instructors allow underachieving students less time to respond to questions, give them less attention, provide them fewer nonverbal supportive behaviors (smiles), and generally interact with them less.[51] As a result, teachers essentially listen less to these students. It comes as no surprise, then, that underachievers often feel their teachers simply don't care about them. Earlier in the text, you learned that feeling valued in a relationship is important to both listening and relationship development. It is unlikely, then, that these students have the motivation to listen in the classroom. It is important to remember that not all underachievers come from disadvantaged families, just as not all disadvantaged students will end up being underachievers. In fact, just the opposite can occur. It is true, however, that students who feel excluded and undervalued by their teachers are more likely to become turned off by school, stop listening, start acting out, or engage in other negative behaviors.

Culture and Ethnicity

Another factor that affects how you interact with your teacher is culture. Classroom communication experts Robert Powell and Dana Caseau wrote, "Culture influences what people know, how they came by that knowledge, what roles they play and how they should play them, what they value, and how they put their values in action ... culture plays a significant role in the education process."[52] For example, teachers in the United States often cultivate an informal relationship with their students, encouraging students to critically evaluate and challenge material presented in class. This approach reflects the Western view that speakers are responsible for the clarity and understandability of their speech. Japanese students have a very different experience. In contrast, the classroom socialization process for Japanese students encourages them to become skilled at attentive listening.[53] In the Japanese classroom, the teacher both supports and facilitates listening by creating opportunities for students to actively listen to their peers and setting an expectation of active listening. It is not unusual for instructors to withhold their own evaluations of student presentations and comments to encourage reaction turns (i.e., peer commentary and response). Thus, students have more autonomy in Japanese classrooms. In fact, teachers who are more directive, who do not foster student spontaneity, or who force their personal opinion onto students are viewed as ineffective and unsuccessful.

The differences discussed above also reflect the differences that exist between high-context and low-context cultures. Most U.S. classrooms reflect the fact that the United States is a low-context culture. **Low-context cultures** focus more attention on verbal expression and pay less attention to nonverbal cues. As a result, U.S. students listen for linearly organized presentations (e.g., topically, chronologically, cause and effect) and clear and explicit directions. Likewise, teachers listen for answers to questions that are understandable, direct, and precise. Teachers and students from **high-context cultures** are challenged in U.S. classrooms because their communication and listening expectations are not dependent on direct or explicit messages; much of the communication is embedded in the situation and is, thus, implied. As a result, they focus more on communicative elements such as nonverbal communication, physical context, environment, or even a speaker's mood.

Often academic listening is hampered by ingrained stereotypes or expectations of what is considered to be appropriate behavior. For example, Asian students are often viewed as polite, motivated, obedient, and modest.[54] As a listener, if you aren't Asian, you should be aware that smiles and laughter can reflect confusion or embarrassment, not excitement or happiness. Also, don't be surprised if your Asian American friend engages in longer periods of silence than you are used to; silence has greater communicative importance in Asian cultures than in most Western cultures. In addition, emotional restraint, formality, and politeness are important guides to Asian social behavior. As a result, students from traditional Asian homes may view their primary role in the classroom as one in which they principally absorb information from their instructor. Challenging a teacher is generally viewed as inappropriate classroom behavior.[55] Thus, students from other cultures, particularly Asian cultures, might think U.S. American students are disrespectful of their teachers.

As the above example illustrates, nonverbal behaviors differ among cultures and can affect our interpretations and perceptions as listeners. For example, Native Americans and Hispanic Americans are taught that it is disrespectful to look at parents and other authority figures directly. However, as Americans, we value and expect direct eye contact. As a culturally sensitive listener, you will want to check how much of your interpretation of the nonverbal messages sent by the other party is based on your biases and expectations rather than your knowledge (or lack of knowledge) of the other culture.

> **THINK ON IT**
>
> Is there a relationship between cultural background and preferred teaching method? Will individuals from some cultures likely prefer the direct method? Indirect? Or some integrated approach?

Special Challenges for Nonnative Speakers

THINK ON IT:

How have cultural differences affected your experiences with other students? With your instructors?

Classes that primarily use a lecture format can be particularly challenging to nonnative-speaking students. Unfortunately for many of these students, they do not receive adequate listening training prior to entering the foreign-language classroom. For example, students are seldom exposed to a spontaneously delivered lecture. Instead, they often listen to scripted lectures delivered at a slow speaking rate rather than a conversational one. As a result, they experience listening-related problems associated with the features of spoken language, instructor interpersonal strategies, how discourse is structured, and media usage.[56]

Spontaneous spoken language can be problematic largely because of the nonverbal elements. For example, nonnative speakers can have trouble reading a professor's kinesics (i.e., body language) since the amount and type of body language varies among cultures. Head nods, eye contact, and the quizzical eyebrow lift can alter the meaning of what a professor is saying, indicate agreement, or signal displeasure. Another major language feature that nonnative speakers can have difficulty addressing occurs at the *microstructure* level of a lecture. This type of structuring is quite different from the conversational speaking and listening required in many foreign-language classes. Microstructuring refers to the unfilled pauses and verbal fillers (e.g., "um," "ah," "OK," "so") that are a natural part of the spontaneous lecture. This type of structure is also marked by numerous incomplete clauses, the use of contractions, and other forms of incomplete thoughts that make up a lecture. Finally microstructure includes our use of false starts, redundancy, and repetition. It is not unusual for us to begin a thought, change our mind in midstream, and begin our thought again. Good teachers will include some redundancy and repetition in their lectures to allow students to catch material they initially missed or give them the opportunity to think on a question that's been asked. However, it can be confusing for the nonnative speaker.

Of course, the examples here primarily apply to nonnative speakers entering an American classroom. If you are considering becoming an exchange student, you will want to research the types and effects of language differences as they occur in the classes you will be attending.

SUMMARY

Whether at home or in the classroom, we all appreciate the feeling that we are listened to. This chapter has primarily focused on the role of listening in classroom and teacher-student interactions. It does not address the overall lack of listening training that students receive during their K–12 years of school. Madelyn Burley-Allen, author of *Listening: The Forgotten Skill,* reported that students are provided, on average, 12 years of writing instruction, seven years of reading instruction, and two years of speech instruction, but less than half a year of listening instruction.[57] As we noted in Chapter 1, listening well is a skill that requires instruction and practice, whatever the context. Unfortunately, as alluded to in the cartoon earlier in the chapter, educators often do not model this important skill nor is it explicitly valued by the educational system. However, every year of school places greater demands on your listening skills, skills that are generally underdeveloped. You're lucky. You are attending a school that values and understands the importance of listening. You have an instructor who is guiding you in skill-building activities. We hope you have the motivation to not only learn the material in this text but to apply it to your daily life.

CONCEPTS TO KNOW

Relevancy
  Personal Relevancy
  Motivation
Learning Styles
  Auditory
  Visual
  Kinesthetic
Kolb's Experiential Learning Model
  Converging
  Assimilating
  Accommodating
  Divergent
Emotional Intelligence
Apprehension
  Communication Apprehension
  Receiver Apprehension
Teaching Methods
  Direct
  Indirect
  Integrated

Academic Attributions
  Effort
  Ability
  Luck
  Difficulty
Internal and External Attributions
Stable and Unstable Attributions
Classroom Climate
  Teacher Self-disclosure
  Teacher Immediacy
  Student Engagement
  Classroom Management
Organizational Lecture Cues
Organizational Clarity
Culture and Diversity
  Gender
  Socioeconomic Differences
  High- versus Low-context
Cultures

DISCUSSION QUESTIONS

1. What differentiates the boring lecture from the interesting one? Are differences related to class size? Topic? Personal interest? How have your teachers gotten you interested and involved? What have you observed about your listening behavior?

2. There is one questioning technique that your instructors probably use quite frequently. It is not a question per se, but it is often attached to the questions they ask. This technique emphasizes the importance of silence. It is called *wait-time*. Wait-time occurs when a teacher asks a question and simply waits. That silence prior to someone answering the question is wait-time. Given enough time, someone in the class will try to answer the question; the silence becomes too much for him or her. Looking back at classes you've had over the past week, did you have an instructor engage in extended wait-time with you? Under what circumstances did it occur? How have previous instructors used wait-time in their classes? Was it tied to the topic? Student interest? Student confusion?

3. Going back to our discussion of teaching methods (direct, indirect, and integrated), how does teaching method affect classroom interactions (e.g., student preparation for class, turn-taking, note-taking, type of listening)?

4. Many professors use multimedia presentations when teaching. What is their potential effect on classroom listening and discussion? When do you find slides to be most useful? Least useful? What types of problems can they cause when you're trying to listen to the lecture?

LISTENING ACTIVITIES

1. Following a short class lecture, compare notes with others in your class (one person or a small group of three to four students). What similarities and differences exist? What does this suggest about how you listen? What explanations do you have for the differences in your note-taking? For explaining the similarities?
2. Practice note-taking. Go to a play and outline the plot, or watch a television program such as *Nova* and note main ideas and subpoints of its content. Both suggestions have their own advantages. Choose a play that is well known enough that you can get a written copy to assess your listening skills or you can record the television programming and review it again while you compare. Focus on identifying main points, primary subpoints, and enough examples or explanations to reflect your understanding of the plot.

3. In groups of four to five people, develop a visual presentation for this chapter. If developing slides, what would you include as main points? Subpoints? What type of background would you use? Font? How many words would you put on the page? Why should you consider these things when developing your presentation? If possible, each group should display two to three slides for the class. Which slides are received the most favorably? What makes them stand out or work for others in the class?
4. During class, chart the microstructures the instructor engages in. Do you normally pay attention to these structures? What effect do you think they might have on the listening for nonnative speakers.
5. Interview one or two nonnative speakers. Do they have problems listening in class? What type of problems do they have? Do they prefer a particular teaching method? Which one and why?

ADDITIONAL READINGS

Baringer, D. K., & McCroskey, J. C. (2000). Immediacy in the classroom: Student immediacy. *Communication Education, 49,* 178–186.

Brophy, J., & Good, T. L. (2000). *Looking in classrooms* (8th ed.). New York: Harper & Row.

Flowerdew, J. (Ed.). (1994). *Academic listening.* New York: Cambridge University Press.

Frymier, A. B., & Houser, M. (2000). The teacher-student relationship as an interpersonal relationship. *Communication Education, 49,* 207–219.

Gay, G. (2002). Preparing for culturally responsive teaching. *Journal of Teacher Education, 53,* 106–116.

Hidi, S., & Harackiewicz, J. M. (2000). Motivating the academically unmotivated: A critical issue for the 21st century. *Review of Educational Research, 70,* 151–180.

Ivey, D., & Backlund, P. (2000). *Exploring gender speak: Personal effectiveness in gender communication.* San Francisco: McGraw-Hill.

Silver, H. F., Strong, R. W., & Perini, M. J. (2000). *So each may learn: Integrating learning styles and multiple intelligences.* Alexandria, VA: Association for Supervision and Curriculum Development.

ENDNOTES

1. O'Hair, O'Hair, & Wooden, 1988; Wolff, Marsnik, Tacey, & Nichols, 1983; Wolvin, Coakley, & Disburg, 1992
2. Janusik & Wolvin, 2009; Emanuel et al., 2008
3. Gilbert, 1988; Imhof, 1998
4. Wolvin et al., 1992; Worthington, 2005
5. Conaway, 1982
6. Newton (1985) reported that first-year college students who took a listening class had significantly higher GPAs than those who did not take the class
7. Imhof, 1998
8. James, 1977
9. Kyle & Rogien, 2004
10. Sadler-Smith, 1997, p. 51
11. Beall, Gill-Rosier, Tate, & Matten, 2008
12. Beall et al., 2008
13. Martin & Potter, 1998; Beall et al., 2008
14. Kolb, 1984; Kolb & Kolb, 2005; Kolb, Boyatzis, & Mainemelis, 2002
15. Diagram adapted from Loo (2002a, 2002b) and McCarthy (1990)
16. Kolb & Kolb, 2005
17. Salovey, Mayer, Caruso, & Lopes, 2003, p. 251
18. Powell & Caseau, 2004
19. Healy, 1998; as described in Goleman, 2005
20. Goleman, 1997; Powell & Caseau, 2004

21. McCroskey & McCroskey, 2002
22. McCroskey & McCroskey, 2002; McCroskey & Andersen, 1976; McCroskey, Booth-Butterfield, & Payne, 1989
23. Chesebro et al., 1992
24. Preiss, Wheeless, & Allen, 1990; Scott & Wheeless, 1977
25. Chesebro & McCroskey, 2001
26. Wheeless, Preiss, & Galye, 1997
27. Moore, 2009
28. Moore, 2009
29. B.E.S.T. Robotics contest (Boost Engineering, Science & Technology)
30. Habibah & Pihie, 2003
31. Van der Veer, 2007
32. Alderman, 1990
33. McNary, Glasgow, & Hicks, 2005
34. Coty, 1994
35. Jalongo, 1991, p. 7
36. Downs, Javidi, & Nussbaum, 1988
37. Long & Hoy, 2006
38. Richmond, 2002, p. 70
39. O'Hair et al., 1988

40. Titsworth, 2004
41. O'Hair et al., 1988, p. 114
42. O'Hair et al., 1988, p. 116
43. Imhof, 1998; O'Hair et al., 1988
44. Titsworth, 2001
45. Cowan, 1995; Kallison, 1986; Mayer, 1977; Scerbo, Warm, Dember, & Grasha, 1992; Titsworth, 2001
46. Kiewra, 1983; Titsworth & Kiewra, 1998
47. American Association of University Women, 1991; Diller, Houston, Morgan, & Ayim, 1996; Powell & Caseau, 2004; Sadker & Sadker, 1994; Wood, 2001
48. Powell & Caseau, 2004
49. Rawlins, 2000
50. Tannen, 1994
51. Gollnick & Chin, 1994; Good & Brophy, 1997
52. Powell & Caseau, 2004
53. Cook, 1999
54. Powell & Caseau, 2004
55. Powell & Caseau, 2004
56. Flowerdew & Miller, 1997
57. Burley-Allen, 1995, as cited in Sandall, Schramm, & Seibert, 2003

REFERENCES

Alderman, M. K. (1990, September). Motivation for at-risk students. *Educational Leadership*, 27–30.

American Association of University Women. (1991). *Shortchanging girls, shortchanging America*. Washington, D.C.: Greenberg-Lake Analysis Group.

Beall, M., Gill-Rosier, J., Tate, J., & Matten, A. (2008). State of the context: Listening in education. *International Journal of Listening, 22*, 123–132.

Chesebro, J. L., & McCroskey, J. C. (2001). The relationship of teacher clarity and immediacy with student state receiver apprehension, affect, and cognitive learning. *Communication Education, 50*, 59–68.

Chesebro, J. L., McCroskey, J. C., Atwater, D., Bahrenfuss, R., Cawelti, G., Gaudino, J., & Hodges, H. (1992). Communication apprehension and self-perceived communication competence of at-risk students. *Communication Education, 37*, 270–277.

Conaway, M. S. (1982). Listening: Learning tool and retention agent. In A. S. Algier & K. W. Algier (Eds.) *Improving reading and study skills* (pp. 51–63). San Francisco: Jossey-Bass.

Cook, H. M. (1999). Language socialization in Japanese elementary schools: Attentive listening and reaction turns. *Journal of Pragmatics, 31*, 1443–1465.

Coty, S. (1994). "Sometimes I wish I'd never did it." Removing communication road blocks from at-risk students. *Voices in the Middles, 1*, 19–25.

Cowan, N. (1995). *Attention and memory: An integrated framework*. New York: Oxford University Press.

Diller, A., Houston, B., Morgan, K. P., & Ayim, M. (1996). *The gender question in education: Theory, pedagogy, & politics*. Boulder, CO: Westview.

Downs, V. C., Javidi, M., & Nussbaum, J. (1988). An analysis of teachers' verbal communication within the college classroom: Use of humor, self-disclosure, and narratives. *Communication Education, 37*, 127–141.

Emanuel, R., Adams, J. Baker, K., Daufin, E. K., Ellington, C., Fitts, E., Himsel, J., Holladay, L., & Okeowo, D. (2008). How college students spend their time communicating. *International Journal of Listening, 22*, 13–28.

Flowerdew, J., & Miller, L. (1997). The teaching of academic listening comprehension and the question of authenticity. *English for Specific Purposes, 16*, 27–46.

Gilbert, M. B. (1988). Listening in school: I know you can hear me—but are you listening? *International Journal of Listening, 2*, 121–132.

Goleman, D. (2005). *Emotional intelligence.* New York: Bantam.

Gollnick, D. M., & Chin, P. C. (1994). *Multicultural education in a pluralistic society* (4th ed.). New York: Macmillan.

Good, T., & Brophy, J. E. (1997). *Looking in classrooms* (7th ed.). New York: Longman.

Habibah, E., & Pihie, Z. A. L. (2003). *Listening competence among university students.* (ERIC Document Reproduction Service No. ED478119)

Imhof, M. (1998). What makes a good listener? Listening behavior in instructional settings. *International Journal of Listening, 12,* 81–105.

Jalongo, M. R. (1991). *Strategies for developing children's listening skills.* (PDK Fastback Series Title 314). Bloomington, IN: Phi Delta Educational.

James, K. (1977). Note-taking in lectures: Problems and strategies. In A. P. Cowie & J. B. Heaton (Eds.), *English for academic purposes* (pp. 99–107). London: BAAL/SELMOUS.

Janusik, L. A., & Wolvin, A. D. (2009). 24 hours in a day: A listening update to the times studies. *The International Journal of Listening, 23,* 104–120.

Kallison, J. (1986). Effects of lesson organization on achievement. *American Educational Research Journal, 23,* 337–347.

Kiewra, K. A. (1983). The relationship between notetaking over an extended period and actual course-related achievement. *College Student Journal, 17,* 381–385.

Kolb, A. Y., & Kolb, D. A. (2005). Learning styles and learning spaces: Enhancing experiential learning in higher education. *Academy of Management Learning and Education, 4,* 193–212.

Kolb, D. A. (1984). *Experiential learning: Experience as the source of learning and development.* Englewood Cliffs, NJ: Prentice-Hall.

Kolb, D. A., Boyatzis, R. E., & Mainemelis, C. (2002). Experiential learning theory: Previous research and new directions. In R. J. Sternberg & L. F. Zhang (Eds.), *Perspectives on cognitive, learning, and thinking styles* (pp. 227–248). Mahwah, NJ: Lawrence Erlbaum.

Kyle, P. B., & Rogien, L. R. (2004). *Classroom management.* New York: Pearson.

Long, J. F., & Hoy, A. W. (2006). Interested instructors: A composite portrait of individual differences and effectiveness. *Teaching and Teacher Education, 22,* 303–314.

Loo, R. (2002a). A meta-analytic examination of Kolb's learning style preferences among business majors. *Journal of Education for Business, 77,* 25–50.

Loo, R. (2002b). The distribution of learning styles and types for hard and soft business majors. *Educational Psychology, 22,* 349–360.

Mayer, R. E. (1977). The sequencing of instruction and the concept of assimilation to schema. *Instructional Science, 6,* 369–388.

McCarthy, B. (1990, October). Using the 4MAT system to bring learning styles to schools. *Educational Leadership,* 31–37.

McCroskey, J. C., & Andersen, J. (1976). The relationship between communication apprehension and academic achievement among college students. *Communication Research, 3,* 73–81.

McCroskey, J. C., Booth-Butterfield, S., & Payne, S. (1989). The impact of apprehension on college student retention and success. *Communication Quarterly, 37,* 100–107.

McCroskey, J. C., & McCroskey, L. L. (2002). Willingness to communicate and communication apprehension in the classroom. In J. L. Chesebro & J. C. McCroskey (Eds.), *Communication for teachers* (pp. 19–34). Boston: Allyn & Bacon.

McNary, S. J., Glasgow, N. A., & Hicks, C. D. (2005). *What successful teachers do in inclusive classrooms.* Thousand Oaks, CA: Corwin Press.

Moore, K. (2009). *Effective instructional strategies.* Thousand Oaks, CA: Sage.

Newton, T. (1985). *Description of the St. Edwards University directed listening skills project.* Paper presented at the International Listening Association Summer Conference, St. Paul, MN.

O'Hair, M., O'Hair, D., & Wooden, S. L. (1988). Enhancement of listening skills as a prerequisite to improved study skills. *International Journal of Listening, 2,* 113–120.

Powell, R. G., & Caseau, D. (2004). *Classroom communication and diversity: Enhancing instructional practice.* Mahwah, NJ: LEA.

Preiss, R. W., Wheeless, L. R., & Allen, M. (1990). Potential cognitive processes and consequences of receiver apprehensions: A meta-analytic review. In M. Booth-Butterfield (Ed.), *Communication, cognition, and anxiety.* (Special Issue), *Journal of Social Behavior and Personality, 5,* 155–172.

Rawlins, W. K. (2000). Teaching as a mode of friendship. *Communication Theory, 10,* 5–26.

Richmond, V. P. (2002). Teacher nonverbal immediacy: Use and outcomes. In J. L. Chesebro & J. C. McCroskey (Eds.), *Communication for teachers* (pp. 65–82). Boston: Allyn & Bacon.

Sadker, M., & Sadker, D. (1994). *Failing at fairness: How America's schools cheat girls*. New York: Charles Scribner's Sons.

Sadler-Smith, E. (1997). Learning style: Frameworks and instruments. *Educational Psychology, 17*, 51–64.

Salovey, P., Mayer, J. D., Caruso, D., & Lopes, P. N. (2003). Measuring emotional intelligence as a set of abilities with the Mayer-Salovey-Caruso emotional intelligence test. In S. J. Lopez & C. R. Snyder (Eds.), *Positive psychological assessment: A handbook of models and measures*. Washington, D.C.: American Psychological Association.

Sandall, N., Schramm, K., & Seibert, A. (2003, May). *Improving listening skills through the use of children's literature*. Master of arts action research project. Saint Xavier University & SkyLight Professional Development, Chicago, IL. (ERIC Document Reproduction Service No. ED482002)

Scerbo, M., Warm, J., Dember, W., & Grasha, A. (1992). The role of time and cuing in a college lecture. *Contemporary Educational Psychology, 17*, 312–328.

Scott, M. D., & Wheeless, L. R. (1977). The relationship of three types of communication apprehension to classroom achievement. *Southern Speech Communication Journal, 42*, 246–255.

Tannen, D. (1994). *Gender discourse*. New York: Oxford University Press.

Titsworth, B. S. (2001). The effects of teacher immediacy, use of organizational lecture cues, and students' note taking on cognitive learning. *Communication Education, 50*, 283–297.

Titsworth, B. S. (2004). Students' note taking: The effects of teacher immediacy and clarity. *Communication Education, 53*, 305–320.

Titsworth, B. S., & Kiewra, K. (1998, April). *By the numbers: The effect of organizational lecture cues on note taking and achievement*. Paper presented at the American Educational Research Association convention, San Diego, CA.

Van der Veer, R. (2007). *Lev Vygotsky: Continuum library of educational thought*. London: Continuum.

Wheeless, L. R., Preiss, R. W., & Galye, B. M. (1997). Receiver apprehension, informational receptivity, and cognitive processing. In J. A. Daly, J. C. McCroskey, J. Ayres, T. Hopf, & D. M. Ayers (Eds.), *Avoiding communication: Shyness, reticence, and communication apprehension* (pp. 151–187). Cresskill, NJ: Hampton.

Wolff, F., Marsnik, N., Tacey, W., & Nichols, R. (1983). *Perceptive listening*. New York: Holt, Rinehart & Winston.

Wolvin, A. D., Coakley, C. G., & Disburg, J. E. (1992). Listening instruction in selected colleges and universities. *International Journal of Listening, 6*, 59–65.

Wood, J. T. (2001). *Gendered lives: Communication, gender and culture* (4th ed.). Belmont, CA: Wadsworth.

Worthington, D. L. (2005). *Listening education: A review of current listening syllabi*. Paper presented to the Communication and Social Cognition Division at the meeting of the National Communication Association, Boston, MA.

Listening in Context

Organizations

Cultural Differences and Organizational Listening

On his way home from work, Mr. Kim, a CPA with an auto parts manufacturing plant, is thinking about the executive team meeting that occurred earlier in the day. The executive team reflects the international nature of the company. Mr. Kim is worried about whether some of the divisions are listening to the needs of their employees and setting the example necessary to have good morale. He really likes working for S&K, a Korean-owned company. He feels culturally connected with the values and work expectations of the organization but worries about his friend Steve Goleman. Mr. Goleman is the vice president of human resources and has expressed concerns about possible differences in the expectations of the employees and the values of the company. Mr. Goleman isn't sure that the company is really tuned in to the needs of the predominately United States–born workers.

This past Sunday the two families had gone on a picnic and their children, Ben and NaMii, had talked about listening as an important part of an organization's culture, a topic that had come up in their listening class. *There just might be something to this,* Mr. Kim thinks as he navigates the traffic. ■

I n the context of our model, Listening MATERRS, we can see that the situation in which an interaction takes place can profoundly affect the process of listening. As the Case Study above illustrates, our concern with listening extends beyond ourselves as individuals to the many situations we find ourselves in. Therefore, we need to focus on how listening is used and the impact of listening (good or bad) on different contexts. This chapter will explore listening in an organization. To do so, we will look at the organization as a listening entity as well as areas of listening that are essential to the success of organizations. However, before we can talk about organizations as a listening context, we need to understand what an organization is. An **organization** is a dynamic system in which individuals engage in collective efforts for goal accomplishment.[1]

Just as individual listening skills are important for a person's success, the willingness of an organization to value listening in its relationship with employees, customers, and any other important groups is a critical aspect of successful organizations. Effective organizational listening leads to improved morale, happier customers, and a healthier bottom line.

To understand organizations as listening contexts, we first need to understand several important organizational concepts: purpose, mission, culture, and climate. Once we have defined these concepts, we will look at organizations in general; how organizations exhibit listening; and how listening as an organizational value can affect communication, conflict, and the day-to-day operations of a business.

UNDERSTANDING ORGANIZATIONS

The degree to which an organization listens is determined by a several factors. Among them are purpose, mission, culture, and climate. We will also address workplace social support and leadership. Even though we think of organizations as a collection of individuals, its unifying purpose, mission, and culture make it a listening entity. As a listening entity, organizations are subject to experiencing communication successes and failures, particularly with two of their main publics: customers and employees. Over the next few pages, we look at these factors and how they affect listening inside and outside the organization. Toward the end of the chapter, we discuss how these factors come together to create the listening organization.

Purpose and Mission

When we talk about the purpose of an organization, we are referring to what the organization exists to do, whether it's manufacturing something, raising funds, or providing services to the public. In our Case Study at the beginning of this chapter, Mr. Kim and Mr. Goleman, the fathers of NaMii and Ben, work for S&K, a company whose purpose is to provide specific auto parts to auto manufacturers. Of course, other companies focus on services such as home health, investment advice, or clothing sales.

An organization's mission statement is a declaration of its purpose. Organization expert John Bryson feels that mission statements should answer six questions:

1. Who are we?
2. What are the basic needs or problems for which we exist?
3. How do we respond to these needs?
4. How should we respond to key stakeholders?
5. What are our core values?
6. What makes us unique?[2]

Similarly, Janel Radtke, author of *Strategic Communications for Nonprofit Organizations*, argued that a good mission statement explains why a company or organization came into being in the first place, what need it was designed to meet.[3] For example, local hospitals were often originally established to provide communities with quality health care, so individuals didn't have to drive an hour to deliver a baby, get stitches for a cut, or get kidney dialysis. Radtke also noted that mission statements should address what needs an organization will be meeting (e.g., building a new hospital). It is important for mission statements to outline the principles or beliefs that guide the work of the organization, in other words, its values (e.g., to provide excellent, committed care to the ill and to identify and proactively address community health issues).

Sometimes companies will make separate values statements or ethics statements that highlight the values and principles on which the organization is built and run. These statements are an extension and refinement of what appears in the organization's mission statement. For example, Ford Motor Company publishes a Standards of Corporate Conduct that is given to all employees and is accessible on their Web site.[4] In 2006 the letter to employees from then chairman and CEO of the company, William Clay Ford, Jr., stated the company had adopted "Business Principles that reflect the values espoused by the Company during our first 100 years. Importantly, the Business Principles also serve as a guide for our decisions and actions globally as we embark upon our second century of delivering excellent automotive products and services. These Business Principles establish standards that we—and others—will use to evaluate our performance in areas that are key to our business."[5] Mr. Ford's statement clearly establishes the organizational values that guide Ford Motor Company's daily operations. His statement also lets readers know that these values reflect the long and proud history of the company.

Radtke also argued that "an effective mission statement must resonate with the people working in and for the organization, as well as with different constituencies that the organization hopes to affect. [Ideally it should] express the organization's purpose in a way that inspires commitment, innovation, and courage."[6] Most organizations, whether for profit or not, have mission statements, and those statements vary tremendously. Imagine the differences between mission statements for retailers Walmart and Nordstrom, or nonprofits such as the American Cancer Society and Susan G. Komen for the Cure. While each pair of these organizations has similar goals, their overall missions differ substantially. Table 9.1 contrasts the missions.

TABLE 9.1	
Selected Mission Statements	
Walmart[7]	Nordstrom[8]
We save people money so they can live better.	Fashion is personal. We don't dictate, we suggest, collaborate, teach, inspire and engage. We're the matchmaker guiding our customers to find "the one." The business of fashion.
Susan G. Komen for the Cure[9]	American Cancer Society[10]
To save lives and end breast cancer forever by empowering people, ensuring quality care for all, and energizing science to find the cures.	The American Cancer Society is the nationwide, community-based, voluntary health organization dedicated to eliminating cancer as a major health problem by preventing cancer, saving lives, and diminishing suffering from cancer, through research, education, advocacy, and service.

The uniqueness or persona of an organization is not just in its purpose and mission but also in the internal aspects of culture and climate.

Organizational Culture

Organizational culture is the study of "an organization's way of life," one created by the history of the organization, its leaders, and employees.[11] Edgar Schein, a noted scholar in the area of organizations, defined culture as "a

THINK ON IT

Look at the mission statements presented in Table 9.1. Do they meet the guidelines established by John Bryson and Janet Radtke? What did you learn about the organizations based on their mission statements? Are any of the mission statements reflective of an organization that values listening?

pattern of shared basic assumptions that was learned by a group as it solved its problems of external adaptation and internal integration, that has worked well enough to be considered valid, and therefore, taught to new members, as the correct way to see, think and feel in relation to those problems."[12] Schein believes that cultural assumptions apply to how an organization sets strategies and establishes goals, selects methods of achieving those goals, measures progress, and controls its output. For example, whether or not S&K establishes its annual production goals by consulting with the various departments in the organization or by board decree will reflect the S&K culture in which Mr. Kim and Mr. Goleman work. Organizatio-nal culture also addresses how an organization deals with behavior that is out of line with either its goals or its accepted norms of behavior. As you know from your experiences in the classroom, such behavior can potentially lead to a conflict situation (e.g., a reprimand from the instructor to the offending student or even worse, a public dressing-down by classmates).

Organizational culture helps shape the context in which all interactions within an organization, even interpersonal exchanges, take place. As such it provides the context in which listening occurs, as illustrated in our Listening MATERRS model. The culture even influences the way people in the organization think and operate. Scholars Eric Eisenberg and H. Lloyd Goodall called this tendency **organizational cognition,** meaning that members of the organization have shared meanings, values, and rules.[13] Thus, Ben & Jerry's (of ice cream fame) encourage their employees to have fun and be a bit goofy, especially when it comes to developing new names and flavors of ice cream. Ford Motor Company, on the other hand, is much more conservative in its day-to-day operations (refer back to the ethics statement above). Shared cognitions allow groups to share the meaning of symbols, metaphors, and stories. A good example of this can be found in your school. Members of the student body know what the school motto means as well as the use of certain insider sayings. At Auburn University the term *War Eagle* is often substituted for "hello" and "good-bye." Current and former AU students (and likely their parents) know these usages, but few people outside of the membership do. Chances are you can identify similar examples in your school. These shared cognitions serve to make people feel they are part of the organizational community.

By looking at the definitions and characteristics of **organizational culture,** we can see that culture is a created "social reality" of how the organization operates, what it considers important, and how it treats its employees and other publics. Underlying this reality are the values of the organization, or the principles on which they operate. These principles can include listening to employees and other

THINK ON IT

Go online and look up the mission statement of three of your favorite companies or organizations. What do they have in common? How do they differ? What company values are reflected in their statements? How might those values affect listening both inside and outside of the company?

important groups and working toward mutually beneficial outcomes. Unfortunately they can also do the opposite and reflect an organization interested in only the year-end financial reports. The importance of values is very evident whether they are formally stated or simply displayed in the day-to-day operation of the organization.

Culture Gaps   When an organization fails to live by its stated values, it exhibits **culture gaps.** Culture gaps are differences in what an organization says it values and what it actually does in its day-to-day operations. These types of organizations are perceived to focus more on their own interests and often devalue listening by their actions. If these perceptions are indeed true, the organization often ends in failure. The 1990s were full of examples of organizations that illustrate what happens when they don't listen and don't live up to their stated values. One of the most visible examples of corporate failure to live by stated values and to listen is Enron. This organization dominated business news during the early 2000s. The scandal became front-page news when the company declared bankruptcy on December 2, 2001. About that same time, a number of current and former top leaders of the organization were charged with numerous counts of defrauding stockholders. In essence, its leaders hid the company's actual financial status by creating numerous dummy organizations and entering into partnerships with those organizations. They did this to hide the level of debt Enron was carrying. Meanwhile, corporate leaders strongly encouraged employees and others to invest in company stock. Needless to say, all this activity made the stock look like a desirable investment. However, the company was essentially operating a false front, one built on the retirement funds of thousands of individuals. At the time, some individuals within the company questioned what was going on. However, these voices were quickly silenced by both corporate leadership and investors who had high hopes of making large profits.

Despite a 65-page statement of organizational ethics stressing fairness and honesty, apparently few, if any, in Enron could raise opposing views or offer contrary suggestions to those in power without being sanctioned in some way.[14] An article in *Forbes* magazine suggested that these values were only spoken, that a giant gap existed between what the leadership wrote and what it did. The British Broadcasting Company also reported that the culture of Enron was anything but caring. Instead, BBC reports characterized the culture as cutthroat and suggested that encouraging the values of fairness and honesty were not incorporated into the day-to-day operations of the organization. The fact that two of the most powerful leaders in the organization, Ken Lay and Jeffrey Skilling, were eventually sentenced to spend substantial time in prison is of little comfort to the thousands of individuals who lost their life savings because they were victims of an organization driven by greed rather than driven by a culture of listening.

Unfortunately this state of affairs is not uncommon. Similar situations have occurred more recently during the mortgage crisis with companies such as A.G. Edwards. Employees who questioned financial practices were either ignored or essentially told to keep their opinions to themselves. Of course, the ramifications were even greater, with eventually the entire national economy being negatively affected.

Organizational Climate

Closely related to culture, **organizational climate** is the perception, usually on the part of employees or organizational members, of how things are in an organization.[15] More specifically, climate is defined as an individual's perception of the important aspects of the work environment.[16] An individual's perceptions are based on his or her judgment of the beliefs, values, behaviors, and skills needed to be effective in the organization.[17] Essentially climate is a response to the culture of an organization. Although we think of climate as an individual reaction, these reactions tend to be shared by members of a group. For example, if you feel that your school is a warm, supportive place, that feeling is probably shared by the majority of other students at the school, particularly those students you hang out with.

As the employees and other people associated with the organization act on their perceptions, they create the climate. Once the climate is created, it influences the way people work or even study in the case of a school. A survey by the Six Seconds Institute for Organizational Performance found a clear relationship between how people feel and how they perform.[18] This survey found that 43 percent of retention of employees is predicted by leadership, alignment, and collaboration. *Alignment* indicates the organization is listening to the needs and values of employees and working with those needs. You might recall from our previous Case Study that Mr. Goleman is concerned about S&K's alignment. *Collaboration* indicates employees work together in a selfless manner. When these conditions exist in an organization, it has a listening environment or climate, and retention of employees is higher. (We discuss leadership later in the chapter.)

On the other hand, if employees are constantly fearful of losing their jobs or being reprimanded by supervisors, the climate is one of fear and dislike. Recently one of our students told us about the unhappy environment of the public relations company she interned with. While she valued the hands-on experience and felt that she had learned a tremendous amount, she did not like how the supervisor talked to others in the group. She specifically said that she felt it was inappropriate for employees to be reprimanded in front of her. Basically this student did not like the organizational climate of the firm.

Of course, most companies have more favorable climates. If people can feel relaxed and playful, the atmosphere is fun and employees tend to be very loyal to the company. It is important to note that a relaxed, playful climate doesn't mean the business isn't serious. Ben & Jerry's is serious about the ice cream business even while encouraging their employees to be creative and playful at work.

Climate can have a profound impact on the individuals in the workplace. One study done in New Zealand found that people who feel a great deal of pressure on the job are more prone to suffer from burnout than those who feel less pressure.[19] Likewise, employees who feel their organization's climate is low pressured, supportive, and cohesive are more likely to enjoy their work. When such a climate exists, it is said to be high in social support.

Organizational Social Support

As you learned earlier in the text, **social support** is based on the social relationships or networks that we develop. In our earlier discussions, we focused on family and friends as primary social support systems. However, good social support in the workplace has a number of positive implications for companies and other organizations. **Organizational social support** focuses on "the informational functions of supportive communication and the role that co-workers play in assisting one another in defining and making sense of their work environment."[20] Terrance Albrecht and Daena Goldsmith noted that social support helps members of an organization to "manage uncertainty."[21] In other words, social support seems to help us maintain a sense of control over our everyday and work lives.

Social support takes a number of different forms but can be summarized in two categories: **action-facilitating support** and **nurturing support.** Action-facilitating support includes instrumental and informational support, while nurturing support covers emotional, esteem, and social network support.[22]

Instrumental support focuses on doing tasks and favors, while **information support** addresses how corporations share and provide information. Clearly there are many ways you can provide this type of support in the workplace. You can conduct an Internet search for a friend; you can contribute relevant information to a discussion or run an errand for someone. As a listener, when you provide a listening ear as someone talks through a problem, you provide instrumental support. Organizations provide instrumental support by making sure employees have access to the resources they need to do their jobs. Coworkers also provide instrumental support for each other when they work cooperatively on a task. When an organization's culture encourages cooperation, this type of support is evident. Innolect, Inc., an organizational consulting firm, fosters a climate of instrumental support. The associates, or members of the Innolect group, also often share information so others can be successful in a job or have a leg up in their effort to work with a particular client.

Unfortunately some organizations are built on a culture of extreme competition and discourage instrumental support among divisions. In cases such as this, there is very little sharing of information or cooperation. Supposedly one large wine producer operated in this fashion several years ago. It pitted the sales and production departments against each other. So production tried to produce more product than sales could sell, and sales tried to sell more than production could produce. While this strategy kept people motivated to bring in big numbers, it created a very stressful work environment. A friend who is an organizational consultant reported a similar situation. In this company one group felt that a smaller division was unimportant to the mission and, consequently, members of the "important" group refused to provide any instrumental support to the smaller division. As one would suspect, this attitude led to long-term, unproductive conflict in the organization (which was one of the primary reasons he was called in to help).

Fortunately many organizations have cultures that encourage positive, supportive social relationships. That is, they encourage **nurturing support.** These organizations tend to be listening-safe climates, or climates in which one is free to express his or her views and to be listened to in a nonjudgmental way. Social support thus becomes an important part of employee relations. A quick look at *Fortune*'s list of the 100 best companies to work for in 2010 will identify organizations that listen. For example, one very familiar organization tops the list: Google. Video clips found online at CNNMoney reveal that the employees at these companies have fun, are encouraged to enjoy their work experience, and are expected to think innovatively.[23] Google's organizational climate has helped make it one of the most financially successful companies in the world.

Listening, Social Support, and Corporate Climate   Although it is the individuals in the network who provide the support, the climate and culture of the organization will either motivate or demotivate the existence of that support. When people feel comfortable at work and enjoy their jobs, productivity goes up. Listening is one of the key ingredients in this type of atmosphere. Research indicates that most distressed individuals don't want advice; they want to be heard. For someone to feel heard, we need to engage in supportive listening. Communication scholar Brant Burleson suggested that this type of listening involves the following:[24]

- Focus attention on the other person, not personal feelings or experiences.
- Stay neutral. Avoid being judgmental or labeling information as good or bad. Staying neutral also includes encouraging the speaker to do the same thing.
- Focus on the speaker's feelings rather than events. More than likely, it is the person's feelings that need exploring.
- Support the other person's feelings rather than trying to fix them or direct them. Express understanding of how the person feels, rather than telling her how she should feel.

This type of listening will help your friends and coworkers express themselves and can even help them work through problems. Your esteem and emotional support can provide a listening-safe zone where people can be open about potentially distressing topics such as flunking out of school or being fired. In addition, it prevents us from discounting what other people feel by our misguided efforts to cheer them up. You might recall from Chapter 2 that we talked about yellow listening, where we acknowledge the other person but don't listen to his real needs. Unfortunately we often engage in yellow listening unless concentrating on providing emotional support. For example, often when someone is talking to us about something unpleasant, we

THINK ON IT

What type of organization would you like to work for? What specific actions or comments would motivate you to continue working for an organization or be willing to put in those extra hours that are necessary to complete a task?

give a yellow response by saying things can't be that bad. Good emotionally supportive listening will allow us to be green listeners, who are supportive of whatever the other person is feeling, whether we, as listeners, are comfortable or not. Some organizations talk about listening to their employees, but they often either only go through the motions or ignore the employee messages altogether. Remember Enron?

 Another type of nurturing support is **social network support,** which involves maintaining ongoing relationships. As students, you probably think of this type of support as your network of friends and family. In an organization this type of network can be colleagues in the business or industry or coworkers. For example, both authors of this book have extensive professional networks. Not only do we, as coworkers, provide support to each other for our teaching and research but we both work with scholars and practitioners in other organizations. We find this network energizes us and keeps us constantly challenged. It keeps us from getting complacent or stuck in the rut of the same type of thinking. Consequently professionally we remain more open to new ideas and approaches. We hope we remain more open as individuals as well. This type of network is an important part of a vital organization.

Modern communication makes maintaining a social network a special challenge. The ability to create virtual communities makes it very easy for us to form a network outside of our particular organization. Chances are you communicate regularly with students at schools other than the one where you are enrolled. This ease of communicating outside of our own organization can also provide some interesting communication and listening challenges.

Recent research by Andy Wolvin and Laura Janusik indicated that we are now spending more than 15 percent of our time with e-mail and the Internet.[25] While scholars haven't decided whether this type of interaction constitutes listening (we discuss this idea more fully in Chapter 12), we can agree that electronic communication mediums provide us with virtual networks. In business settings these networks allow people to communicate about key issues, particularly when time is short and distances are great. However, using technology too much can cause people to become overly reliant on using the medium and not reaching out to people within the same organization. Electronic networking can also lead to misunderstandings since receivers don't have access to all of the information, such as facial expressions and vocal tones, needed to truly interpret someone's remarks. McDonald's is very sensitive to these concerns. Recognizing the importance of face-to-face interactions, it had no e-mail system at its headquarters as late as 1996.[26]

Several years ago, Professor Fitch-Hauser was hired by an organization because they were having trouble with miscommunication among employees. After observing the situation, she discovered that many of the employees communicated with each other solely by e-mail. Employees seemed to think that it was a waste of time to actually go into someone's office and have a face-to-face discussion, even if the person was in the next office. So while e-mail can save time, misuse of it can lead to communication problems. Think about it, if your "context" is limited to your office or cubicle, you might feel there is no need to actually go down the hall to talk with someone. It makes sense that if your sense of place and belonging is defined by a communication medium—e-mail—and your office, then it becomes easy to feel threatened. Your feelings are likely due to your lack of non-text-based information (e.g., nonverbal information) or a social network to help define the message. This may well be why so many of you prefer MySpace and Facebook to e-mail since they provide a little more context.

The previous example of the overuse of e-mail clearly illustrates the importance of social support to an organization. In the example the networks were weakened by an overreliance on e-mail. The absence of face-to-face interaction created a context in which it was impossible to listen fully. Subsequently both employee morale and productivity were negatively affected.

Leadership

Climate and culture are profoundly affected by an organization's leadership. Not only do leaders of an organization reflect its values but they also have a

Sir, the creative meeting's over!

Managers must commit themselves to listening sensitively!

critical role in defining those values. As one would expect, listening organizations have listening leaders. As John Yokoyama, owner of Pike Place Fish Market in Seattle, said, "If I am not listening actively to my crew, I fail to create an environment where they will listen to one another and to our customers. If I don't listen to the needs and concerns of my staff, I can't reasonably expect them to listen to those same needs of their team members and our customers. My behavior sets the tone for our company."[27] Clearly Mr. Yokoyama understands the effect of organizational context on listening.

Witt Communications, a consulting firm, addresses listening leaders on their Web site.[28] They suggest that for leaders to be successful in contemporary business, they have to be good listeners. If they listen, they are able to identify problems before they get out of control, uncover causes of miscommunication and conflict, understand people, build rapport, gather and evaluate information, and generate solutions. The company also suggests that listening leaders build organizations that value collaboration. Witt Communications' stance is supported by research that indicates that leaders spend up to 89 percent of their time communicating with subordinates.[29]

Sometimes leaders have to shift an organization's culture so it starts to value listening. The giant Korean electronics company Samsung is an excellent example of how a leader can lead the charge to redefine organizational values and direction. In the early 1990s, Samsung was known for producing cheap, discounted goods, not innovative, high-quality, well-designed electronics. Today the organization is one of the fastest-growing companies in the world and the recipient of numerous design awards.[30] As we look at the internal moves behind this transformation, we can find listening leaders who have developed a listening organization. Kun-Hee Lee, chairman of Samsung, knew that things at the company had to change. He wanted to help the company create a distinctive identity, one built on innovative design that could meet global demand while at the same time reflecting the ancient culture of Korea. In essence, he shifted the focus to designing and balancing opposite forces, commonly known as yin and yang. One of the major changes he introduced was the creation of a collaborative work environment where employees know enough about other employees' jobs and related concerns that they mutually and willingly seek to address them. For example, designers at Samsung now take a year of mechanical engineering so they will think about how the product works, not just what it looks like. Engineers also have to become familiar with design concerns so they have a realistic idea of how their products will be packaged. Now engineers and designers work together to produce products that are electronically innovative and have pleasing, distinctively functional designs; that is, they balance their opposing forces.

Organizations that value this type of collaboration are typically based on cultures that value inquiry and listening. **Inquiry** is the art of asking questions. Asking questions becomes an art when the questions are the right questions, those that link values with actions and results by opening up thoughtful exploration of possibilities and actions. The type of listening that is needed is open to what is truly being said, what needs to be expressed, and what is not being said.[31] Then not only will the organization provide a listening-supportive context, it will be a listening organization.

Merrie Jo Pitera
Chief Executive Officer
Litigation Insights
Overland Park, Kansas

As a CEO of a midsized litigation consulting firm, listening to and understanding our employees is key to better communication and a smooth working environment. Because we have a diversified office in terms of generation, gender, and ethnicity, everyone in our office has a different listening style based on their culture, experiences, and sensibilities. Therefore, to ensure effective communication, and thus leadership, I have to take these differences into consideration when assigning projects and providing general instructions.

As for our clients, it is important to be a good listener. Our clients often communicate their goals for their projects. If we do not adequately understand those goals, we could effectively lose a project because we were not being responsive to their concerns. Therefore, listening to a client's goals and ensuring we have adequately heard those goals are critical to the success of running our business.

THE LISTENING ORGANIZATION

If we look at organizations closely, we can see that organizations, like people, make choices about whether or not to listen. They choose to listen to their employees, customers, competitors, or the community just like the listener in our model, Listening MATERRS. As an entity with definable groups of people with whom it wants to build a relationship, an organization can be considered a party in potential listening situations. For a listening situation to exist, the organization and the group it wants to communicate with must have some type of relationship in which the actions of either the organization or the public will have an effect on the well-being of the other.[32]

Organizational listening can be described as the responsiveness of an organization to the needs of its public. When organizations listen, they tend to have better reputations, more productive employees, better-quality products, and a happier customer base.

As we noted at the beginning of the chapter, an organization is a dynamic system in which individuals engage in collective efforts for goal accomplishment.[33] The organization of the 21st century has undergone and continues to experience a number of technological changes affecting how it communicates with its employees and other publics. Today virtual organizations are as viable as their more traditional brick-and-mortar counterparts. The advent of virtual organizations, organizations in which the work and employees are connected by a network rather than a physical plant or office building, requires us to reexamine how we define organizations. In such organizations an employee can work out of her home in Albany, New York, be supervised by someone in Seattle, and have clients in Detroit, Atlanta, and New Delhi. Regardless of how we define organizations, it is the process of communication that keeps them current, competitive, relevant, and viable. And of course, an important part of that process is how well organizations listen to important groups or publics.

> **THINK ON IT**
>
> Colleges and universities, like all organizations, reflect the changing boundaries of what defines the institution. For example, does your school offer online courses? If so, are you taking any of those courses? How do online classes differ from the ones that require your physical attendance? What type of relationship do you have with your teacher? To get the other side of the story, ask one of your teachers who teaches an online course about the differences in teaching the two types of classes. See if you can identify the listening challenges that are part of each context.

To get us focused on organizations as listeners, we need to examine a model of how organizations interact with their publics. Public relations scholars James Grunig and Todd Hunt proposed a model of public relations that can easily be applied to the listening organization.[34] This model, the **two-way symmetrical model of public relations,** reflects an organization that engages in two-way communication with its many publics. **Publics** in this setting are any groups of people with which the organization has an interdependent relationship (e.g., employees, customers, community). The assumptions of this model underscore the strength of the interdependence of an organization with its various publics. These assumptions include *telling the truth, seeking joint understanding,* and *managing the perceptions of the various viewpoints* represented in an organization or business relationship.

Applied to this context, a listening organization is one that fully engages in developing and maintaining two-way symmetrical interactions between it and the public. This type of interaction requires a great deal of listening so the organization can develop a relationship with the particular public in question. Just as people have relationships, organizations have relationships with groups with which they are interdependent. For example, your school has an interdependent relationship with you, the faculty, and numerous other groups. An interdependent relationship suggests that both parties, the organization and the public, make important contributions necessary for the organization to achieve its goals. However, it is unlikely that these goals can be achieved if the different publics themselves are unwilling to listen. A balanced perspective, one in which the needs of the public are balanced against the needs of the organization, is crucial. And listening is the means by which such a perspective can be achieved. Just as caring people engage in good listening behaviors in their relationships, organizations also engage in activities that reflect good relational listening. In essence, effective listening can cut across the boundaries that traditionally separate organizations and their publics (e.g., customers and employees, employees and upper management). Listening, then, allows organizations to remain in touch with and responsive to their employees, their customers or clients, and any other important public.

In the Case Study at the beginning of this chapter, Mr. Goleman is concerned about whether S&K is tuned in to the needs of a crucial public, the employees. If S&K is a good listening organization, it will listen to its employees and work to find mutually satisfactory ways of operating.

If we take the perspective that listening is a characteristic that helps an organization be responsive, we need to look at how organizations "listen" as well as the effect that organizational listening can have on both company morale and company profits. An analysis of research exploring various aspects of organizations and their critical relationships reveals a clear connection between the quality of communication and the nature of the relationship an organization has with its publics.[35] Other research suggests that an organization's relationship with its important publics can be assessed by *how dynamic* they are; *how open* they are; *how satisfied* both the organization and the public are; and *how well each side understands, agrees, or arrives at consensus* with each other.[36] Other important elements in these relationships are *trust* and *credibility*.[37]

A little later in this chapter, we will look at some specific publics with whom organizations have relationships. Before we do that, however, we need to look at what determines whether or not an organization chooses to listen. Just as individuals are motivated to make choices to attend to a message, organizations also make these decisions. This type of decision is usually based on the culture and climate that exists within the organization.

The Learning (Listening) Organization

We previously discussed several important aspects of organizations that can affect how organizations communicate and listen. They included the purpose, mission, culture, and climate of an organization, as well as social support and leadership. Fundamental to all of these elements is learning. Much has been written about learning organizations.[38] However, a review of the literature highlights one fundamental issue: listening. In fact, as you will see in the pages below, we feel that a more accurate label for these learning organizations is **the listening organization.**

As we noted earlier, an organization that strives to maintain two-way symmetrical relationships listens to its publics and operates as a listening entity. Just as a good listener is one who keeps an open mind to changes in the world around her, a listening organization does the same. Such organizations are open to creating and acquiring knowledge and converting it into organizational changes and new ways of behaving. Listening organizations listen to the information and find ways to incorporate it into appropriate adaptations to meet the publics' needs. Think about why a school would offer online courses. First, they learn about the technology, about the changes in the population that have led to a demand for the courses, and the willingness of faculty to work in that platform. Then based on the mission and values of the school, they will change how they deliver classes to meet the publics' need to take classes at times convenient to them, not the school.

A listening organization must possess a certain level of emotional intelligence (EI). As you remember from Chapter 4, emotional intelligence reflects our "ability to recognize and express emotion, and to regulate emotion in the self and others."[39] A listening organization, then, not only listens to information but it also has a good grasp of the changes in the business climate and the emotional ups and downs of its employees and other publics. As you can see, a lot of listening goes on in these organizations. However, to help us understand the concept of listening organizations, let's look at fundamental processes associated with learning organizations.

According to *The Superintendent's Fieldbook,* there are several ways to recognize a learning (listening) organization:[40]

- People in the organization ask a lot of questions and *listen* to one another.
- Employees have access to pertinent, accurate, and timely information.
- Individuals can explain their thinking when they share ideas with others.
- Employees are aware of what's going on in all parts of the organization.
- People in the organization embrace the rituals of the organization's culture.
- Members of the organization use language and metaphors appropriate to that organization in their conversations.
- Organizational members at all levels take improvement seriously.
- Individuals tend to approach conflict in a constructive, straightforward manner.
- Finally employees should be self-motivated and open to giving and receiving accurate and truthful feedback.

Organization Structure and Change

Organizations that exhibit the above characteristics of learning and listening find they are better able to adapt to the changes they encounter. One challenge facing all organizations is the shift in **organizational structure** that is occurring. Organizational structure refers to the alignment of personnel, or who reports to whom, who works with whom on what tasks, and so forth. As noted above, organizations are moving away from traditional structures aligned to a specific place, to networks that literally span the globe. Such changes have been spurred on by the exponential changes occurring in technology that make it possible for employees to work without being in the physical camp of the company. Telecommuting is on the rise. The U.S. Bureau of Labor reports that the number of people telecommuting at least one day a month rose from 28.7 million in 2006 to 33.7 million in

THINK ON IT

Do you know of a business in your area that would qualify as a listening organization? What qualities does it possess that leads you to think so?

2008 (a 17 percent increase in two years and a 43 percent increase from 2003).[41] Gartner Dataquest estimates suggest that by the time of publication of this book, more than 14 million people will telecommute one day a week from home.[42] Worldwide, the number is estimated to have exceeded 100 million.[43] This shift in the shape and definition of the workplace has forced organizations to face the challenge of adapting their operating and communication methods to meet the changing needs of employees. It appears that different communication strategies are needed with employees, depending on whether they work on-site or telecommute.[44] Specifically organizations must be able to adapt their communication strategies to meet the differing needs of the workers. For example, the concept of openness needs to be applied differently. People on site tend to want to know more information about the organization's objectives, policies, performance evaluations, and other day-to-day operating information. This type of information seems to enhance employee morale. However, it appears to have the opposite effect on telecommuters.[45]

A listening organization will recognize the possible effect of the changing structure of the workplace and make changes necessary to keep the morale of employees high. They will also recognize that workplace needs are changing and make organizational changes to support those needs. For example, if a company has a large number of employees who telecommute, they might adjust the location of their training. Instead of holding training sessions at the home office in Des Moines or at a set facility in Dallas all the time, they can choose to do regional meetings, so employees across the country have an easier time getting to the meetings. Alternatively the company could use webcasts or other similar technology to provide necessary training. Professor Fitch-Hauser experienced something similar to this when she worked directly with an organization's employee at the employee's home rather than at the organization's home office, which was in a different state. Because of this arrangement, not only did the company not have to bear the cost of travel in time and money, the employee was able to work her personal and business life around the work-related training.

Another characteristic of a listening organization is that it is better able to make other changes as well, including **systemic changes.** One type of systemic change is how an organization handles large-scale organizational conflict. PECO Energy, Pennsylvania's largest utility, faced an interesting challenge in the mid 1990s.[46] The International Brotherhood of Electrical Workers campaigned to unionize the employees. Even though the attempt failed and PECO retained its nonunion status, the company listened to their employees and instituted changes in how it handled employee conflict.

Listening and Organizational Conflict

As we can see in the PECO example, another hallmark of a listening organization is being able to manage conflict when it occurs. Just as all interpersonal relationships will encounter conflict, all organizations will encounter conflict. Any time you have interdependent parties (or departments), you have a situation that is ripe for conflict. Listening organizations realize that all conflicts can be managed and

CASE STUDY 9.2

When Corporate Cultures Collide

Steve Goleman gets home from a difficult day and finds his son, Ben, studying at the kitchen table.

Hey, Dad, you look beat. Have a rough day at work?

Well, I am a bit frazzled. I'm working with the new managers from the Ulsan, South Korea, plant, and I'm having some problems getting them to listen to me about the labor issues we are facing.

Well, have you tried talking with them?

Of course I have, but they keep wasting my time by talking about their experience and background and asking questions about mine. I don't understand why they are stalling and aren't willing to face the issues. I know they have been successful in dealing with labor problems in Ulsan.

Oh, Dad, you're good in situations like this. I'm sure you'll come up with a solution. How about a snack while we wait on dinner?

Is there an organizational listening problem? If so, what is it? What type of listening behavior is Mr. Goleman exhibiting toward the Korean management team?

What type of listening is Ben exhibiting toward his father? What are some possible responses Ben could have given that would have modeled good listening behavior for his father?

Hint: Remember the discussion of red, yellow, and green listening in Chapter 2. ∎

---

encourage climates that foster open communication, trust, and acceptance. In effect, these companies establish **listening-safe zones.** To better understand how conflict can be managed, we need to take a good look at listening in this context. Case Study 9.2 addresses this topic.

To manage conflict, an organization must use the type of listening that creates an atmosphere in which information can be exchanged freely and solutions emerge. Workplace dispute expert Erik Van Slyke suggested that we should define this type of listening as

> the process of becoming aware of all the cues that another party emits. It is a process of allowing another person to communicate the conscious and subconscious, both what the other person knows and what she or he may not yet understand. It is the act of attending to what another person is saying and what he or she is not saying. Listening demands work, but is the key to constructive conflict resolution.[47]

Listening plays two critical roles in conflict resolutions. First, it is the channel we use to *get the information* we need to resolve a conflict. If an organization or its representatives don't take the time to gather the necessary information, they won't have a clear understanding of what the root of the conflict is or what the other party really wants. Listening organizations care enough to want to resolve a conflict so all parties' needs are met. This doesn't mean they cave in to all demands, but they listen to discover what the real underlying issues are and work to find mutually beneficial solutions.

The second critical role of listening is to *reduce the personal issues* of conflict. All conflicts, even organizational ones, have objective issues and personal issues.[48] **Objective issues** deal with facts, data, and information. Consequently they are easier to resolve. **Personal issues,** on the other hand, are just that—personal—and are typically based on emotions. When an organization or an individual takes the time to listen, it tends to calm the emotional mind, according to Van Slyke. He contended that active listening that is voluntary and "involves recognizing, understanding and accurately interpreting the messages received" gives the emotions in a conflict situation time to slow down and let the rational mind catch up.[49] In such cases we can focus greater attention to rational processing of information and less on affective processing. Depending on the nature of the situation, we could also engage in dual processing. Parties who feel they are being listened to feel more trust and willingness to work toward a solution.

While all organizations will face conflict, a listening organization will resolve conflict in a manner that manages the situation. These organizations are sensitive to the multitude of factors that affect conflicts such as cultural sensitivity and personality types. Case Study 9.2 presents a situation that calls for cultural sensitivity. Once Mr. Goleman recognizes that part of the conflict he thinks he perceives is based on cultural differences, he will be able to resolve it in a manner that will be satisfactory to all parties. And once Ben completes his listening class, he will recognize his father's need for an empathetic, green response rather than the yellow one he gave.

Employee Relations

Many of the examples used in the previous section emphasize the importance of listening to employees. Employees are also an important public in any organization. To be economically viable, companies have to focus on reducing employee turnover (it's expensive to continually train new ones), maintaining employee morale (related to increased productivity), and keeping its employees long term (encouraging outstanding employees to stay). To do this, companies must not only listen to their workers, regardless of whether they are happy or angry, but they must also engage in appropriate follow-through. For example, after receiving complaints about rudeness on the part of certain employees, one city implemented a range of customer service training for all city employees. When asked what happened when an employee received praise, the response from city management was that a letter is placed in the employee's file and later used during the employee's annual review. When another organization was asked the same question, the response was one of surprise; the thought of catching employees doing something right had never entered the organizational mind.

Listening to an employee or coworker who is angry is a special challenge. Good listening skills are the base of being able to successfully handle the angry person. Chapter 5 outlined steps suggested by Jeff Bannon to handle conflict.[50] We briefly touch on them again. First, *inquire*. Let your coworker talk while you actively listen. Second, *empathize*. People like to feel that you can connect to them emotionally, particularly when they are feeling strong emotions such as anger. Third, *ask permission*. Don't assume that a coworker wants or needs additional information or explanation. Asking implies control, something that people who are angry or upset may feel they lack. By listening carefully, you can help ensure that you *respond appropriately* (e.g., "What would help you make a decision?") and that you are positioned to move toward the final step suggested by Bannon, *explaining and offering choices* (assuming they are desired). Again, we provided more in-depth coverage of these steps in Chapter 5.

Customer Satisfaction

Recently a friend of ours called a local pizza company to place an order. After repeatedly explaining his order to the person on the other end of the phone, he became exasperated and asked to speak to the manager. He wanted to tell the manager about the employee's rude behavior. The manager cut him off and asked for his order. Our friend explained that he would never order pizza from that company again and hung up. So because the manager would not take a few minutes to listen, they have lost a longtime (more than 10 years), loyal customer.

This example emphasizes another critical target public that an organization must listen to: its customers. Listening organizations focus on developing customer relations. These relationships are critical today because consumers have easier access to more choices than ever before. So companies must really listen to their customers and respond quickly to remain competitive.

The survey by the Institute for Organizational Performance we mentioned earlier found that 47 percent of the difference in low and high scores on customer service was caused largely by customer trust. For an organization to generate trust in its customers, the organization must listen. Listening is essential in customer service because it is the only way for an organization to identify what the needs and wants of the customers are.[51] Organizations need to focus on how customers describe their specific complaints. Only by listening carefully to customers can the organization address tough, customer-focused problems and challenges, such as dissatisfaction. The goal of good listening is to have satisfied customers.

In his classic business book, *What They Don't Teach You at Harvard Business School: Notes from a Street-smart Executive,* Mark McCormack suggested that businesspeople should listen aggressively to get insight about people in general.[52] He felt that businesses that could find a responsive chord then respond to it are more successful in business. McCormack's ideas were echoed a decade later when authors Robert Kriegel and David Brandt suggested that companies should try to give customers something they didn't expect.[53] To do so, they felt that companies had to listen to their customers, be truly willing to receive information, and use that information to build empathetic relationships with their customers.

Let's look at a very traditional business, banking, to see how important listening to customers can be. Biff Motley, senior vice president of retail banking and marketing with Whitney Bank in New Orleans, looked through many customer comments and found that customers who were satisfied with their banks reported feeling that bank employees cared about them, listened to their needs, and went beyond just the job description.[54] Consequently he became an advocate of "listening banks."

Another excellent example of the importance of listening to customers can be seen in the Pike Place Fish Market mentioned earlier in this chapter. John Yokoyama made the following statement about the importance of listening to customers.

> To make a difference, a salesperson has to listen to the customer. And genuinely want to help that person. The salesperson needs to take an interest in the customer, not as a means to an end but as an end in itself. . . .
>
> If you are going to listen powerfully to your customers, you can't do it in order to make more money. If you do listen for that reason, it is just a form of manipulation. You are going to listen through the filter of "Come on, say yes."

Or "Come on! You can spend more than that." When you truly listen to someone, you hold that person in high regard. You see him or her as naturally valuable with something significant to contribute.[55]

As the above quotation indicates, listening is critical in building trust with customers. Research by Rosemary Ramsey and Ravipreet Sohi and others suggest that perception of a salesperson's listening behavior influences customer satisfaction with the salesperson and whether or not the customer would do future business with that individual.[56] *Business Week* columnist Michelle Nichols feels that good salespeople engage in "round-trip communication where both parties interact and connect—that is both parties listen and talk."[57] She recommended that businesspeople, particularly sales staff, use "whole-body listening" that goes beyond hearing the words and includes tuning in to the nonverbal signals the customer is sending. Using this skill helps the salesperson "hear" the tone of voice and other things the customer isn't saying. For example, a good whole-body listener will notice whether a customer's face lights up or looks confused. This type of information is critical to the salesperson in knowing what to do next. Salespeople who listen have customers who buy.

Failure to Listen

Unfortunately not all organizations listen. When organizations don't maintain two-way symmetrical relationships with their publics, just like humans, they are subject to experiencing communication failure. Miscommunication or communication failure can be caused by a range of problems, such as failure to receive all or part of the message or failure to understand the message. Any of these problems can have a profound impact on an organization's relationships with its employees and customers. A brief look at miscommunication will help us better understand this problematic occurrence and its effect on listening at the organizational level.

Research on miscommunication has focused on interpersonal communication. However, we can find a number of parallels between the way organizations communicate with their receivers and the way people interact. Early research identified two types of communication failures: input and model.[58] **Input failures** involve incorrectly perceiving or interpreting information. When an organization misreads market research or feedback from employees or other important parties, the organization suffers from input failure. **Model failure** occurs when the incoming information fails to fit with expectations or fit into the listener's existing schema. When this happens, the listener may make inappropriate inferences or reach the wrong conclusions about the information. On an organizational level, model failure can occur if an organization focuses more on its own ideas of product needs than on changing trends. For example, when the automotive industry continues to manufacture large SUVs rather than smaller, more fuel-efficient vehicles when gasoline prices skyrocket, they are exhibiting model failure. The companies seem to be focused on their plans to produce large SUVs. News that gas prices were increasing and consumers were concerned didn't fit with their expectations.

Miscommunication can also occur in cross-cultural settings. For organizations to be successful when they do business in other countries, they must shift their models to incorporate cultural concerns. One reason international companies such as

BMW, Mercedes, Toyota, Honda, and Hyundai are so successful in their U.S. manufacturing plants is they took the time to study U.S. expectations and customs. They knew that simply importing their business models to the United States wouldn't work, so they were smart enough to incorporate U.S. business models into their United States–based companies while maintaining key components of their own organizational models. As we saw in our previous Case Study, Mr. Goleman certainly hopes that S&K follows the example of other international firms.

Research on miscommunication shows we understand or interpret actions and discourse by making inferences about the goals we think the other party has and the plans they have for attaining those goals.[59] As listeners, organizations also attempt to understand their relevant publics by interpreting actions and feedback. They make inferences about their customers' goals and the goals of other important groups. When an organization practices two-way symmetrical communication, or actually listens to their publics, they are much more likely to make smart business decisions. Those organizations that fail to listen will be more likely to make decisions that alienate their customers and employees and more likely to get embroiled in conflict.

Becoming a Listening Organization

Several times in this chapter, we have used Seattle's Pike Place Fish Market as an organization that practices listening. The fish market is a small market in an area where other vendors also sell fish. However, this particular market sets itself apart by the effort it puts into listening to its customers. In fact, this small company is the model for a series of books on customer service and motivation (as seen in our use of earlier examples). The owner of the market, John Yokoyama, suggested that one of the elements that make the market so famous and so popular is that the organization is built on being a listening organization. The following is a summary of how Yokoyama and the fish market became a listening organization.[60]

The transformation began when all of the employees of the market defined their vision to become world famous. Yokoyama had to make a decision to be open to employee ideas. In essence, he had to listen to them and their ideas. As a listening leader, he had to listen to more than just the words; he had to listen to the entire message, whether he agreed with it or not. He had to and continues to work on suspending judgment and remaining open to ideas, which have ranged from reducing the number of hours in a workweek to installing a webcam in the market.

This transformation called for speaking and listening responsibly. In essence, this means everyone who works there has to take responsibility for his own experience and perceptions and be able and willing to recognize the difference between blame and personal responsibility. In a regular organization, we might expect to hear employees playing the blame game. If anything goes wrong, it must be someone's fault (usually someone else's or another department's). In a listening organization, each person takes personal responsibility to address problems and challenges. This certainly doesn't mean that every employee has to "fix" the problem; it means he has to be committed to working as a team member toward the team's efforts. For this to happen, employees have to be willing to express their frustrations and make it safe for all employees to say anything they feel needs to be said.

They have to have a listening "safe zone." Certainly they can become upset by some of the things that are said. However, they have to commit to being quiet and to listening. The listener has to take responsibility for his own reactions and feelings.

Listeners who take responsibility for their own reactions as listeners must have a high level of emotional maturity and be of high emotional intelligence. As they listen to fellow workers, they understand that they, as listeners, are attaching emotional energy to the words in the message. This emotional energy has a direct effect on how they react. They also realize that individuals hear the same words but often make different choices about how to react to those words. An emotionally mature crew in an organization such as the fish market takes control of its emotional reactions. So when a customer (or fellow crew member) is having a bad day and takes his or her frustration out on the crew, they are able to create a listening-safe zone in the workplace. As a result, they are less likely to get defensive when a customer gets angry or unpleasant. They know that the more they listen, the sooner the other person will become calmer.

An emotionally mature listener can, in turn, become a more responsible speaker. So instead of using blaming language when discussing a problem or a reaction to something, the emotionally mature speaker takes responsibility for his or her reactions. **Blaming language** is language that focuses the blame and responsibility on the other person. A phrase such as "you make me so mad" is an example of this type of language. Such phrases suggest that the other person has power over the speaker. As a good listener, you should try to communicate in a less threatening and more emotionally mature way. So you would use a response such as "I perceive your comment in this way, and I feel this way about it. I'm expressing this to you because it is hindering my working effectively with you."

However, before organizations can build empathetic relationships with customers, they need to have systems in place to listen to the customer. Marketing scholars Leonard Berry and A. Parasuraman suggest organizations need to listen to three categories of customers: external, internal, and competitors' customers.[61] The listening system should be able to get a picture of these groups and their needs from numerous perspectives.

An example of a listening organization that has excellent customer relations is Virgin Atlantic Airways. One of the few financially successful airlines in the world, this company listens to the needs of its customers. By empathizing with customers, Sir Richard Branson has built an airline that provides little extras that keep customers coming back. For example, knowing how uncomfortable it can be to be strapped into a seat for a long time, Virgin Atlantic Airways instituted stand-up bars in their cabins. In addition, they offer nail treatments and massages on board long flights. The airline was also the first to offer seatback videos so fliers could watch movies they wanted to watch when they wanted to watch them.[62] How did all these innovations occur?

Any organizational listening system should allow an organization's managers to get involved with customers in such a way they can get valuable information from the customers' perspective. To do this, an organization should gather information that is relevant, precise, useful, credible, understandable, and timely. Today organizations listen to their customers by conducting focus groups or surveys, monitoring calls and e-mails to their customer service centers, establishing chat rooms and blogs for real-time interaction with customers, and monitoring other sites where their companies are being discussed. Getting the information isn't enough to improve customer relationships, however. Organizations must respond appropriately and in a timely manner and address challenges while they are still important, before they morph into something more serious. Being responsive to customer needs directly affects the customer and, it is hoped, leads to increased satisfaction. However, additional benefits are increased employee morale and good public relations. Responsive companies get noticed, whether by word of mouth, in the blogosphere, or some other type of public recognition. So good listening can lead to good news, and good news can lead to increased profits, a win-win situation for an organization and all of its publics.

SUMMARY

This chapter has looked at how organizations listen. Just as listening is a critical competency for an individual communicator, it is a critical aspect of being a successful business. Intelligent organizations listen to the needs of their employees and have lower turnover rates and better overall morale. Likewise, companies that listen to their customers build stronger relationships and achieve higher satisfaction ratings. Listening isn't just a human skill; it is also a critical business skill.

Although this chapter focuses on organizations as the listening entity, we can learn to be better listeners by using a listening organization as a model. We offer the following three suggestions:

■ Within ourselves we need to develop a sense of deep inquiry. That requires us to not just acknowledge what the other person is saying by giving appropriate feedback; it requires us to ask the right questions. "Be careful what you ask for; you might just get it." Well, a deep inquirer will craft questions to get exactly what he or she needs to know. So the questions will go beyond the superficial and "socially rote."

■ In addition, the questions will be accompanied by a calm and receptive mindset that is indicative of deep listening. Suspending judgment and bias are critical competencies used by the listening leader.

■ Listen to the whole message. Whether we are serving a customer or not, the people to whom we are listening want to say what they want to say. If we interrupt them, finish ideas for them, or zone out because we think we know what they are going to say, we provide a disservice and won't be able to meet their needs.

CONCEPTS TO KNOW

Organization
Misstatement
Organizational Cognition
Organizational Culture
Culture Gaps
Organizational Climate
Organizational Social Support
    Action Facilitating
    Instrumental
    Informational
    Nurturing
    Inquiry

Organizational Listening
Organization
Publics
Listening Organization
Organizational Structure
Systemic Changes
Listening-safe Zones
Objective Issues
Personal Issues
Input Failure
Model Failure

DISCUSSION QUESTIONS

1. Think of two incidents where you had a negative experience with a company: one where the ultimate outcome was negative and one where it ended more positively. What occurred? What differentiated the two outcomes? The two companies? Did you feel listened to by both companies? Why or why not? What type of listening occurred (red, yellow, or green)?

2. Think of a recent place you have worked. Would you describe the company or organization as having a listening culture or climate? Why or why not?

3. Keeping in mind our description of organizational climate, culture, and so on, describe the "perfect company" that you would like to work for. How does your description explicitly or implicitly focus on listening?

LISTENING ACTIVITIES

1. Check out paper or online job listings for customer service representatives. How do they (or don't they) emphasize listening skills?

2. In groups of three to four, identify three or four companies that have good or positive public images. What makes you identify them as "good" companies? What characteristics do they share? Do these characteristics suggest they value organizational listening? Are these characteristics reflected in the company mission statements?

3. During the recent Gulf oil spill, British Petroleum received a lot of negative publicity for how they handled the disaster. In groups of three to four, research some of the negative stories associated with the disaster. What do they suggest about input or model failure on the part of BP?

ADDITIONAL READINGS

Cooper, L. (1997). Listening competency in the workplace: A model for training. *Business Communication Quarterly, 60,* 75–84.

Duzer, C. V. (1997). *Improving ESL learners' listening skills: At the workplace and beyond.* Retrieved from Center for Adult English Language Acquisition Web site: www.cal.org/caela/esl_resources/digests/LISTENQA.html.

Dwyer, J. (2008). *Business communication handbook* (8th ed.). Black Forest, Australia: Pearson.

Gauld, D., & Miller, P. (2004). The qualifications and competencies held by effective workplace trainers. *Journal of European Industrial Training, 28,* 8–22.

Guffey, M. E., Rhodes, K., & Rogin, P. (2006). Workplace listening and nonverbal communication (Ch. 3). In Guffey, M E, Rogin, P. & Rhodes, K. (2010). *Business communication: process & product* (3rd brief Canadian ed.). Toronto: Nelson Education Ltd.

Jamblin, F. M., & Putnam, L. L. (Eds.). (2001). *The new handbook of organizational communication.* Thousand Oaks, CA: Sage.

Nohria, N., & Khurana, R. (Eds.). (2010). *Handbook of leadership theory and practice.* Boston: Harvard Business School.

ENDNOTES

1. Shockley-Zalabak, 2006
2. Bryson, 1995
3. Radtke, 1998
4. Ford, 2007
5. The Ford Standards for Corporate Conduct are updated periodically. This letter is no longer available online. However, the latest ethical statements and letter from Ford's current CEO are available from the company at www.ford.com/doc/corporate_conduct_standards.pdf.
6. Radtke, 1998
7. Walton, 2009
8. Nordstrom, 2006
9. About Us, 2010
10. ACS Mission Statement, 2008
11. Littlejohn & Foss, 2005, p. 258
12. Schein, 2004, p. 17
13. Eisenberg, Goodall, & Trethewey, 2010
14. Enron Code of Ethics, 2000
15. Furnham & Goodstein, 1997

16. Ashforth, 1985
17. Van Maanen & Schein, 1979
18. Freedman, 2003
19. Johnston & Johnston, 2005
20. Eisenberg, Goodall, & Trethewey, 2004, p. 213
21. Albrecht & Goldsmith, 2003
22. du Pré, 2010
23. 100 Best Companies, 2009
24. Burleson, 1994
25. Janusik & Wolvin, 2006
26. Kriegel & Brandt, 1996, p. 115
27. Yokoyama & Michelli, 2004, p. 87
28. Witt Communications, 2008
29. Gardner et al., p. 569
30. Breen, 2005
31. Walters, 2005
32. Ledingham & Brunig, 1998
33. Shockley-Zalabak, 2006
34. Grunig & Hunt, 1984
35. Grunig, Grunig, & Ehling, 1992; Grunig, Grunig, & Dozier, 2002
36. Ledingham, Bruning, & Wilson, 1999; Grunig, 1993
37. Grunig et al., 1992
38. O'Keeffe, 2002; Serenko, Bontins, & Hardie, 2007; Wang & Ahmed, 2003

39. Salovey, Mayer, Caruso, & Lopes, 2003
40. Cambron-McCabe, Cunningham, Harvey, & Koff, 2004
41. As cited in Telework Trendlines, 2009
42. Tahmincioglu, 2007
43. Robert Half International, as reported by CNN, 2006
44. Rosenfeld, Richman, & May, 2004
45. Rosenfeld et al., 2004
46. Lipsky, Seeber, & Fincher, 2003
47. Van Slyke, 1999, p. 98–99
48. Van Slyke, 1999
49. Van Slyke, 1999, p. 101
50. Bannon, 2003
51. Tschohl, 1994
52. McCormick, 1984
53. Kriegel & Brandt, 1997
54. Motley, 2005
55. Yokoyama & Michelli, 2004, pp. 98–99
56. Malshe & Pryor, 2004; Ramsey & Sohi, 1997
57. Nichols, 2006
58. Ringle & Bruce, 1980
59. Berger, 2001
60. Yokoyama & Michelli, 2004
61. Berry & Parasuraman, 1997
62. Conley, 2005

REFERENCES

100 best companies to work for. (2009). Fortune: CNNMoney.com. Retrieved from http://money.cnn.com/magazines/fortune/bestcompanies/2009/full_list/.

About Us. (2010). Susan G. Komen for the Cure. Retrieved from http://ww5.komen.org/AboutUs/AboutUs.html.

ACS Mission Statement. (2008). American Cancer Society. Retrieved March 5, 2010, from www.cancer.org/docroot/AA/content/AA_1_1_ACS_Mission_Statements.asp.

Albrecht, T. L., & Goldsmith, D. J. (2003). Social support, social networks, and health. In A. Marshall, K. I. Miller, R. Parrott, & T. L. Thompson (Eds.), *Handbook of health communication* (pp. 263–284). Hillsdale, NJ: Lawrence Erlbaum.

Ashforth, B. E. (1985). Climate formation: Issues and extensions. *Academy of Management Review, 10*, 837–847.

Bannon, J. (2003, October). Anger at work: Whether it's others' or your own, here's how to deal with it. *Training & Development*. Retrieved from http://findarticles.com/p/articles/mi_m0MNT/is_10_57/ai_108787970/.

Berger, C. R. (2001). Miscommunication and communication failure. In W. P. Robinson & H. Giles (Eds.), *The new handbook of language and social psychology* (pp. 177–192). Chichester, U.K.: Wiley.

Berry, L. L., & Parasuraman, A. (1997). Listening to the customer: The concept of a service-quality information system. *Sloan Management Review, 38*, 65–76.

Breen, B. (2005, December 1). The Seoul of design. *Fast Company*. Retrieved from www.fastcompany.com/magazine/101/samsung.html.

Bryson, J. (1995). *Strategic planning for public and nonprofit organizations*. San Francisco: Jossey-Bass.

Burleson, B. R. (1994). Comforting messages: Features, functions, and outcomes. In J. A. Daly & J. M. Wiemann (Eds.), *Strategic interpersonal communication* (pp. 135–161). Hillsdale, NJ: Erlbaum.

Cambron-McCabe, N., Cunningham, L. L., Harvey, J., & Koff, R. H. (2004). *The superintendent's fieldbook:*

A guide for leaders of learning. Thousand Oaks, CA: Corwin Press.

Conley, L. (2005, October 1). Profitable player runner-up: Virgin Atlantic. *Fast Company.* Retrieved from www.fastcompany.com/magazine/99/open_customer-virgin.html?#.

du Pré, A. (2010). *Communicating about health: Current issues and perspectives* (3rd ed.). New York: Oxford University Press.

Eisenberg, E. M., Goodall Jr., H. L., & Trethewey, A. (2010). *Organizational communication: Balancing creativity and constraint* (6th ed.). New York: Bedford/St. Martin's Press.

Enron Code of Ethics. (2000). Enron Corporation.

Ford standard of corporate conduct. (2007). Ford Motor Company. Retrieved from http://www.ford.com/doc/corporate_conduct_standards.pdf.

Freedman, J. (2003). Case study: Emotional intelligence at the Sheraton Studio City Hotel. Six Seconds Institute for Organizational Performance.

Furnham, A., & Goodstein, L. (1997). The organizational climate questionnaire (OCQ). *The 1997 Annual: Volume 2, Consulting,* (pp. 163–181). San Francisco: Jossey-Bass.

Grunig, J. E. (1993). On the effects of marketing, media relations, and public relations: Images, agendas, and relationships. In W. Armbrecht, H. Avenarius, & U. Zabel (Eds.). *Image und PR* (pp. 263–295). Opladen, Germany: Westdeutscher Verlag.

Grunig, J. E., & Hunt, T. (1984). *Managing public relations.* New York: Holt, Rinehart & Winston.

Grunig, L. A., Grunig, J. E., & Dozier, D. M. (2002). *Excellent public relations and effective organizations: A study of communication management in three countries.* Mahwah, NJ: Lawrence Erlbaum.

Grunig, L. A., Grunig, J. E., & Ehling, W. P. (1992). What is an effective organization? In J. E. Grunig (Ed.), *Excellence in public relations and communication management* (pp. 65–90). Hillsdale, NJ: Lawrence Erlbaum.

Janusik, L. A., & Wolvin, A. D. (2006). 24 hours in a day: A listening update to the time studies. *International Journal of Listening, 23,* 104–120.

Johnston, A., & Johnston, L. (2005). The relationship between organizational climate, occupational type and workaholism. *Journal of Psychology, 34,* 181–188.

Kriegel, R. & Brandt, D. (1996). *Sacred cows make the best burgers.* New York: Warner Books.

Ledingham, J. A., & Bruning, S. D. (1998). Relationship management in public relations: Dimensions of an organization–public relationship. *Public Relations Review, 24,* 55–65.

Ledingham, J. A., Bruning, S. D., & Wilson, L. J. (1999). Time as an indicator of the perceptions and behavior of members of a key public: Monitoring and predicting organization—Public relationships. *Journal of Public Relations Research, 11,* 167–183.

Lipsky, D. B., Seeber, R. L., & Fincher, R. (2003). *Emerging systems for managing workplace conflict.* San Francisco: Jossey-Bass.

Littlejohn, S. W., & Foss, K. A. (2005). *Theories of human communication.* Belmont, CA: Wadsworth.

Malshe, A., & Pryor, S. (2004). Relational listening and impression management in salesperson-customer relationships. *Advances in consumer research, 31,* 447–448.

McCormick, M. (1984). *What they don't teach you at Harvard business school: Notes from a street-smart executive.* New York: Bantam.

Motley, L. B. (2005, October). The benefits of listening to customers. *ABA Bank Marketing, 37,* 43.

Nichols, M. (2006, September 14). Listen up for better sales. *Bloomberg Businessweek.* Retrieved from www.businessweek.com.

Nordstrom 2006 Annual Report Introductory Flash presentation. Nordstrom, Inc. Retrieved from http://about.nordstrom.com/annual_report/2006/scorecard.asp.

O'Keeffe, T. (2002). Organizational learning: A new perspective. *Journal of European Industrial Training, 26,* 130–141.

Radtke, J. M. (1998). *Strategic communications for nonprofit organizations: Seven steps to creating a successful plan.* Philadelphia: Wiley.

Ramsey, R. P., & Sohi, R. A. (1997). Listening to your customers: The impact of perceived salesperson listening behavior on relational outcomes. *Journal of the Academy of Marketing Science, 25,* 127–137.

Ringle, M. H., & Bruce, B. C. (1980). Conversation failure. In W. G. Lehnert & M. H. Ringle (Eds.), *Strategies for natural language processing* (pp. 203–221). Hillsdale, NJ: Lawrence Erlbaum.

Robert Half International. (2006, March 3). Making the case for telecommuting. CareerBuilder.com. Retrieved from www.cnn.com/2006/US/Careers/03/03/cb.telecommuting/.

Rosenfeld, L. B., Richman, J. M., & May, S. K. (2004). Information adequacy, job satisfaction, and organizational culture in a dispersed-network organization. *Journal of Applied Communication Research, 32,* 28–54.

Salovey, P., Mayer, J. D., Caruso, D., & Lopes, P. N. (2003). In S. J. Lopez & C. R. Snyder (Eds.), *Positive psychological assessment: A handbook of models and measures* (pp. 251–265). Washington, D.C.: APA.

Serenko, A., Bontis, N., & Hardie, T. (2007). Organizational size and knowledge flow: A proposed theoretical link. *Journal of Intellectual Capital, 8,* 610–627.

Schein, E. (2004). *Organizational culture and leadership* (3rd ed.). San Francisco: Jossey-Bass.

Shockley-Zalabak, P. (2006). *Essentials of organizational communication* (6th ed.). Boston: Allen & Bacon.

Tahmincioglu, E. (2007, October 5). The quiet revolution: Telecommuting. MSNBC. Retrieved from www.msnbc.msn.com/id/20281475/.

Telework Trendlines (2009, February). *A survey brief by WorldatWork.* Retrieved from www.workingfromanywhere.org/news/Trendlines_2009.pdf.

Tschohl, J. (1994). *Achieving excellence through customer service.* Englewood Cliffs, NJ: Prentice-Hall.

Van Maanen, J., & Schein, E. H. (1979). Toward a theory of organizational socialization. In B. Staw (Ed.), *Research in organizational behavior* (vol. 1, pp. 209–264). Greenwich, CT: JAI Press.

Van Slyke, E. (1999). Listening to conflict: Finding constructive solutions to workplace disputes. New York: AMACOM.

Walters, J. (2005). Fostering a culture of deep inquiry and listening. *Journal for Quality & Participation, 28,* 4–7.

Walton, R. (2009). WalMart 2009 annual report: Message from Rob Walton. Retrieved from http://walmartstores.com/sites/AnnualReport/2009/message.html.

Wang, C. L., & Ahmed, P. K. (2003). Organizational learning: A critical review. *The learning organization, 10,* 8–17.

Weinstein, B. (2010, February 12). How to solve work-at-home ethical dilemmas. *CNN.* Retrieved from www.cnn.com/2010/LIVING/02/03/opinion.weinstein/index.html.

Witt Communications. (2008). Retrieved from www.wittcom.com/index.htm.

Yokoyama, J., & Michelli, J. (2004). *When fish fly: Lessons for creating a vital and energized workplace.* New York: Hyperion.

Listening and Health

Psychological and Physical Realities

CASE STUDY 10.1

The Physician's Office

This discussion takes place in an examination room at a doctor's office. NaMii Kim's grandmother hasn't been feeling well, so she has gone to see her primary care physician, Dr. Julia Moore.

Dr. Moore: *Hello, Mrs. Kim. What seems to be wrong today?*

Mrs. Kim: *I haven't been feeling very good lately. It seems, uh, it seems that . . .*

Dr. Moore is looking at her chart and interrupts

Mrs. Kim: *Hmm, I see your temperature is OK and your*

blood pressure has stabilized. The medicine we have you on seems to be doing the trick. Is something else bothering you today?

Mrs. Kim: *I just don't feel good and I don't . . . uh . . . my back hurts some . . . and . . .*

Dr. Moore: *Well, let's draw some blood and run some tests. It's been a while since we've done that. Let's see what it tells us. After the nurse takes the blood, make an appointment to come back next week to get the test results. Talk to you soon.* ■

The most recent data available, a 2005 National Ambulatory Medical Care Survey by the Centers for Disease Control, reports that 963.6 million medical visits occurred that year.[1] Unfortunately many of these visits likely reflected the type of interaction presented in the Case Study above. Mrs. Kim's interaction also illustrates several startling statistics about how patient interviews actually take place. An early study by medical researchers Howard Beckman and Richard Frankel found that doctors tend to let their patients talk for only an average of *18 seconds* before interrupting them. The longest time any doctor in their study listened was 2.5 minutes.[2] Follow-up research, done more than a decade later, found that the amount of time physicians let their patients talk before interrupting them had increased to a whopping *23 seconds*.[3] In related research, Frankel found that 15 out of 16 patients who were interrupted failed to resume what they were talking about after they were interrupted.[4] This last piece of information shouldn't surprise anyone who knows the importance of listening to an interaction. In the Case Study, Dr. Moore failed to engage in either active or empathetic listening. How do you think Mrs. Kim felt after this encounter?

Fortunately researchers and the health-care industry are trying to improve the communication element of health care. Health communication is one of the fastest-growing areas of research in the field of communication. Good communication affects our health both psychologically and physically. As the above example shows, listening also plays a critical role in the quality of the health care we receive. In this chapter we look at the effect of listening on health. We will first examine the general importance listening has to your health. Next we'll examine listening and psychological health. Finally we'll look at patient–health-care provider communication and how listening affects your physical health. While we will look at these areas separately, you should keep in mind that they are dynamic and necessarily tied together with one influencing the other.

THE IMPORTANCE OF HEALTH COMMUNICATION

We cannot overstate the importance of good communication to your overall physical well-being. Research conducted at the University of California, Irvine, shows that good doctor-patient communication leads to lower blood sugar levels in diabetics and lower blood pressure in hypertensive patients.[5] Another example of the importance of communication can be seen in the infant "wasting-away disease," marasmus, which was found to be directly caused by a lack of nonverbal touch communication between baby and caregiver. In fact, without this tactile stimulation, infants actually died. Today we refer to this type of problem as failure to thrive.[6] The cure? Active communication with the child.

Communication is also central to successful health-care encounters.[7] We have to be able to communicate our symptoms and physical ailments. Research in this area has consistently found that good communication with health-care providers increases patient compliance with treatment plans, leads to improved symptoms, and results in improved management of chronic diseases.[8] Our overall satisfaction with both the people and the process of health-care delivery is directly related to good communication.

Satisfaction, in turn, affects a number of patient-to-doctor communication factors. Important factors are the level of respect and trust we feel toward health professionals as well as the level of openness we have with them. Patients who actively work with their health-care providers are more likely to report that they are satisfied with their physicians, more likely to trust their physicians' diagnoses, and more inclined to follow their treatment plans.[9] These communications are even more important for those individuals with low health literacy, those who have difficulty reading medical directions or using other health information.[10] The financial impact of low health literacy is estimated to be as much as $73 billion in health expenses each year. Health literacy involves more than the ability to read and write; it includes having both access to health information as well as the willingness to research and use it effectively. Athena du Pré argued that effective interpersonal communication can help these patients avoid costly medical errors and delays as well as the associated pain and loss of quality of life that might occur. In short, good listening is critical in compensating for the effect of low health literacy.

Social changes have also affected how we approach health care and have resulted in major changes in how health care is managed. Because of the dramatic increase in medical cost over the past 50 years or so, the practice of managed care was introduced to cut costs.[11] By the early 2000s, 88 percent of U.S. physicians were associated with some type of managed health-care system.[12] One of the results is that doctors and other health-care providers are now responsible for seeing many more patients, as many as 15 to 20 in an hour if not more. Obviously such a schedule creates problems for providers who want to listen and communicate well with their patients and for patients who want to relay in-depth information.

Social changes have also affected our perceptions of physicians. At the beginning of the 20th century, doctors were viewed as godlike individuals who dispensed good health. This **paternalist** approach affected the doctor-patient relationship in many ways. For example, good patients did not question their physicians, and they were expected to do as they were told. During the 1970s, '80s, and '90s, the attitude toward doctors shifted as did their relationships with patients. Many patients and doctors developed and expected a more **consumeristic** approach. As consumers of medicine, patients were expected to actively participate in their health. Today patients and physicians are encouraged to take a more **collaborative** approach, jointly working toward good health.

The increasing emphasis on collaborative communication reflects a growing interest in patient–health-care provider communication, an interest further reflected in the research published in medical, nursing, and other allied health journals, which more and more focus on the importance of and ways to improve listening and other communication skills in health-care contexts.[13] We look at a few of these findings as they are related to our psychological and physical well-being.

LISTENING AND PSYCHOLOGICAL WELL-BEING

While listening is important in any health-related encounter, it can be critical to those who work in the helping or therapeutic professions (e.g., psychiatrists, psychologists, social workers, marriage and family therapists). As psychologists and counselors Steven Graybar and Leah Leonard wrote, "If the foundation of successful psychotherapy is the therapeutic relationship, then the mortar of the therapeutic relationship is listening."[14] This thought is also reflected in our interview with psychologist Bill Fish.

Bill Fish, MA
Individual and Marriage Therapist
Sheridan, Wyoming

In my practice as a therapist, I listen intently to each client. Listening in my profession translates into caring. If they think you don't care, why should they talk to you? While listening, I quite frequently say, "So it sounds like you are saying . . ." because even though I do my best to be attentive, sometimes I misinterpret what he or she is saying to me. If I get it wrong, I can't help them. They may choose not to continue meeting with me or may not disclose something important about their problem.

Ideally I teach my clients to listen more effectively. Whether it is a couple having problems or parents and children experiencing difficulties, they have to be able to determine what the real problem is; only then can they solve it. Listening is the key.

We covered many of the concepts associated with this aspect of health care earlier in the book when we addressed therapeutic and relational listening and social support. Now we will address a few issues central to psychological and psychiatric counseling.

The most prevalent approach to counseling today is the patient- or client-centered approach.[15] This approach focuses on the client as the primary source of identifying means to solve his or her problem. With the counselor's help, patients and clients can arrive at a solution that is the most workable for them.

As you can see, the quality of the relationship between the patient and counselor/therapist is important. In fact, one study found it to be the strongest predictor of a positive outcome for the patient, no matter the treatment regimen.[16] Graybar and Leonard argued that listening is the foundation of psychotherapy. As they wrote, "Listening and being listened to are the cornerstones of psychological development, psychological relatedness, and psychological treatment."[17] They went on to assert that people who see therapists often do so because they "have been listened to far too little in their lives."[18] This statement poignantly illustrates that sometimes we need to be listened to by someone who is separate from our daily lives, someone who can listen compassionately but do so in such a way as to allow us to assess our lives, the situation, or the events so we can develop methods of effectively addressing our problems. Essentially by listening, counselors and therapists can help identify the underlying problems patients or clients might have and empower them to address their problems meaningfully.

All therapists use important communication skills, most of which are related to relational listening. The skills include asking questions, reflection, selective reflection, empathy building, and checking for understanding.[19] Questions, particularly **open-ended questions,** are quite important. They allow us to expand on our story or comments and encourage us to continue speaking. **Reflection,** also known as echoing, includes restatement and paraphrasing. This type of repetition is important in counseling sessions because it not only signals that the counselor is listening but also acts as a verbal prompt, encouraging the individual to continue speaking. **Selective reflection** is a more refined type of reflection. Counselors use this technique to identify information that the client appears to be emphasizing or that is emotionally charged. **Empathy-building statements** allow therapists to acknowledge their clients' feelings and indicate they understand those feelings. This aspect of counseling can be quite important, especially if the person is from cultures such as North America or England, where we are taught that we are supposed to control our feelings.

THINK ON IT

Think back on the last time a friend came to you with a personal crisis. How did you help him? Did you engage in any of the communication skills therapists use? If not, how might you approach a similar situation in the future?

Finally **checking for understanding** can be an important method of ensuring accuracy. It is not unusual in counseling sessions for patients to quickly introduce a number of topics into a discussion. As a result, the counselor might want to do a verbal check to determine if he or she has identified the primary issues troubling a person. This technique is also used by counselors to review topics that have been covered over the course of a session.

What sets the best therapists apart? Swiss psychologists Daniel Gassmann and Klaus Grawe suggested that the best therapists are able to assess their clients' strengths and abilities.[20] As they assist their clients in recognizing and accepting their problems, they remind clients of their strong points while pointing out the support available to them. It is important to note they use this technique throughout the counseling session, not just at the end. It is no surprise, then, that effective listening is an important skill for those in the helping professions, professionals and volunteers. Another important quality is empathy, both empathetic concern and empathetic understanding. (We covered empathy earlier in the text.)

The importance of empathy and empathetic listening can be seen in the findings of a recent study at a mental health facility in Hong Kong.[21] This research found that psychiatric inpatients were more likely to have a positive perception of being physically restrained if the staff displayed concern for them, actively listened to them, and provided information about the restraint while it was in use.

We have only introduced you to the nuances of listening in psychotherapy, social work, and other related fields. If you are interested in a counseling career, check out the list of additional readings at the end of the chapter. Next we briefly explore the effect of listening on our physical health.

LISTENING AND PHYSICAL WELL-BEING—EXPLORING THE PATIENT-PROVIDER RELATIONSHIP

There are times when we get sick and have to see a health professional. Our illness might be as simple as a cold or as complex as a terminal illness. In this section we're going to address communication issues between health-care providers and patients, highlighting the importance of listening on both sides of the health team. The negative outcomes for poor listening can range from mild to severe. For example, as a patient, you could take food with your medicine (when you shouldn't have) and end up with a stomach ache. Or the consequences of not listening can be life threatening. One real-life example of poor listening happened to Professor Worthington's brother. At the time, Bill worked at a manufacturing plant. One day he pulled a muscle while repairing a piece of equipment. His supervisor sent him to visit the company doctor. At the office, Bill told both the nurse *and* the doctor that he was severely allergic to aspirin. The doctor gave him samples of medication along with a prescription. On his way home (a 30-minute drive), Bill decided to wait to take the medicine because he did not have anything in the car to drink. As soon as he got home, he took the medicine and immediately knew aspirin was included in the medication and that he was in trouble. He stopped breathing when he got to the hospital emergency room. Bill was luckier than some patients; he

"You're not listening to what you're hearing."

lived and suffered no lingering ill effects from his experience. This example is only one of the many medical errors estimated to occur every day in this county. While estimates vary widely, the Institute of Medicine reports that as many as 98,000 people die yearly from medical errors. (This figure addressed only errors associated with hospital care.) The majority of these mistakes are attributed to communication errors of some type, including poor listening.[22]

In this book we have covered a number of aspects of listening that have implications for health-related interactions. For instance, in Chapter 1 we discussed the role of recall as an important aspect of Listening MATERRS. The type of information we receive appears to affect our ability to recall it. For example, patients seem to recall information about their medication better than other information (e.g., how to wrap a bandage, what to eat or avoid eating). In addition, the more information that was provided, the greater the chance for information overload and the less a patient can remember. Of course, the more serious the illness, the more likely a patient will be overwhelmed and misunderstand or simply not process the physician's message.

Another listening-related matter can be found in Chapter 3, when we addressed schema formation. Your schema about physicians will affect how you interact with your doctors. For example, if you believe that physicians have a higher status than you, you will likely feel at a disadvantage when interacting with them. This feeling may keep you from getting the full benefit you need from the medical visit. Keep in mind, while they know a lot about medicine, you know your body and your illness; you are both experts in your own way. Combining your expertise can lead to better health for you.

One important schema is the one we hold for our personal health. Do you view yourself as a "healthy" person? Would you describe your health as excellent, great, good, or poor? What happens if you are diagnosed with a chronic illness (e.g., allergies, asthma, cystic fibrosis)? What if it is an acute illness (e.g., cold, flu, sprained ankle)? The schemata we hold for ourselves are important ones, and as you know, they are difficult to change. Like all schemata, they have a way of shaping how we listen to information. So if you consider yourself to be healthy, you will probably expect to hear that whatever is bothering you is temporary and will go away. You may have difficulty listening to anything to the contrary.

Factors Affecting Patient-Provider Interactions

In addition to patient/health-care provider schema, a number of other factors can influence how patients communicate with health-care providers.

Nature of the Visit   Why you are visiting your doctor and the diagnosis can affect how you listen.[23] If you have a general checkup and the physician says all is fine, you may not pay much attention to her directions to cut down on fatty foods in your diet because of a slightly elevated cholesterol level. If, on the other hand, she tells you that you have a chronic kidney disease, it is unlikely that you will really hear much she says after making the diagnosis. Such a message creates both anxiety and fear, both of which interfere with your ability to attend to the message.

Gender   Men and women differ in their use of the medical system and views of health care. For example, women are more likely than men to go to their physicians.[24] At least one study suggests that women's greater contact with health-care providers and the health system leads them to expect greater involvement in health-care decisions and to develop a more consumeristic approach to patient-provider interactions.[25] Case Study 10.2 on the next page illustrates this tendency.

As you can see in Case Study 10.2, Deena felt she was not being listened to by this physician. In fact, based on her description, it would appear that Deena preferred to be very active in her medical encounters. Unfortunately her doctor was unable to meet her dual needs for involvement and control in her personal health care. Not only did the physician end up with a very dissatisfied patient but he also actually lost a patient. Patient satisfaction is only one of the outcomes that might be affected by poor communication with health-care providers.

Effect of Culture   Culture is another factor that affects how we view health and illness. Athena du Pré wrote, "Misunderstandings can occur when people have different ideas about the nature of disease, how people are supposed to act in health-care situations, and how illness reflects on people in the community."[26] For example, people from Eastern cultures refuse to acknowledge mental illness; in Malawi, in southern Africa, women who openly discuss sex are seen as bad mannered and promiscuous, and in other parts of the world, men and women must see physicians of the same sex, a major difficulty when physicians of both sexes are in short supply. Not surprisingly the problem is most severe for women patients.

Different cultures also view health differently. For example, many Western societies have adopted an organic or biomedical view of health. Based on this view,

CASE STUDY 10.2

Deena's Story

When I was 29, I had a cousin die of skin cancer—melanoma. He had felt a lump under his arm but didn't think too much about it. When it got uncomfortable, he finally went to the doctor to have it checked on. It was too late. Surgery removed much of his chest wall, lymph nodes, and shoulder. The chemo was awful. He died six months after he was diagnosed.

Pretty much everyone in the family went to be checked out by his or her dermatologist. My mom bugged me enough that I eventually went. After I got back to the exam room, I told Dr. "Smith" what happened. I also told him about how different skin cancers seem to run in the family. Both my mother and grandmother were diagnosed with basal cell and squamous cell (skin) cancers. Several years back I had two moles removed because they had changed in size, and after testing, we found out they were precancerous.

After giving him all this history, basically all he did was a cursory check of a few of my visible moles and told me everything would be fine. What he didn't know and still doesn't know is that I am an informed patient. I know what a full-body check is. (It is when the dermatologist physically checks every inch of your skin and charts all skin characteristics.) My mom has one done every year. I felt that I had reached the age where I needed to have one to establish a baseline for future changes in my skin. I suggested this to Dr. Smith, but he didn't agree. He didn't act concerned at all. I felt like a child who was being patted on the head and told, "There, there, now." On hearing about my cousin, it was clear that this doctor had decided I was a hysterical female who was simply overreacting or running scared.

I could have forced the issue and insisted on a full-body check. But why bother? I never wanted to see him again and couldn't get out of the office fast enough! Although it is inconvenient and almost an hour drive, I now go to my mother's dermatologist. He takes me seriously. ■

---

health-care providers seek to identify signs of ill health (e.g., fever, bacteria, rash). Health is seen more in terms of "health versus illness." If you don't have the signs or symptoms, then you are assumed to be in good health. Of course, you know that some days you feel better than others, you know that some colds are worse than others (even though the symptoms can be exactly the same), and you know that some sprained ankles are more severe than others. Thus, health (and illness) is on a continuum. However, the organic model does not do a good job of addressing this continuum. This model is evidence based. If you lack evidence of being sick, then you must be well. The observable is what is important.

Other cultures take a more holistic approach, conceptualizing "health as harmony."[27] Health incorporates more than just signs and symptoms of illness. It is based on a combination of our physical, social, and psychological well-being. Thus, the next time you are ill, your Asian friends might tell you that you need to focus on your Qi (pronounced chee). Qi refers to the life force or energy that resides within the body. Health is related to life energy, life rhythms, and maintaining a balance within one's body. This perspective actually emphasizes strong communication between patient and provider. Through communication and listening, the caregiver can identify what area of

THINK ON IT

What are the implications of these two views of health to patient-provider interactions? What is emphasized? Deemphasized? What are the implications for listening? Rapport building and so forth?

the patient's life is "out of balance." While some mainstream providers have incorporated aspects of the harmony perspective into their practices, it is more commonly found in practices of alternative medical specialists.[28]

Race and Ethnicity   In addition to culture, race and ethnicity also seem to affect health and medical care.[29] Research reveals differences in who does or does not receive prescriptions, health information, or access to certain medical facilities.[30] Racial stereotypes can also affect how we listen to messages and the quality of the interaction. For example, previous research indicates that patients get more involved in medical decision-making when the doctor is the same race they are.[31]

Race differences can be compounded for individuals who are not native English speakers (or speak it poorly). Not surprisingly language differences can lead to avoidance, misdiagnoses, improper treatment, and lower patient satisfaction.[32] For example, a study by Donald Rubin and his colleagues found that the accent and ethnicity of the physician can affect how North American patients respond to physicians of non-Western ethnolinguistic backgrounds (e.g., Turkish, Chinese, Indian).[33] One recent survey found that one in four visits to office-based physicians were to international medical graduates.[34] Thus, the odds of a North American patient coming in contact with a nonnative physician at some point in his or her life are fairly high.

Not surprisingly language proficiency can affect patient compliance; it is difficult to follow instructions that you do not understand. However, there is some question about whether stereotyping on the part of the patient affects his or her listening ability.[35] For example, one recent study found that participants rated the Anglo physician (who spoke standard American English) higher in interpersonal attractiveness than his Asian counterpart. Intuitively it would seem that interpersonal attractiveness (i.e., overall likeability) could affect patient health-care interactions. Likeability is a component of source credibility, and we are less likely to question the recommendations of someone whom we find interpersonally attractive.

Age   Understanding health issues related to older adults is of increasing importance. According to the U.S. Administration on Aging, by 2050 25 percent of our population will be over the age of 65.[36] Not everyone, including many of those who will be in this cohort, see this as a positive event. Just as people can be discriminated against because of their race or gender, they can also be discriminated against because of their age. Many Americans hold negative views of the elderly, which are unfortunately reinforced by media portrayals.[37] Overall, these negative stereotypes tend to present older individuals as cranky and dour, often lonely and unhappy. In addition, these individuals often believe the elderly are commonly ill and befuddled. As a result, providers may treat their elderly clients as if they cannot care for themselves or as if they are not interested in or cannot understand health information.[38]

One way this is often manifested is through "elderspeak." Elderspeak occurs when people use terms such as *sweetie* and *dear* or when they talk slower to someone just because the person is older.[39] Many older people find it demeaning and upsetting, in part because it suggests they are incompetent. Kristine Williams, a nurse gerontologist at the University of Kansas's School of Nursing, noted that health-care workers are often among the worst offenders.

Communication patterns between the older patient and health-care providers can be affected by several other factors.[40] For example, older individuals are often not assertive during medical encounters, despite their wish to be informed. They may also be less assertive when a family member accompanies them to a medical appointment. It is not unusual for the older patient to be "sidelined" while the family member and provider converse. In fact, some physicians perceive the patient's companion as a "patient substitute," who provides biomedical information about the patient.[41] While there do not appear to be major differences in what is discussed during the visit, the older patient is often implicitly excluded from the conversation, as evidenced by the fact that providers do not directly address them but refer to them as "she" or "he."[42] In essence the sidelined patient feels he or she isn't being listened to.

Problems associated with caring for elderly patients are exacerbated when the patient is also chronically ill. Obviously, then, it is important that these patients follow their treatment plans and take their medications correctly. But without good communication, there is little chance the older patient will comply.[43] Doctors can increase the probability of their elderly patients' compliance by providing more information about the medication and its purpose. When physicians listen, treatment programs can be adapted to important aspects of the elderly patients' lives, such as their cognitive and physical abilities, daily schedules, and living arrangements. We had a good friend, Fran, who lived in assisted living. She chose to go into assisted living because she recognized that she needed help meeting her physical and medical needs. Her physician, once she made him aware of the exercise and health facilities available to residents of the facility, worked with Fran to establish an exercise program to help her address problems she had with maintaining her balance. By focusing on finding common ground, Fran's physician found an exercise program that fit her living circumstances and provided a quality treatment program that addressed his diagnosis of her medical condition. His attention to the details of her situation, coupled with the empathy and encouragement he provided her, contributed to Fran's being both a compliant and highly satisfied patient.

WHAT YOU CAN DO AS A PATIENT

As you have seen in previous sections of this chapter, many factors affect health communication. This section will look at five things you can do to enhance your listening effectiveness in future health-care encounters.

First, **be aware of your schemata** about the physician-patient relationship, your attitude toward health care, and the illness you are diagnosed with. Remember we process information via our mental schemata of things, and as a result, they can have a major impact on our interpretation of information and our interactions with health-care providers.

Second, **come prepared.** Write down your symptoms or any questions you may have. As the mother of a young child, Professor Worthington does this all the time so she doesn't forget to mention symptoms her daughter has or other medical concerns she has. It is easy to get distracted at the doctor's office, so a list of simple notes can help keep you on track. Most health-care providers will not mind and are actually pleased when you do so. They take it as a sign you want to follow their instructions. Having questions also makes you appear more competent, which in turn has a positive effect on other aspects of the interaction, such as history-taking.[44] However, if you have a lot of questions or concerns, you might want to consider making more than one appointment. Health-care providers are more likely to address concerns when there are only a few to address.[45]

Of course, if you do not understand something, then you cannot follow instructions. So the third thing you should do is **be assertive.** Be direct in stating your symptoms and in asking your questions. Many patients ask indirect questions, questions that are disguised as statements. So if you've ever told your physician, "I think my stomach is always upset because of the stress I'm under," you are using an indirect question. The problem with these types of questions is that your physician may not recognize them for what they are: a question or an indirect way of seeking information. While you may use this technique because you don't want to appear foolish or ignorant, keep in mind that it is OK to ask questions.[46] Take the plunge and be direct.

The fourth way to have a better health encounter is to **make sure you have the physician's complete attention.** In the United States, eye contact is a good check on this final suggestion. Doctors often turn away to wash hands, come in making notes, or even speak to nurses or other office personnel. However, to make an accurate diagnosis, your caregivers need to do more than hear you; they need to really listen. When they turn away or if you are unsure if you have their full attention, pause. Most of us tend to look at people when they unexpectedly stop talking to determine what's going on.

Finally, **use the information-verifying skills** you've learned. Double-check your information by using restatements, summaries, and paraphrases. Personally summarize the information. It will help you in recalling it later. If your caregiver does not have a convenient information brochure on your condition or the treatment regimen that she suggests, write down the information and review it with her. This can save you an extra call to the office asking for clarification, and it can save you further illness or aggravation because you did not follow the treatment plan as you should have. If you want to be a cooperative patient, one who is active in caring for your health, you have to not only be willing to comply with the doctor's suggestions but you need to have the correct information in the first place and be able to recall it. Information-verifying skills allow you to do this.

Of course, when assessing these suggestions, keep in mind that they are based on and are most appropriate for health-care providers in Western cultures and need to be adapted if you are in other parts of the world. Ultimately you and your caregiver are responsible for working together to achieve your good health. If you feel that you are doing everything you can to reach that goal but that your relationship with the health professional is not helping you to achieve that end, then perhaps you should seek advice elsewhere. Such a decision does not imply that you believe that your physician is incompetent but is simply be a sign that the two of you approach your health in different ways. Some individuals want a physician who is efficient, direct, and to the point, while others want someone who spends more time with them and expresses greater empathy.

THINK ON IT

Looking at the above suggestions, what advice would you give to Deena the next time she visits her physician? What could she have done differently when visiting the dermatologist?

PROVIDER COMMUNICATION AND LISTENING

As you learned in Chapter 1, many of us are poor listeners. Health-care providers are no exception to this. As we see in Case Study 10.3, Dr. Holmes was not very responsive to Susan's concerns. At the same time, however, Susan did not assert herself. As we mentioned at the beginning of this chapter, patient-caregiver communication is transactional in nature. Susan was not assertive; Dr. Holmes was not responsive. However, neither Susan nor Dr. Holmes was aware of the influence on the other's responses.

Case Study 10.3 illustrates a number of things that can affect our attitude toward health professionals and the health-care process. Caregivers are also influenced by other factors. One important factor is simply attending medical school, which affects providers' schemata of health-care practice and patients.[47] While schools in some health areas, such as nursing, operate from more of a patient-centered perspective, others generally do not (e.g., medical, dentistry) or do so minimally (e.g., physical, occupational, speech therapy).[48] In addition, few curricula, particularly medical schools', provide in-depth training in patient-provider communication.[49] At the same time, while in school, future providers undergo an intense socialization process, which includes identification with a prestigious position and experiencing overwhelming responsibilities.

CASE STUDY 10.3

Susan's Story

Susan, an 18-year-old university student, has come to visit her new doctor. Susan has experienced what she calls a racing heart a couple of times over the past month. She decided that she needed to be checked out, so she made an appointment. Dr. Holmes is part of a large clinic with six doctors and eight nurses and other support staff.

Prior to meeting her doctor, Susan filled out a number of insurance forms and medical background forms. She waited approximately 45 minutes to meet the doctor.

Dr. Holmes enters the exam room. He says hello to Susan and asks how she is. Overhead, the intercom calls Dr. Holmes's name. He excuses himself, only to return 15 minutes later. He looks at the chart and says, *"So you're in for a physical. Let's get started."* So far Susan has only said hello. Dr. Holmes asks Susan how she is doing. Susan says, *"My heart races sometimes. I don't know if it's really anything, but—"* Dr. Holmes interrupts, *"Let's see what your physical tells us."*

As the interview continues, Dr. Holmes asks Susan about her physical activity, vices and habits (e.g., smoking,

drinking), medications, and so forth. He gives her a prescription for an allergy medication. Susan responds to all the questions. *"I run two miles a day, lift weights three times a week." "I don't smoke." "I was diagnosed with seasonal allergies five years ago."*

Finally as the interview ends, while he is writing notes in Susan's chart, Dr. Holmes asks, *"Is there anything else?"* Susan again mentions her racing heart. Dr. Holmes interrupts and notes that everything seems fine with her physical. *"You're probably just overdoing it. Students tend to burn the candle at both ends. Eventually it catches up with you. Make sure you're eating and sleeping the way you ought to."* He laughs. *"Don't wait till the last minute to do your assignments like I used to do."*

Susan doesn't tell Dr. Holmes that she doesn't wait till the night before to write her papers or study for an exam. Overall, she was not satisfied with Dr. Holmes's response but did not say anything. She took her prescription and left. ∎

Caregivers frequently become data driven. In other words, they rely on the results of physical exams and other medical tests. As a result, they come to use and depend on what Howard Waitzkin calls the **"voice of medicine."**[50] Oftentimes caregivers become so comfortable with this "voice" (i.e., discussing symptoms, test results, medications, treatment options) that they are unwilling to listen to the **"voice of the life-world"** from their patients (e.g., personal or family issues, fears). Care providers may feel these concerns, such as those associated with family and friends, are not relevant to the patient's condition or that they are out of the caregiver's control, so they ignore them or turn the discussion back to topics where they feel greater control.

Finally medical socialization can lead future health-care providers, particularly physicians, to see themselves as authorities whose opinions should not be questioned. In addition, the stress of medical school can actually lead medical students to engage in listening avoidance.[51] Listening takes time and energy; medical students have relatively little of both as they pursue their goals of becoming doctors, nurses, or other allied health professionals.

Not surprisingly research shows that physicians get little communication training. One survey found that 75 percent of the surveyed physicians had never been exposed to a communication class of any type.[52] Those who were exposed to communication training most often learned about listening, observing patients, and interviewing. This lack of training is reflected in findings showing that while approximately one-third of a medical encounter focuses on the physician providing information and instructions, general practitioners almost never attempt to determine their patients' viewpoints or opinions either prior to or after providing medical information.[53]

Most physicians tend to engage in physician-centered talk.[54] This "I'm in charge" communication approach has the provider doing the majority of the talking, controlling what gets discussed (topics), and determining when the interaction ends.[55] In addition, doctors tend to be assertive, interrupting more, using touch more, asking questions more, but answering questions less.[56] Roughly 91 percent of questions during a health interview are asked by physicians.[57] As we saw in Susan's story, Dr. Holmes engaged in a number of physician-centered behaviors. Unfortunately most of these behaviors (e.g., interrupting, stereotyping her as a college student) send clear signals to Susan that Dr. Holmes is not really listening to her concerns.

Part of the problem that physicians face is that they have to balance two roles: one technical and the other interpersonal.[58] During their information interview, or history taking, with a patient, the primary task is generally gathering evidence about the illness (e.g., date of onset, symptoms). However, it is mediated by the interpersonal role adopted by the doctor. This role is based on the overall communication style of the physician. Researchers and writers suggest that in meeting the demands of these two roles, it is almost as if physicians should use one ear to listen to a patient's biomedical information while the other attends to a patient's psychosocial information.[59]

It is important to note that some providers, including doctors, adopt a patient-centered approach and are open to the listener's needs. Caregivers adopting this approach are more likely to self-disclose to their patients and express empathy to them. Physicians of this type are also more likely to provide desired information and discuss treatment regimens.[60] The patient-centered approach has other important implications for physicians. Doctors who develop ongoing relationships with their patients have higher job satisfaction, feel more valued, and are less likely to experience job burnout.[61] Also, they are less likely to be sued. Other researchers actually argue that primary care physicians who are unable or unwilling to take the time to develop quality patient-provider relationships should consider areas where long-term patient-caregiver relationships are unlikely (e.g., emergency medicine, anesthesiology).[62] Finally one Swedish study indicated that a patient-centered consultation style (e.g., listening to patients, providing information, discussing treatment effects) may be related to fewer unnecessary antibiotic prescriptions.[63] This patient-centered style is evidenced in our interview with cardiologist Dr. Allan Schwadron.

Allan Schwadron, MD, FACC, FCCP, FSCAI
Cardiologist
Auburn, Alabama

When it comes to what I do, listening is critical. It is also one of the most demanding skills that a physician uses. Much of what we need to know about a patient can be elicited from a good detailed history. I think the skill that it takes to just sit down and ask a patient questions, allow him time to answer those questions, and then have his answers prompt you to ask questions makes a huge difference. Importantly, medical schools are realizing that you can't take people who are extremely bright but don't have social skills and expect them to care for patients.

How do I listen to patients? The first thing I do is to make my patients comfortable. I try to establish a social-type atmosphere when I talk to them. I try to look for clues in the patient's manner and speech. For example, does anything suggest that she is being evasive about her answers or that she is unsure (even though her tone of voice sounds really definite). I also want to make sure my patients really pay attention because a major portion of what I do involves teaching my patients. I think that that's important because if you have an understanding of what's wrong with you and why you're being treated a certain way, you're more likely to continue the therapy.

I also ask questions. However, you have to be careful with questions because they focus the discussion on specific details. If I am too directive in the questions I ask, I run the risk of missing something that may be important to properly diagnosing them. So at some point, people need to ramble a little bit. Then you can pick out clues from their rambling.

Finally, I often use visual aids. I'll show them how we put the balloon in, put the stent up, and then I'll show them the result afterward. I believe patients are more likely to listen to what I'm saying if they can visualize it.

PATIENT OUTCOMES: SATISFACTION AND COMPLIANCE

Research indicates that patients value good communication skills as much as they value good clinical skills and that patient satisfaction is more dependent on the providers' communication skills than on their clinical skills.[64] It is important to note that a patient can be satisfied with his or her care but actually dissatisfied with the communication that occurs during the office visit. In a recent article, Calvin W. Roberts, a professor of ophthalmology and a practicing ophthalmologist, argued, "The quest for satisfaction begins with listening." As a physician, he actively works to create an office environment "that enhances communications and fosters satisfaction."[65] In his practices he follows what he calls the QuEST model to address patient dissatisfaction. This model reflects a patient-centered approach in that it suggests that physicians, "**qu**estion and acknowledge, **e**valuate, **s**et a course of action, and **t**alk and discuss" patient concerns and problems. He went on to say that an open dialogue with patients allows them to at least have an opportunity to express their needs and concerns, and the physician to validate the patient's feelings. A pragmatic man, Dr. Roberts noted that not only are satisfied patients more likely to follow treatment plans, but they are more likely to return for follow-up care and to refer their family and friends.

Communication skills that appear to positively influence patient satisfaction include overall friendliness of the communication; increased interpersonal involvement; low communicative dominance; less interrupting; focused active listening; clear, detailed explanations; acknowledgment of patient concerns; avoiding technical jargon; and maintaining eye contact.[66] While you might think these skills are self-evident, the fact is that numerous studies indicate that health-care providers, especially doctors, do not use them.[67]

A recent review of health communication literature identified a number of important communication factors associated with patient satisfaction, including "a caring and understanding manner on the part of the health care provider . . . a balanced inquiry into psychosocial and biomedical concerns . . . and the expression of patient and provider expectations."[68] Of course, aspects such as medical competency also factor into patient satisfaction. In addition, immediacy behaviors (e.g., smiling, eye contact, reduced physical distance) and perceived listening are positively related to patient satisfaction with care and with provider communication.[69]

THINK ON IT

Probably a few of you reading this book have been hospitalized or have had a relative hospitalized. Think back on that experience. What were the most memorable positive and negative experiences you had? Were they related to your communication with health-care workers?

How do patients express their dissatisfaction? They often will change physicians. One study found that 20 percent of newly established patients (i.e., they had been seeing their physician for one year or less) indicated they changed physicians because they were unhappy with their previous doctors.[70] Of these patients, almost 30 percent indicated they were dissatisfied with the attitude or personality of their previous physicians, while approximately 25 percent indicated they changed physicians due to dissatisfaction with their previous treatment regimen. Three communication factors—empathetic communication, listening, and immediacy—seem to predict patient satisfaction with not only their doctors but also nurses and other hospital staff.[71] These behaviors help reduce the uncertainty and relieve the anxiety often associated with hospital stays.

Clearly, listening and communication skills positively affect the patient-provider relationship. For example, in one nursing home, residents reported higher levels of satisfaction with nursing home assistants when the assistants had been exposed to listening training. Residents reported improvements in several areas, including increased eye contact, increased personal self-disclosures, positive use of silence, positive feedback, and reduced advice-giving.[72]

What Health-care Providers Can Do

As you have learned, empathy and empathetic listening are important to our overall well-being. Careful active listening is an important component of the patient-provider encounter, not only for the patient's satisfaction and health, but also for the well-being of the provider. Fortunately medical, nursing, and pharmaceutical schools as well as hospital and hospice volunteer programs are increasingly providing interpersonal training.[73]

Those of you who are contemplating either volunteering with or entering a health-care profession should keep in mind that all the following advice is designed to convey one important thing to patients (and their families): respect. A number of factors are related to building respect; arguably the most important is establishing trust. Trust is one of the strongest items associated with patient reports of improved health.[74] Trust affects a number of related health issues, including overall satisfaction with doctors, willingness to disclose sensitive information, and willingness to stick to a treatment program. For adults, a trusted physician is seen as competent, honest, and committed to maintaining confidentiality. Adolescents respond to physicians in much the same way as their parents do. They describe trusted physicians as people they respect, who are honest, and who know what they are doing. However, one significant difference between adults and adolescents is that adolescents are more likely to stress the importance of confidentiality of health and personal information.[75] One likely reason for this concern is that adolescents may be uncertain about what physicians can and/or will tell their parents or guardians. Adolescents worried about confidentiality concerns may not fully inform their physicians about their symptoms or may not fully comply with treatment because they do not want to miss out on activities such as Friday night's dance or a double date with friends.

Here are some pointers for building trust. First, **be aware of personal schemata.** This piece of advice echoes what we suggested to you as patients. For example, physicians sometimes focus so much on one illness that another unrelated illness is ignored or goes undiagnosed. In a recent story, one doctor admitted focusing so much attention on a patient's severe depression that he didn't follow up on other secondary symptoms. Those symptoms, as it turned out, were caused by cancer. The patient died from the cancer, not the depression.[76] In addition, just like everyone else, health-care providers are touchy about some topics. Imagine a hospice volunteer facing the family member of someone whose mother has just died, when his own passed away recently. Knowing yourself means you'll be aware of issues that might inadvertently affect your relationship with others. There are many ways to volunteer at hospitals and with hospice. The volunteer in the previous example might be more effective answering phones or running errands until he is able to fully deal with his grief.

Second, **look interested (use immediacy behaviors).** Generally speaking, patients respond better when health-care providers appear interested in and supportive of what they say. For example, patients are more likely to speak freely and disclose when physicians and nurses maintain eye contact with them.[77] Other nonverbal behaviors associated with active listening include an open posture, confirming head nods, interested facial expressions, and appropriate gestures and touch. Nonverbal communication (i.e., immediacy behaviors) is one technique caregivers can use to validate patients' experiences and confirm that they understand patients' needs.[78]

Providers can also **listen for distress markers.** While nonverbals can tell us much about how others are feeling, nonfluencies can tell us a lot as well. For example, patients often stutter or stammer and sometimes have extensive pauses when building up to important disclosures.[79] Health communication scholar Athena du Pré suggested that caregivers avoid changing topics until they can determine what the disclosure addresses. Another strategy is to **use silence** (carefully). Silence can be golden when used positively. It opens space for someone to think and express an idea. However, silence can be quite negative as well. Oftentimes disapproval is tied to silence. Have you ever had a parent or friend offer silence as a response to something you said or did? If so, you know what we are talking about.

You'll want to **avoid abruptly changing topics.** Changing topics quickly, as our Dr. Holmes did in Case Study 10.3, can make patients feel out of control. It certainly is not a way to encourage peer-oriented, collaborative communication and subsequently is unlikely to lead to a trusting relationship.

As we've noted several times throughout the book and in this chapter, **be empathetic.** Empathy and empathetic understanding have been discussed in detail in several other chapters of this text. In the health-care setting, empathy has been described as a primary dimension of developing a caring relationship, which is based on acceptance and respect for the patient.[80] Obviously, based on this description, collaborative, or patient-centered, communication must necessarily involve empathetic understanding, the attempt to understand health and illness from the patient's perspective. Engaging in empathetic communication is especially important when working with children and elderly patients. Caregivers should strive to establish a supportive environment that empowers patients. This involves several factors, including acknowledging patients as individuals (at a level they can understand), being aware of their values and beliefs, and working with family members and significant others in assisting the patient in meeting a mutually agreed upon treatment plan.

Of course, it is important to **listen more than you talk.** We're not suggesting this just because you are reading a listening text. Remember that physicians, on average, interrupt their patients within 18 seconds of beginning their health interview.[81] It's no wonder 75 percent of patients say they did not tell their physician everything they planned to tell them. It is interesting to note patients who are allowed to finish speaking tend to speak for only about two minutes. As we noted earlier, patients sometimes use indirect questions when they want to avoid appearing ignorant or foolish. It is important then to "listen between the lines" for these types of requests for information. Volunteers need to be particularly good listeners. As a volunteer, you might interact with physicians; nurses; orderlies; family members; and of course, the patient. They all have different needs and concerns, and it might sometimes be difficult to sort through conflicting information.

Much of this chapter's discussion boils down to control issues during the health interview. Questions are a mainstay of the health-care interview; however, "health professionals should be cautious so as not to control interviews through the use of questions."[82] **Allowing patients some control** (i.e., allowing them to talk) during the interview emphasizes the responsibility that both parties have in receiving and disclosing information as well as in requesting and providing information. One method physicians use to emphasize the importance of patient contributions to their own health care is to treat them as equals and use collaborative communication.[83] We're more likely to be open with people we see as equals.

It always helps to **take steps to ensure understanding.** Ensuring understanding is particularly important because medical interactions often include medical jargon, which can be incomprehensible to patients and their families. As you learned earlier in the text, asking for feedback is an important way of ensuring that others understand us. It is also a method of empowering patients. When patients share in health-care decision-making, they feel not only respected but that they are a partner who can make meaningful contributions to their health-care and treatment decisions.[84] As you learned, paraphrasing and restating information are also an excellent method of ensuring that you (and others) have heard and fully understood the other's message.

> **THINK ON IT**
>
> In this section we've provided you with several suggestions for communication with patients (and their families). Based on what you've read elsewhere in the text, what other suggestions would you make? Develop a list of four to six additional tips, providing a justification for why each should be included and giving an example to illustrate each.

SUMMARY

While it is beyond the scope of this chapter, you should be aware that listening in the medical context goes beyond the patient-provider relationship. In other chapters we discuss the importance of social support systems, listening across the life span, and listening and the media. All of these areas have important applications to how we interact with health-care professionals. In addition, how doctors, nurses, social workers, and other health-care professionals interact and work together can have a significant effect on a person's health. Health-care activities have to be coordinated; multiple physicians and support staffs could be involved. Subsequently developing cooperative relationships among all these health-care "players" is important in achieving the goal of patient comfort and health. As we noted at the beginning of this chapter, breakdowns in communication can lead to medical errors, some minor, some fatal. If you are interested in learning more about health communication, check out the additional readings listed at the end of this chapter.

CONCEPTS TO KNOW

Paternalistic Approach
Consumeristic Approach
Collaborative Approach
Open-ended Question
Reflection
Selective Reflection
Empathy Building
Checking for Understanding

Factors Affecting Patient-Provider Interactions
Tips for Patients
Voice of Medicine
Voice of the Lifeworld
Patient Satisfaction and Compliance
QuEST Model
Tips for Providers

DISCUSSION QUESTIONS

1. This chapter discusses the importance of listening for both the patient and the health-care provider. Is it more important for the health-care provider to be a good listener or the patient? Why?
2. Do you have more of a paternalistic or consumeristic approach to health care? What makes you think so? What are the advantages and disadvantages of each approach?
3. Do you think your approach to health care changes with context? For example, would you interact with your health-care provider differently if you had a clear-cut problem, such as a broken leg, as opposed to something more ambiguous, such as unexplained abdominal pain? What about something more serious, such as lupus?

LISTENING ACTIVITIES

1. Visit three to four different medical school Web sites. If available, check out their mission statements. Do these statements address patient-provider communication in any way? If so, how? Now look at course offerings, course descriptions, and so forth. Do they offer communication skill–building classes to students? Are they required or electives? If required, how many are students required to take? If there are no required classes, do course descriptions suggest they touch on communication issues? You might also consider doing the same for other medical schools (e.g., nursing schools, dental schools).

2. Doctor-patient interactions (as well as nurse-patient interactions) are portrayed in many prime-time dramas, soap operas, and comedies. Choose two different types of shows (e.g., a comedy and a drama, a drama and a soap), and watch an episode of each. Do they portray patient-provider interactions similarly or not? Looking at what we've covered in this chapter, which does the best job of illustrating good listening? How? If you were to rewrite a scene from one of the shows you watched to better exemplify the advice in this chapter, what would it look like? What would you want to emphasize or do differently? Why?

ADDITIONAL READINGS

Burnard, P. (1992). *Effective communication skills for health professions*. New York: Chapman & Hall.

Cegala, D. J., & Broz, S. L. (2003). Provider and patient communication skills training. In T. L. Thompson, A. M. Dorsey, K. I. Miller, & R. Parrott (Eds.), *Handbook of Health Communication* (pp. 183–204). Mahwah, NJ: Lawrence Erlbaum.

Cegala, D. J., Post, M. D., & McClure, L. (2001). The effects of patient communication skills training on the discourse of older patients during a primary care interview. *Journal of the American Geriatrics Society, 49*, 1505–1511.

Hummert, M. L., & Nussbaum, J. F. (Eds.). (2001). *Aging, communication, and health*. Mahwah, NJ: Lawrence Erlbaum.

Jackson, L. D., & Duffy, B. K. (Eds.) (2001). *Health communication research*. Westport, CT: Greenwood.

Kohn, L. T., Corrigan, J. M., & Donaldson, M. S. (Eds.). (2000). *To err is human: Building a safer health system*. Washington, D.C.: National Academy Press.

Makoul, G. (1998). Communication research in medical education. In L. D. Jackson & B. K. Duffy (Eds.), *Health communication research: A guide to developments and directions*. Westport, CT: Greenwood.

Nussbaum, J. F., & Coupland, J. (Eds.) (2004). *Handbook of communication and aging research* (2nd ed.). Mahwah, NJ: Lawrence Erlbaum.

Petronio, S. (2002). *Boundaries of privacy: Dialectics of disclosure*. Albany, NY: SUNY Press.

Thompson, T. L., Dorsey, A. M., Miller, K. I., & Parrott, R. (2003). *Handbook of health communication*. Mahwah, NJ: Lawrence Erlbaum.

Whaley, B. B. (Ed.). (2000). *Explaining illness: Research, theory and strategies*. Mahwah, NJ: Lawrence Erlbaum.

ENDNOTES

1. Cherry, Woodwell, & Rechtsteiner, 2007. Down-loadable files and other related information can be found at www.cdc.gov/nchs/ahcd.htm.
2. Beckman & Frankel, 1984
3. Levine, 2004
4. Beckman & Frankel, 1984; Dyche & Swiderski, 2005; see also Li, Krysko, Desroches, & Deagle (2004).
5. Levine (2004) provides an easy-to-read summary of select research findings on the effect of doctor-patient communication on patient health, medical risks, and malpractice.
6. Richmond & McCroskey, 2004
7. du Pré, 2010
8. Brody, Miller, Lerman, Smith, & Caputo, 1989; Burgoon, Birk, & Hall, 1991; Frank, 1988; Greenfield, Kaplan, Ware, Yano, Haskard, & DiMatteo, 2009
9. Cecil, 1998; Frankel & Beckman, 1984; Young & Klingle, 1996
10. "Health Literacy," 2003
11. du Pré (2010) provides an excellent, brief overview of 20th-century changes in American health insurance and managed care.
12. Trends and Indicators, 2004
13. See, for example, Boyd (1998); Denning (2001); Dennis (2004); Dykes (2004); Lloyd (2003); Lundkvist, Åkerlind, Borgquist, & Mölstad (2002); Roberts (2004); Sifton (2002).
14. Graybar & Leonard, 2005, p. 2
15. Burnard, 1997
16. Krupnick, Sotsky, Simmens, Moyer, Elkin, Watkins, & Pilkonis, 1996
17. Graybar & Leonard, 2005, p. 3
18. Graybar & Leonard, 2005
19. Bernard, 1997, p. 64
20. Gassmann & Grawe, 2006
21. Chien, Chan, Lam, & Kam, 2005
22. Kohn, Corrigan, & Donaldson, 2000; Sutcliffe, Lewton, & Rosenthal, 2004
23. Robinson, 2003
24. Nussbaum, Ragan, & Whaley, 2003
25. See Nussbaum, Ragan, & Whaley (2003) for a review of the effect of gender on patient-provider interactions.
26. du Pré, 2010, p. 203
27. du Pré, 2010
28. du Pré, 2010
29. Health and race differences are primarily social in nature. Bhopal (1998) found that biological dif-

ferences among races are not the primary reason for differences in illness. See also Schulman et al. (1999).
30. Barber et al., 1998; Engelberg, Flora, & Nass, 1997; Flores, Abreu, Olivar, & Kastner, 1998; Govindarajan et al., 1999
31. Cooper-Patrick et al., 1999
32. Weech-Maldonado et al., 2003; Flores et al., 1998
33. Rubin, Healy, Gardiner, Zath, & Moore, 1997
34. Hing & Lin, 2009
35. Ray & Bostrom, 1990
36. "Aging Statistics," 2010. For additional aging statistics, visit the Department of Health & Human Services Administration on Aging at www.aoa.gov/AoARoot/Aging_Statistics/index.aspx.
37. Mulac & Giles, 1996; Nussbaum, Thompson, & Robinson, 1989
38. Baltes & Wahl, 1996; Charles, Goldsmith, Chambers, Haynes, & Gauld, 1996; Nussbaum et al., 1989
39. Leland, 2008
40. Greene & Adelman, 2001; Nussbaum et al., 1989; Nussbaum et al., 2003
41. Hasselkus, 1992
42. Greene & Adelman, 2001
43. Beisecker & Thompson, 1995; McLane, Zyzanski, & Flocke, 1995
44. Cegala, Gade, Broz, & McClure, 2004
45. Rost & Frankel, 1993
46. Cegala, 1997; Frankel, 1990
47. du Pré, 2010
48. Bryan, 1991; Drass, 1988, du Pré, 2010, Robertson, 1996
49. Bryan, 1991
50. Waitzkin, 1991
51. Watson, Lazarus, & Thomas, 1999
52. Zimmerman & Arnold, 1990
53. Goss, Mazzi, Del Piccolo, Rimondini, & Zimmerman, 2005
54. du Pré, 2010
55. Arnold & Shirreffs, 1998, p. 3
56. Cegala, 1997; du Pré, 2010; Goss et al., 2005
57. West, 1993
58. Ong, de Haes, Hoos, & Lammes, 1995
59. Arnold & Shirreffs, 1998
60. Kinnersley, Stott, Petters, & Harvey, 1999
61. Brown, Stewart, & Ryan, 2003; Dykes, 2004
62. Gray, Evans, Sweeney, Lings, Seamark, Seamark, Dixon, & Bradley, 2003
63. Lundkvista, Åkerlind, Borgquiat, & Mölstad, 2002

64. Matthews, Sledge, & Lieberman, 1987; Tarrant, Windridge, Boulton, Baker, & Freeman, 2003
65. Roberts, C. W., 2004, p. 64
66. Bowker, 1996; Charles et al., 1996; Conlee, Olvera, & Vagim, 1993; Grant, Cissna, & Rosenfeld, 2000; Jadad & Rizo, 2003; Ray & Donohew, 1990; Williams, 1997
67. Bowman & Ruben, 1986; Ruben, 1989; Welch, 2010
68. Brown et al., 2003
69. Wanzer, Booth-Butterfield, Gruber, 2004
70. Weiss & Blustein, 1996
71. Wanzer et al, 2004
72. Trahan & Rockwell, 1999
73. Bowles, McIntosh, & Torn, 2001; Chambers-Evans, Stelling, & Godin, 1999; Garcia de Lucio et al., 2000; Ito & Lambert, 2002; Rogan & Timmins, 2004; Roter, 2000
74. Trust in patient-physician relationships has been addressed by a variety of researchers. The following provides a sample of articles for additional review: Safran et al. (1998); Hall et al. (2002); Hall et al. (2001); Thom & Stanford Trust Study Physicians (2001); Mechanic & Meyer (2000); Ginsburg, Menapace, & Slap (1997); Rosser & Kasperski (2001).
75. Klostermann, Slap, Nebrig, Tivorsak, & Britto, 2005. This finding appears to hold true in other Western-based cultures; see Farrant & Watson (2004).
76. Lester, Tritter, & Sorohan, 2005
77. Bensing, Kerssens, & van der Pasch, 1995; Burnard, 1997; Sidell, 2001
78. Wanzer, Booth-Butterfield, Gruber, 2004
79. du Pré, 2010, p. 70
80. Brown et al., 2003; Corbett, 2001
81. Beckman & Frankel, 1984
82. Northouse & Northouse, 1992, p. 167
83. du Pré, 2001
84. Rogan & Timmins, 2004; Edwards, Elwyn, Smith, Williams, & Thornton, 2001

REFERENCES

Aging Statistics. (2010). Department of Health & Human Services Administration on Aging. Retrieved from www.aoa.gov/AoARoot/Aging_Statistics/index.aspx.

Arnold, W. E., & Shirreffs, J. H. (1998). Patient perceptions of patient-physician communication with allopathic and naturopathic physicians. *International Journal of Listening, 12,* 1–11.

Baltes, M. M., & Wahl, H. (1996). Patterns of communication in old age: The dependence-support and independence-ignore script. *Health Communication, 8,* 217–231.

Barber, K. R., Shaw, R., Folts, M., Taylor, K., Ryan, A., Hughes, M., Scott, V., & Abbott, R. R. (1998). Differences between African American and Caucasian men participating in a community-based cancer screening program. *Journal of Community Health, 23,* 441–451.

Beckman, H. B., & Frankel, R. M. (1984). The effect of physician behavior on the collection of data. *Annals of Internal Medicine, 101,* 692–696.

Beckman, H. B., Markakis, K. M., Suchman, A. L., & Frankel, R. M. (1994). The doctor-patient relationship and malpractice: Lessons from plaintiff depositions. *Archives of Internal Medicine, 154,* 1365–1370.

Beisecker, A. E., & Thompson, T. L. (1995). The elderly patient-physician interaction. In J. F. Nussbaum & J. Coupland (Eds.), *Handbook of communication and aging research* (pp. 397–416). Mahwah, NJ: Lawrence Erlbaum.

Bensing, J. M., Kerssens, J. J., & van der Pasch, M. (1995). Patient-directed gaze as a tool for discovering and handling psychosocial problems in general practice. *Journal of Nonverbal Behavior, 19,* 223–242.

Bhopal, R. (1998, June 27). Spectre of racism in health and health care: Lessons from history and the United States. *British Medical Journal, 7149,* 1970–1973.

Bowker, J. (1996). Cancer, individual process, and control: A case study of metaphor analysis. *Health Communication, 8,* 91–104.

Bowles, N., Mackintosh, C., & Torn, A. (2001). Nurses' communication skills: An evaluation of the impact of solution-focused communication training. *Journal of Advanced Nursing, 36,* 347–354.

Bowman, J. C., & Ruben, B. D. (1986). Patient satisfaction: Critical issues in the implementation and evaluation of patient relations training. *Journal of Healthcare Education and Training, 1,* 24–27.

Boyd, S. D. (1998, June). Using active listening. *Nursing Management, 55.*

Brody, D. S., Miller, S. M., Lerman, C. E., Smith, D. G., & Caputo, G. C. (1989). Patient perception of involvement in medical care: Relationship to illness attitudes and outcomes. *Journal of General Internal Medicine, 4,* 506–511.

Brown, J. B., Stewart, M., & Ryan, B. L. (2003). Outcomes of patient-provider interaction. In T. L. Thompson, A. M. Dorsey, K. I. Miller, & R. Parrott (Eds.), *Handbook of health communication* (pp. 141–161). Mahwah, NJ: Lawrence Erlbaum.

Bryan, G. T. (1991). Physicians and medical education. *Journal of the American Medical Association, 266,* 1407–1408.

Burgoon, M., Birk, T. S., & Hall, J. R. (1991). Compliance and satisfaction with physician-patient communication. *Health Communication Research, 18,* 177–208.

Burnard, P. (1997). *Effective communication skills for health professionals* (2nd ed.). New York: Chapman & Hall.

Cecil, D. W. (1998). Relational control patterns in physician-centered clinical encounters: Continuing the conversation. *Health Communication, 10,* 125–150.

Cegala, D. J. (1997). A study of doctors' and patients' communication during a primary care consultation: Implications for communication training. *Journal of Health Communication, 2,* 169–194.

Cegala, D. J., Gade, C., Broz, S. L., & McClure, L. (2004). Physicians' and patients' perceptions of patients' communication competence in a primary care medical interview. *Health Communication, 16,* 289–304.

Chambers-Evans, J., Stelling, J., & Godin, M. (1999). Learning to listen: Serendipitous outcomes of a research training experience. *Journal of Advanced Nursing, 26,* 1421–1426.

Charles, C., Goldsmith, L. J., Chambers, L., Haynes, R. B., & Gauld, M. (1996). Provider-patient communication among elderly and nonelderly patients in Canadian hospitals: A national survey. *Health Communication, 8,* 281–302.

Cherry, D. K., Woodwell, D. A., & Rechtsteiner, E. A. (2005). *National ambulatory medical care survey: 2005 summary.* Advance data from vital and health statistics (no. 387). Hyattsville, MD: National Center for Health Statistics. Retrieved from www.cdc.gov/nchs/ahcd/physician_office_visits.htm.

Chien, W. T., Chan, C. H. H., Lam, L. W., & Kam, C. W. (2005). Psychiatric inpatients' perceptions of positive and negative aspects of physical restraint. *Patient Education and Counseling, 59,* 80–86.

Conlee, C. J., Olvera, J., & Vagim, N. N. (1993). The relationships among physician nonverbal immediacy and measures of patient satisfaction with physician care. *Communication Reports, 6,* 25–33.

Cooper-Patrick, L., Gallo, J. J., Gonzalez, J. J., Vu, H. T., Power, N. R., Nelson, C., & Ford, D. E. (1999). Race, gender, and partnership in the patient-physician relationship. *Journal of the American Medical Association, 282,* 583.

Corbett, T. (2001). The nurse as a professional career. In R. B. Ellis, J. Gates, & N. Kenworthy (Eds.), *Interpersonal communication in nursing: Theory and practice* (pp. 91–105). London: Churchill Livingstone.

Denning, J. J. (2001). How to improve your listening skills, avoid mix-ups. *Ophthalmology Times, 26,* 28.

Dennis, S. (2004). Active listening is key to client-centred care, but how often do we make the effort? *Nursing Standard, 19,* 22–23.

DiMatteo, M. R. (1994). The physician-patient relationship: Effects of the quality of health care. *Clinical Obstetrics and Gynecology, 37,* 149–161.

Drass, K. A. (1988). Discourse and occupational perspective: A comparison of nurse practitioners and physician assistants. *Discourse Processes, 11,* 163–181.

du Pré, A. (2001). Accomplishing the impossible: Talking about body and soul and mind during a medical visit. *Health Communication, 14,* 1–22.

du Pré, A. (2010). *Communicating about health: Current issues and perspectives* (3rd ed.). New York: Oxford.

Dyche, L., & Swiderski, D. (2005). The effect of physician solicitation approaches on ability to identify patient concerns. *Journal of General Internal Medicine, 20,* 267–270.

Dykes, J. R., (2004, September). Making time to listen. *Family Practice Medicine.* Retrieved from www.aafp.org/fpm.

Edwards, E., Elwyn, G., Smith, C., Williams, S., & Thornton, H. (2001). Consumers' views of quality in the consultation and their relevance to 'shared decision-making' approaches. *Health Expectations, 4,* 151–161.

Engelberg, M., Flora, J. A., & Nass, C. I. (1997). AIDS knowledge: Effects of channel involvement and interpersonal communication. *Health Communication, 7,* 73–91.

Farrant, B., & Watson, P. D. (2004). Health care delivery: Perspectives of young people with chronic illness and their parents. *Journal of Paediatrics and Child Health, 40,* 175–179.

Flores, G., Abreu, M., Olivar, M. A., & Kastner, B. (1998). Access barriers to health care for Latino children. *Archives of Pediatric & Adolescent Medicine, 152,* 1119–1125.

Frankel, R. (1990). Talking in interviews: A dispreference for patient-initiated questions in physician-patient encounters. In G. Psathas (Ed.), *Interaction competence* (pp. 231–262). Washington, D.C.: International Institute for Ethnomethodology and Conversation Analysis & University Press of America.

Garcia de Lucio, L., Garcia Lopez, F. J., Marin Lopez, M. T., Hesse, B. M., & Caamano Vaz, M. D. (2000). Training programme in techniques of self-control and communication skills to improve nurses' relationships with relatives of seriously ill patients: A randomized controlled study. *Journal of Advanced Nursing, 32,* 425–431.

Gassmann, D., & Grawe, K. (2006). General change mechanisms: The relation between problem activation and resource activation in successful and unsuccessful therapeutic interactions. *Journal of Clinical Psychology and Psychothreapy, 13,* 1–11.

Ginsburg, K. R., Menapace, A. S., & Slap, G. B. (1997). Factors affecting the decision to seek health care: The voice of adolescents. *Pediatrics, 100,* 922–930.

Goss, C., Mazzi, M. A., Del Piccolo, L., Rimondini, M., & Zimmermann, C. (2005). Information-giving sequences in general practice consultations. *Journal of Evaluation in Clinical Practice, 11,* 339–349.

Govindarajan, A., & Schull, M. (2003). Effect of socioeconomic status on out-of-hospital transport delays of patients with chest pain. *Annals of Emergency Medicine, 41,* 481–490.

Grant, C. J.,III Cissna, K. N., & Rosenfeld, L. B. (2000). Patients' perceptions of physicians' communication and outcomes of the accrual to trial process. *Health Communication, 12,* 23–39.

Gray, D., Evans, P., Sweeney, K., Lings, P., Seamark, D., Seamark, C., Dixon, M., & Bradley, M. (2003). Towards a theory of continuity of care. *Journal of Royal Society of Medicine, 96,* 160–166.

Graybar, S. R., & Leonard, L. M. (2005). In defense of listening. *American Journal of Psychotherapy, 59,* 1–18.

Greene, M. G., & Adelman, R. D. (2001). In M. L. Hummert & J. F. Nussbaum (Eds.), *Aging, communication, & health* (pp. 101–120). Mahwah, NJ: Lawrence Erlbaum.

Greenfield, S., Kaplan, S. H., Ware, J. E., Yano, E. M., & Frank, H. J. (1988). Patients' participation in medical care: Effects of blood sugar control and quality of life in diabetes. *Journal of General Internal Medicine, 3,* 448–457.

Hall, M. A., Dugan, E., Zheng, B., & Mishra, A. K. (2001). Trust in physicians and medical institutions: What is it, can it be measured, does it matter? *Milbank Quarterly, 79,* 613–639.

Hall, M. A., Zheng, B., Dugan, E., et al. (2002). Measuring patients' trust in their primary care providers. *Medical Care Research Review, 59,* 293–318.

Hanh, B. A. (1995). Children's health: Racial and ethnic differences in the use of prescription medications. *Pediatrics, 95,* 727–732.

Haskard, K. B. Z., & DiMatteo, M. R. (2009). Physician communication skills and patient adherence to treatment: A meta-analysis. *Medical Care, 47,* 826–834.

Hasselkus, B. R. (1992). Physician and family caregivers in the medical setting? Negotiation of care? *Journal of Aging Studies, 6,* 67–80.

Health literacy of America's adults: Results from the 2003 national assessment of adult literacy. (2003). U.S. Department of Education Institute of Education Sciences National Center for Education Statistics. Retrieved from http://nces.ed.gov/pubsearch/pubsinfo.asp?pubid=2006483.

Hing, E., & Lin, S. (2009). *Role of international medical school graduates in providing office-based medical care: United States, 2005–2006.* (NCHS data brief no. 13). Hyattsville, MD: National Center for Health Statistics. Retrieved from www.cdc.gov/nchs/data/databriefs/db13.htm.

Ito, M., & Lambert, V. (2002). Communication effectiveness of nurses working in a variety of settings within one large university teaching hospital in western Japan. *Nursing and Health Sciences, 4,* 149–153.

Jadad, A. R., & Rizo, C. A. (2003). I am a good patient believe it or not. *British Medical Journal, 326,* 1293–1294.

Kinnersley, P., Stott, N., Peters, T. J., & Harvey, I. (1999). The patient-centeredness of consultations and outcome in primary care. *British Journal of General Practice, 49,* 711–716.

Klostermann, B. K., Slap, G. B., Nebrig, D. M., Tivorsak, T. L., & Britto, M. T. (2005). Earning trust and losing it: Adolescents' views of trusting physicians. *Journal of Family Practice, 54,* 679–687.

Kohn, L. T., Corrigan, J. M., & Donaldson, M. S. (Eds.). (2000) *To err is human.* Washington, D.C.: National Academy Press.

Krupnick, J. L., Sotsky, S. M., Simmens, S., Moyer, J., Elkin, I., Watkins, J., & Pilkonis, P. (1996). The role of the therapeutic alliance in psycho-therapy and pharmacy-therapy outcome: Findings in the National Institute of Mental Health Treatment of Depression collaborative research program. *Journal of Consulting and Clinical Psychology, 64,* 532–549.

Leape, L. L., Hiborne, L. J., Bell, R., Kamberg, C., & Brook, R. H. (1999). Underuse of cardiac procedures: Do women, ethnic minorities, and the uninsured fail to receive needed revascularization? *Annals of Internal Medicine, 130,* 183.

Leland, J. (2008, October 7). In "sweetie" and "dear," a hurt for the elderly. *New York Times Online.* Retrieved from www.nytimes.com.

Lester, H., Tritter, J. Q., & Sorohan, H. (2005, April 20). Patients' and health professionals' views on primary care for people with serious mental illness: Focus group study. *British Medical Journal, 330,* 1122+. Published online. Retrieved from www.bmjjournals.com.

Levine, M. (June 1, 2004). Tell the doctor all your problems, but keep it to less than a minute. *New York Times Online.* Retrieved from www.nytimes.com.

Li, H. Z., Krysko, M., Desroches, N. G., & Deagle, G. (2004). Reconceptualizing interruptions in physician-patient interviews: Cooperative and intrusive. *Communication & Medicine, 1,* 145–157.

Lloyd, R. C. (2003). Improving ambulatory care through better listening. *Journal of Ambulatory Care Management, 26,* 100–109.

Lundkvist, J., Åkerlind, I., Borgquist, L., & Mölstad, S. (2002). The more time spent on listening, the less time spent on prescribing antibiotics in general practice. *Family Practice, 19,* 638–640.

Matthews, D. A., Sledge, W. H., & Lieberman, P. B. (1987). Evaluation of intern performance by medical inpatients. *American Journal of Medicine, 83,* 938–944.

McLane, C. G., Zyzanski, S. J., & Flocke, S. A. (1995). Factors associated with medication noncompliance in rural elderly hypertensive patients. *American Journal of Hypertension, 8,* 206–209.

Mechanic, D., & Meyer, S. (2000). Concepts of trust among patients with serious illness. *Social Science Medicine, 51,* 657–668.

Mulac, A., & Giles, H. (1996). "You're only as old as you sound": Perceived vocal age and social meanings. *Health Communication, 8,* 199–215.

Northouse, P. G., & Northouse, L. L. (1992). *Health communication: Strategies for health professionals.* Norwalk, CT: Appleton & Lange.

Nussbaum, J. F., Ragan, S., & Whaley, B. (2003). Children, older adults, and women: Impact on provider-patient interaction. In T. L. Thompson, A. M. Dorsey, K. I. Miller, & R. Parrott (Eds.), *Handbook of health communication* (pp. 183–204). Mahwah, NJ: Lawrence Erlbaum.

Nussbaum, J. F., Thompson, T., & Robinson, J. D. (1989). *Communication and aging.* Cambridge, MA: Harper & Row.

Ong, L. M. L., de Haes, J. C. J. M., Hoos, A. M., & Lammes, F. B. (1995). Doctor-patient communication: A review of the literature. *Social Science and Medicine, 40,* 903–918.

Ray, E. B., & Bostrom, R. N. (1990). Listening in medical messages: The relationship of physician gender, patient gender, and seriousness of illness on short- and long-term recall. In R. Bostrom (Ed.), *Listening behavior: Measurement and applications* (pp. 128–143). New York: Guilford.

Ray, E. B., & Donohew, L. (1990). *Communication and health: Systems and applications.* Hillsdale, NJ: Lawrence Erlbaum.

Richmond, V. P., & McCroskey, J. C. (2004). *Nonverbal behavior in interpersonal relationships* (5th ed.). Boston: Pearson.

Roberts, C. (2004). 'Only connect': The centrality of doctor-patient relationships in primary care. *Family Practice, 21,* 232–233.

Roberts, C. W. (2004, October). The QuEST for satisfaction begins with listening. *Review of Ophthalmology, 11*(10), 64–68.

Robertson, D. W. (1996). Ethical theory, ethnography, and differences between doctors and nurses in approaches to patient care. *Journal of Medical Ethics, 22,* 292–299.

Robinson, J. D. (2003). An international structure of medical activities during acute visits and its implications for patients' participation. *Health Communication, 15,* 27–58.

Rogan, F. C., & Timmins, F. (2004). Improving communication in day surgery settings. *Nursing Standard, 19*(7), 37–42.

Rosser, W. W., & Kasperski, J. (2001). The benefits of a trusting physician-patient relationship. *Journal of Family Practice, 50,* 329–330.

Rost, K., & Frankel, R. (1993). The introduction of the older patient's problems in the medical visit. *Journal of Aging and Health, 5,* 387–401.

Roter, D. (2000). The medical visit context of treatment decision-making and the therapeutic relationship. *Health Expectations, 3,* 17–25.

Ruben, B. D. (1989). The health caregiver-patient relationship: Pathology, etiology, treatment. In E. B. Ray & L. Donohew (Eds.), *Communication and health: Systems and applications* (pp. 51–68). Hillsdale, NJ: Lawrence Erlbaum.

Rubin, D. L., Healy, P., Gardiner, T. C., Zath, R. C., & Moore, C. P. (1997). Nonnative physicians as message sources: Effects of accent and ethnicity on patients' responses to AIDS prevention counseling. *Health Communication, 9,* 351–368.

Safran, D. G., Taira, D. A., Rogers, W. H., Kosinski, M., Ware, J. E., & Tarlov, A. R. (1998). Linking primary care performance to outcomes of care. *Journal of Family Practice, 47,* 213–220.

Sidell, M. (2001). Supporting individuals and facilitation change: The role of counseling skills. In J. Katz, A. Peberdy, & J. Douglas (Eds.), *Promoting Health: Knowledge and Practice* (2nd ed.). London: Palgrave.

Sifton, C. B. (2002). Lessons on listening: The art of communication. *Alzheimer's Care Quarterly, 3,* iv–vi.

Sutcliff, K. M., Lewton, E., & Rosenthal, M. M. (2004). Communication failures: An insidious contributor to medical mishaps. *Academic Medicine, 79,* 186–194.

Tarrant, C., Windridge, K., Boulton, J., Baker, R., & Freeman, G. (2003, June 14). How important is personal care in general practice? *British Medical Journal (Clinical Research Edition), 326,* 1310.

Thom, D. H., & Stanford Trust Study Physicians. (2001). Physician behaviors that predict patient trust. *Journal of Family Practice, 50,* 323–328.

Trahan, B. C., & Rockwell, P. (1999). The effects of listening training on nursing home assistants: Residents' satisfaction with and perceptions of assistants' listening behavior. *International Journal of Listening, 13,* 62–74.

Trends and indicators in the changing health care marketplace. (2004). Health insurances/costs. Kaiser Family Foundation. Retrieved from www.kff.org/insurance/7031/print-sec5.cfm.

Waitzken, H. (1991). *The politics of medical encounters: How patients and doctors deal with social problems.* New Haven, CT: Yale University Press.

Wanzer, M. B., Booth-Butterfield, M., & Gruber, K. (2004). Perceptions of health care providers' communication: Relationships between patient-centered communication and satisfaction. *Health Communication, 16,* 363–384.

Watson, K. W., Lazarus, C. J., & Thomas, T. (1999). First-year medical students' listener preferences: A longitudinal study. *International Journal of Listening, 13,* 1–11.

Weech-Maldonado, R., Morales, L. S., Elliott, M., Spritzer, K. L., Marshall, G., & Hays, R. D. (2003). Race/ethnicity, language and patients' assessments of care in Medicaid managed care. *Health Services Research, 38,* 789–808.

Weiss, L. J., & Blustein, J. (1996). Faithful patients: The effect of long-term physician-patient relationships on the costs and use of health care by older Americans. *American Journal of Public Health, 86,* 1742–1747.

Welch, S. J. (2010). Twenty years of patient satisfaction research applied to the emergency department: A qualitative review. *American Journal of Medical Quality, 25,* 64–72.

West, C. (1993). "Ask me no questions . . .": An analysis of queries and replies in physician-patient dialogues. In A. D. Todd & S. Fisher (Eds.), *The social organization of doctor-patient communication* (2nd ed., pp. 127–157). Norwood, NJ: Ablex.

Williams, S. A. (1997, June). The relationship of patients' perceptions of holistic nursing caring to satisfaction with nursing care. *Journal of Nursing Care Quality, 11,* 15–29.

Young, M., & Klingle, R. S. (1996). Silent partners in medical care: A cross-cultural study of patients' participation. *Health Communicator, 8,* 29–53.

Zimmerman, R., & Arnold, W. E. (1990). Physicians' and patients' perceptions of actual versus ideal physician communications and listening behaviors. *Journal of the International Listening Association, 4,* 143–164.

Listening in Legal Contexts

Shooting at Merc's Department Store

Hey, Radley. Is your mom's station going to cover any of that woman's trial? You know the one accused of shoplifting from Merc's Department Store and then shooting the security guard? My mom is going to be one of the witnesses. She saw the whole thing and gave statements to the police right after it happened. And Tamarah in our listening class group was the 9-1-1 operator who took the initial call from Merc's.

Wow! I didn't realize we were so connected to that shooting. I'm pretty sure the station will cover the story, NaMii, but Mom hasn't mentioned anything about working on that particular one. But then again, she doesn't always tell me what stories she's working on. Is your mom nervous about being a witness? I wonder if the lawyer will rough her up like in the trial scenes of Law and Order.

Oh, Radley, you watch too much television. My dad has to work with his company's legal counsels all of the time, and he says they are easy to work with. And my mom said the officer who took her statement was really nice. He asked clear questions and listened to what she had to say. I think he is also going to be a witness. The really funny thing is that some of the parents of our group have been called for jury duty. Ben's dad and Carter's mom are in the jury pool. I wonder if they'll end up as jurors. ■

When you think about listening in a legal context, what springs to mind? A courtroom such as the one Radley thought of in the case above? A police interrogation? We take a very broad approach to listening in the legal context. While we do talk about listening in law enforcement and the courtroom, we also address mediation, an alternative type of dispute resolution. We examine interactions among a variety of individuals who work in legal contexts, including attorneys, jurors, negotiators, mediators, law enforcement personnel, 911 operators, EMTs, and the general public. If you think there is a potential overlap among these areas, you are right. Take the scenario in Case Study 11.2.

To Catch a Vandal

Wendell called 911 to report that his car had been vandalized. He told the operator he had seen a man, about 5'10" wearing a yellow jacket in his front yard. The hood of the jacket was up, so he hadn't been able to see the man's face. A few minutes later, Jeff, a young man walking in the neighborhood and wearing a yellow jacket was stopped and detained by police officer Frank Long. After speaking with Jeff, Officer Long was suspicious and asked Jeff to go to the station with him. On their arrival, Jeff called his attorney, Joe Palmer, who met him at the police station. ■

Think of all the areas where listening occurs during this brief scenario: the 911 operator listens to Wendell, Wendell listens and answers the operator's questions, Officer Long listens to his dispatcher and to Jeff, Jeff listens to Officer Long, Jeff's attorney listens to both the officer and Jeff. All of these listening opportunities occur, and Jeff hasn't even be formally charged with a crime. Regardless of whether Jeff simply wore the wrong color jacket at the wrong time or is accused of and tried for the vandalism, there will be many more listening opportunities before the situation is resolved. Let's take a look at some of the possible listening situations.

PUBLIC SAFETY OFFICIALS

Law Enforcement Officers

Often the first legal-related person we have contact with is a police officer. Most police officers undergo 12 to 14 weeks of training to learn their job.[1] This training includes a significant communication component, including mediation training, which includes a great deal of listening training. Clearly an officer's duties are more than crime prosecutions and prevention, maintaining order (e.g., traffic flow and violations, keeping the peace), and other services (e.g., medical, missing persons, assisting motorists). The following sections demonstrate how listening plays a key role in the field of law enforcement. It is important to note many of these skills can be applied to similar contexts in other fields.

Investigative Interviewing   Law enforcement officers work with members of the public in many ways. When you watch a crime drama, you often see an officer interviewing an eyewitness about the particulars of a crime, as is the case with NaMii's mother in the Case Study at the beginning of the chapter. This type of situation involves both the listening of the officer as well as the observation skills of the witness. Eyewitnesses face a number of challenges. The account in Case Study 11.3 of an office invasion witnessed by Professor Worthington illustrates several problems.

Office Invasion

Recently a friend and I were working on a Saturday evening in my office. As we sat there (with the door open), a young man came out of the department's instructional resource center across the hall. First, I was greatly surprised; then I tried to figure out who he was. I did not recognize him as a graduate student and knew he was not related to any of the department's faculty. He headed for the front door of the building, opened it, and let someone else in. I stopped him in the hall and asked him what he was doing. He said he and his friend were going to study. (His friend was standing behind him.) When I asked him why he was in the IRC, he said he came through an open window to get to the front door to let his friend in (the front doors were locked). Obviously all kinds of warning bells were going off in my head. As I was telling him that the building was off limits to students on the weekend and that he had to leave, I was trying to memorize everything I could about him. I've studied problems with eyewitness testimony and know how events can affect our memory. For the first time, I experienced them. While I can remember the one dark-haired student-type, I can't remember anything about his friend except that he was about 5'10" and had sandy-colored hair. ■

Two weeks later the department was burglarized. Was it the same young men? We don't know. However, as seen here, events typically happen within minutes, if not seconds. Adrenaline is coursing through your system, and as seen with Professor Worthington, you often center your attention on just a few things. Keep in mind that what happened to Professor Worthington is not particularly shocking or unusual. Witnessing an actual assault, robbery, or severe car accident is traumatic for everyone involved. Consequently the observation and attending skills of any witness are tested to their limits. To complicate matters, witnesses often focus on different things, causing police officers to interview as many different people at the scene of an accident as they can. Therefore, an officer has to be particularly careful as both a listener and a questioner.

How an investigator asks a question can shape the response of the witness. Therefore, a witness such as Mrs. Kim in Case Study 11.1 should carefully listen to the questions and be mindful of the potential effect of the wording. Research indicates that listeners often integrate into their own memories what officers, other witnesses, and other parties involved with a case say to them. Elizabeth Loftus, a highly respected cognitive psychologist, and others have found that if a questioner introduces the existence of an object that was not at the original scene, the eyewitness will integrate the information into his or her memory of events. As an example, if the police officer had asked Professor Worthington in the situation mentioned earlier, "And what color was the young man's baseball cap?" she might have added the presence of the baseball cap to her memory of events that night. Fortunately the police officer who interviewed her simply asked, "What can you tell me?" thus allowing for a free-flowing response and, it is hoped, more accurate recall on her part. The lesson here for law enforcement officials is to *listen and not lead the other person*; less talking and more listening aids a witness's ability to accurately recall events and details. In these types of situations, comprehensive listening allows officers to gain accurate understanding of what occurred, building a picture of events leading to the incident. And critical listening helps the witness separate what he or she remembers from anything that might be included in a question. Officer Natalie Blackstock McKinley offered additional advice in her interview in this chapter.

Much of the research on eyewitness testimony focuses on two types of information: estimator variables and system variables.[2] **Estimator variables** are elements not under our control but directly related to the crime events. Examples of estimator variables include the type and severity of crime, complexity of the event, and familiarity with surroundings as well as the race, attractiveness, sex, and age of the accused. As we discussed earlier in the text, any of these factors can affect how we perceive both auditory and visual information. In the example at the beginning of the chapter, Mrs. Kim's answers to the officer's questions would have been influenced by the fact the crimes happened in her place of employment, a department store, her relationship with the guard who was shot, and her perceptions of the accused.

System variables, in contrast, are related to events within the criminal justice system. They include factors such as the time lapse between when someone witnesses the event and the eventual testimony, interviewer question structure, and police lineup instructions. For example, one early study in this area found that when recalling a filmed murder, witnesses are 91 percent accurate when they are allowed to freely elaborate their recall of the event without any questions. When an interviewer used open-ended questions, the accuracy dropped to 83 percent. Accuracy dropped even more, to 72 percent, when the witnesses responded to leading questions.[3] This research gives even more support to the point we made earlier about the importance of a witness using critical listening to identify potential biasing effects of questions.

Like witnesses, officials also use a variety of types of listening. For example, following an accident or crime, people are naturally shaken by events. It is important that officers take time to engage in empathetic listening to calm witnesses. In Case Study 11.1, Mrs. Kim witnessed a coworker get shot. Chances are she was very upset by what she had seen. Therefore, a good police officer would recognize her heightened emotional state and work to calm her emotions before asking questions. People who are calm (or at least somewhat calmer) are more likely to recall events and recall them more accurately. Of course, officers also use their critical listening skills to assess the veracity of a witness's statement as well as identify any missing information. This combination of empathetic and critical listening not only helps the officer get the information; it will also help him or her during the testimony phase of the trial if the situation ends up in court.

Natalie Blackstock McKinley
Patrol Officer, Crisis Negotiator, and D.A.R.E. School Resource Officer
LaGrange Police Department
LaGrange, Georgia

Police officers have to listen very carefully. We listen for tone and inflection and try to determine if someone is lying to us or not. In hostage negotiations, we listen to everything, including background noise. Over my career, I've learned that close listening encourages people to talk. And the more people talk, the more they may reveal.

What is the most significant piece of advice I can offer to the public? When you are in an emergency, *slow down*. People tend to talk very fast, and their words come out in a rush when they are excited, scared, mad, and so on. It can be hard, but if you take a few deep breaths before explaining something, it can actually speed up the interview process. A deep breath gives you time to collect and organize your thoughts and to determine what you really need to say. This means we may not have to ask so many questions and can address your emergency even more quickly.

Crisis Negotiation

As the previous section indicates, there are many ways that listening is important to the jobs of those involved in public safety. A specific area where listening is critical is in a crisis situation. Fortunately law enforcement officers now receive substantial training in crisis negotiation. Examples of crisis negotiations include hostage taking, some instances of domestic violence, suicide attempts, and standoffs. Arthur Slatkin, a police and criminal psychologist, noted that today's negotiators have psychology and counseling backgrounds and strong communication skills.[4] Fortunately research shows that FBI agents trained in hostage negotiation have stronger active listening skills and a lower tendency to engage in problematic behaviors such as problem-solving.[5] (Problem-solving is problematic if someone jumps to solving the situation before listening to all sides of the issue.) It is important for us to note Slatkin acknowledged the fundamental role listening plays in these types of negotiations when he wrote the following:

> "[A]t the heart of negotiation and negotiator trained skills is 'active listening,' a way in which a listener communicates demonstrably that he is listening . . . that he acknowledges the other person, is taking in what is being said, is trying to understand what is being said, and cares about the person saying it."[6]

The crisis negotiator uses her training to connect with persons in crisis to bring them to a more balanced state with the expectation of bringing the crisis to a conclusion that will preserve some of the individual's self-respect. This suggests that relational listening is an important part of what crisis negotiators do. Through relational listening, crisis negotiators make a connection with the party in crisis using specific techniques. A negotiator's communication techniques can be broken down into three categories: listening, action, and sharing.[7] You are already familiar with the basic *listening techniques:* clarification, paraphrasing, reflection, and summarizing. *Action techniques* involve probing, confrontation, interpretation, information giving, and instructions. Finally *sharing responses,* which reflect relational listening, include self-disclosure, immediacy, and reinforcement.

Most of these techniques appear self-evident. However, they are specially adapted to crisis negotiations. For example, **confrontation** is used in a very specific manner to address inconsistencies or discrepancies in a person's statements, in behaviors, or between statements and behaviors (e.g., "You say you don't want to hurt anyone,

THINK ON IT

Even as a student you sometimes talk with people who are experiencing a crisis. Sometimes these crises are romances that break up, family upheavals, or negative medical news. How can you use crisis negotiation listening in such situations?

but you shot out the window twice"). Similarly, when a negotiator engages in **self-disclosure,** it is strategically done to further the negotiation. For example, the negotiator could model personal disclosure to encourage someone threatening suicide to disclose back. Remember earlier in this book we discussed the reciprocal nature of self-disclosure and the societal pressure we typically feel to respond in a similar manner. Thus, when an officer discloses seemingly personal information, the other person might feel he should as well without fully realizing why. Such information can give the officer important insight into the person and the situation. **Immediacy responses** involve statements of the negotiator's feeling about the individual at that particular time. For example, one of the characters we have followed throughout this book, Tamarah Jackson, works as a 911 operator in public safety. If Tamarah receives a call from someone reporting a break-in, she might say something such as the following if the caller has stopped talking on the phone: "Do you know that when you stop talking to me, I think that something has happened and it really upsets me?" **Reinforcement,** on the other hand, encourages someone to start or continue with a behavior (e.g., "You really showed good faith when you released that hostage"). As you can see, one of the primary ways in which negotiators attempt to defuse a crisis situation is by connecting with the individual. As we learned earlier, we all want to feel that we are valued, respected, and important. People in crisis are no different. Of course, the ultimate goal of all negotiators is to end the crises safely for everyone involved, and their listening and communication reflect that goal.

ATTORNEY-CLIENT COMMUNICATION

While not all of you will have contact with someone in public safety, the odds are that at some point in your life you will have contact with an attorney. You might want to have a will drawn up, a contract reviewed, or get divorced. Good listening skills—on both your and your attorney's parts—results in a more effective and satisfactory relationship.

Legal commentators David and Cindy Victor noted, "An attorney is only as effective as his or her ability to communicate."[8] Certainly it is important for an attorney to know the law; however, the Victors argued that communication is central to almost all attorney tasks. Until recently attorney-client relationships received little, if any, formal attention in law schools. As a result, younger attorneys often failed to recognize the importance of listening.[9] Consequently attorneys fresh from law school were often less people oriented and more research focused. As they matured as lawyers, they learned the importance of good communication and strong listening skills in gaining and maintaining their client relationships.

Fortunately law school professors, attorneys, and other legal professionals today have come to recognize the importance of establishing and maintaining a quality relationship with their clients.[10] Listening is considered a central communication skill in attorney-client relations.[11] In fact, active listening is the guiding force behind effective communication between attorneys and their clients. Gerald Riskin, a consultant specializing in client-relation skills, argued that "active listening creates a unique and priceless bond with a client."[12] The following sections are designed to look at listening and communication skills and behavior for both attorneys and clients.

Diane F. Wyzga, RN, JD
Trial Consultant and Founder
Lightning Rod Communications
San Clemente, California
www.lightrod.net

When I teach critical listening skills to lawyers, I ask them to listen with awareness. Why should we listen with awareness instead of merely hearing? Perhaps it's because, as one litigator told me, "Law is a win-lose game. What happens when we come in second place? Our client has had one opportunity to have his story told. We listen so our client gets a better chance at being heard even when we come in second place."

For attorneys, one of the key principles to listening well begins with setting up an atmosphere conducive to the clients' believing they are listened to. Our job is to listen to the client to understand what they want or need to say. "Tell me more" is the most invaluable statement you can ever use to encourage someone to speak. It takes the burden off you to keep crafting questions and allows the client's narrative story to emerge. And if you listen with intention, you will hear the content, as well as the context, of the story, which will help you assess the viability and worth of the case.

Advice for Attorneys

For those of you who think you want to become lawyers, here are some good suggestions for developing your listening skills. The rest of you will find the suggestions are applicable to most professional settings and interactions. We have organized our advice around the three stages of an attorney interview: developing rapport, gathering information, and counseling.[13] You will notice that attorneys tend to begin the interview using relational listening then moving to comprehensive listening and finishing with critical listening.

Interviewing—Stage One   The initial contact between attorneys and their clients and witnesses is very important.[14] It is here the interview focuses on establishing a relationship, while later stages address understanding and assessing a client's case. The primary purpose of this first stage of the interviewing process is to **establish rapport** with clients.[15] If clients feel that the attorney is unresponsive or indifferent about their cases, it is unlikely they will remain clients for very long. Thus, it is important that attorneys help clients relax and establish a supportive communication climate. Attorneys must assess the merits of a case and the needs of the client during the initial stages of the interview. In an effort to get adequate and accurate information, attorneys attempt to establish rapport by doing the following:

- *Putting clients at ease by presenting a professional image and keeping distractions to a minimum.* Inappropriate clothing, ringing phones, loud conversations, and other external noises can interfere with a quality interview. In Chapter 3 we discussed the effect of these types of stimuli on information processing. Most attorneys begin a visit by using icebreakers such as a warm welcome and a few minor personal questions (e.g., "Is this your first time visiting an attorney?" "Did you find the office OK?" "I hope you didn't have to wait too long"). This social exchange sets the tone for the rest of the interview.

- *Allowing the client to direct the initial part of the interview.* This lets the client establish his comfort zone. The attorney should focus on active listening and asking open-ended questions that encourage the client to talk. Of course, an attorney who is listening to the client will let the other person talk and use this type of question sparingly since they tend to interrupt the flow of information. While some visits will be straightforward (e.g., reviewing a business contract), other cases could be more volatile. The attorney interview is the first time the client has been able to purge the emotions associated with the case, whether it is a divorce, an arrest for DUI, or a wrongful death. At this stage, the primary goal is to "build empathetic identification and rapport."[16]

- *Engaging in relational listening.* Depending on the type of case, attorneys can find themselves playing the role of counselor.[17] It is easy to see how divorce, child custody, or sexual abuse cases require lawyers to focus on the emotional effect on their clients as well as attempting to gather information about the case. It is no surprise that in these types of cases clients experience great emotional distress, and lawyers must be able to address this distress. However, other more common types of cases (e.g., contract disputes, personal injury, bankruptcy) can be emotionally upsetting as well. When emotions run high, a good listener will use empathetic silence. Head nods and other nonverbals assure clients that the lawyer is listening, while silence encourages them to continue speaking. Of course, a good listening attorney will be attuned to when the client has truly finished talking, is uncomfortable opening up, or expects him or her to direct the interview.[18] As you can see, empathetic or therapeutic listening is an important part of attorney-client interviews.[19] Attorney Merit Bennett encourages his clients to "talk themselves out." He finds that not only does he learn about the events surrounding the case but he often can learn what type of outcome they will be satisfied with.[20] Other attorneys also note the importance of expressing empathy while engaging in active listening. Through paraphrasing and direct assertions of empathy, lawyers can acknowledge not only the content of the client's communication but the underlying emotions as well.[21]

Interviewing—Stage Two   The next stage of the attorney-client interview focuses on *information gathering.* Here comprehensive and critical listening are most useful. Comprehensive listening is central to translating or interpreting a client's communication and is necessary for fully understanding the client's needs. An easy pitfall at this stage is premature counseling or problem solving.[22] Counseling, or giving advice, too soon can prevent an attorney from getting needed facts. Problem solving, or listening in the yellow fix-it mode discussed in Chapter 2, can be viewed as an indication that the attorney is more focused on his or her assessment than on the client's information. Critical listening is important in this stage so lawyers can evaluate the information and ask for needed clarification. The following suggestions will help attorneys and others maximize listening:

- *Briefly outline the purpose and goals of the interview.* By letting the client know what to expect in the interview, the attorney helps establish a framework from which the client can listen and process the information. Most clients, particularly first-time clients, have only media portrayals to shape their expectations of the process, and such portrayals are generally inaccurate. For example, if our friend Radley, who has watched too many courtroom dramas, were to be interviewed by a lawyer, his expectation of being "grilled by the attorney" might make him defensive. So an outline of what to expect would help Radley relax and listen to the questions. The overview also provides a good transition from relational to comprehensive and critical listening. Of course, attorneys should use everyday language and avoid legalese as they address information gathered from the client's narration of events and ask for further clarification or expansion. A good listener will use summary statements and paraphrasing to ensure full understanding of the client's needs.

- *Ask questions.* While asking questions is important, the wording of the questions is critical. As you recall from earlier in the chapter, leading questions tend to predispose the client to answer in a particular way. Consider, for example, "Isn't it true that John played high-stakes poker regularly?" versus, "Did John like to gamble?" These questions carry different implications and will consequently get different responses. Probing questions don't have to lead the client to answer in a specific manner. Asking someone to elaborate or complete his or her thoughts opens the door for more accurate information. Whatever the type of question or technique, the primary function is to keep the discussion moving to gather necessary information. Consequently, as in all listening situations, attorneys should keep interruptions to a minimum. The client has the information the attorney needs, and allowing him or her to freely talk will oftentimes help the attorney identify important topics to explore later.

- *Take brief notes (if necessary),* but avoid writing down large amounts of information. Clients might slow their narratives to match the speed of note-taking or start wondering about what is being written; either way, it can become a distraction.

- *Be respectful.* While this isn't a listening skill per se, being respectful helps an attorney (and others) establish a climate in which the client is able to give the necessary information, regardless of how painful it may be. Because the topic might be very emotional, both attorneys and clients may need to take a break to emotionally gather themselves. Professor Fitch-Hauser once gave a lengthy deposition as an expert witness to an attorney who tended to become angry when he didn't get the answer he wanted. Fortunately he was professional enough to realize when he needed to take a break, so he wouldn't say anything that would be harmful to his client's case. Being respectful also includes being polite to clients. People want to be acknowledged as respected individuals.[23] Saying "please," apologizing for delays, and giving your full attention to the client when listening are just a few ways of achieving this goal.

- *Listen for truthfulness, accuracy, omissions, and contradictions.* Clients need to feel comfortable enough to disclose their cases with all their negatives. However, clients do forget, misremember, and occasionally outright lie. As attorney Merit Bennett noted, omitted information is potentially detrimental to a client's case.[24] For example, an attorney should not find out in court that his client has previously been ticketed for driving under the influence. This information will likely lead jurors to question his client's credibility. The attorney who knows possibly negative information in advance can plan for it and deal with it accordingly. Through active listening, attorneys can better assess the strengths (and weaknesses) of a client's story and identify and address any contradictions.

- *Avoid prejudging.* Attorneys, like all of us, have biases that can affect the interpretation of messages. Few attorneys have the option of working with only clients they approve of. Even if they do, they will be required to interview other individuals, work with other attorneys, or have cases tried before judges they simply do not like. Consequently it is important for attorneys to assess their biases and determine if they can listen without prejudice and effectively handle the case.[25] If they cannot, the ethical attorney will refer the case to a colleague. In addition, attorneys need to be aware of the effect of cultural differences on communication and their assessment of the case. As law professor Susan Bryant noted, "all lawyering is cross cultural," requiring a nonjudgmental approach to the attorney-client relationship. One way to achieve this is by focusing on the facts of the case, not the judgment of the client.[26] Thus, it is important for attorneys to recognize the effect of their own schemata on their perceptions and listening when they start a relationship with a new client.

Interviewing—Stage Three The final stage of the attorney-client interview involves **counseling** the client. It is here that attorneys move from comprehensive listener to adviser and problem solver. Please note, however, this does not mean they stop listening; they simply listen differently.

- Perhaps the most important aspect of this stage is *evaluating the facts of the case.* First, the attorney must use critical and comprehensive listening to assess whether the situation should go into the legal system at all, and if so, is it one that is "provable" and worth pursuing. For example, in Chapter 10 Professor Worthington described her brother's experience with medical malpractice. The doctor who prescribed the incorrect medication came to visit him, took personal responsibility for what happened, and apologized. Because he was the company physician, all medical bills were paid, and her brother received full pay while recuperating. He suffered no lasting physical or neurological damage. If he had chosen to sue, it is unlikely an attorney would take the case. One attorney friend calls these types of incidents "no harm–no foul" cases. They take time and money to pursue and are unlikely to result in a monetary return that makes it worth everyone's time and effort.

- Counseling a client also entails *assessing viable courses of action open to the client.* Through active listening and closely watching the client's nonverbals, an attorney can better assess client responses to the different options and resulting scenarios (e.g., best-case versus worst-case scenario). Attorneys use their listening and related observation skills as well as their knowledge of the legal system to realistically analyze risks, costs, time, effort, and other realities of taking a case to court (or negotiations). Once attorneys make this assessment, they then present the information to the client in such a way the client can listen

THINK ON IT

While the above suggestions were applied to attorney-client interviews, how might the advice be applied to other interviewing contexts?

and absorb the truth of that assessment even when the client doesn't want to hear it. Attorney Lucinda Jesson noted the importance of managing client expectations.[27] It is important that a client clearly understand the possible *realistic* outcomes of her case. A good attorney will do his or her best, but none promise a win.

Advice for Clients

Many more of you will be clients than attorneys. Listening will be just as important for you as it is for the attorney. Like the attorney, you will want to set the stage for effective listening by being prepared. This will include having all pertinent documents organized and with you when you meet with the attorney. The more accurate and in depth the information you provide, the better attorneys will be able to do their job.[28] It will also be helpful if you create an outline of the situation to help you remember and to present a balanced overview of the situation. Here are a few other suggestions that will help you be a better listener:

- *Recognize your own biases and the strength of your emotions.* In other words, be as accurate and objective as you can as you present information about your case to the attorney. Being objective also means trying to keep emotions from clouding your description of events. The attorney is there not to judge you, but to evaluate the viability of your case, determine your needs, and present viable options. If you are not honest or misrepresent facts, then she cannot properly do her job.[29]
- *Look for an attorney who listens.* A lawyer who does not fully understand the situation cannot offer you adequate advice or appropriate legal options. If you are continually interrupted by staff and phone calls or if your attorney spends all the time talking, then you might want to think twice about using him as your representative.
- *Engage in comprehensive and critical listening.* After listening to your information, your attorney will generally offer you an assessment of the merits of your case. If she feels the case is meritorious, she will present several options on how to proceed. You will need to understand and evaluate the relative merits of each option. If she turns your case down, use the responding aspect of listening to ask why. It could be that there are additional materials or facts she needs.
- Be sure you *fully understand the attorney retainer and fee agreement.* When you are under stress or emotionally charged, as people often are when they talk with attorneys, it is easy to zone out on information that doesn't specifically address the case, such as information about fee agreements. One friend was rudely awakened when she discovered the emotional purging she engaged in while on the telephone with her attorney cost her several hundred dollars; the attorney was charging her an hourly rate for each call. Her attorney was an excellent relational listener and offered great emotional support, but it came at a price. If the attorney takes your case, you have several means of resolving

> **THINK ON IT**
>
> How does the advice for clients apply to interactions you may have with professionals or situations you are currently facing. For example, how can you use this information when you apply for a job or when you talk with one of your instructors?

it. You might end up litigating it (going to trial), or you could engage in one of several types of alternative dispute resolution (ADR) methods. We start our discussion looking at the role listening plays in the courtroom context.

LISTENING CHALLENGES OF THE JURY

The Jury as Audience

The jury process begins with jury selection, or **voir dire**. Every jurisdiction has what is commonly called a venire, or jury pool. The jury pool is composed of individuals from the community, and the actual jury is selected from this pool. In Case Study 11.1, both Mr. Goleman and Mrs. Bishop will be in the jury pool. During voir dire, the attorneys, clients, and judge meet potential jurors. Generally potential jurors are questioned in an open courtroom about their backgrounds, attitudes, and other experiences related to the case. Listening on the part of attorneys and potential jurors is very important during this process.

Voir dire is more than just selecting who will actually serve on a jury. Attorneys also use it to build or establish their cases, introduce case themes, and favorably introduce their clients. The goal of both sides is to impanel jurors who will be the least biased against their cases. Therefore, attorneys listen for any information that might indicate a potential bias or predisposition against their clients. Jaine Fraser, a jury consultant and trial psychologist, suggested that attorneys use the **80-20 rule of listening** during voir dire: listen 80 percent of the time and talk 20 percent of the time. New Mexico attorney Randi McGinn offered even more specific advice.[30] She tells attorneys that they should ask open-ended questions, avoid speaking legalese, and avoid being judgmental. Most important, she tells attorneys they should listen, allowing jurors to talk, and avoid note-taking while jurors are speaking.

If You Are Called for Jury Duty

If you are ever called for jury duty, our first suggestion is to go. It's a fascinating look at our legal system at work. Just keep in mind that you bear the responsibility of listening carefully so you can reach a fair decision. Here are some suggestions that can help you be a better listener:

- *Use comprehensive listening.* During jury selection, the judge and attorneys will introduce the case, general background, and primary players. You need to pay close attention at this time for at least two reasons. First, there could be a legitimate reason for you to be excused (e.g., you were cited for driving under the influence, you were the victim of a robbery, you know one of the individuals involved). Second, this information provides you with background on the case if you are actually picked for jury duty.
- *Be aware of potential biases and schemata.* Remember that the attorneys are introducing their cases and trying to influence how you interpret evidence. After all, attorneys do have an obligation to put their clients' cases in the best light possible. Of course, you will also want to be honest about your own biases and the experiences that have caused you to have these biases. For example, one of Professor Worthington's good friends was killed by a

drunk driver. She is the first to admit that she has no tolerance for driving under the influence. Consequently she would not be the best candidate to serve as a juror on a DUI case.

- *Stay focused.* The voir dire process is full of distractions. You might wonder why the person next to you was dismissed or what the judge and bailiff are discussing. Like most listening situations, it takes concentration to stay focused on the task at hand. Active listening will help you to accurately answer questions and can help you learn even more about a case.

- *Ask for clarification.* Keep in mind that responding is an important part of listening. If during the voir dire you don't understand what the attorney is asking or a word being used, ask for clarification. Judges and attorneys are so accustomed to using legal language that they sometimes forget that most of us are not familiar with those terms. Since you can't evaluate and respond to a judge's or attorney's questions without first understanding them, it's OK to say, "I'm not sure what that word means" or "Could you rephrase that? I don't understand." Odds are others in the jury pool could use the clarification as well.

- *Volunteer information if it is needed.* If you are asked a question, be direct in answering it. However, as a comprehensive and critical listener, you will recognize that the question requires more than the obvious answer. For example, if asked, "What do you do for a living?" the authors of your book would most likely respond that they are college professors. However, we also do some litigation consulting. Professor Fitch-Hauser has worked as an expert witness on several cases, and Professor Worthington assists in witness preparation and is an active member of the American Society of Trial Consultants. So we would need to reveal these activities in our responses to the question.

COURTROOM CONTEXT

If you are selected to serve on a jury, once the trial begins, you will want to be prepared to listen to the different stages of the trial. Attorney and litigation consultant Richard Waites argued, "Listening in the courtroom is critical to the process of communication and persuasion."[31] In the following sections, we focus on stages of the trial where juror listening is critical: attorney opening statements and closing arguments, witness examination, judicial instructions, and jury deliberations.

Opening Statements

Each side starts the trial by presenting opening statements or arguments. You will probably be motivated to listen because of your curiosity about the case. As a responsible listener, you will want to use this motivation to focus on the schema formation aspect of the opening statements. Attorneys often strategically organize their openings in a narrative format because it is believed that a strong story has the greatest potential for influencing juror decisions. By presenting an overview of the case and introducing the story, or theory of the case, opening statements provide a framework through which later evidence and information are interpreted.[32] Researchers in trial advocacy agree that opening statements can have a great influence on the jury.[33]

Schema activation naturally occurs during opening statements. They affect what information we attend to, what meaning we assign to incoming information, how we draw inferences (i.e., connect information or fill in gaps), and how we organize and store information in memory. If you think about the Listening MATERRS model presented in Chapter 1, it becomes clear that the listeners will look for motivation to listen to the testimony as well as begin putting schemata in place that will help them translate and evaluate it. How attorneys frame their opening statements significantly impacts how jurors listen to their cases.

The Importance of Stories and Schemata   Listeners' use of schemata continues throughout the testimony phase of a trial. The **story model of jury decision-making** helps us understand how jurors process information during the predeliberation stage of the trial.[34]

Why are stories so important? For listeners, stories provide a way to keep track of and make sense of all the information in the trial.[35] Attorney Richard Waites also noted that the underlying themes in a story "help jurors organize case information along the lines that the [attorney] wishes, and help them to overcome disputes or conflicts with specific evidence."[36]

Unfortunately not all information in a trial is presented in order. The story then helps listeners reorder the information into an easier-to-understand narrative format. Years of research reveals that that when we hear information out of order, we naturally reorder it into a standard story format.[37] In general, storing things in memory in a narrative format makes it easier for us to remember, and what we remember will affect the decisions we make as jurors.

The stories become very helpful when the jurors go in to deliberation after they have heard the evidence. Deliberation is often a process of constructing the most plausible story that fits the case facts and explains case events. And as psychologists Patricia Devine and Thomas Ostrom noted, memory of information can be quite important because verdicts are primarily based on the jurors' shared recollections of trial events.[38] Stories help us identify and process important information (such as motives or means) and pay less attention to background or less important information (what the defendant and the victim ate for dinner at the restaurant).

At the heart of every story are themes. In a trial these themes are called *case themes*. Waites argued that compelling themes "are at least as important as the key facts of the case."[39] In general, we can classify case themes as **evaluative** (characterizing character traits, behaviors, and motivations) or **more powerful than fact** (characterizing the evidence).[40] Powerful stories include the most powerful themes and evidence in a way that coincides with juror life experiences. Whether the theme is taken from a fairy tale ("The Boy Who Cried Wolf"), a biblical story ("David and Goliath"), or a historical event (Rosa Parks's refusing to give up her seat), it should be "easy to remember, appeal to common sense, [be] in accord with jurors' concepts of fairness and justice, and [be] consistent with the evidence."[41]

As you can see, using stories actually aids the listening process. We find it easier to remember trial evidence when it is organized narratively. In fact, trial simulations suggest that jurors take the many bits and pieces of the trial (evidence and testimony) and construct their own stories. In addition, attorneys will attempt to prime the schemata we draw upon to process and evaluate trial evidence. In other words, if one attorney's version of events (story) is more compelling, we will likely engage and use schemata that are in keeping with that story. When this occurs, we will pay greater attention to some evidence and testimony than others. We will also work harder to make that evidence fit with that story, dismissing any that doesn't fit.

Testimony

After the opening statements, each side presents the evidence supporting its case. As you know from watching movie and television court scenes, this evidence takes many forms (photographs, diagrams, physical evidence). The most influential is witness testimony, especially when it is live testimony rather than written or recorded. Eyewitnesses recount events, identify suspects, and provide important background information. Listening to testimony can teach us many lessons about critical listening. Jurors, as they listen to both sides, need to evaluate all of the testimony, especially when it is contradictory. They have to assess witness credibility by following the attorneys' questions and evaluating witness responses, all while closely watching the witness's nonverbals. As you can see in Case Study 11.4, in addition to factual contradictions, jurors also often have to deal with emotional conflicts. Imagine the listening challenges of balancing and evaluating all of the contradictory information.

Closing Arguments

Just as opening statements are influential in their ability to frame a dispute, closing arguments are influential in their ability to synthesize trial information and remind jurors of evidence deemed important to an advocate's case. Here attorneys openly attempt to affect attitude change. Good-listening jurors will want to listen closely (and be aware of) attorney attempts to persuade them to adopt a certain version of the case facts. Attorney Richard Waites noted that closings allow attorneys to highlight key elements of their cases and reinforce themes and theories, while John Crawford suggested that strategic "planned redundancy" aids jurors' memories during deliberation.[42]

> ### CASE STUDY 11.4
>
> # Silicone Breast Implant
>
> During the testimony phase of a class-action lawsuit against silicone breast implant makers, women testified that their implants had leaked or burst. They alleged the silicone had traveled in their bodies and caused a host of illnesses and autoimmune disorders, such as chronic fatigue syndrome, depression, fibromyalgia, and other ailments. These witnesses had clearly suffered emotional and physical trauma. Their emotional trauma was further supported by psychologists who testified about the psychological effects of removing the implants. On the other hand, the companies being sued presented experts who countered the alleged victims' claims. They had research scientists testify about the causes of autoimmune diseases and statisticians testify about the probabilities of developing specific symptoms or diseases.
>
> Of the evidence described above, accounts of trauma, research reports, and statistics, which do you believe would be most influential? Why? How does it fit in with our previous discussion of listening and storytelling? ■

Judicial Instructions and Jury Deliberations

After all of the testimony and closing arguments, judges give juries instructions for deliberation and decision making, and the jurors retire to deliberate. By this point of the trial, jurors' energy level is typically pretty low. After all, they have been listening for a long time, and listening takes a lot of energy. However, it is important to engage in close, comprehensive listening. The judge's instructions ultimately guide jury deliberations and affect the type of verdict a jury reaches. So at this point focusing on concentrating and using comprehensive listening is very important as they listen to the judge's instructions.

The fact that jurors get to talk for the first time in the trial process can sometimes cause them to focus on talking rather than discussing and listening. However, our experience as researchers (and as actual jurors) suggests that people work hard to be fair during jury deliberations. In the next few paragraphs, we offer some suggestions for enhancing listening during the deliberation process. Drawn from the work of Aubrey Fisher, as an added bonus, these suggestions can be adapted to many other group discussions.[43]

Fisher's Phases   If not appointed, the first thing a jury does after retiring to the jury room is to select a foreperson. This individual typically helps facilitate the discussion and will ultimately deliver the jury's verdict to the court official (a bailiff). Once this is done, the deliberation begins. However, jurors should avoid jumping into immediate discussions about the case. During this initial **orientation phase**, they need a few minutes to decompress from the events of the trial and get to know one another a bit. And as in any setting, it is more comfortable talking with and listening to people whom we know at least a little bit about. One way to break the ice is to have each person introduce him- or herself and tell everyone what he or she would be doing if not in the jury room that day.

Jury deliberation can involve conflict and debate. At the early stages of deliberation, people are uncomfortable engaging in this type of exchange. Consequently during the **conflict phase**, juries generally should *avoid early votes*. In fact, judges will often tell you *not* to take an early vote, but to discuss the evidence first. This is excellent advice for several reasons. First, since the jury members aren't ready to engage in a debate about the evidence, they could be influenced by others in the group before they make up their own minds. This in turn can prevent them from listening with an open mind to what others have to say. You can see this happen in the movie *Twelve Angry Men* when the group takes a vote (for the death penalty) as soon as they sit down. Hands slowly go up around the table. It is clear that some individuals are unsure, but they almost vote to send the young man to the electric chair anyway. If it were not for Henry Fonda's character (in the original film version), the group would have reached what is called a *false consensus* (i.e., group members think they agree when in actuality they don't), and the defendant would have received the death penalty.

Second, early votes often can have a polarizing effect on jury decision making.[44] Individual jurors know where everyone stands but have no clue why. They haven't had a chance to find out. Since the act of publicly committing to a position can have a detrimental effect on discussion, they also might never be able to find out. People do not want to appear indecisive or wishy-washy, so they often become firmly committed to their publicly stated position and be less willing to listen to others. When they do listen, it is more than likely going to be selective listening for information that supports their position. As a result, they ignore important ideas and evidence. Juries who reach decisions in this manner are labeled **verdict driven.**

Listening juries are **evidence driven.** Here jurors actively listen to one another, engage in argumentation, openly debating the validity of the evidence and how it fits with the judge's instructions. Not surprising, active listening techniques are important to this type of jury, as is critical listening. This type of jury *focuses on the evidence* and engages in **substantive conflict,** or debating over ideas, and avoids **affective conflict,** which focuses on personality differences. Members are careful to avoid prejudging either ideas or the jury members who are delivering the ideas. They are able to do so because they know the important work of the group is to deliver a fair verdict. Consequently they carefully listen to the points made regardless of who originates the idea. Of course, it is important for all members of the jury to participate. An observant listener will listen for what's not being said as well as to what is being said. For example, if a juror notices someone rolling his or her eyes and looking out the window, the juror should follow up to find out what her counterpart is thinking.

Jury deliberation can be tense and emotionally taxing. Therefore, it's important for the group to *take breaks when necessary,* particularly if emotions are running high because of heated debate. It's difficult to listen when we are upset or angry. Taking a break, getting a soft drink, or engaging in some other activity can help everyone relax and lead to better listening and group decision making.

The behaviors that are appropriate for any group discussion are even more important during jury deliberation. Most juries will eventually enter an **emergence phase.** At this time jurors will begin to "emerge" from conflict. One way jurors can determine if they are emerging from conflict is to listen for *preludes to agreement.* People seldom abruptly change their positions during deliberations. Usually they provide both verbal and nonverbal indications that they are moving toward the opposing position. They might nod their heads at an opposing point, shrug to indicate they are unsure, or say something such as, "I can see your point," or, "I haven't thought about it that way before." These types of ambiguous statements allow jurors to change their minds but in a way that helps them save face. It is also important for jurors to demonstrate they are listening by engaging in nonverbal behaviors that show they are being attentive. These behaviors might include such things as leaning forward, nodding in agreement, or in some other manner acknowledging the points of other jurors.

Another good listening behavior (throughout deliberations) that enhances the jury experience is to *avoid interrupting.* As trial consultants, we see jurors in simulated trials do this frequently. They are so intent on presenting their own positions that they interrupt or cut off what others are saying. Verdicts are a joint decision. Interruptions disrupt listening and inhibit the ability to fully understand and evaluate what is being said. Eventually most juries will reach a verdict. An important aspect of the **reinforcement phase** is acknowledging and bonding over the decision that has been reached. Here jurors will compliment each other for a job well done and recognize the hard work they've accomplished. It's important, when possible, for jurors to engage in this type of supportive listening as it increases satisfaction with the verdict that was made and with the overall legal and jury process.

Being on a jury is a unique opportunity to actively participate in the American legal system. If called, serve. Every case allows you to offer your personal contribution in rendering justice in a criminal case or resolving a civil dispute. However, as we mentioned earlier, litigation is only one method of resolving disputes. In reality, most cases never reach the courtroom. People can resolve conflicts through several other alternative dispute methods in the legal system. Next, we introduce you to alternative methods of resolving disputes. Because many of the listening skills hold true across the varying methods, we will focus on listening in one particular method: mediation.

ALTERNATIVE DISPUTE RESOLUTION

Alternative dispute resolution is the term used to describe a number of methods of resolving disputes without litigation. The two major approaches used are mediation and binding arbitration.[45] Other approaches include mediation-arbitration, nonbinding arbitration, minitrials, partnering, and early neutral evaluation. The greatest differences in these methods are the amount of input and freedom in participation and outcomes. Figure 11.1 illustrates the level of outcome control associated with each type of ADR and litigation.

Types of Disputes

The choice of which ADR method to use should be based on the type of dispute. Three broad areas or disputes are issue oriented, emotion oriented, or a blend of the two.[46] **Issue-oriented** dispute resolution is connected to rules, regulations, or the guidelines we follow in everyday life. It is not unusual for judges and arbitrators or your boss, principal, or teacher to take on the role of an evaluator in these instances. When there is a schoolyard fight, the teacher or principal steps in; when we have a significant on-the-job dispute, the boss could become involved; if a neighbor is shooting off late-night fireworks, we call the police. Whoever is called on to resolve the dispute, that person relies on listening to all sides to be fair, unemotional, and objective when deciding the outcome.

Emotionally oriented dispute resolution calls on professionals such as counselors, psychologists, social workers, ministers, or others in the helping professions to assist in resolving the dispute. These helping professionals are trained in therapeutic, empathetic, and other types of listening needed to resolve these very personal disputes. A primary focus of the problem in these types of disputes is the emotions involved. Thus, a marriage counselor may mediate for a distressed couple, coaches may work with the disappointment of the loss of a state championship, or grief counselors may be called in when students die in a car accident. In these cases, emphasis is placed on the emotions themselves rather than any underlying issues.

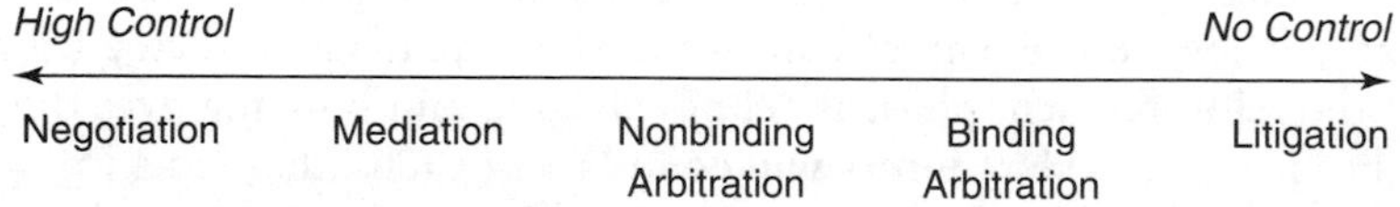

High Control   *No Control*

| Negotiation | Mediation | Nonbinding Arbitration | Binding Arbitration | Litigation |

FIGURE 11.1
Level of Outcome Control and ADR Type.

Issue-emotion dispute resolution addresses both issues and emotions. In this type of dispute, there is something about the dispute that makes it difficult for parties to address their problems. Consequently a neutral third party (e.g., mediators, professional negotiators) is needed to help individuals to resolve their differences. Usually the neutral third party aids in facilitating an open dialogue among those involved while ensuring the discussion is fair and balanced. Ideally the process allows everyone an equal input into discussion and equal input into mutually agreeable resolution options. Of course, equal input calls for equal listening.

We summarize the different types of resolution in Table 11.1.

Listening and ADR

Professional mediator Louise Phipps Senft argued that listening is a fundamental component of mediation. "Listening is more important . . . than speaking."[48] However, she noted that not only are mediators responsible for engaging in good listening skills but so are clients and the attorneys who represent them. She noted that in many cases, the parties coming to negotiations and mediation are so focused on proving their points that they fail to listen to the other side or the mediators. She asserted that it is through listening that parties are able reach a fair and workable

TABLE 11.1		
Issues, Emotions, and Dispute Resolution[47]		
Type of Dispute	Examples of Professional Roles	Primary Attributes
Issue Oriented	Judge, Arbitrator, Supervisor	Focus is on rules, gathering evidence, being objective, maintaining social order.
Emotionally Oriented	Counselor, Social Worker, Psychologist	Focus is on understanding the emotional climate, stabilizing emotions, neutralizing negative emotions and/or other emotional impediments to resolution. Mediator will personally intervene as needed.
Issue and Emotionally Oriented	Mediator, Diplomat, Intermediary, Negotiator	Conducted by a neutral third party, focus is on equitable discussions stressing fairness and mutual areas of interest. Identifies and addresses issue-oriented and emotionally oriented topics. Defuses or neutralizes emotions impeding resolution. Mediator might personally intervene.

solution. Individuals become people instead of being viewed as the enemy. Mediator William Logue agreed by suggesting that when listening is evident, the parties involved feel acknowledged and that their beliefs and feelings have been accepted, creativity is boosted, and the number of emotional outbursts are reduced.[49]

Mediation

In this type of ADR, a neutral third party—a mediator—facilitates negotiations between two or more parties in hopes of reaching a mutually satisfactory resolution. Disputes that revolve around conflicts of interest are particularly appropriate for mediation. These conflicts typically stem from a situation of scarcity. Both parties want the same thing, but there is not enough of it to be had by all. Thus, someone wants more money for a property than another wants to pay, you disagree with your insurance agent about how much the insurance should pay for the damage to your car, and so forth. These types of conflict are particularly prone to compromise, in part because bargaining is not associated with deep-seated values (ethical, moral, or religious differences). Cases that focus on the principle of the matter are usually over values and are consequently difficult to settle. We don't want to look like we are willing to compromise our principles. An illustration of the difference in issue-oriented and principle-based approaches can be seen in a divorce case. If the parties are issue oriented, not focused on the morality of the behavior that led to the divorce, they can focus on interests of dividing the estate fairly. If they focus on the morality aspect of the situation, they will more than likely get bogged down in the blame game and fail to listen to the needs of the other party in such a way that a fair settlement can be reached.

Mediation differs from other types of legal and ADR methods in that while there is a mediator who helps to facilitate negotiations, the mediator is not charged with imposing a solution on the disputing parties. Mediators play an important role in helping each party to step outside of their schemata. In other words, a skilled mediator has the ability to get the parties involved to see beyond the events leading up to the mediation (e.g., who breached the contract first, how much damage a company suffered) to develop creative solutions to the problem(s) for a win-win situation for everyone involved. The example in Case Study 11.5 does an excellent job of distinguishing mediation from other types of ADR.

CASE STUDY 11.5

Kathryn and Indigo's Problem[50]

Kathryn and her cousin Indigo are arguing over the last orange in the basket on the kitchen table. Indigo's mom, Sydney, hearing the argument, tells the children they know the importance of being able to share, so she carefully slices the orange, giving half to each child. The children were not any happier. Imagine for a moment that a mediator had handled the situation.

The mediator would have first asked the children, "Why do you want the orange?" Kathryn, the cook in the family, wants to make marmalade, while Indigo is thirsty. With this information, the mediator would suggest that Indigo juice the orange then give the rind and pulp to Kathryn, a win-win situation for both young girls. ■

Why Do People Choose Mediation?   Generally mediation follows a failed attempt at direct, unassisted negotiations.[51] Sometimes the failure is due to poor listening by one or both parties. In these cases a mediator steps in to listen to both sides and assist them in reaching a mutually agreeable outcome. It also is often used in a variety of other types of disputes, such as the following:

- One or both parties
  - want to avoid the high costs of going to trial.
  - wish to maintain confidentiality and/or avoid publicity.
  - need to continue a working relationship with the other party.
  - know that litigation will not fully address the issues.
  - recognize that those involved are so emotional that it is doubtful that they could negotiate a settlement on their own.

Mediators do not "decide what is best" for the disputing parties, nor do they attempt to impose a resolution.[52] They do, however, assist those involved in reaching a mutually agreeable outcome.

Most important, mediation works.[53] While success rates vary with the context, research suggests that, overall, mediation leads to between 40 and 70 percent of disputes reaching a lasting, formal agreement. The parties tend to be more satisfied and believe the agreements are fairer, in part because both parties have contributed to the outcome and solution. As a result, they are more likely to comply with the settlement terms.

What Makes Mediation Work?   Fundamentally the introduction of a neutral third party who listens changes the communication between the disputing parties.[54] Civility is usually a ground rule of discussions. Mediators are better able to see the bigger picture, including aspects of the conflict that go beyond legal issues to underlying areas of interest to both parties. Because mediators **listen to both sides,** they are often in the best position to not only identify barriers to resolution but also recognize the "blinders" parties in a dispute might have. Mediators point out unrecognized areas of interest, barriers to resolution, and other perceptual stumbling blocks, and both parties can address these areas in open discussion.

The best mediators are impartial, supportive, active listeners.[55] Mediator and author Peter Ladd described three primary mediation skills: paraphrasing, reframing, and reviewing.[56]

However, these skills are necessary for effective listening between competing parties. As you can see, these skills are basic to and reflect good listening. *Paraphrasing* is important because it allows the mediator to essentially pause the mediation process and sum up and point out the primary points in a concise manner. Ladd noted that it is especially useful when the involved parties become

> **THINK ON IT**
>
> Do you know someone who seems to be a natural mediator? Which of the characteristics and skills described here are reflected in his or her behaviors?

overly emotional or communication between the parties begins to stall. By providing a summary of what has occurred or agreed-upon main points, mediators can provide a sense of forward motion, simultaneously conveying what has been covered as well as pointing out continued areas of difference. *Reframing* is necessary when disputants use language or messages that could potentially inflame the discussion or lead to a breakdown in the dialogue. Generally the mediator attempts to reframe the message so it is more acceptable for the opposing party, thus allowing the mediation to continue. For example, let's say Darryl claims, "You promised you would fix my computer. You worked on it, and now it does not run at all! You cheated me out of $200." If you were mediating between Darryl and Jameth, you might tell Jameth, "Darryl is trying to say that it was her understanding that the work you did on her computer was guaranteed but that the guarantee has not been honored." Finally *reviewing* goes beyond a general paraphrasing of issues. Mediators tend to use the technique when an extended silence occurs during discussion. Essentially you review the major issues or themes that have been discussed. Reviews such as these help identify new topic areas as well as help put discussion back on track.

Finally if you ever find yourself in a mediation situation, you should keep in mind that you are not there to win over the mediator. Good mediators work hard to help both sides reach an amicable and long-term agreement.

SUMMARY

This chapter has examined how listening plays a critical role in several legal contexts. Not surprising, listening is critical in law enforcement, all phases of a trial, and alternative dispute resolution situations. So whether you talk with someone in public safety, an attorney, a judge, or a mediator, you will notice that listening contributes to the success of that interaction. If you plan to go into law enforcement or become an attorney, listening will be a critical communication competency for you. It is important to note, however, many of the skills discussed in this chapter go beyond the legal context to other professional encounters. Whether working in a small group, attending a professional seminar, or listening to a workplace dispute, a clear understanding of listening in legal contexts can aid your comprehension, assist in evaluating information, and enhance group problem solving.

CONCEPTS TO KNOW

Eyewitness Testimony
    Estimator Variables
    System Variables

Negotiator Communication Techniques
    Listening Techniques
    Action Techniques
    Sharing Responses

Attorney Interview Stages
    Establishing Rapport
    Information Gathering
    Client Counseling

Advice for Clients

Advice for Jurors
    80-20 Rule
    Listening During Voir Dire

Opening Statements
    Role of Schemata
    Effect of Stories/Storytelling

Trial Themes
    Evaluative
    More Powerful than Fact

Jury Deliberation (Fisher's) Phases
    Orientation
    Effect of Early Votes
    False Consensus
    Conflict
    Affective versus Substantive
    Taking Breaks
    Emergence
    Preludes to Agreement
    Reinforcement

DISCUSSION QUESTIONS

1. Natalee Halloway was allegedly murdered by Joran Van der Sloot in 2005. (You can do an Internet search on the case if you are unfamiliar with it.) They never found her body. Imagine that he has come to trial and you have been hired as a communication consultant by his defense attorney. Address the following questions based on the material covered in the chapter.
2. What type of biases would you want to explore during voir dire? Rank them from most important to least important. Why did you choose these biases, and why did you rank them this way? How could such biases affect juror listening during the trial or juror decision making during deliberations?
3. What type of story or theme(s) might you develop to aid jurors while listening during the trial? How might different themes address different issues (or biases) associated with the trial (e.g., death penalty, drug use, no body has been located)?
4. How comfortable would you be aiding in the defense of Mr. Van der Sloot? If you are uncomfortable, how might that affect your ability to fully listen to him? To provide him with solid/effective advice?

LISTENING ACTIVITIES

1. View a movie or television program portraying courtroom communication. Drawing on material from this and earlier chapters of the book, which of the characters presented portrayed the best listening skills? The worst? As a listening expert, what advice would you give to improve the listening of characters portraying poor listening skills?
2. Using the same video material from above, what biases do you see evidenced by the judge, attorneys, witnesses, or jurors? How might such biases affect the testimony of a witness? The rulings by a judge? Questioning by an attorney? Verdict discussions of a juror?
3. Write a one- to two-page description of your current schema of courtrooms and what occurs within them. Next watch actual trial proceedings by going to the local courthouse or, if you're unable to view an actual trial, try viewing trial proceedings on television channels such as truTV. Does what you observe match up with your original schema? How was your schema confirmed? What did you find surprising?
4. Watch the movie or read the play *Twelve Angry Men*. Does the group follow the decision-making process described by Fisher? Do they go through each of the four phases? What actions, behaviors, comments, and so forth by the characters support your claims? Would you say they were an evidence-driven jury? What could they have done differently to improve their decision-making process? To improve individual and group listening?

ADDITIONAL READINGS

Brewer, N., & Williams, K. D. (2005). *Psychology and law: An empirical perspective*. New York: Guildford.
Deutsch, M., & Coleman, P. T. (2000). *The handbook of conflict resolution: Theory and practice*. San Francisco: Jossey-Bass.
Gelfan, M., & Brett, J. M. (Eds.). (2004). *The handbook of negotiation and culture*. Stanford, CA: Stanford University Press.
McMains, M. J., & Mullins, W. C. (1996). *Crisis negotiations: Managing critical incidents and hostage situations in law enforcement and corrections*. Cincinnati, OH: Anderson.
Madonik, B. G. (2001). *I hear what you say, but what are you telling me? The strategic use of nonverbal communication in mediation*. San Francisco: Jossey-Bass.

Mayer, B. (2000). *The dynamics of conflict resolution: A practitioner's guide.* San Francisco: Jossey-Bass.

Silkenat, J. R., & Aresty, J. M. (Eds). (2000). *ABA guide to international business negotiations: A comparison of cross-cultural issues and successful approaches.* Chicago: American Bar Association.

Spangle, M. L., & Isenhart, M. W. (2003). International negotiation. *Negotiation: Communication for diverse settings.* Thousand Oaks, CA: Sage.

ENDNOTES

1. Police and Detectives, 2008–2009
2. Wells, 1987; Wells & Olson, 2003
3. Lipton, 1977; Also see Wells (1987) and Pansky, Koriat, & Goldsmith (2005) for a review of related research on eyewitness recall and testimony.
4. Slatkin, 2005
5. Van Hasselt et al., 2006
6. Slatkin, 2005, p. xi
7. Slatkin, 2005, ch. 2
8. Victor & Victor, 1997, p. 286
9. Seckler, 2008
10. Arenson, 2002
11. See, for example, Ritter & Wilson (2002); Herman (1995); Wagner (2001).
12. Riskin, 2001
13. Matlon, 1988
14. Dinerstein, Ellmann, Gunning, & Shalleck, 2004
15. Wagner, 2001
16. Matlon, 1988, p. 25
17. Bayles, 2002
18. Matlon, 1988, p. 26
19. Keeva, 1999
20. Keeva, 1999
21. Dinerstein et al., 2004
22. Matlon, 1988
23. Lore, 2005
24. Keeva, 1999
25. Keeva, 1999
26. Bryant, 2001
27. Lore, 2005
28. MADD Victim Services
29. MADD Victim Services
30. McGinn, 2005
31. Waites, 2003, p. 21
32. Frederick, 2005; Spiecker & Worthington, 2003, 2008
33. Spiecker & Worthington, 2008
34. Pennington & Hastie, 1992. See also Williams & Jones (2005) for a brief review of trial strategy and tactics.
35. Waites, 2003
36. Waites, 2003, p. 139
37. For a summary of this research, see Fitch-Hauser (1990).
38. Devine & Ostrom, 1985
39. Waites, 2003, p. 139
40. Waites, 2003
41. Waites, 2003, p. 140
42. Waites, 2003; Crawford, 1996
43. Adapted from Fisher's (1970) decision-making model, these suggestions are based on newly formed groups where members have had little or no previous prior contact.
44. Hastie, Penrod, & Pennington, 1983; Levett, Danielsen, Kovera, & Cutler, 2005
45. Picker, 2003
46. Ladd, 2005
47. Adapted from Ladd, 2005, p. 5, figures I.1, I.2, I.3
48. Senft, 2005
49. Logue, 2003
50. This example is adapted from one appearing in Picker (2003) and attributed to Fisher, Roger, & Ury (1981) in *Getting to Yes: Negotiating Agreement without Giving In.*
51. Picker, 2003
52. Mayer, 2000
53. Mayer, 2000; Spangle & Isenhart, 2003
54. Lewicki, Hiam, & Olander 1996; Mayer, 2000; Spangle & Isenhart, 2003
55. Conley & O'Barr, 1998
56. Teply, 1991

REFERENCES

Arenson, K. W. (2002, January 13). The fine art of listening. *New York Times,* Section 4A, Education Life Supplement, 34.

Bayles, F. (2002, July 31). Abuse victims flock to lawyers. *USA Today,* D1.

Bryant, S. (2001). The five habits: Building cross-cultural competence in lawyers. *Clinical Law Review, 8,* 33–107.

Conley, J. M., & O'Barr, W. M. (1998). *Just words: Law, language, and power.* Chicago: University of Chicago Press.

Devine, P. G., & Ostrom, T. M. (1985). Cognitive mediation of inconsistency discounting. *Journal of Personality and Social Psychology, 49,* 5–21.

Dinerstein, R., Ellmann, S., Gunning, I., & Shalleck, A. (2004). Connection, capacity and morality in lawyer-client relationships: Dialogues and commentary. *Clinical Law Review, 10,* 755–804.

Fisher, B. A. (1970). Decision emergence: Phases in group decision making. *Speech Monographs, 37,* 53–66.

Fitch-Hauser, M. (1990). Making sense of data: Constructs, schemas, and concepts. In R. N. Bostrom (Ed.), *Listening behavior: Measurement and application.* New York: Guilford.

Frederick, J. T. (2005). *Mastering voir dire and jury selection* (2nd ed.). American Bar Association Press.

Hastie, R., Penrod, S., & Pennington, N. (1983). *Inside the jury selection* (2nd ed.). American Bar Association. Cambridge, MA: Harvard University Press.

Herman, R. M. (1995, June). Stop . . . look . . . listen: Interviewing and choosing clients. *Trial, 31,* 48–56.

Keeva, S. (1999, January). Beyond the words: Understanding what your client is really saying makes for successful lawyering. *ABA Journal,* 60–63.

Ladd, P. D. (2005). *Mediation, conciliation, and emotions: A practitioner's guide for understanding emotions in dispute resolution.* Lanham, MD: University Press of America.

Levett, L. M., Danielsen, E. M., Kovera, M. B., & Cutler, B. L. (2005). The psychology of jury and juror decision making. In N. Brewer & K. D. Williams, *Psychology and law: An empirical perspective.* New York: Guilford.

Lewicki, R., Hiam, A., & Olander K. W. (1996). *Think before you speak: A complete guide to strategic negotiation.* New York: John Wiley.

Lipton, J. P. (1977). On the psychology of eyewitness testimony. *Journal of Applied Psychology, 62,* 90–95.

Logue, W. D. (2003, March 24). What's it worth? Listen and learn. *Connecticut Law Tribune.* Retrieved from www.law.com/jsp/article.jsp?id=900005382952.

Lore, M. (2005, October 17). Legal professionals offer advice on how to maintain good relations with clients. *Minnesota Lawyer.* Retrieved from www.minnlawyer.com/article.cfm?recid=73599.

MADD Victim Services. *Selecting a Civil Attorney.* Retrieved from www.madd.org/victim-services/finding-support/victim-resources/selecting-a-civil-attorney.pdf www.madd.org/victims/1639.

Matlon, R. J. (1988). *Communication in the legal process.* New York: Holt, Rinehart, & Winston.

Mayer, B. (2000). *The dynamics of conflict resolution: A practitioner's guide.* San Francisco: Jossey-Bass.

McGinn, R. (2005). *Cause strikes: How to discover jurors' true beliefs and eliminate those who deny justice.* ATLA Toronto 2005 Annual Convention Papers.

Pansky, A., Koriat, A., & Goldsmith, M. (2005). Eyewitness recall and testimony. In N. Brewer & K. Williams (Eds.), *Psychology and law: An empirical perspective* (pp. 93–150). New York: Guilford.

Pennington, N., & Hastie, R. (1992). Explaining the evidence: Tests of the story model for juror decision making. *Journal of Personality and Social Psychology, 62,* 189–206.

Picker, B. G. (2003). *Mediation practice guide: A handbook for resolving business disputes* (2nd ed.). Washington, D.C.: American Bar Association Section of Dispute Resolution.

Police and Detectives (2008–2009). *Occupational outlook handbook, 2008–09 edition.* Bureau of Labor Statistics. Retrieved from www.bls.gov/oco/ocos156.htm.

Riskin, G. A. (2001, January 22). Mastering new skills: Actively listening to colleagues and clients is the *Sine Qua Non. Legal Times.* Retrieved from www.marcusletter.com/Riskin%20Legal%20Times.htm.

Ritter, R. H., Jr., & Wilson, P. A. (2001). Developing the fine art of listening. *Texas Bar Journal, 64,* 897–900.

Seckler, S. (2008). Questions to ask when it's time to listen. *BCG Attorney Search Newsletter.* Retrieved from www.bcgsearch.com.

Senft, L. P. (2005, March 11). Commentary: The negotiation table—Turning problems into opportunities: Listening, mediator style. *Baltimore Daily Record.* Retrieved from www.mddailyrecord.com/2005/03/08/the-negotiating-table-turning-problems-into-opportunities-listening-mediator-style/.

Slatkin, A. A. (2005). *Communication in crisis and hostage negotiations.* Springfield, IL: Charles C. Tomas.

Spangle, M. L., & Isenhart, M. W. (2003). *Negotiation: Communication for diverse settings.* Thousand Oaks, CA: Sage.

Spiecker, S. C., & Worthington, D. L. (2003). The influence of opening statement and closing argument organizational strategy on juror decision-making. *Law and Human Behavior, 27,* 437–456.

Spiecker, S., & Worthington, D. L. (2008). Explorations of juror reasoning: The influence of attorney opening statement/closing argument organizational strategy. *Communication Law Review, 8,* 52–63. Retrieved from www.commlawreview.org.

Teply, L. L. (1992). *Legal Negotiation.* St. Paul, MN: West.

Van Hasselt, V. B., Baker, M. T., Romano, S. J., Schlessinger, K. M., Zucker, M., Dragone, R., & Perera, A. L. (2006). Crisis (hostage) negotiation training. *Criminal Justice and Behavior, 33,* 56–69.

Victor, D. A., & Victor, C. R. (1997). The lawyer-client encounter: Listening for facts and relationship. In M. Purdy & D. Borisoff (Eds.), *Listening in everyday life* (2nd ed.) (pp. 285–294). Lanham, MD: University Press of America.

Wagner, F. (2001, October 15). Listen to prospective clients. *New Jersey Law Journal, 166,* 27.

Waites, R. C. (2003). *Courtroom psychology and trial advocacy.* New York: ALM.

Wells, G. (1987). Applied eyewitness-testimony research: System variables and estimator variables. In L. S. Wrightsman, C. E. Willis, & S. M. Kassin (Eds.), *On the witness stand.* Newbury, CA: Sage.

Wells, G. L., & Olson, E. (2003). Eyewitness identification. *Annual Review of Psychology, 54,* 277–295.

Williams, K., & Jones, A. (2005). Trial strategies and tactics. In N. Brewer and K. D. Williams (Eds.), *Psychology and law* (276–322). New York: Guilford.

Transforming Listening

Future Directions

Looking Back, Looking Forward

NOLVIA: Can you believe our class is almost over? Only one more week!

BEN: Yeah, just our group presentation tomorrow and the final exam. It seems like we just started the semester and just got into our group.

NOLVIA: It's been fun. I really liked the family listening diary that we did.

BEN: Well, I liked the personality profiles we filled out. I'm minoring in psychology and liked learning about myself. I'd never thought about how my personality could affect how I listen.

NOLVIA: I liked learning about Grice's maxims and how they affect our conversations. They help explain why some of my conversations with my cousin Abelson seem awkward. He's constantly breaking the conversational rules. At least now I know what part of the problem is.

What about you, Tamarah?

TAMARAH: I don't know if I can pick out one thing. I knew listening was important before I got here. As a 9-1-1 operator, my job and people's lives depend on it. I also liked the material on social support, what makes for good support

and bad support. Looking back to some of my arguments with my family, I know there have been times when I wasn't always being as supportive as I should have been or could have been.

What about you, Ben? Do you feel like you're a better listener now?

BEN: Yes and no. I know a lot more about listening and all the distractions that are out there. If anything, I know how bad I can be at it sometimes. It's really hard work to truly listen to others. Of course, I pay a lot more attention to how I listen and how others listen as well. I'd like to think I'm a better listener now.

NOLVIA: I feel the same way. Carter and I were working together last night, and I found my attention wandering. I just winced and said to myself, 'Nolvia, focus!'

BEN: I know exactly what you mean. I think I've got a better handle on one of my really bad habits: interrupting. It can be really hard, but I keep working at not interrupting others unless I absolutely have to. I've found that if

(Continued)

NOLVIA:

I keep my mouth shut, I learn a lot more about people, and I think I help them more too.

Hey, that's like that *NCIS* episode we watched in class where Gibbs didn't say a word during his entire conversation with Abby. She gave him that big hug and told him how great he was at helping her out with her problem. I had basically the same thing happen with my friend Shelly last weekend. It was weird having

watched the show. Sometimes you really can be a better friend if you just listen and stop trying to solve the other person's problems.

TAMARAH: Yeah, I know one thing: I'll never think of listening the same way again . . . and I'll work hard to be a better listener too.

BEN: Speaking of solving problems, this looks like the rest of the group headed this way. We need to iron out the last of our presentation. Hey, Radley! ■

The goal of this book has been to introduce you to the importance of listening in your everyday life. Over the course of this text, you've learned about important underlying features that affect how you listen, and you've learned about aspects of listening in specific contexts such as the workplace and the classroom.

Our understanding of listening continues to change, in part because of new and exciting research that is being conducted by prominent listening scholars. As we noted in Chapter 1, listening is a relatively new area of study. As a result, theory and conceptual development lag behind those of other, more established areas of communication study (e.g., interpersonal, persuasion, health communication).[1] As more listening research is conducted and as new technologies emerge, our notion of what it means to listen will likely change significantly. In this chapter we examine new areas of research and how they affect how we conceptualize listening and study listening in the future.

EXPLORING NEW CONCEPTS

In previous chapters we have discussed how our schemata of an issue, event, or person can affect how we listen. Laura Janusik, a professor at Rockhurst University, and Margarete Imhof, a professor at Johannes Gutenberg University in Germany, believe that understanding how individuals conceptualize listening is important to understanding both how they listen and what listening behaviors they are willing to enact. For example, our listening schemata affect a number of listening processes outlined in our Listening MATERRS model, such as attention and translation. To further our understanding, Imhof and Janusik recently developed the **Listening Concepts Inventory**.[2] Tests of their new measurement found that the students they surveyed believe listening and listening behaviors are based on four central beliefs about the role of listening: *organizing information, building relationships, learning/integrating information,* and *critiquing messages*. The work of Imhof and Janusik reflects much of our earlier discussions in this book. Using listening to build relationships, learn information, and evaluate messages is not that surprising. However, the emphasis on organizing information is not as intuitive. As students, why do you think organizing information was rated as a significant factor? What elements from your lives might make organizing information an important element of your listening lives?

Clearly understanding how we think about listening is important. As noted in Chapter 1 and elsewhere in the text, researchers continue to work to uncover the building blocks of listening and listening processes.

We also need to better understand the **physiology of listening.** Listening disabilities can be caused by both physiological and neurological dysfunctions with the auditory system. In addition to the traditional hearing loss mentioned in earlier chapters, listeners need to know more about auditory-processing disorders and language-processing disorders. These types of disabilities can occur at any age and are often quite difficult to diagnose. Unfortunately they can have devastating results. Even a small hearing loss can affect the language development in children and lead to feelings of social isolation in adults. In addition, hearing loss can affect children's ability to learn to read and write and how they interact with others. Young adults with auditory-processing problems could find their career choices limited and the potential for workplace problems increased.

Our understanding, however, must go beyond the physical makeup of the ear and related auditory reception to include what happens in the brain once we have received a message stimulus. What elements affect the way information is recorded? How does the *temporal lobe,* the auditory area of the brain, effectively retrieve and retain a message in a coordinated way?[3] What factors affect the physiology of listening? Obviously factors such as hearing loss or brain damage can affect how we translate and process incoming messages. What is unclear is what additional physiological features may impact our listening behaviors. As MRIs and other brain imaging technologies become more sophisticated, we will learn more about the physiology of listening and how it influences how we listen to and process incoming messages.

Researchers are also beginning to look closely at how listening can change with the type of relationship involved. The *Active-Empathy Listening Scale* is an example of how current researchers are focusing on listening in specific contexts and relationships. Graham Bodie, a professor at Louisiana State University, described **active-empathetic listening** "as the active and emotional involvement of a listener during a given interaction, an involvement that is conscious on the part of the listener but is also perceived by the speaker."[4] Thus, this type of listening combines the best of both active listening and empathetic listening and, at its core, is other oriented. The scale developed by Dr. Bodie provides scholars with a means of examining the role of listening in close relationships.

Other researchers also emphasize the importance of the listening situation and factors associated with each participant.[5] For example, the **BFF Situational Assessment Scale** considers traditional listening elements such as the *relationship between listeners* and *sharing information.* However, it also focuses on the *power* differential between those involved. While this might be considered an element of the relationship, the scale developers treat it as distinct and separate for several reasons. The primary reason is that power shifts from situation to situation. For example, at times you will have greater knowledge or skill in a particular area than other members of a group. At other times you might have the power to reward or punish others. Finally the scale also measures the *feelings* associated with the person or situation. As a patient, pain can literally make it difficult for you to listen. In other situations, you could be having a great day (or a really bad one). Thus, the concept of feelings reflects both the feelings *between* the communicants and the feelings the speaker holds for himself, the environment, others, or events.

Other communication concepts are being reinvented and applied to the field of listening to help further our understanding of listening processes. **Interaction involvement (II)** affects how others perceive your communication. Individuals low in interaction involvement tend to be less attentive to others, are less responsive during conversations, and tend to have problems choosing the most effective conversational strategy to use.[6] In addition, those with a low II are believed to have a greater self-centered focus, while those high in II tend to engage in more proactive, other-oriented behaviors.[7] The **interaction involvement scale** assesses three elements assumed to be associated with II: responsiveness, perceptiveness, and attentiveness. **Responsiveness** refers to how well you appropriately respond during a conversation, while **perceptiveness** addresses your ability to translate or assign meaning to the other's behavior. **Attentiveness** has the most obvious relationship to listening. We, along with colleagues with ties to South Korea, Finland, and Germany, have used this construct to explore how individuals in these countries (and the United States) differ in their mobile phone use.[8] Results of our survey suggest that students from these four countries do differ in their interaction involvement. For example, U.S. and Korean students had the lowest overall combined interaction involvement scale scores, while Finns and Germans had the highest. Of the four nations studied, U.S. participants had the lowest attentiveness subscale scores and the highest perceptiveness subscale scores. Responsiveness, attentiveness, and perceptiveness have the potential to help explain cultural differences in listening.

In this section we have introduced you to a handful of innovative areas of listening research. However, listening does not occur in a vacuum. As seen with the BFF Situational Assessment Scale, context affects listening processes. In the next section, we explore a number of contextual factors, particularly those associated with mediated communication.

EXPLORING NEW CONTEXTS

Perhaps the most exciting area of listening research addresses the myriad of ways technology and media now affect our daily lives. Technological changes over the past two decades have introduced a number of listening challenges. For example, mobile phones (called "mobiles" in many other countries) were first developed by Dr. Martin Cooper approximately 40 years ago.[9] Mobile phones have fundamentally altered the way we communicate with others. Today we often expect instant access to family and friends. You carry on conversations while in line at the grocery store, at dinner with friends, and as you move from one class to another. In this respect this technology has both expanded and contracted our world. Today when you sit waiting for a class to start, you may

LEARN MORE

If you would like to know more about the invention and development of early mobile phones, you can view a CSPAN interview with Dr. Cooper available at www.youtube.com/watch?v=1CZ4oLw58ek.

be talking on your phone or using it to text someone. As a result, you're not communicating with those around you. So while you can reach out and touch someone across the country or around the world, you are not getting to know the person sitting next to you in class. Your world becomes smaller when you lose the opportunity to interact and communicate with new others in your world. The fact is that most of us communicate with a small, select group of individuals on a daily basis. When you fail to expand this group, you miss opportunities to meet the person who could be your new best friend, study partner, or spouse. Of course, the mobile phone is only one of many new technologies that you have grown up with. The question is how do these technologies affect your interactions with others?

From a listening perspective, you have likely noticed that when you're on the phone, it is often difficult to focus on those around you. When you focus on the **absent other** (the person on the other end of the connection) rather than those around you, **caller hegemony** occurs.[10] The caller, or absent other, becomes your immediate focus and priority, often to the detriment of your conversations with friends or family.[11] As mentioned above, we explored the effect of mobile phones on listening processes along with three colleagues.[12] Our study examined cultural differences in student usage of mobile phones in the United States, South Korea, Finland, and Germany. As we noted previously, students from these four groups differed in their interaction involvement. A number of other differences were also identified. For example, ideas about when it was appropriate (and inappropriate) to use a mobile phone varied across the four countries. German and U.S. students tended to view phone usage while eating out with friends as inappropriate, while Koreans thought it was normal to use phones while dining out. Finnish students felt the appropriateness of doing so depended on the situation. These results suggest that not only do conventions for mobile phone use vary from country to country but the expectations of where listeners should focus their attention also varies by culture.

Another context that will be familiar to you is listening to music. While technology has certainly changed how music is delivered to us, the effect of how we listen to music is also being explored. You've probably already seen reports about the damage that loud noise can cause to your hearing. So you are likely aware of the physiological damage that a loud concert might have on your listening mechanisms. Unfortunately many of us also listen to car stereos, televisions, and MP3 players at sound levels that can damage our hearing.

Researchers are interested in much more than just sound levels. Research into the psychology of listening to music suggests that listening to music at work positively affects work performance and, what is more important, music tends to put us in a good mood.[13] What type of music do you think is the most beneficial? Classical is often what springs to mind. You might have heard or read something about the **Mozart Effect,** which is a popular term to describe supposed increases in intelligence following listening to Mozart's sonatas. Unfortunately the effect isn't that clear cut (or we'd all be listening to Mozart). Overall this research suggests that there might be some very short-term gains in spatial-temporal reasoning.[14]

Other research suggests that listening to upbeat music is the key. Generally such music positively affects individual mood.[15] As genres, rap and hip-hop often get a bad rap (pardon the pun) and likely unfairly. While the music videos often give older adults pause, much of the music has positive or at least neutral messages.

However, it is true that some music does deserve at least part of its negative reputation. Many music lyrics advocate violence (particularly toward women), drug abuse, and similar counterculture behavior. There is some evidence that listening to this type of the music does affect individual cognitions and perceptions, increasing hostile or aggressive thoughts and actions.[16] Whether listening to it leads to negative, antisocial behavior is less clear.

One recent study suggests, however, there are direct positive benefits to listening to music with prosocial messages. Psychologist Dr. Tobias Greitemeyer reported that students who listened to **prosocial music** were more likely to engage in helping behaviors.[17] What types of music did the students listen to? Michael Jackson's "Heal the World," the Beatles' "Help," and Liveaid's "We are the World."

Drawing on this and other research on emotional intelligence, music professor Susan Kenney argued that music can also help teach children **delayed gratification.** She suggested that songs such as "Patty Cake" use actions and rhyme to teach children anticipation and the importance of waiting for the climax of a song.[18] Earlier research in emotional intelligence provides tangential support for her claim. In his book *Emotional Intelligence,* Daniel Goleman reported results of a longitudinal study (a study that lasts several years) that found that children who were able to delay gratification at age four tended to become adolescents who exhibited better coping skills and conflict-resolution skills, were more self-assertive, and had higher self-esteem. Unfortunately no one has directly tested the relationship between listening to the types of childhood music mentioned by Dr. Kenney and an increased ability to delay gratification as adults. However, her ideas provide an intriguing topic for future listening study.

Computer-mediated communication is the focus of another growing body of research. The long-term effects of CMC on communication and listening behaviors are still unclear. What we do know is that it plays an important function in our professional, educational, and personal lives. As early as 1995, the former chairman of the MIT Media Laboratory and founder of One Laptop One Child, Nicholas Negroponte, predicted that e-mail would eventually approach if not surpass the voice as the primary means of interpersonal communication.[19] Think about your own daily lives. When you think of your interactions on Facebook, texting, and regular e-mail interactions, how much time do you actually spend directly communicating with others? What if you take away classroom communications?

Another group of researchers is exploring the effect of features of television and radio and CMC on how we listen and how they affect information processing.[20] For example, access to the Internet has changed the way we access and process information. How many times do you have multiple windows open on your computer or try to study while constantly checking your e-mail or returning texts? One of the newest areas of research in brain development examines how such multitasking affects how we process information. One proposed change in our cognitive

THINK ON IT

Dr. Greitemeyer's study suggested there is a direct relationship between what we listen to and how we behave. What do you think? Make a list of your five favorite songs and get the lyrics of each. Examining the lyrics, how might what you listen to affect your own behavior?

LEARN ABOUT YOURSELF

If you'd like to test your ability to focus and multitask, try two online interactive tests presented by the *New York Times.* Both were published in the June 6, 2010, online edition. The easiest way to locate them is to search for the following two titles: "Test How Fast You Juggle Tasks" and "Test Your Focus."

processing is that multitasking affects our ability to concentrate or focus on a project. If true, it could affect our ability to read books, to engage in extended projects, or to listen to a longer speech. Of course, it could also affect how we listen to others.

Another interesting area of research in mediated communication addresses how we process commercials. Viewers and listeners tend to find **compressed advertisements**—advertisements with faster speaking rates and fewer pauses— more interesting, more persuasive, and easier to remember. Other research suggests that slower speaking rates in advertisements allow listeners to focus on specific facts, while higher rates lead listeners to develop more global impressions of a message or speaker. In a study testing the effect of speaking rate on the effectiveness of radio advertisements, Professor Christopher Skinner and his colleagues concluded that ad designers should keep the goal of the ad in mind when making decisions about how much the speaking rate of an ad should be compressed. For example, if the goal is to teach a consumer a step-by-step process, then a slower rate might be needed. This advice is especially pertinent for designers of public service announcements and other health messages. Faster rates are fine when the goal of the ad is to establish or alter a listener's general opinion of a product, person, or event.[21]

Other research examines how media can affect schema formation and how those schemata can influence message processing. For example, one legal study by Kimbelianne Podlas found that when individuals who are heavy viewers of *syndicated court programming* such as *Judge Judy* or *Judge Joe Brown* are called for jury duty, they expected judges to act similarly.[22] In other words, these viewers believed that judges were opinionated and they voiced those opinions. The fact is that judges are instructed to act in exactly the opposite way of these television judges. The Model Code of Judicial Conduct instructs judges to avoid expressing any biases or prejudices via their oral communication or nonverbals. Thus, most judges tend to be silent unless one of the parties asks for a ruling or something occurs in the courtroom that must be addressed. How do you think these viewers interpret silence during actual legal proceedings? Podlas's research suggested that jurors who watch syndicated court television programs tend to interpret silence as agreement.

> **THINK ON IT**
>
> What are the courtroom implications for schemata based on television programs such as *CSI, Law & Order,* or *Judge Judy*?

Schemata about courtroom proceedings are not the only perceptions affected by television viewing. Certainly attitudes toward money, family, health, sex, and sexual behaviors have also been studied. Have any of you watched reality dating programs? Have you ever considered how such programming could affect your view of dating and dating behaviors? Of sex and sexual behaviors? One study by Eileen Zurbriggen and Elizabeth Morgan found that heavy viewers of programming such as *The Bachelor* and *Elimidate* were more likely to hold gender stereotypical views and beliefs of dating and dating relationships.[23] They were also more likely to see dating as an adversarial activity. Zurbriggen and Morgan's findings held true for both men and women and held particularly true for individuals who report watching the programming primarily with the goal to learn dating techniques rather than for

> **THINK ON IT**
>
> While many of you will end up in long-term relationships with individuals you meet in class or at work, others might try speed dating or online dating. Do you think these types of programming might affect how you approach a blind date? Your schema of dating?

entertainment purposes. If you think about the highly sexual nature of many of these types of programs, you might not find the researchers' results very surprising. The compressed nature of the program (an evening or even a week of activities compressed to 50 minutes or fewer of programming) results in a high concentration of sexually suggestive activities and content (e.g., kissing, groping, stripping, suggestive dancing, language).

EXPLORING LISTENING AND EDUCATION

After taking a listening class, you tend to have a more realistic perception of the quality of your own listening. If you were asked to rate your listening competency at the beginning of this semester, you likely rated yourself as a fairly competent listener. However, if you rate yourself now, it wouldn't be unusual for you to actually rate your listening competency lower! As we can see with Ben's comments in the Case Study at the beginning of this chapter, this decline in your perception of your listening is believed to be caused by a better understanding of what goes into being an effective listener.[24]

As we noted at the beginning of this text, few of you had the opportunity to take listening classes prior to the one you are currently enrolled in. In addition, listening training was probably not available and was seldom, if ever, emphasized in your other classes. Our text has sought to offer you a taste of our current understanding of the art and science of listening. As you can see in our discussion above and elsewhere in the text, research in listening is at a new and exciting nexus. Young scholars are expanding our knowledge of what it means to listen, which in turn will shape what is taught in the listening classes in the future. Organizations such as the International Listening Association and the National Communication Association provide forums to introduce emerging listening research to established and new listening scholars, many of whom are teaching classes similar to the one you are enrolled in.

In addition, media available to instructors and students continue to transform the listening classroom. Sites such as YouTube and Hulu can provide numerous video clips, which can serve as examples of listening concepts for both teacher presentations and student projects. If you see a particularly good listening example during a television program, it is not unusual for it to be available online within a few days of its airing. For example, while working on this chapter, Professor Worthington watched an episode of *House* ("Baggage"). In the episode, House interacts with a psychotherapist in his usual hostile and acerbic fashion. Their interaction, however, is a good example of several contexts and types of listening, including health, friendship, translation of messages, and social support. Of course, episodes that aren't available online often can be downloaded, or the DVD can be rented or purchased.

The educational aspects of listening unfold in other ways as well. For example, computer programs are being developed to help small children improve their listening skills. One such program, **Phonomena**, was designed to help children with language problems.[25] The computer game, developed by Dr. David Moore of Oxford University, teaches children to better differentiate between *phonemes*.

Some children have problems distinguishing between sounds such as the "i" in the word *bit* and the "e" in the word *bet*. Moore's computer game has them listen to the original phoneme then choose from several examples the word that sounds most like the phoneme they first heard. Similar activities have long been available for children, but they are typically presented in either a written format and, thus, rely on children "hearing" the sound in their heads or having an adult read off the phonemes and the child choose from among those provided. Of course, problematic pronunciation (i.e., dialects, accents) might make identification more difficult for children. These types of computer programs make a game of learning and listening, using a familiar computer game format, and tend to be well received by children (and adults).

Another proposed strategy for increasing listening performance is **Listening across the Curriculum.** Many colleges and universities have **Writing across the Curriculum** and **Oral Communication across the Curriculum** programs. These programs were developed to help students hone their communication skills so they will be effective communicators when they enter the workplace.[26] Such programs encourage or require instructors across disciplines to include writing or speaking assignments in their classes to improve students' skills in these areas. Unfortunately few institutions have incorporated Listening across the Curriculum programs.[27]

> **THINK ON IT**
>
> What might be some of the difficulties in instituting a Listening across the Curriculum program? What challenges might be faced by faculty? By students?

Dr. Janice Newton of Canada's York University believes that listening education should go beyond a single class.[28] She argued that to truly master listening, listening skills need to be incorporated in university core classes. Assigned to teach in two different departments, Dr. Newton has personal experience doing just this. She includes listening activities and skills practice in both her political science and her women's studies courses. Listening and critical thinking are closely related. Ideally improving your listening skills will assist your critical thinking and ultimately your classroom performance.

Instituting Dr. Newton's suggestion represents an ideal for educators who value listening. However, there are a number of challenges that face listening classes included in current, more traditional communication curriculum. For example, the majority of listening classes are taught at the junior and senior college level.[29] While it's good to have the benefit of listening training prior to graduation and beginning your career, wouldn't it be nice to have the benefit of such training throughout your college career? As we discussed earlier in Chapter 8, improved listening has been associated with improved classroom performance.

An additional issue in listening education addresses the **role of the college textbook.** Researchers differ in the underlying goal that a college textbook should serve: to help produce additional knowledge of a field *or* to present what is known and has been proven about a field.[30] As listening scholar Laura Janusik noted, either of these views assumes that the material presented in the textbook is accurate and based on solid research. Unfortunately the listening chapters presented in many communication textbooks (e.g., public speaking, small-group communication, health communication) are not supported by research.[31] Most instructors trust the quality of the material being presented in these chapters, so few review the research presented in them. Writers of listening textbooks also experience problems. We are often faced with a lack of research or with conflicting research from various disciplines. Psychologists study listening as related to counseling and witness examination. Political scientists study the effects of listening on mediation and arbitration. Medical researchers study listening in doctor-patient interviews. And of course, communication scholars study the effect of listening in all of these areas and more. Laura Janusik best summed up the relationship between the teaching and research of listening when she wrote, "Thus, as a field, we have approached a crossroads because much of what we have believed to be true about listening is not supported, and without supported knowledge, new knowledge cannot be created."[32] She argued that we need to focus greater attention on researching listening, what it is and how it works.

Scholars in both the United States and abroad are accepting Janusik's charge. Findings from their recent studies are presented throughout this book. We have worked hard to bring you research by scholars from a variety of disciplines and have drawn on established research wherever possible. We have extensively reviewed listening research with the goal of providing you with knowledge of the current state of the field while synthesizing research from areas outside communication. From the beginning, we hoped to broaden your understanding of listening and to provide you with the means of improving your own listening skills.

CONCLUDING THOUGHTS

Listening and what it means to listen continue to change. Do you "listen" to your "inner voice," to those conversations you have with yourself? Some listening scholars suggest that when you attend to these conversations, you are "listening."[33] Similarly the development of interactive media has led the act of listening to be transformed into a metaphor to describe these other communication activities. For example, do you consider yourself "listening" to text messages? When you read your e-mail? When posting to social networking sites (or reading posts)? In these contexts, listening has become a metaphor used to describe our act of paying attention to online communication.[34] Kate Crawford, a professor at the University of New South Wales in Sydney, Australia, specializes in research addressing the technologies of listening. She argued that the metaphor of listening is useful for describing how we receive and process online interactions, such as those associated with various social media. It is true that how we pay attention and what we pay attention to evolves in response to social and technological changes.[35] Yet the use of this metaphor is problematic. How does it muddy our understanding of listening? Of course, this begs the question of how we should reference these types of online communication. If we call them conversations, then the language associated with descriptions of conversations (e.g., talk, listen) is naturally engaged. However, when we equate listening to paying attention, we ignore what makes listening a unique aspect of communication. So we conclude this book with one last call to *Think on It:* Should we use the metaphor of listening when referencing how we pay attention to electronic communication? To our inner voice? If not, why not? If so, why?

CONCEPTS TO KNOW

Listening Concepts Inventory
Physiology of Listening
Temporal Lobe
Active-empathetic Listening
BFF Situational Assessment Scale
Interaction Involvement
  Responsiveness
  Perceptiveness
  Attentiveness

Absent Other
Caller Hegemony
Mozart Effect
Prosocial Music
Delayed Gratification
Computer-mediated Communication
Compressed Advertisements
Phonemena
Listening across the Curriculum

DISCUSSION QUESTIONS

1. We introduced you to several new listening measurements. In your opinion, which of the measurements appears to have the greatest ability to help us learn more about how people listen and process information?
2. We discussed the effect of computer-mediated technology on how we listen. How do your instructors feel about mobile phone and computer use in the classroom? How do you feel when a mobile phone buzzes or rings in class? What about computer use? How does it affect listening in the class?
3. We discussed reading, writing, and listening across the curriculum programs. If you could institute only one of these three programs, which would you institute first? Second? Why?

LISTENING ACTIVITIES

1. Chart your computer use for two days. Try to be as in depth as possible. How many applications do you have open at any one time? Do you concentrate on the assignment you are working on, or do you tend to flip between programs, check e-mail, Facebook, and so on. Do you feel the way you work could have an effect on the way you listen?
2. Listening across the Curriculum programs provide listening training and activities in classes from all areas and majors. In groups of three or four individuals, design an outline of a program for your college or university. You should include ideas for sample assignments, identify the primary classes that should be included, and develop a one- to two-page justification for the program you design.

ADDITIONAL READINGS

Berko, R., Wolvin, A. D., & Wolvin, D. (2010). *Communicating: A social, career and cultural focus.* Boston: Allyn & Bacon.

Brownell, J., & Wolvin, A. D. (2010). *What every student should know about listening.* New York: Pearson.

Wolvin, A. D. (2010). *Listening and human communication in the 21st century.* New York: John Wiley.

ENDNOTES

1. Bodie, in press a, 2009, 2008
2. Imhof & Janusik, 2006
3. See Wolvin (2010), ch. 1, for a fuller discussion of physiological processes of listening.
4. Bodie, in press b
5. Bentley, Fitch-Hauser, & Flynn, 2006
6. Cegala, 1981, 1984; Villaume, Jackson, & Schouten, 2006

7. Sidelinger, Ayash, Godorhazy, and Tibbles, 2008
8. Worthington, Fitch-Hauser, Kim, Välikoski, & Imhof, 2009
9. Benesh, 2001; Ellis, 2008
10. Hopper, 1992
11. Gergen, 2002
12. Worthington et al., 2009
13. Lesiuk, 2005
14. See Pryse-Phillips (2003) for a review.
15. Thompson, Husain, & Schellenberg, 2001
16. See Timmerman, Allen, Jorgensen, Herrett-Skjellum, Kramer, & Ryan (2008) for a meta-analysis of related studies.
17. Greitemeyer, 2009
18. Kenney, 2009
19. Negroponte, 1995
20. See Skinner, Robinson, Robins, Sterling, & Goodman (1999) for a brief review.

21. Skinner et al., 1999
22. Podlas, 2001
23. Zurbriggen & Morgan, 2006
24. Ford, Wolvin, & Chung, 2000
25. Graham-Rowe, 2003
26. Helsel & Hogg, 2006
27. One notable exception is Alverno Collego. For a full description of Alverno's Integrated Listening Model, see Thompson, Leintz, Nevers, & Witkowski (2010).
28. Newton, 2010
29. Janusik, 2010
30. Alfred & Thelen, 1993; Connors, 1986
31. Janusik & Wolvin, 2002
32. Janusik, 2010
33. Robson & Young, 2007
34. Crawford, 2009
35. Crary, 1999

REFERENCES

Alfred, G. J., & Thelen, E. A. (1993). Are textbooks contributions to scholarship? *College Composition and Communication, 44,* 466–477.

Benesh, P. (2001, September 19). Cell phone inventor: Industry needs new focus. *Investor's Business Daily,* A5.

Bently, S., Fitch-Hauser, M., & Flynn, J. (2006). *Effective listening: Identifying component factors and relevant/appropriate behaviors.* Paper presented at the annual meeting of the International Listening Association, Salem, OR.

Bodie, G. D. (in press a). The understudied nature of listening in interpersonal communication research: Introduction to a special issue. *International Journal of Listening.*

Bodie, G. D. (in press b). The Active-Empathic Listening Scale (AELS): Conceptualization and evidence of validity with the interpersonal domain. *Communication Quarterly.*

Bodie, G. D. (2008, March). *The concept of theory in listening: What is it and how can we tell if we have one?* Paper presented at the annual meeting of the International Listening Association, Portland, ME.

Bodie, G. D. (2009). Evaluating listening theory: Development and illustration of five criteria. *International Journal of Listening, 23,* 81–103.

Cegala, D. J. (1981). Interaction involvement: A cognitive dimension of communicative competence. *Communication Education, 30,* 109–121.

Cegala, D. J. (1984). Affective and cognitive manifestations of interaction involvement during unstructured and competitive interactions. *Communication Monographs, 51,* 320–338.

Connors, R. J. (1986). Textbooks and the evolution of the discipline. *College Composition and Communication, 37,* 178–194.

Crary, J. (1999). *Suspensions of perception: Attention, spectacle, and modern culture.* Cambridge, MA: MIT Press.

Crawford, K. (2009). Following you: Disciplines of listening in social media. *Continuum: Journal of Media & Cultural Studies, 23,* 525–535.

Ellis, J. (2008, April 3). Watson, can you hear me now? In just three decades, cellular phones have taken charge: 84 percent of us own them. *Portland Press Herald,* A1.

Ford, W. Z., & Wolvin, A. D., Chung, S. (2000). Students' self-perceived listening competencies. *International Journal of Listening, 14,* 1–13.

Gergen, K. (2002). The challenge of absent presence. In J. E. Katz & M. Aakhus (Eds.), *Perpetual contact: Mobile communication, private talk, public performance* (pp. 227–241). Cambridge, MA: Cambridge University Press.

Graham-Rowe, D. (2003, August 30). The listening game. *New Scientist, 179*(2410), 10–11.

Greitemeyer, T. (2009). Effects of songs with prosocial lyrics on prosocial behavior: Further evidence and a mediating mechanism. *PSPB, 35,* 1500–1511.

Hopper, R. (1992). *Telephone conversation.* Bloomington: Indiana University Press.

Helsel, C. R., & Hogg, M. C. (2006). Assessing communication proficiency in higher education. Speaking labs offer possibilities. *International Journal of Listening, 20,* 29–54.

Imhof, M., & Janusik, L. A. (2006). Development and validation of the Imhof-Janusik Listening Concepts Inventory to measure listening conceptualization differences between cultures. *Journal of Intercultural Communication Research, 35,* 79–98.

Janusik, L. A., & Wolvin, A. (2002). Listening treatment in the basic communication course text. In D. Sellnow (Ed.), *Basic communication course annual, 14* (pp. 164–210). Boston: American Press.

Janusik, L. A. (2010). Listening pedagogy: Where do we go from here? In A. D. Wolvin (Ed.). *Listening and human communication in the 21st century* (pp. 193–224). Malden, MA: Wiley-Blackwell.

Kenny, S. (2009). A marshmallow and a song. *General Music Today, 22,* 27–29.

Lesiuk, T. (2005). The effect of music listening on work performance. *Psychology of Music, 33,* 173–191.

Negroponte, N. (1995). *Being digital.* New York: Knopf.

Newton, J. (2010, March). *Listening across disciplines: How do we teach it?* Paper presented at the International Listening Association Conference, Albuquerque, NM.

Podlas, K. (2001). Please adjust your signal: How television's syndicated courtrooms bias our juror citizenry. *American Business Law Journal, 39.* Retrieved from www.allbusiness.com/legal/837058-1.html.

Pryse-Phillips, W. (2003). *Companion to clinical neurology.* London: Oxford University Press.

Robson, D. C., & Young, R. (2007). Listening to inner speech: Can students listen to themselves think? *International Journal of Listening, 21,* 1–13.

Sidelinger, R. J., Ayash, G., Godorhazy, A., & Tibbles, D. (2008). Couples go online: Relational maintenance behaviors and relational characteristics use in dating relationships. *Human Communication, 11,* 341–355.

Skinner, C. H., Robinson, D. H., Robinson, S. L., Sterling, H. E., & Goodman, M. A. (1999). Effects of advertisement speech rates on feature recognition, and product and speaker ratings. *International Journal of Listening, 13,* 97–110.

Thompson, K., Leintz, P., Nevers, B., & Witkowski, S. (2010). The integrated listening model: An approach to teaching and learning listening. In A. D. Wolvin (Ed.), *Listening and human communication in the 21st century* (pp. 266–286). Malden, MA: Wiley-Blackwell.

Thompson, W. F., Husain, G., & Schellenberg, G. (2001). Arousal, mood, and the Mozart effect. *Psychological Science, 12,* 248–251.

Timmerman, L., Allen, M., Jorgensen, J., Herrett-Skjellum, J., Kramer, M., & Ryan, D. (2008). A review and meta-analysis examining the relationship of music content with sex, race, priming, and attitudes. *Communication Quarterly, 56,* 303–324.

Villaume, W. A., Jackson, J., & Schouten, T. G. (2006). Issue-event extensions and interaction involvement text-based and meaning-based discourse strategies. *Human Communication Research, 15,* 407–427.

Wolvin, A. D. (2010). Listening engagement: Intersecting theoretical perspectives. In A. D. Wolvin (Ed.), *Listening and human communication in the 21st century* (pp. 7–30). Malden, MA: Wiley-Blackwell.

Worthington, D. L., Fitch-Hauser, M., Kim, S., Välikoski, T. R., & Imhof, M. (2009). *Mobile telephony, privacy management, and interaction involvement: A cross-cultural comparison of Finnish, German, Korean, & U.S. American students.* Paper presented at the National Communication Association, Chicago, IL.

Zurbriggen, E. L., & Morgan, E. M. (2006). Who wants to marry a millionaire? Reality dating television programs, attitudes toward sex and sexual behaviors. *Sex Roles, 54,* 1–17.

AUTHOR INDEX

SUBJECT INDEX

compressed advertisements, 269
computer-mediated communication, 268
delayed gratification, 268
Mozart effect, 267
prosocial music, 268
Turn-taking, 119

U
Underaccommodate, 92
Understanding checking, 216
Unstable attributions, 172

V
Validation, 150
  active understanding, 150
  general sharing, 150
  open-ended questions, 150
Values, 45
Van Slyke's levels of listening
  active listening, 36
  empathetic listening, 37
  passive listening, 34–35
  reflective listening, 37
  responding listening, 35
  selective listening, 35

Verbal assurances, 146
Verdict driven, 253
Voice of lifeworld, 224
Voice of medicine, 224

W
WFH model. *See* Listening Worthington Fitch–Hauser (WFH) model
Working memory, 12, 46
Writing across curriculum, 271

Y
Yellow listening, 30